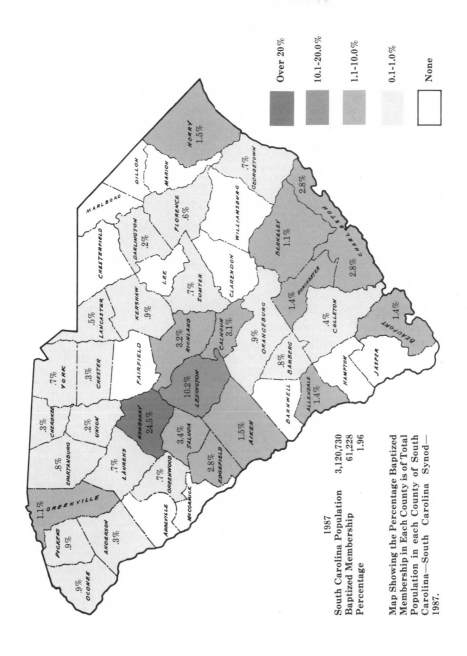

Over 20%

10.1-20.0%

1.1-10.0%

0.1-1.0%

None

1987

South Carolina Population   3,120,730
Baptized Membership   61,228
Percentage   1.96

Map Showing the Percentage Baptized
Membership in Each County is of Total
Population in each County of South
Carolina—South Carolina Synod—
1987.

A HISTORY
OF THE
LUTHERAN CHURCH
IN
SOUTH CAROLINA
1971-1987

SOUTH CAROLINA SYNOD
Lutheran Church in America

1003 Richland Street
P. O. Box 43
Columbia, South Carolina 29202

A HISTORY

OF THE

LUTHERAN CHURCH

IN

SOUTH CAROLINA

1971-1987

"The principal function of the Synod shall
be the shepherding of its Congregations
and Ministers." . . . .

—*From the Constitution of the
South Carolina Synod of the
Lutheran Church in America,
1980.*

Published by
THE SOUTH CAROLINA SYNOD
OF THE
LUTHERAN CHURCH IN AMERICA

Prepared and Edited by
HISTORY OF SYNOD COMMISSION

1988

Printed by
THE R. L. BRYAN COMPANY
COLUMBIA, SOUTH CAROLINA
1988

Preface

As it became clearer and clearer that the Lutheran Church in America would be involved in a merger with other Lutheran bodies, the 1982 Convention, upon the recommendation of the bishop and the executive board, authorized the establishment of a History of Synod Commission and the funding for the writing and publication of such a history. This volume is to be a companion volume to *A History of the Lutheran Church in South Carolina*, 1971, which gives a detailed history of Lutheranism in South Carolina from the early years of the 1700's until its publication in 1971. This volume, therefore, begins at the point the 1971 volume concludes and ends with December 31, 1987, the effective date of the end of the Lutheran Church in America.

After a slow and difficult start that included the resignation of the first two chairpersons, the commission began its work in earnest in 1984. Biographical information was already being gathered from the pastors who had served in the synod since 1971, and work now needed to proceed on the congregational histories and the general work of the synod. The work of the commission was divided as follows:

Editor and Writer . . . . The Rev. James B. Park
Pastoral Biographies . . . . Miss Mary Boozer and
                                          the Rev. James B. Park
Congregational Histories . The Rev. Russell B. Kleckley,
                                    Mrs. Kathleen Fesperman, and
                                    the Rev. Dr. Douglas Johnson
Committees and Synodical History . . Mrs. Virginia Aull
Institutions and Auxiliaries . . Miss Margaret Paysinger
Statistical Data . . . . The Rev. Dr. James S. Aull
Pictures and General
    Counsel . . . . The Rev. Dr. Herman W. Cauble
Index and Research . The Rev. Dr. W. Richard Fritz, Sr.

In the narrative section, we have sought to describe the general work of the synod, the committees, auxiliaries, institutions, and agencies. Congregational histories have been written to reflect the scope of the ministry of each congregation since 1971. Statistical data for each congregation as of December 31, 1971, and December 31, 1987, is included in Appendix 3. Biographical data was gathered on all pastors who were at any time on the Roll of Ministers of the South Carolina Synod since 1971. Some of these were ordained by the synod and transferred to another synod for service; others came to this synod after retirement. In either case, specific places and dates of service outside the South Carolina Synod before or after their being a part of this synod have not been included. A listing of the Certified Lay Professionals as of December 31, 1987, along with some biographical information, has also been included.

We have also included in Appendix 6 corrections to the 1971 volume as they have been reported to us and verified. We hope that errors in this volume are few, but we do request that any noted be reported to the Editor or the synod office.

I am deeply indebted to all the pastors and lay persons who provided us with information for this volume. I am particularly indebted to the members of the Commission who provided their time and talents to the development of this volume, and to Bishop Cauble for his continued support and interest in our work. We also thank Mrs. Carolyn Huntley and Mr. Timothy Yount for their early leadership of this commission.

James B. Park,
Editor

Camden, S. C., 1988.

vi

Contents

Contents—*continued*

Chapter One—The Synod

With over two hundred and fifty years of history as a foundation, the Lutheran Church in South Carolina moved into the 1970's and 80's as a part of the Lutheran Church in America, and continued the growth, both in congregations and ministry programs, that had characterized the earlier years. The most notable area of growth for the synod was in the Grand Strand area—along the beaches of South Carolina. Only one congregation had served that area since 1956, and the growth of the area, both in tourism and in permanent residents, brought the need for additional congregations. In 1975 and 1976, two congregations were organized along the Grand Strand, one at the south end, Shepherd of the Sea, Garden City in November, 1975,[1] and one at the north end, King of Glory, North Myrtle Beach in November, 1976.[2] These two congregations grew rapidly, and were joined in their service to the beach area by St. Peter, Pawleys Island in 1984[3] and Christ the Servant, Conway in 1986.[4] The Charleston area of the South Carolina coast had also experienced tremendous growth around its perimeters, and the development of new congregations in that area was also a key part of the Lutheran church's ministry during this time. Christ, Hilton Head was organized in 1973[5] to serve that new community and was soon joined by the congregations of Peace, Ladson (North Charleston) in 1974,[6] All Saints, Mt. Pleasant in 1975,[7] and A Mighty Fortress, Sangaree (Summerville) in 1981.[8] But growth was not limited to the coastal areas of the state. The Piedmont section experienced the development of two new congregations with Redeemer, Greer being organized in 1972[9] and St. Matthias, Easley, organized in 1974.[10] Cross and Crown expanded the ministry of the Lutheran church in the Florence area with its organization in 1981,[11] and Christus Victor was established in the new community of Harbison, northwest of Columbia in 1986.[12] In the summer of 1987, a new mission field was entered when a pastor/developer under call of the synod began work in the northeastern part of Columbia.

With support from the Division for Mission in North America of the LCA, Living Springs Lutheran Church began worship services on November 15, 1987. The worshipers look forward to their organization as a congregation of the Evangelical Lutheran Church in America.

Pastor Larry Bost worships at synod convention with sign language.

But the most distinctive new congregation for South Carolina Lutherans resulted from the development of the Ministry with the Deaf in Columbia in 1985.[13] Organized as a congregation, these Lutherans provide a special ministry for people with hearing disabilities and their families. They are led by a hearing-impaired pastor who not only ministers to their needs, but also extends his ministry to much of the hearing impaired community in Columbia, including those in hospitals and prisons. This congregation worships in the Chapel of St. Paul, Columbia. (See page 169.)

Interest in, and support for, the development of new Lutheran congregations was demonstrated by members of the South Carolina Synod throughout these years by their participation in several special projects.

The 1974 LCA Convention in Baltimore adopted the program of "Strength For Mission," and in 1976 the LCA Convention in Boston set the goal at $25 million for a campaign during 1977-78. Money from this campaign was used to strengthen this mission of the LCA in North America and overseas.[14] The South Carolina Synod pledged over $670,000 to this campaign, exceeding the LCA guideline for the synod. Mr. Arthur W. Sedler, a layman of the synod, served as director of the synodical campaign.[15]

A special Reformation Offering to be received in October 1984, was approved by the synod convention challenging

LCA President Robert J. Marshall (center) meets with "Strength For Mission" leaders, including Mr. Arthur Sedler (right), Director for South Carolina.

each congregation to make a gift amounting to at least $1.00 per confirmed member in addition to its regular benevolence offerings, to be divided equally between support for new LCA congregations and support for the LCA World Mission program.[16]

A second campaign, called "One in Mission," with payments to be made from July 1986-June 1989, was conducted throughout the LCA and the South Carolina Synod. The LCA goal of $36 million was earmarked for new mission congregation development ($30 million) and as a birth gift for the Evangelical Lutheran Church in America ($6 million). In the South Carolina Synod the goal was $1.4 million with $933,333 designated for the LCA goals, $311,111 for Newberry College, and $155,556 for Southern Seminary.[17] The Rev. Hugh E. Baumgartner served as general chairman. Again the synod exceeded its goal with pledges of over $1.7 million.[18]

Throughout all of these years, the primary purpose of the Lutheran Men of South Carolina has been the financial support of mission congregations through their Loan and Gift Funds. In the years of 1971 to 1987, nineteen different congregations received low interest loans of over $777,000 and twenty-six different mission congregations received gifts of over $233,000 (see page 62).

Upon the retirement of the Rev. Dr. Herman W. Cauble as Bishop of the South Carolina Synod, the Executive Board authorized the establishment of the Herman W. and Elizabeth Petrea Cauble Mission Trust Fund. Over $17,000 has been contributed to this fund in honor of Dr. and Mrs. Cauble (see page 6).

In addition to these special projects, the congregations of the synod have supported the development of mission congregations through special gifts made directly to them. All of these are evidence of the strong sense of mission in South Carolina.

But growth of the Lutheran church in South Carolina was not limited to the development of these new congregations. During the period 1972 to 1987, the baptized membership grew each year from 51,606 in 1972[19] to 61,282 in 1987, with 38,481 communing, contributing, confirmed members.[20]

Officers and Staff

Through these years, the synod continued to enjoy strong leadership from its elected officers, pastors, and laity. The Rev. Dr. Herman W. Cauble had been elected President of

Bishop Herman W. Cauble is flanked by Secretary James S. Aull (left), and Treasurer James B. Wessinger (right).

the synod in 1971, and the Rev. Paulwyn L. Boliek was elected to succeed Dr. Cauble as secretary of the synod.[21] With the Rev. Lloyd W. Mitcham, Jr. as the Executive Secretary of Christian Education, and Mr. James B. Wessinger as Treasurer, they provided the synod with the effective leadership that was needed to move through the 1970's. In 1979, Secretary Boliek resigned to become pastor of Resurrection, Augusta, Georgia, and the Rev. Dr. James S. Aull was elected Secretary of the Synod.[22] The office of president was changed by the convention of the LCA in 1980 to bishop.[23] In 1981, Mr. Wessinger retired as treasurer after

Treasurer Raymond S. Caughman.   *Assistant to the Bishop Robert L. Dasher.*

20 years of service. A scholarship at Newberry College was established in his honor, and over 500 people attended a dinner honoring Dr. Wessinger and Mrs. Carolyn Sanders, bookkeeper.[24] Mr. Raymond S. Caughman was elected treasurer by the synod convention in 1981.[25] Pastor Mitcham resigned as Executive Secretary of Christian Education and Youth Ministry in 1984 to accept a call in North Carolina. The executive board authorized a change in the title and responsibilities for this position, and in 1985, called the Rev. Robert L. Dasher as Assistant to the Bishop.[26]

Bishop Cauble receives a cross upon his retirement from the Rev. Guy C. Cruse, Chairman of the recognition committee.

The Rev. Dr. Herman W. Cauble retired as Bishop of the South Carolina Synod on December 31, 1987. A banquet in his honor was held at Newberry College on October 18, 1987 with about 400 in attendance. In addition to small, personal gifts to him and Mrs. Cauble, along with a Book of Letters from people throughout the synod, the Herman W. and Elizabeth Petrea Cauble Mission Fund was established to help new mission congregations in South Carolina.[27]

The Rev. Dr. James S. Aull was elected to serve as the Bishop of the new South Carolina Synod of the Evangelical Lutheran Church in America.[28]

In addition to these people, the synod has been faithfully served by people working on the various committees and boards of the synod to develop the ministry programs and enhance the outreach and witness of the Lutheran church in South Carolina.

On November 23, 1983, the Rev. Dr. Karl W. Kinard, President Emeritus of the South Carolina Synod, died. He was only the second full-time president of the synod, having served from 1943 to 1971. Prior to that he had served as the secretary of the synod, 1935 to 1943, in a part-time position. His wife, Esther, had died in July 1983.[29]

January 14, 1974, marked the 150th anniversary of the organized Lutheran synod within the boundaries of South Carolina. In recognition of this anniversary, a special program of celebration was held on Sunday, January 13, at the Carolina Coliseum in Columbia. Over 8,000 people attended this service that included the Rev. Dr. Robert J. Marshall, President of the Lutheran Church in America, as the speaker, an afternoon concert before the service, and a spe-

150th Anniversary celebration at Carolina Coliseum.

cial anniversary hymn composed by Professor Gordon Beaver of the Lutheran Theological Southern Seminary. An historical pageant with Holy Communion was held at the Township Auditorium on Sunday, April 28, as the opening of the synod convention, with an anniversary reception following at St. Paul Lutheran Church. Music for this special service was provided by the seminary choir, a joint handbell choir, and the Airport High School Chorus. Ushers were from the youth of the synod, and the reception was provided by the Lutheran Church Women. A special thankoffering was received by the congregations of the synod on the sunday before Thanksgiving, 1974, in honor of the 150th anniversary and designated for the Loan Fund for mission congregations in South Carolina.[30]

For years, the synod had been operating with five districts. In 1975, after a study by the Committee of Deans, the synod convention approved a realignment that resulted in eight districts to be organized by not later than October 15, 1975.[31] The purpose of each district was to "assist in caring for and developing the church on its territory, to provide liaison between the synod and the congregations of the district, and to perform such other functions, . . . , as the synod may assign to it." [32] Each district met twice a year, elected a dean, secretary, and cabinet, which was composed of the clergy and lay representatives to the five operational committees of the synod. The deans of the districts served as a committee to review and act on the status of pastors "whose status is subject to reconsideration," represent the district at congregational and auxiliary events, and other tasks as were needed for the ministry of their districts.[33]

The business of the synod was transacted at an annual convention held in the spring of the year. For years these conventions were held at various congregations throughout the synod, but in 1982, the conventions were moved to Newberry College where they have been held since. In 1974, the convention authorized an additional lay delegate for every

The synod in convention at Newberry College.

congregation with an active confirmed membership of over 250.[34] With the growth in the number of congregations and pastors, and the addition of these lay delegates, the synod soon outgrew the facilities of most congregations. Newberry College provided the synod with the necessary facilities for meetings, overnight accommodations, and meals. The time for these conventions was moved to a date after college commencement, and alternated between weekend and weekday conventions, with the various districts serving as hosts.

In 1973, the Church House at the corner of Richland and Park streets in Columbia was free of debt for the first time since its erection in 1958 and expansion in 1964. Here the offices of the bishop and other synod staff, the synodical film library, and other related offices are housed. In 1987, the building underwent a complete renovation at a cost of $100,000, paid for by a loan of $75,000, and synod reserves.[35]

Inclusive Ministry

Throughout these two decades, the synod experienced a growing awareness in the area of inclusive ministry—that is ministry with minorities, especially blacks and women. The executive board approved the idea of a mission congregation in the Eau Claire section of Columbia to serve the needs of those residents, particularly the blacks. In 1971, the Committee on American Missions, in cooperation with the Board of American Missions of the LCA, called the Rev. William Batterman, who carried on a short-lived mission in that area.[36]

In 1979, a Task Force on Minority Ministries was formed by the Social Ministry Committee of synod, and in 1985, it became an autonomous committee of synod.[37] The committee began its work by surveying and noting the positive changes throughout the synod in the area of racial inclusiveness. Beginning in 1980, it began work on an Equal Employment Opportunity Statement that was adopted by the synod convention in 1981. This statement calls for the executive board of synod to engage employees without regard to sex, race, or nationality, ethnic or religious background, except in instances in which preference should be

The Rev. Garey Green (right), newly ordained, and his sponsor, the Rev. Dermon A. Sox, Jr. (left).

given to members of Lutheran congregations. That convention also adopted a Statement on Racial Inclusiveness that commits the South Carolina Synod to "the elimination of all racial barriers and to the opening of the doors of all congregations to all people." [38] This statement was reaffirmed at the convention in 1984.[39] In 1982, a resolution was adopted calling for congregations to affirm the inclusiveness of its ministries to all the people of its communities.[40] In 1983, the first black person was ordained by the South Carolina Synod.[41]

As a result of the 1976 Convention action, the synod secretary was asked to compile and report statistics concerning the levels of participation by women in the leadership roles of congregations and the synod.[42] The Secretary reported increasing numbers of women in positions of responsibility in the church, but still far less proportionately than their membership numbers. This growth in women's inclusiveness is evidenced by the following: in 1972, of the 128 lay delegates to the South Carolina Synod Convention, 13 (10%) were women; in 1976, of 189 delegates, 42 (22%) were women; in 1972, of the 8 lay delegates from South Carolina to the LCA Convention, only 1 (12.5%) was a woman; in 1976, of the 8 lay delegates, 4 (50%) were women.[43]

Conventions of the synod adopted several resolutions dealing with issues before the people and the legislature of the state. Among them were 1982 Convention actions opposing the storage of nuclear waste from other states in South Carolina[44] and supporting the bilateral freeze on the development and deployment of nuclear weapons;[45] 1983 Convention action opposing any attempt to legalize gambling in South Carolina;[46] action expressing opposition to the sale of children in South Carolina by the 1984 Convention;[47] and the support of reform of the adoption laws of South Carolina by the convention of 1985.[48] The synod also adopted a resolution supporting significant minority representation in the South Carolina Senate;[49] and a resolution supporting the removal of the Confederate flag from the top of the State House was adopted in 1986.[50]

Ecumenism

Ecumenism was certainly an area of growth during the decades of the 70's and 80's. Most of this work was carried out through the Christian Action Council of South Carolina, of which the South Carolina Synod is a supporting member. The purpose of this Council has been to enhance the cooperative efforts among churches and individual Christians and to identify common concerns and to develop avenues for working together to translate those concerns into action. Legislative seminars and programs for new pastors in the state are but two of the Council's programs.[51] In 1971, the Council faced a financial crisis when the Internal Revenue Service ruled that it was not a "religious" agency, and must, therefore, pay taxes, although contributions to it were tax exempt as "educational charitable" deductions. An appeal of this ruling resulted in the overturning of the IRS ruling in 1972.[52] The 50th anniversary of the Council in 1983 showed that involvement by the South Carolina Synod began in 1952 with support steadily growing through the years. The relationship with the Lutheran Church was strengthened in 1983 when the council moved into rented quarters at Southern Seminary.[53] In 1985, the Rev. Dr. Howard McClain resigned as Executive Director after over 35 years of service. The Rev. Dr. Russell B. Norris became the Executive Minister in 1986, the first Lutheran to hold that position.[54] Eighteen church bodies, with more than 6,000 congregations and nearly 1.8 million Christians across South Carolina, support the work of the Council.

One of the biggest steps in ecumenism occurred in 1984 with the development of the Episcopal-Lutheran Dialogue. A statement endorsing this document and establishing procedures by which Lutherans and Episcopalians could share in the celebration of Holy Communion was adopted and signed by the Bishops of the Upper and Lower Diocese of the Episcopal Church and the Bishop of the South Carolina Lutheran Synod. A conference on this dialogue and document was held in Columbia, and since then a number of shared services of Holy Communion have been celebrated throughout the state.[55]

Episcopal Bishops William A. Beckham and C. FitzSimons Allison (left and right), and Bishop Cauble sign "Guidelines for the Joint Celebration of the Eucharist between Lutheran and Episcopal Churches in South Carolina."

In 1987, another ecumenical highlight was the visit of Pope John Paul II to Columbia. Although the synod was not officially involved in the preparations for this visit, four national Lutheran leaders attended a conference with other leaders of the Christian and Jewish churches in America and the Pope at the University of South Carolina. A number of Lutheran clergy and laity shared in the Christian prayer service that was held at Williams-Brice Stadium. The next day, Southern Seminary hosted a meeting of the Christian leaders who had come to Columbia to discuss further the road of ecumenism. Over 300 people attended the conference.

Midlands Lutheran Council

Because the Columbia metropolitan area, like many other cities, is undergoing enormous changes and is presenting an increasing challenge to our congregations to witness effectively, in August 1984, Bishop Cauble formed an Area Mission Study Committee to examine the community and how to enhance the ministry of the Lutheran church in, and around, the area. Years of hard, sophisticated work, with the assistance of the Rev. Boyce Whitener of the LCA's Division for Mission in North America, resulted in the publication of the *Midlands Area Mission Strategy, 1986-1996*, a proposed plan for ministry. Detailed data on the demographic composition of congregations and parishes provided concrete basis for planning. Also came a proposal that the area congregations, which have long cooperated informally, work together on a more formal basis as the Midlands Lutheran Council. To guide the new Council, the study committee drew up a Statement of Mission, Principles of Mission, and a set of goals toward enhancing the cooperative ministry of the Lutheran church in the community and with other denominations. The Midlands Lutheran Council first met in May 1987, at Ebenezer Church, Columbia. The Statement of Mission, Principles of Mission, and Goals were approved, and the Board of Directors with four clergy and eight lay members was elected. Representatives of the bishop, Newberry College, LTSS, Lutheran Social Services of Central South Carolina, the Lowman Home, and the LCA Division for Ministry in North America are also members of the board. The board met monthly in 1987 drawing up ideas for ways to serve the Lutheran church in the Columbia area. In late June 1987, the Council met again to advise the board on a variety of projects and proposals. With the Council's approval, the board has worked on promotion and publicity for the 1987 Reformation services and plans for the 1988 Reformation service; a survey of congregations to discover unique and common areas of ministry; long-range planning; and "professional leadership events" for pastors and other church leaders. Thirty-six area congregations are participating in the Midlands Lutheran Council.[56]

The South Carolina Lutheran

The Synod Executive Board elected the Rev. D. Murray Shull, Jr. as the "interim editor" of the *South Carolina Lutheran* on August 30, 1966. The subsequent convention of synod confirmed the appointment by electing him Editor and re-electing the Rev. G. B. Corley as Business Manager,[57] a position he had held since 1957. The new editor reported to the synod convention of 1968: "The position of editor ... is a sobering responsibility. By the news printed or omitted is inferred what is relevant, or not relevant, to the life of the synod and its congregations." [58]

Editions during the first few years under Pastor Shull revealed only slight changes in the design, omission of the "Editorial," use of occasional guest editorials (usually from other church publications), and the addition of "The Worship Corner," a regular feature for about four years. In 1969, the number of pages was increased from eight to twelve in six of the eleven issues.

At the end of 1968, the subscriptions numbered 11,505, and for the next ten years there was a steady increase in the number of subscribers. By 1976, when the growth reached over 14,000, the Newberry Observer Company, which had printed and mailed the publication for forty years, found it necessary to request that another firm be engaged to do the work. Crown Printing Company of Greenville took over the printing function, with computer printed address labels supplied by Data Systems, Inc., also of Greenville, until Mr. Fred Lester of Newberry took over this function.

The changes brought on by the increased subscriptions evolved into an exciting transition in 1977 that offered expansion at a reasonable cost into the occasional use of color and art work, additional pages, coded labels, and printouts by congregations and districts. "It's been a year of extra work and rewards as we have grown in providing a quality publication to serve the people of the South Carolina Synod," reported Editor Shull.[59] At the end of 1977, the subscription list numbered 15,229, and only 34 out of 150 congregations were not on the Every Home Subscription Plan.

Funding of a synodical publication reflects many factors in its history. *The Lutheran Messenger,* the original predecessor periodical, "published monthly in the interests of the Evangelical Lutheran Synod of South Carolina," in 1922 distributed 5,000 free sample copies of its first issue among the congregations. The initial annual subscription price was fixed at fifty cents.[60] Synod records show that for just over twenty years there were three sources of income for *The South Carolina Lutheran*: subscriptions, synod (budgeted allocation), and the women's auxiliary of synod. The records show an annual contribution that ranged from $50.00 to $150.00 per year from the women from 1954 through 1975. In 1970, synod gave an additional allocation above the budgeted amount to underwrite increased costs, and in 1977, extra monies were authorized to finance the changeovers mentioned above. The 1982 Convention of synod adopted a budget for 1983 that doubled the funding for the *South Carolina Lutheran* from $6,000 to $12,000. Increased to $13,000 in 1984, the budget allocation dropped back to $12,000 in 1985 through 1987. Mounting postal costs during this period had a definite impact on publications of this type.

Subscription rates fall into two categories: a congregational (when every member home is included) and an individual subscription rate. In 1971, increasing costs forced a rate increase to $1.00 per year for the congregational plan, and $1.50 for the individual plan. By 1980, those rates had doubled; but the 1982 rates of $2.50 for the congregational plan, and $3.50 for the individual plan were still in effect in 1987.

Subscription numbers likewise reflect the acceptance and support of congregations and members. Peaking in 1978 at 15,286 (possibly in response to the addition of color, improved type styles, etc.), there was a period of leveling off until 1983 when the 15,000 mark was reached again with 130 churches on the congregational plan. At the end of 1987, there were 16,971 subscriptions with 132 on the congregational plan and 30 on the individual plan.[61] It took 32 years (1922-1954) to reach the initial goal of 3,000 subscriptions for the synodical publication,[62] and in the next 32 years, that number increased more than five times.

While the 1980's were years of increased support through increased funding by the synod and increased numbers of subscriptions, there were other indications of the success of the *South Carolina Lutheran*. Editor Shull reported to the 1982 Convention: "It has been a great year for the *South Carolina Lutheran*. We were the top winner among all Lutheran Church in America synod publications in the LCA sponsored contest last October (1981)." [63] In 1983, the total number of pages printed each year increased from 116 to 120, with some color pages in every issue.

Editor Shull in his annual reports to the synod regularly expressed his appreciation to the district reporters who channel news from congregations to the "Sandlapper Soul Scenes" columns and to the bishop and staff of synod for their support. In 1985, he wrote: "I am very grateful for the growing numbers of persons who are occasionally and regularly writing feature articles.... You enable us to have a broader coverage across the synod and to feature more often persons, events, and institutions that are meaningful in the life of our constituency." [64]

During the 1980's, there has also been more coverage of items pertaining to the life and work of the national church. As developments led to establishing the new Evangelical Lutheran Church in America in January 1988, the synodical paper devoted generous space to articles that informed the members of the synod of all phases of the merger and transition.

In 1987, the Rev. G. B. Corley marked 30 years as Business-Circulation Manager, and Editor Shull's 20th Anniversary passed in 1986. These tenures are indicative of the confidence placed in these men who are recommended by the Publications Committee of the Executive Board and elected by the synod in convention for two year terms. The Publications Committee is given the responsibility for the *South Carolina Lutheran*. It serves in an advisory/supervisory capacity. Decisions on purpose, policy, general guidelines, etc. are determined cooperatively by the publication's staff and the committee.

Pastor Shull also serves as the official synod correspondent for the LCA's publication, *The Lutheran*.

Other Programs

A Synod-Wide Bicentennial Banquet was held as part of the 1976 Convention at the Omar Shrine Temple in Charleston. Over 600 people attended this evening that included entertainment by the Madrigalians and the Jazz Ensemble from Newberry College, an address by the Rev. Dr. Robert J. Marshall, President of the LCA, and the fellowship of those assembled.[65]

The Executive Board authorized the commissioning of artist Leon Loard of Montgomery, Alabama, to paint a portrait of Dr. Herman W. Cauble.[66] The portrait was presented to the synod at a banquet as part of the 1979 Convention by the Rev. Earl H. Loadholdt on behalf of the Executive Board. Mrs. Cauble unveiled the portrait, and Dr. Cauble responded with words of appreciation.[67] The portrait was later hung in the Synod House.

The call process is one that affects every pastor and congregation. A resolution adopted by the 1981 Convention called on the Executive Board to appoint a special committee "to study the call procedures currently being used in our synod and other synods." [68] The Executive Board appointed James N. Hallman, chairman; the Rev. Henry M. Moody, Jr.; and Reid S. Wingard to this committee. They made a progress report to the 1982 Convention.[69] The Executive Board approved the final product, "Guides for the Call Process," set July 1, 1983 as the implementation date, and authorized the distribution of the guides to all pastors and church councils of the synod.[70] This guide has been a valuable tool to pastors, congregations, and the synod staff in working through the call process.

On March 28, 1984, a devastating tornado hit South Carolina with the most severe effect being felt in Newberry and Marlboro counties. Over $40,000 was channeled through the synod from congregations and individuals in the synod for disaster relief in the hard hit areas.[71]

A special ministry at the South Carolina Central Correctional Institution (CCI) in Columbia is carried out by a pastor of the South Carolina Synod and is supported by individuals and congregations of the synod. Having gradu-

Frankie San visits an inmate at CCI.

ated from LTSS in 1966 and having completed additional studies at the University of South Carolina, Kyuzo Miyaishi (Frankie San) was ordained by the synod in 1973 with a Call to Special Service as a "Tent Making Ministry" at CCI. Frankie San was born in Tokyo, Japan. At age 30, he became a Christian, graduated from Hosei University in Tokyo in 1961, and came to the United States to begin his studies at Columbia Bible College. In 1962, he transferred to LTSS and completed his internship at the Lutheran Children's Home of the South in Virginia.

Frankie San began visiting CCI while a student, proclaiming the message, "Christ loves you; I love you." Upon graduation, he began spending his days at the prison as an adult education instructor and later as a library assistant, teaching the prison illiterates the three R's, and introducing the meaning and value of brotherly love to the prison population. At Christmas, he dons a Santa Claus suit and distributes gifts he has collected from individuals and congregations. He regularly visits throughout the synod sharing the impact of his ministry, and publishes a regular Christmas report for the synod.

He has spent hours on Death Row, in the prison infirmary, in the Maximum Security section, and throughout the prison, writing letters to family and friends, giving encouragement, and proclaiming to all "Christ loves you; I love you." His legacy will continue through a foundation, currently valued at $800,000, established to ensure the continuation of this type of ministry.

The Merger

While continuing its full programs for ministry, the South Carolina Synod actively participated in the discussions and studies that would eventually lead to the formation of the Evangelical Lutheran Church in America in 1988, and to a restructuring of the South Carolina Synod organization. At the 1981 Convention of Synod, the Rev. Dr. Albert Haversat, Assistant to the Bishop of the LCA, addressed the convention on the proposals for Lutheran merger. At the conclusion of his report, an opinion poll was conducted, with 222 delegates voting in favor of a merger of the three Lutheran churches in some form, 44 preferring separate structures, and 11 undecided.[72] Reports from the Commission on Lutheran Unity (CNLC) to the 1982 and 1983 Conventions kept the synod informed of the progress that was being made, and of the direction that the merger was taking. At the 1984 Synod Convention, a more intensive review in small group forums and discussion on the floor of the convention were held concerning the CNLC report.[73] As a result of this, several sense motions expressing the feeling of the South Carolina Synod in convention were adopted for review by the CNLC. These motions included:

1) "that every ordained minister be a delegate in local and small regional assemblies, and ordained ministers have a fifty percent representation in the national and large regional assemblies" (243 for, 51 against, and 10 abstaining);

2) "that the quota aspect (which called for equal male and female representation) of the assemblies should be eliminated" (259 for, 44 against, and 8 abstaining);

3) "that the South Carolina Synod of the LCA supports only one level of specific ministry, that of those who are set apart for the ordained ministry, in the new Lutheran church;" at the same time affirming the priesthood of all believers and supporting those who serve in the lay ministry of the church (273 for, 19 against, and 4 abstaining);

4) "that membership in this church shall be defined as baptized members of its congregations" (280 for, 10 against, and 4 abstaining);

5) "that the new Lutheran Church should include an organization for women" (293 for, 0 against, and 5 abstaining);

6) "that a Lutheran Men's auxiliary be developed as a part of the new Lutheran Church" (297 for, 0 against, and 2 abstaining);

7) "that the congregation remain the sole base from which the new Lutheran church organizational structure is built" (135 for, 128 against, and 14 abstaining);

8) "that the CNLC establish an organization for youth as an auxiliary of the new Lutheran church" (298 for, 0 against, and 2 abstaining); and

9) "that, while we are against the quota system..., we support the spirit of the commission in attempting to establish fair representation of all persons," and ask the commission to carefully consider other alternatives that might achieve the same goals (202 for, 44 against, and 35 abstaining).

The voting was concluded with the adoption of a motion stating that the synod "confidently believes that God is guiding us to do His will in forming a new Lutheran church; we thank the commission for its laborious and diligent ministry; and we pray God's continuing guidance and blessing on their work." [74]

The Rev. Dr. H. George Anderson, a member of the CNLC, reported to the 1985 Convention on the work of the commission noting how they had responded to the input made through sense motions by the South Carolina and other synods. He also "reviewed the major areas where a consensus has not yet been reached." [75] Again, several sense motions were adopted by the convention:

1) "that satisfaction and pleasure be expressed concerning the proposed boundaries for Synod B of the Regional Center for Mission IX" (245 yes, 1 no);

2) "that it is the strong desire of the South Carolina Synod to have the state of Virginia included in Regional Center for Mission IX" (245 yes, 0 no);

3) "that it is the wish of the South Carolina Synod to share and be strengthened through our new Lutheran church with a relationship with the churches of the Carib-

bean, and that they be included within Regional Center for Mission IX" (243 yes, 2 no);

4) "that the ordering of ministry within the new Lutheran church reflect the primacy of the ministry of the whole people of God and the unique importance of the ordained ministry of Word and Sacrament. In synod assemblies, ordained ministers of Word and Sacrament be given voice and vote by virtue of their office and all commissioned ministers be considered lay persons eligible for election as delegates from their congregations. In the national assembly, commissioned ministers be considered as lay persons, eligible for election as lay delegates, and the delegates elected from the 'roster of ministers' be ordained ministers of Word and Sacrament. The new Lutheran church commit itself to the professional support of its commissioned ministers, allocating adequate resources for their preparation, continuing education, recognition, and constant support" (245 yes, 0 no); and

5) "that it is the sense of the South Carolina Synod to favor strongly Option A, which states 'each seminary be a seminary of this church, shall be incorporated, and shall be financed by synods of this church. Each seminary shall be governed by a Board of Regents, elected by the supporting synods, except that two regents shall be elected by the Division for Ministry from outside the supporting synods.'" (240 yes, 5 no).[76]

Earlier a motion had been adopted calling for all ordained ministers to have a vote at the Synod Assembly.[77]

By 1986, the intensity of the work toward merger had reached the point that the Executive Board appointed a task force to work for the transition of the South Carolina Synod into the new church.[78] This Transition Team, composed of the Rev. John L. Setzler, chairperson, with Mr. James N. Hallman, the Rev. David A. Donges, the Rev. Dr. James S. Aull, the Rev. Robert L. Dasher, and the Rev. Walter Wist as members, began a long and exhaustive process of looking at the synod in the framework of what the mission is, how the synod should be organized, and how it should operate. To do this, several task forces were appointed to work through the various aspects of the synod's ministry and organizational structure. At the 1986 Convention, three major steps were taken:

1) following the report of the CNLC, presented by the Rev. Dr. Reuben Swanson, Secretary of the LCA, the convention adopted a resolution strongly reaffirming the synod's support of the efforts being made to join together The Lutheran Church in America, The American Lutheran Church, and the Association of Evangelical Lutheran Churches, by January 1, 1988. The standing vote showed only 6 negative votes and 3 abstentions;[79]

2) the convention adopted a Mission Statement for the new South Carolina Synod of the Evangelical Lutheran Church as proposed by the Transition Team and amended;[80] and

3) a resolution approving the merger of the South Carolina Synod, LCA into the South Carolina Synod, ELCA was approved by more than the two-thirds vote required.[81]

Again several sense motions concerning the proposed merger were adopted by the convention. Five of them had been submitted by the Executive Board:

1) six recommendations concerning the governing documents of the ELCA, in view of the synod's understanding of the nature of the church, composed the first motion that was adopted (the actual motion adopted was a substitute motion offered from the floor);

2) a motion relating to the ordained ministry was adopted;

3) a motion calling for more articulate statements affirming a commitment to the development of ecumenical relationships was adopted;

4) support for inclusive representation in assemblies, councils, boards, committees, and governing bodies of the ELCA was approved; and

5) items related to the Pensions and Other Benefits were addressed.

Other sense motions included:

1) a recommendation "to include all ordained ministers as delegates at synod assemblies;"

2) a recommendation that the "constitution for congregations of the ELCA provide for the option of either the

pastor or a lay person serving as president of the congregation;"

3) a call for the reconsideration of the CNLC's "decision to locate the headquarters of the new church in Milwaukee;" and

4) a recommendation that the "primary location of the Lutheran Theological Southern Seminary continue to be in Columbia, South Carolina." [82]

All of this synod action, combined with the work of the CNLC, the South Carolina Synod Transition Team, and action by the conventions of the LCA, ALC, and AELC, and the Constituting Convention of the ELCA, culminated in the Constituting Convention of the South Carolina Synod of the ELCA at Newberry College on May 29-30, 1987. At this convention, the constitution, bylaws, and continuing resolutions were adopted; the Rev. Dr. James S. Aull was elected Bishop; Mrs. Mary Ann Shealy was elected Vice-President; the Rev. James W. Addy was elected Secretary; Mr. Raymond S. Caughman was elected Treasurer; members of the Synod Council and Boards of Trustees for Institutions and Committees of Consultation and Discipline were elected; representatives to the Regional Council were elected; a budget was adopted; the location of the synodical offices was approved; and other business was conducted by the voting delegates of lay men, lay women, certified lay professionals and clergy representing the 161 congregations of the LCA and the one congregation and one mission under the development of the ALC.[83]

Chapter Two—Committees

Committees carried out a large portion of the synod's work. As they engaged in the planning and execution of ministry programs for the synod, they enhanced the ability of congregations to function in its communities. Five of these committees were operational committees, and the membership included one lay person and one clergy person from each of the eight districts, and up to one additional person appointed by the bishop.[1]

American Missions

Bishop Cauble and the Rev. Joseph Holt break ground for the first unit at Cross and Crown, Florence.

The American Missions Committee, for which the bishop served as chairman, worked to foster and cultivate a "mission" spirit among the members of the South Carolina Synod. Working closely with the Division for Mission in North America's Regional Staff Person for South Carolina, this committee monitored and supported the development of mission congregations throughout South Carolina. It also provided financial aid for older congregations which were unable to maintain an adequate ministry on their own. Beyond that, this committee was also responsible for the summer ministry at camp sites in Myrtle Beach, and for supporting the Rural Mission, Incorporated, an ecumenical effort on John's Island.[2] The Rev. David F. Johnson served as the LCA's Deployed Staff

person for many years until his death in 1981. The Rev.
Boyce C. Whitener was later appointed to that position.

Evangelism

A major continuing project of the Evangelism Committee
has been the Carolinas' Evangelism Conference, sponsored
every two years by the North and South Carolina Synods.
These conferences began in 1966, and have brought to the
area some of the leading persons in the field of evangelism
to conduct workshops and worship services for congregational evangelism leaders. A Rally to open the conference
has been the highlight of this event for the past several
years. In 1973, a special evangelism emphasis called "Key
'73" was led by this committee. During this year, special
emphasis was placed on evangelism with workshops and
skillshops being held to equip members of the congregations with the skills needed to do person-to-person evangelism.[3] EvangALIVE in '75 was the key emphasis of evangelism that included five cluster clinics on inactive members,
prospective members, climate building, year round planning, and person to person witnessing.[4] A "Year Full of
Evangelism" was designated for 1984-85 to encourage every
congregation to develop an intentional program of evangelism to the unchurched, to the inactive, and for the integration of new members.[5] This followed action in 1976 when
the LCA and the ALC began working together on a joint
evangelism emphasis called Evangelical Outreach. An EO
coordinator was appointed by the synod with work to include emphasis on Bible study and witness through the
Word and Witness Program, the use of mass media for
evangelism, the training of parish callers, and the use of the
catechism for the training of new members.[6] EO was continued as a special project of the Evangelism Committee.
Additionally, this committee has regularly sponsored retreats, conferences, and workshops on evangelism, as well
as the publication of several evangelism guides for the congregational committees.[7]

Social Ministry

The Social Ministry Committee provided leadership for the synod and the congregations in various social areas and concerns that faced the people of South Carolina during these years. They did so by studying the issues and presenting resolutions to the synod conventions for adoption and implementation, and by developing programs for the congregations to use in their communities. Much of the work of this committee was done through the development of "task forces" and included work in areas of Native American Indian concerns, Ministry with the Aging, Alcohol and Drug Abuse, Literacy, Hospital Visitations, and many others. Three programs that the committee worked most diligently with deserve special note.

The committee sponsored the attendance of two deaf members of the synod at a Convention of the International Lutheran Deaf Association as a "first step" toward providing a broader ministry for the hearing impaired of South Carolina.[8] Work in this area grew until, with the assistance of DMNA, a mission congregation was organized in Columbia for people with impaired hearing and their families (see pages 2 and 169).

The Task Force on Minority Ministries began as a part of the Social Ministry Committee in 1979, and in 1985, became a committee of the synod (see page 9).

The most involved on-going ministry of the Social Ministry Committee has been that of child care. The 1970 Synod Convention directed the Executive Board to set up a special committee to study the synod's relationship with the Children's Home of the South and the availability of alternative services in South Carolina for child care. This committee recommended, and the conventions of synod in 1971 and 1972 approved, the withdrawal of support from the Children's Home because of the distance to the home in Virginia and because of comparable services available in South Carolina.[9] The synod's withdrawal became effective July 1, 1972, and the committee began to formulate its own program for child care in South Carolina. On January 1, 1974, the Social Ministry Committee began purchasing the services of the

Executive Director of the Lutheran Social Ministry Agency of Greater Columbia for one day per week as the Child Care Ministry Coordinator for the synod.[10] This relationship continued until the reorganization of the Social Ministry Agency into the Lutheran Social Services of Central South Carolina, which, while interested in the child care program, did not have the staff to carry out its work. The synod then hired a part-time person to carry out this ministry program.[11]

In addition to child care, the Social Ministry Committee became an advocate for many issues facing the South Carolina Legislature. One such issue revolved around concern over the fact that children could be legally bought and sold in South Carolina. A resolution expressing this concern was adopted by the 1984 Synod Convention (see page 10), and the result of this and other outcries from citizens of the state was the passage of measures to halt this practice and a review of the adoption laws of the state. The 1985 Convention approved a resolution in support of these actions.[12]

Also through the efforts of this committee, several special projects in the state have received grants for their work. Two examples of these are a grant of $10,000 to the South Carolina Literacy Association and a $3,000 grant to the Columbia Urban Service Center from the Board of Social Ministry, LCA.[13]

The on-going ministry team on aging expanded its ministry in the late 1980's. June 1983-May 1984 was adopted as "The Year of the Older Lutheran" by the 1983 Convention. As an affirmation of this recommendation, the convention rose and read a "Credo on Aging." [14] At the 1985 Convention, the Social Ministry Committee's recommendation calling for each congregation to appoint a "Senior Staffer" and to carefully review its program ministry with the aging was adopted.[15] Mr. Raymond L. Boozer served as Synod Senior Staffer,[16] and through his leadership, surveys of activities in the congregations for "seniors" were conducted; synod wide programs for "seniors," and workshops for developing programs for the aging in the congregation and community were held.

Educational Ministry

One of the most active of the synod's operational committees was that of Educational Ministry (formerly Parish Education). The oversight of many synodical programs that affect every congregation, from teacher training to supervising the synod's media center, to supporting the camping program at Lutheridge, became the primary concern of a full-time staff person for many years. The Rev. Lloyd W. Mitcham came to the South Carolina Synod as Executive Director of Christian Education in 1968.[17] He served in this area with expanded responsibilities to include Youth Ministry until his resignation in 1984.[18]

A Vacation Church School workshop at Camp Kinard.

Through the years this committee has conducted workshops, mini-labs, retreats, and other special events to train Sunday School teachers, to help Vacation Church School leaders, to promote confirmation ministry programs, to help develop educational ministry programs for all congregations, and to cooperate with the Division for Parish Services in introducing new curricular and programs to congregations. Some of these activities and programs include seminars on confirmation ministry and First Communion instruction with the development by the LCA of a new statement and policy regarding communion as early as the fifth grade and with the introduction of new teaching materials for these classes.[19] A conference on Christian Family Life was the highlight of 1979, featuring Dr. Charlie Shedd, a well-known authority in that area.[20] Resource teams were also developed to assist congregations and clusters of congregations in developing leadership training programs.[21] A special observance of the 200th anniversary of the Sunday School in 1980 included the Rev. Dr. James R. Crumley,

Bishop of the LCA, as the speaker for a rally day program.[22] "Strive for Five/Shoot for Ten" was a program that over 80 congregations participated in to stimulate the growth of the Sunday Church School program.[23] In 1984, acting on the recommendation of this committee, the synod convention passed a resolution calling for every congregation to appoint an Educational Ministry coordinator to oversee the entire educational ministry program within that congregation.[24]

The Church School Teacher of the Year Award was started in 1980 and named for Edwin Ricks in 1984. This award, given in memory of a South Carolinian who worked with the LCA in Parish Education for many years, is given annually to that person nominated by his or her congregation and selected by a panel, as the outstanding church school teacher for that year.[25]

The film library continued to be operated out of the Synod House "vault," [26] under the direction of this committee by the work of a part-time staff person, Mrs. Virginia Aull. Efforts have been made to keep the library up-to-date with religious film material, VCR equipment, and other materials and equipment for congregational use.

Dr. G. F. Schott conducts a worship service for the Scout Retreat in the newly constructed shelter.

Scouting has been an active part of the total ministry program for many of the congregations in the synod. For years, the Committee on Scouting has worked to promote scouting as a part of the Christian ministry for young boys and girls. This committee began a Boy Scout Retreat for Lutheran Scouts in South Carolina in 1970, and have held such a retreat at Camp Kinard in December of each year until 1987. At these weekend retreats, boys learn camping skills, share in recreation and fellowship, and have a Sunday Worship Service, with the offering each year going to the World Hunger Appeal. In 1971, the retreat had a bicentennial theme, with each troop presenting a skit on the theme. On May 16, 1987, a "work day" was held with troops camping out over the weekend of May 15-17. At this work day, a shelter was built to serve as the Retreat Center for the scouts. The 1987 Scout Retreat was scheduled for January 1988. The scouts had previously been responsible for getting the drive started to build the large shelter at Camp Kinard. Other "work days" have been held to clean up and repair the outpost area of Camp Kinard.

The Scout Committee is also responsible for promoting and publicizing the "Pro-Deo et Patria" and "God and Family" scout awards, and national scouting events. They have also been a consultant to congregations, encouraging them to make scouting a part of their ministry program. While many people have served diligently on this committee, the Rev. Dr. Fred Schott has been the leading advocate for scouting in the Lutheran Church in South Carolina.

Stewardship

The stewardship program of the synod has always been strong. Even in the difficult economic times of the state and

A stewardship display at synod convention.

the nation, the programs of the church have been carried out because of the generous support of the members of the synod, and because of the hard work of the Stewardship Committee. Since the Lutheran Church in America was formed in 1962, the South Carolina Synod has set as its top priority in the area of stewardship the full payment of the synod's benevolence quota to the LCA. That quota has been paid by 100% and more every year. The synod's Stewardship Committee regularly communicated with the congregations and members of synod through a newsletter called "Ship Shape," and conducted workshops for congregational members and pastors. Mr. Thomas J. O'Brien became the LCA's deployed staff person for stewardship in the Southeast in 1975 and made his office at the synod house, serving other synods in the area as well.

In addition to the operational committees, several standing committees worked within the synod to provide program support and leadership for the congregations and pastors. These committees were appointed by the bishop with the approval of the Executive Board.[27]

Worship

The Committee on Worship provided pastors and congregations with much valuable information throughout the years, as well as leadership for various special worship opportunities in the synod and the districts. District workshops gave worship leaders and participants from various congregations the opportunity to come together and hear about ways of enhancing congregational worship, developing choirs, and providing ways in which the laity can become more involved in worship leadership. They also gave members an opportunity to share ideas about what was happening in worship in the various congregations, providing new ideas for others. Each year the Worship Committee was called upon to plan and coordinate the Ordination Service for the synod as well as the Service of Holy Communion at each synod convention. Some years these two services

Members of the Worship Committee line up participants for the procession of the Opening Worship Service of a synod convention.

were combined at the synod convention; at other times they were held separately. The committee also provided displays and forums at synod conventions on worship; published articles in the *South Carolina Lutheran* on worship; helped sponsor conferences on Worship, Music and the Arts; provided each congregation with a listing of hymns that were appropriate for each Sunday of the three year cycle, as well as those Sundays of the Lesser Festivals;[28] and began a Worship Notebook for each congregation about the seasonal worship opportunities.

The biggest project of this committee was the introduction of the *Lutheran Book of Worship* to the congregations of the synod in 1978. The arrival of this "green book" weighing 2 lbs. and 6 ozs.[29] was greeted with mixed emotions throughout the synod. While the *Service Book and Hymnal* had been in use for only twenty years, many people had developed a deep attachment to its forms of worship and hymn selections and were reluctant to make the change to the "green book." However, with the well organized and trained work of several leadership groups, the transition into this new book of worship was very smooth and complete. The use of the three settings within the book is widely divided throughout the synod, with some congregations using more than one setting during the year.

In 1982, the synod adopted a resolution encouraging all congregations to provide ways for each active member to "invite, encourage, and bring others who are inactive or unchurched to worship." [30]

World Missions

The Rev. James L. Brady, his wife, Lynne, and their children, Mary and Anna, at the Service of Commissioning held on May 25, 1986. Pastor Brady serves as a pastor-teacher, and Mrs. Brady serves in a ministry program with the deaf. Other participants in the service were (pictured in the background) Pastors Larry Bost, Henri Bishop, and Robert Dasher.

While world missions continued to be a strong part of the Lutheran church's ministry and was widely supported by congregations within the South Carolina Synod, the emphasis of this ministry shifted from Americans serving in these mission fields to local nationals providing the leadership for the Lutheran church in their own countries. As a result, the number of missionary families from the United States has decreased, and since 1971, only seven missionary families from South Carolina have served overseas. In 1986, the synod celebrated the commissioning of the Rev. and Mrs. James L. Brady as missionaries.[31] Missionary families from the synod have included:

The Rev. and Mrs. Henri Bishop in Malaysia and Singapore serving as a pastor, returning home in 1979;

Mr. and Mrs. Stanley Frick serving as teachers in Japan until 1973:

Mr. and Mrs. Herbert W. Heyse serving as teachers in Tanzania until 1978;

The Rev. and Mrs. Jerry C. Livingston still serving as a pastor in Japan;

The Rev. and Mrs. William Peery serving as a seminary
professor in India;

Mr. and Mrs. Larry Freeze serving as a maintenance
manager in Liberia until their return home in 1986;

The Rev. and Mrs. James Brady currently serving as a
pastor in Malaysia.

Although the overseas missionary scene has changed,
support for the world missions program has remained high
through the work of the World Missions Committee of
synod and the individual congregations that support these
missionaries. In 1983, for example, the South Carolina
Synod had the highest percentage of congregations in the
LCA supporting overseas missionaries through Designated
Advanced Gifts.[32] This support continues as congregations
provide funds and personal contact in support of the missionaries and their ministry. Congregation support for
world missions through Designated Advanced Gifts in 1986
was $93,300.[33]

In 1977, a Global Missions Event was held at Newberry
College. Sponsored by six synods in the Southeast in cooperation with DMNA and DWME of the LCA, this event
focused on the work of missionaries and the support needed
from the American congregations. Almost 500 people attended this conference.[34] In 1984, the synod adopted a resolution challenging each congregation to receive a special
Reformation Offering amounting to at least $1.00 per con-
firmed member that would be divided equally between the
development of new congregations in the United States and
support of the world missions work of the LCA.[35]

A bequest from the estate of James M. Holman was received by the synod in 1979. Parcels of land in Calhoun
County were sold, and the proceeds ($151,660.03) were in-
vested with the interest of this fund designated for the
support of missionary work in Japan.[36] The synod has had
other close ties with the work of missionaries in Japan. In
1971, Dr. and Mrs. Chitose Kishi visited South Carolina. Dr.
Kishi, a 1926 graduate of Southern Seminary, is former
President of the Japan Evangelical Lutheran Church and
Japan Lutheran Theological College and Seminary. His

visit was sponsored by the Board of World Missions and their Missionary-in-Residence program. Dr. Kishi taught at Southern Seminary in the spring quarter of 1971 and visited throughout the synod with the World Missions Committee making those arrangements.[37]

A delegation of visitors from the Lutheran Church in Japan made a "roots" tour of the southern United States in the fall of 1983. The visit was developed because the Japanese Lutheran Church had its beginnings through missionaries sent by the United Synod of the South, commissioned at services held at St. John, Charleston. Again the World Missions Committee served as hosts for part of this tour.[38]

In 1986, a group of 18 girls and 2 teachers from the high school in Kumamoto, Japan visited in the synod for two weeks, staying with host families in the Charleston and Columbia areas.[39]

World Hunger

A discussion of the World Hunger program.

Brought to the forefront by news reports from especially hard hit countries, a task force was set up in 1974 to direct the work of the synod in the area of world hunger. Congregations and individuals were strongly encouraged to participate in the fight against hunger throughout the world. In 1974, approximately $27,000 was given[40] with that amount rising to over $66,000 in 1975.[41] In 1982, the task force became a committee of synod,[42] and with the World Hunger Program extended through 1990—a decade of commitment—support for the program from the South Carolina Synod reached a high of $241,000 in 1985.[43] For several years the synod led the LCA in per capita giving to World Hunger.

In 1984, the committee published a World Hunger Resource Book for all congregations,[44] and in 1985, co-sponsored with Southern Seminary a conference on root causes of hunger to educate people to the condition and its causes.[45] While hunger remains a severe problem throughout the world, including parts of the United States and South Carolina, this committee has continued to educate members of the synod's congregations about the needs and means of meeting those needs through the World Hunger Program.

Professional Leadership

Preparing professional leaders for the church continued to be a vital part of the synod's overall ministry. This work was done by three different committees whose names and structures changed during this period primarily because of restructuring at the national level, but that in some form helped prepare persons for the full-time ministry, helped full-time church workers continue their education and sharpen their skills, and provided guidelines and support for financial compensation packages for pastors.

The Professional Leadership Preparation Committee was a combination of the Church Vocations and Examining Committees.[46] This committee worked with people, sometimes as early as high school, who felt the desire to pursue some type of church vocation as their life's work. Contact with these individuals continued through their college and seminary years by conducting interviews, providing appropriate testing, and making endorsements for entrance into seminary. Their work also included the final examination of students before certifying to the synod that they met all requirements for ordination.

Providing Continuing Education for clergy and lay professionals was the primary task of the Professional Leadership Services Committee, formerly the Continuing Education Committee.[47] In 1972, Pastors' Retreats at Camp Kinard were well received,[48] and the committee began mak-

Bishop Cauble talks with Pastors Paul Slice (right) and Buzz Van Horne (left), during a break at a pastors' retreat.

ing them an annual event, expanding them to include lay professionals. The committee also encouraged congregations to provide time and funds for these continuing education events, and encouraged each pastor to receive three Continuing Education Units each year.[49] The retreats offered opportunities for study, spiritual reflection, skill development, and fellowship. They attracted many pastors and a number of outstanding leaders. The committee also sponsored pastor/spouse conferences, pre-retirement seminars, first-year-in-ministry retreats, church management seminars, orientation workshops for new pastors in the synod, and professional counseling, free and on a confidential basis, for pastors and spouses.

For several years the Pastoral Support Committee annually compiled data on the compensation of pastors and reported their findings to the synod convention and congregations, making recommendations about budget considerations for pastoral support. Of particular concern were the number of pastors at the lower end of the compensation scale. The 1971 Synod Convention directed the Pastoral Support Committee to address itself to the question of the adequacy of pastors' compensation, and to study and make recommendations for the same. In 1970, the average total compensation was $8,759.[50] Following this mandate, the committee developed a Guideline for Minimum Pastoral Compensation. At the 1977 Convention, several pastors submitted a three part resolution through the Committee on Reference and Counsel. Part I recommended the establishment of a parish-pastor relations committee in each congregation with responsibilities outlined, and Part III recommended that $25,000 be added to the 1978 Budget to be used to supplement pastors' salaries which fell below the recommended levels, and that the Pastoral Support Committee develop guidelines for supplementing pastors' salaries. These two parts were adopted. Part II, which was referred to the Pastoral Support Committee, set forth a compensation scale that included a base salary (based on years of ordained ministry and size of congregation), housing and utilities, business and professional expenses, and benefits.[51] The 1977 Convention also adopted a resolution calling for the Executive Board to give top priority to an allocation at the end of the year for the establishment of an emergency fund for pastoral support. As a result, the Executive Board authorized the President of synod to inform pastors of such funds and requesting that pastors present their needs. In January 1978, $15,000 was set aside for this emergency fund. The Pastoral Support Committee sent a letter to the 35 lowest paid pastors informing them that supplementary funds were available for those who needed it. Six responses were received. Two indicated that they did not need such supplemental support, but that the discussion of pastoral compensation with their councils had proven to be beneficial. Financial supplements were given to four pastors plus two mission pastors recommended by the American Missions Committee.[52] The Pastoral Support Committee developed guidelines for a "Pastoral Service Committee in the Congregation," a "Minimum Pay Package" for 1979 with challenge goals, and "Guidelines to Supplement Pastors' Salaries." These were presented to the 1978 Convention and were adopted.[53] Since that convention, the committee has annually submitted "Recommended Pay Packages" with challenge goals. The committee has also been active in providing clergy and congregations with information con-

cerning the impact of Social Security and tax law changes
on the pastoral support package.

Parish Life and Ministry Development

Parish Life and Ministry Development (P.L.M.D.) began
with a retreat in 1973, and was so well received that the
Executive Board was encouraged to establish a committee
to provide assistance to congregations through the P.L.M.D.
program.[54] This program is a "combined effort of congregations, synods, and churchwide agencies to develop parish

A PLMD committee at work.

life and ministry in a comprehensive way. The heart of the
experience is an on-going process of planning and imple-
menting, out of which parish life and ministry emerges and
is continually renewed." In 1976, a special committee appointed to study the need for additional synod staff recommended that the synod employ a part-time staff person in
the area of P.L.M.D.[55] Dr. D. J. Haigler was employed as the
P.L.M.D. staff person in 1977[56] and served until 1984 when
he was succeeded by Mrs. Jackie Lybrand.[57] Church council
cluster retreats and individual council retreats in the local
setting, as well as the use of LCA resources such as *Renewing*, have been focal points for the P.L.M.D. work.

Camp and Conference Ministries

Camp and conference ministries within the territory of the South Carolina Synod had for two decades been largely limited to the ministry of Lutheridge. However, in 1967, 100 acres were purchased and 100 acres received as a gift from the O. R. Boozer estate.[58] On this 200 acre site near Leesville, S. C. has been developed the Karl W. Kinard Conference Center named to honor the long-time president of the synod. The desire of the synod was to provide year-round facilities at which groups within the synod and congregations could conduct retreats, conferences, meetings, and learning experiences. Development plans for Kinard Conference Center were presented to the 1969 Synod Convention. The convention authorized the promotion of these plans and the borrowing of $150,000 to construct the main conference center building.[59] The conference building and first cottage were built in 1970 with the cottage being a gift of the Lutheran Men of the synod. The men also contributed labor and resources to enlarge an existing lake and construct a second lake.[60]

Eagerness to have such a conference center was shown by the more than 3,500 people in 94 groups who used Kinard Conference Center in its first year of operation. The Rev. L. W. Mitcham, Jr., synodical Secretary of Christian Education, handled reservations for using the center. In January 1971, Mr. and Mrs. Simmie Amick began duties as resident caretaker and cooks. The second cottage constructed was provided by four Columbia churches: St. Paul, Reformation, St. Andrew, and Ebenezer. Two more cottages were donated from the estate of Mrs. Clarence H. Wertz of Orangeburg.[61] A dedication service for all the facilities at Kinard Conference Center constructed up to that time was held on April 16, 1972.[62]

The youth of the synod began an effort in 1972 to raise funds for the construction of a swimming pool. Their goal was to collect a dollar from every confirmed member within the synod. Over a thousand youth and adults gathered in August, 1973, for groundbreaking services for the pool.[63] The pool was used the next summer and dedicated on Sep-

The swimming pool at Camp Kinard is dedicated.

tember 8, 1974. Final cost of the pool was nearly $40,000.

A fifth cottage, completed in 1973, was a gift of five West Columbia area churches: St. David, Mt. Tabor, Emmanuel, Our Saviour, and Mt. Hermon. The sixth and last cottage was constructed in 1974-75 and was a gift from an anonymous donor in honor of Dr. Carl B. Caughman.[64]

The family camping center was first used in 1973. This area with 13 campsites and bathhouse was provided by churches in the Ridge area including Wittenberg, Leesville; Grace, Gilbert; St. Peter, Batesburg; Faith, Batesburg; Cedar Grove, Leesville; and St. Mark and Corinth, Prosperity.[65] A tennis and volleyball court was also developed at this time. The outpost area was cleared and developed by Boy Scout troops from across the synod. The large picnic shelter and nearby restroom in the outpost area were partially provided by a one-time appeal in the congregations in 1975.

A change in the administration of Kinard Conference Center occurred in August 1973, when Pastor Harold G. Skinner accepted the call to become pastor of Wittenberg, Leesville. Involved in the call was an agreement with the executive board of synod to purchase 20% of his time to serve as Coordinator of Kinard Conference Center.[66]

The 1975 Synod Convention approved a synod wide appeal for Camp and Conference Ministries to begin no earlier than 1978.[67] In order not to begin too closely after the start of the LCA's Strength for Mission appeal, the 1977 Convention set the time for the Camp and Conference Appeal to begin its congregational phase in the summer of 1979 with a 24-month pledge period.[68] Its basic goal was $750,000. The challenge goal was $1,000,000.

The Lodge Complex at Camp Kinard is dedicated by (left to right): Pastors Harold Skinner, Camp Coordinator; James S. Aull, Synod Secretary; James W. Addy, Chairman, Camp and Conference Ministries Committee.

Incarnation, Columbia, provided funds for the building of the first unit in the Lodge Complex at Kinard Conference Center. The unit, constructed in 1978, consisted of four motel-type rooms with 2 double beds each, individual room heating/cooling, and private baths.

Mr. and Mrs. Simmie Amick resigned their positions at Kinard Conference Center in May 1979. Mr. and Mrs. Harold Benson began nearly two years of service as Food Preparation Director and assistant. Mr. Edward O. Barber served as resident Caretaker from September 1979 through December 1981. The resignation of Pastor Skinner as Coordinator effective December 31, 1981, had led to a decision by the Management Committee to seek a resident Camp Director. The duties of administering the conference center had grown too large to be handled by only 20% of a person's time. Mr. Jerry A. Freeze was chosen as Camp Director, a position which combined administrative and maintenance duties. He assumed these duties on April 1, 1982.

Along with a $30,000 gift from the Self Foundation of Greenwood, funds from the camping appeal provided the second unit in the Lodge Complex at Kinard Conference Center. Appeal funds were also used to pave a major portion of the road system at Camp Kinard. During 1981, Kinard Conference Center received "through a very generous arrangement by Miss Laura Brodie" ownership of an additional 93.5 acres of land adjacent to the conference center.[69] Use of the conference center grew in 1981 to over 8,300 people in 249 different groups. The third unit in the Lodge Complex at Kinard Conference Center consists of four bedrooms and a meeting room, which can be converted into two bedrooms at a future date. This unit was constructed in 1982.[70] One of the bedrooms is being used as an office. In 1982, the residence on the grounds at Kinard was vastly remodeled in order to be suitable for the Camp Director's home. Construction of a maintenance building was also begun that year.

A one-week Lutheridge Satellite camp for junior campers was held for the first time in 1982. Other special summer programs at this time included a camping program known as Camp Kemo for children with cancer, two camps for mentally retarded children, and camps for autistic and diabetic children.[71]

Twenty-five acres across Two Notch Road from the entrance to Kinard Conference Center were purchased in 1985 to assure an attractive entrance to the center. A small picnic shelter adjacent to the main conference center and a recreational field near the outpost shelter were added at Kinard Conference Center in 1985. In 1986, Mr. Jerry Freeze resigned as Camp Director, and Mr. Herbert Loadholdt became the new Director in April 1987.[72]

Upon the urging of the Charleston area pastors, the Executive Board considered the purchase of the former property of St. Mark, Sullivan's Island for use as a retreat center. The congregation had relocated to the Isle of Palms. The executive board recommended to the 1974 Synod Convention that the former church property be purchased for $22,500 and two adjacent lots owned by the town be purchased for $600 each. The convention approved the recommendation.[73] Volunteers from Charleston area churches prepared the former parish building for use as a retreat center and maintained it as well. This temporary center, therefore, was self-supporting at the low rate of $1 per day per person or $5 per group for day use.

Plans for developing the Sullivan's Island property into a

retreat center were rejected by that town's zoning commission. Thus, other suitable property was sought in the Charleston area. The 1978 Synod Convention approved the purchase of 1.47 acres of land at the corner of 21st Avenue and Palm Boulevard on the Isle of Palms at a net cost of $100,000. The Town Council of the Isle of Palms had given permission to develop the property as a retreat center.[74] The executive board was authorized to sell the Sullivan's Island property.

General concepts and plans for the Coastal Retreat Center were approved by the 1980 Synod Convention. It also authorized the borrowing of $400,000 to complete the center.[75] Groundbreaking for the new Coastal Retreat Center

Ground is broken for the Coastal Retreat Center by (left to right): Mr. John S. Rodenberg and the Rev. E. Armand Shealy, members of the building committee; Mr. Charles A. Curl, representative of Stanley Smith and Sons, Inc., contractors; Bishop Cauble; the Rev. Eugene Kern, member of the building committee; Mr. Harry Stoudenmire, chairman of the building committee; and the Rev. James W. Addy, chairman of the Management Committee for Camp and Conference Ministries.

was held on March 1, 1981. The completed center contains twenty bedrooms with the necessary meeting rooms, kitchen, etc. It was first used in January 1982, and was dedicated on March 27, 1982. Groups using the Coastal Retreat Center provide their own linens and prepare their own meals. In its first year of operation, nearly 3,000 people in 117 groups used the center. Mr. and Mrs. Edwin (Kathryn) Mohrmann donated three years' service as managers of the retreat center.

Use of the Coastal Retreat Center grew to over 250 days in 1983. Such use allowed payments on the debt and the construction of a recreational court costing approximately $19,000. Mr. and Mrs. Robert (Marlene) Park served as managers of the retreat center for seven months in 1985. Mr. and Mrs. Cy (Martha) Kaemmerlen assumed the duties of the managers in November 1985.

The executive board, late in 1985, approved the installation of an elevator at the Coastal Retreat Center in order to better accommodate all of the various groups which use the center. In 1987, they also approved the purchase of the property at 2105 Palm Blvd., adjacent to the center, to be

The Coastal Retreat Center.

used as a residence for the managers of the center. Through the gift of Mr. and Mrs. Walter A. Sigman, Jr. of Clinton, this purchase was completed, and the residence was named "The Sigman House" in their honor.[76]

For several years, management of the camp and conference centers had been the responsibility of an appointed committee. At the 1977 Convention, a resolution was adopted calling for the Executive Board to give serious consideration "to the establishment of an elected board of trustees for the Karl W. Kinard Conference Center and/or the Sullivan's Island Retreat Center ... to oversee their administration." [77] In 1978, first reading approval was given to a constitutional amdendment establishing a nine member Management Committee for Camp and Conference Ministries elected by the convention.[78] Final approval was given at the 1979 Convention,[79] and the first committee was elected. This committee has since had the responsibility for overseeing the camp and conference ministries of the synod.

Certified Lay Professionals

An important support group within the church's ministry program has been the lay people who work in the church in various ministry areas. They have worked in areas such as music, educational ministry, youth ministry, visitation, administration, etc. The use of these lay professionals has grown through the years, so that some congregations have full-time persons, and some congregations have several part-time persons. By meeting guidelines established by the LCA, these persons could become "Certified Lay Professionals" (CLP's). In 1983, the Executive Board authorized the Professional Leadership Preparation Committee to study the relationship of the CLP's to the synod.[80] The 1985 Convention approved an amendment to the synod's constitution giving CLP's seat and voice at conventions.[81]

Campus Ministry

The campus ministry program of the synod works to provide Lutheran youth at the non-Lutheran colleges and universities in South Carolina with a program designed to strengthen the faith and maintain the worship experiences of these Lutheran students. While the programs are varied throughout the state because of the numbers of students involved and the setting in which they live and study, the overall program can be divided into three basic groups.

At the University of South Carolina in Columbia, the synod maintains a fulltime ministry through a Lutheran Campus Pastor. In 1968, Pastor Carl Ficken resigned from that position,[82] having seen the growth of Lutheran campus ministry at the university and at Columbia College grow both in quality and quantity. The synod, in cooperation with the National Lutheran Campus Ministry, an agency of the LCA and ALC, continued the strong pastoral leadership at these two schools by first using two seminarians, Hollis Miller and Larry Yoder,[83] and then by calling the Rev. Robert Dasher as the Lutheran Campus Pastor for the Columbia area, beginning his work in January 1969.[84]

In the seventies, USC experienced tremendous growth and transition. The Campus Center and ministry provided a way for many students to make the change from home to campus. The center became a "home away from home." Student unrest during the seventies made its way to USC, and campus ministry served a mediating role, and the Lutheran Center made headlines as students operated a first aid station during the disturbances of 1970.

The campus pastor during this time continued to meet with a small group of students at Columbia College. Professor D. J. Haigler, a faculty member at Columbia College, provided leadership for the campus ministry.[85]

As one examines the first part of the seventies, the ministry at USC served many students through meals provided by local congregations, challenging programs, a warm and beautiful center which was a home built in the early 1900's, innovative liturgies, opportunities for service projects, pastoral counseling, contact with international students and interracial exchanges, and relationship with national and international student movements.

A dramatic threat came to the ministry in 1974. USC needed the Campus Center property at 1529 Pendleton Street. For many, the Center was more than a building; there were students who felt that they would not have survived college if it had not been for the Center; and many students met their spouses at the Center. Unfortunately, the synod had no recourse due to the university's power of eminent domain. However, the issue of what the property was worth had to be settled in court. A jury of the Richland County Court of Common Pleas directed the university to pay the synod $117,500 for damages. After deducting attorney's fees and other costs related to selling the building, the balance was divided between the synod and the National Lutheran Campus Ministry based on the percentage each had contributed to the original purchase of the building. The synod has invested its share of $55,884.58 with the income being used to help finance the ministry's annual operations.[86]

A tradition called "Fireside" was last held on December 15, 1974, and helped a group of over one hundred say thanks for the past and goodbye to the building as, through tears, they looked to the future. Beverly Alexander, then a student and now a campus pastor in North Carolina, wrote both an obituary and a birth announcement as the Lutheran Ministry moved from its Center to the Wesley Foundation. Appearing in the *South Carolina Lutheran* were these words: "All it took was one man to attach a cable—another to drive a massive machine and the building which was once the Lutheran Student Center at the University of South Carolina soon became past history. What man had created, man also destroyed. The building has served with dignity and warmth." [87]

For the next few years Lutheran Campus Ministry was housed at the Wesley Foundation cooperating in some programs, in addition to offering distinctive programs. During this period, the Lutheran Campus Ministry sign was replaced with one that read "The ELM Center" with ELM being formed by the first letters of the three denominations housed in the Wesley Foundation—Episcopal, Lutheran, and Methodist.[88] The ELM ministry provided an excellent environment for students to deepen their own traditions but also to learn from each other. Worship was always a strong commitment for the ministry. Study groups, support groups, counseling, social activities, leadership development, service projects, faculty luncheons, seminars for clergy, retreats, forums, and Bible study all helped shape the ministry from the middle seventies to the eighties.[88]

At the end of 1984, Pastor Dasher resigned,[89] and, again, the ministry was served by seminarian Shawn Norris until the new Campus Pastor, John Hougen, began his work in August 1986.[90] Prior to Pastor Hougen's arrival, the ELM ministry was dissolved with the Episcopal Church moving their ministry to the recently completed Diocesan House in Columbia. Thus began "The Lutheran/United Methodist Campus Ministry" [91] which has continued to provide ministry to the university's students as they struggle with life's development in a university setting.

At Clemson University, the Campus Ministry program is a cooperative one with the University Lutheran Church in Clemson. With support from the synod's Campus Ministry Committee, this program has grown with the addition of a second staff person as they continue to minister to a growing Lutheran population at the University and in the community. Through the years, an active Lutheran Student Movement has provided the framework for many programs for the Lutheran students at Clemson. Special programs for "Young Marrieds,"[92] special worship services for the students, weekly Bible study programs, and retreats,[93] plus shared programs with the congregation, have made the campus ministry program at Clemson an active and important ministry of the synod. (See University Church, page 264).

At other colleges within the state, part-time staff persons and contact pastors from local congregations have provided ministry to the Lutheran students "at home, away from home." Winthrop, The Citadel, and the College of Charleston have part-time staff persons, while contact pastors have provided ministry and program support at Claflin, South Carolina State, Furman, Converse, Wofford, Erskine, Lander, Coker, Limestone, Presbyterian, and Francis Marion. All of this work is done in cooperation with the Division of Campus Ministry of the Lutheran Council in the U.S.A., and its representative, Dr. Robert Walker.[94]

Communications

Publicity for major synod events was coordinated through the synod office by the Publicity Committee. This committee was especially responsible for the distribution of news releases to the major news centers of the state before, during, and after each convention. In 1975, the committee arranged for each delegate to have a picture taken with a representative of the synod for publication in the hometown newspaper. That year the committee also began the publication of "Convention Notes" which was mailed to each delegate and congregation immediately following the convention giving a synopsis of the convention's actions.[95] A brochure "Lutherans in Action" was published by the committee in 1976.[96] In 1986, the name of the committee was changed to the Committee on Communications, reflecting more accurately its duties and responsibilities.[97] That year, a workshop on the preparation of church newsletters and general news releases was conducted.[98]

Youth Ministry

Youth in recreation at a retreat at Camp Kinard.

Throughout these years, the Youth Ministry Committee has been responsible for coordinating programs within the synod "to provide opportunities for young people and adults to better equip themselves"[99] to live within their communities as a part of God's people. Until 1978, there was no youth organization in the synod, and this committee held the sole responsibility for providing these programs. The Migrant Ministry program, youth rallies and conferences, training conferences for adult leaders, coordinating regional youth gatherings, leading the project to raise funds for the swimming pool at Camp Kinard, were all a part of this committee's work to "expand and develop ministries with youth"[100] so that they could be more effective in their congregations and in their daily lives. The addition of the Youth Staffer enabled the committee to expand its ministry with and for youth.

In response to convention action, the committee appointed an Implementation Committee to establish a state-wide youth organization.[101] This was completed with the organization of the Lutheran Church Youth in August 1978 (see page 60).

Lutheran youth participate in MR Camp at Camp Kinard.

In 1987, as a part of the transition process relating to the synod's becoming a part of the ELCA, the youth ministry program was thoroughly studied, and recommendations for modifications of the program were adopted. The major change was the employment of a part-time Youth Ministry Coordinator for the synod, in place of the Youth Staffer program. Mrs. Nancy Padgett began her work in September 1987,[102] working through this committee and with the LCY to maintain consistency in the youth ministry program in the synod, and to facilitate youth programs through "networking"—putting people with needs in touch with people with the appropriate skills to meet those needs. The Youth Ministry Committee has continually provided programs for youth, enabling them to experience opportunities for learning, fellowship, and leadership development.

Ministry of the Laity

The 1984 LCA Convention adopted a ministry statement on "God's People Called to Ministry" as a result of their baptism, through their vocations, using the different gifts of the Holy Spirit in their daily lives. As a part of this statement, each synod was called upon to appoint a task force to assist the church in its support of God's people in their ministry in the world, with attention to ways in which the programs, priorities, and emphasis of the church can support that ministry. In South Carolina, such a task force was appointed, and they set several goals for their work.

They included: a process of identifying the laity; deepening the understanding of ministry in daily life and exploring ways to support that ministry; affirming the ministry of the laity in its various expressions; and sharing that ministry. The task force immediately began to plan, discuss, and implement these goals by sending publicity to pastors, LCW and LM presidents, and others concerning the Ministry of the Laity; making presentations at district meetings and synod conventions; promoting the third Sunday of November as Laity Sunday; conducting a workshop at Newberry College on February 16, 1985; and encouraging pastors and lay people to attend a leadership conference on "Connections," a word and witness type of study designed for use in the congregation for 32 weeks. A seminar on "God's People in Ministry" in September 1986, with Dr. Marilyn Ascarza from LTSS as the leader, provided participants with ideas on the ministry of the laity, discussion groups, devotions, and Bible Study.

There has been a great increase in interest and participation in lay ministry within the synod. More congregations have participated in Laity Sunday, received materials, heard presentations at district meetings, attended forums and seminars, used the Living Faith Series, *Monday's Ministries*, and other ministry of laity books, and in general raised their awareness of the laity and their role within the church's ministry programs.[103]

Blue Ribbon Committee

In 1972, the Blue Ribbon Committee was established to help coordinate the ministry programs of the synod. Composed of the district deans, the chairpersons of each committee of synod, the editor of the *South Carolina Lutheran*, and the presidents of the auxiliaries, the committee had an annual retreat with the officers and staff of the synod at Camp Kinard. Here program planning and discussion of the ministry profile of the synod led to coordination of programs and scheduling as well as planning for synodwide and district meetings. This committee provided a great deal of "feed in" to the executive board throughout the years.

Chapter Three—Auxiliaries

Among the most active people within the synod are those persons involved in the three auxiliaries—Lutheran Church Women, Lutheran Church Youth, and Lutheran Men. As a part of the individual congregations, they provide opportunities for small group programs and discussions, fellowship, worship, and program support for the various ministries within the congregation. They have been an effective way for members to find avenues of ministry in their church and community. As a part of the South Carolina Synod, these auxiliaries provide support for the ongoing ministry of the church with special emphasis in certain ministry areas. They are also a valuable resource for persons with leadership skills and experience. South Carolina has been especially fortunate to have three very active and effective auxiliaries within its ministry program.

Lutheran Church Women

Since 1962 when it was reorganized, the Lutheran Church Women has been growing, working, and serving with love, concern, and enthusiasm. Through the years new programs have been developed by the auxiliary. Increasing importance has been placed on service to the people of the world through involvement in social concerns. South Carolina Lutheran Women have been in leadership roles in the literacy program in the state since 1962. They have sponsored workshops for training tutors, have served as tutors themselves, have aided the program financially, and have cooperated with the State Literacy Association. Like the LCA, the women's organization has been deeply concerned about world hunger, peace, justice, and fair treatment for all human beings. Projects to send material help to specific groups in mission fields, within the state or through Lutheran World Federation, have been supported by the organization in recent years. Migrant missions, ministry to the deaf, and aid to Native Americans have been areas of

53

Bernice Shealy, Gloria Rast and Betty Bradley pack sewing kits made by the LCW.

particular interest in this state. Because of the wide scope of social missions, Key Women have been named for each district to assist the unit committee and to aid the local organizations in this area of work. Wide interest in social ministry expresses the continuing active love and concern which have marked women's work in South Carolina from its beginning.

Communication between the synodical organization and the local groups has been a challenge throughout the history of women's work in South Carolina. However, in recent years there has been a more concentrated effort by LCW to improve lines of communication. Since 1973, the synodical unit has published its own newsletter. Known as the *GOOD-NEWSletter*, it is published four times a year. In addition, LCW information has been included in each issue of the *South Carolina Lutheran*. In 1970, the unit board began each year to send the *Calendar of Events* which has served as a reminder to local groups of important events, dates, and other suggestions to help in planning activities at the local level. Various publications, sent regularly from the auxiliary to unit and local leaders, have provided a constant flow of information and guidance. *Lutheran Women*, the auxiliary's national magazine, has been widely read by women from 73% of the congregational organizations. District assemblies, held each fall, and the annual conventions have not only been wonderful sources of information but have provided inspiration and joy which cannot be measured.

The Lutheran women of the South Carolina Unit, like the synod itself, have established an outstanding record of stewardship. Although there have been a few rough years in financial giving (usually corresponding with periods of difficulty in the economy), there have been several years when the SCLCW gave more than 100% of budgeted funds to the auxiliary while meeting all obligations at home. Probably the real key to the stewardship of the women has been the overwhelming proportion of contributions given to "others" as contrasted with monies retained for the use of the congregational groups. At the convention of SCLCW, delegates adopted a 1987 budget of $88,975.00, with $75,625.00 to be spent for "others."[1]

Members of the LCW put their Thankoffering in the Treasure Chest during worship at their convention.

One phase of giving which has grown tremendously since its beginning has been "Thankoffering." When Lutheran Church Women was organized in 1962, the decision was made to combine all offerings into one gift. But in 1970, the idea of a special offering to be received during Lent and Thanksgiving was adopted by SCLCW. So successful was the idea that at the National Triennial Convention in 1971, the auxiliary adopted South Carolina's idea as a channel for "special gifts." Today the ingathering of Thankoffering has become one of the highlights of each convention. At the 1987 convention this offering amounted to over $20,800.[2]

Stewardship emphasis, however, has come to include not only the stewardship of money, but of time and talents as well. This extended emphasis has overlapped with new forms of stewardship training. Synodical leaders have been instructed so that they are able to give leadership training to women in congregational organizations. A facet of this training has been increased participation of synodical leaders in national workshops sponsored by the auxiliary. Another expression of this leadership has been the cooperation between the synod and the women's organizations, especially as LCW board members serve as observers to all major synodical committees.

The South Carolina Unit has sent delegates to each of the Triennial Conventions of Lutheran Church Women. At the first such meeting in 1965, Mrs. Herman Cauble was elected to a three-year term on the Board of Directors. Mrs. Harry Crout and Mrs. James B. Shealy have also served on that Board from South Carolina. In addition to these ladies, a number of SCLCW members have served on various committees for the auxiliary.

In 1981, the historical records of women's work in South Carolina were deposited in the archives of Dacus Library on the campus of Winthrop College in Rock Hill.[3] At the time an historian was appointed to collect historical items and deposit them with the library at ten-year intervals. Although records are cared for by Dacus Library, the agreement between Winthrop College and SCLCW stated that they remain the property of SCLCW.

During these years as South Carolina Lutheran Church Women, the organization has been blessed with outstanding Christian leadership. Local leaders, district assembly leaders, unit officers and board members have all combined with the membership to make the women's auxiliary of the South Carolina Lutheran Synod live up to its purpose "... to be a community of women which, in response to the Holy Spirit, engages in the mission of proclamation and reconciliation through its life and work and through the life and work of the LCA." At the close of these twenty-five years as Lutheran Church Women, there are 149 active organizations in the 160 congregations of synod with a total membership of over 6,200 women.[4] Growth during these years has been slow but steady. In 1987, instead of having the unit (synodical) convention, which had been held each year at

LCW officers: Gloria Rast, President; Betty Bradley, Vice-President; Linda Summers, Secretary; and Carolyn Torrence, Treasurer.

Newberry College with delegates from each congregational organization, an LCW Rally was held at the Radisson Hotel on May 23, to which all South Carolina Lutheran Church Women were invited and at which there was a pageant depicting the history of the SCLCW.[5] Later in the summer a constituting convention was held as a first step in the organizing of the new women's auxiliary. The SCLCW now is ready to take part in a new organization of women as Lutherans in America take another step in becoming "One" in the Lord's work.

PRESIDENTS OF LUTHERAN CHURCH WOMEN

1971-1973 .... Mrs. J. Harry Crout
1973-1975 .... Mrs. James B. Shealy
1975-1979 .... Mrs. D. Murray Shull, Jr.
1979-1981 .... Mrs. Thomas R. Peacock
1981-1983 .... Mrs. Wilbur Shealy
1983-1985 .... Mrs. Charles B. Shealy
1985-1987 .... Mrs. Heber Rast

Lutheran Church Youth

From 1968 to 1978, there was no synodical youth organization as such, but many youth were involved in the life and ministry of the church through the efforts of the synodical Youth Ministry Committee. Youth were asked to serve on LCA boards, synodical committees, congregational committees, and church councils. They assumed responsible roles in local congregations and were elected as delegates to LCA conventions.

The Rev. Lloyd W. Mitcham, Jr., who had been added to the synod staff in 1968 as Executive Secretary for Christian Education and Youth Ministry, played a vital role in the success of Youth Ministry in South Carolina, considered to be one of the most effective youth programs in the LCA. One of the weaknesses of youth ministry was the lack of an LCA or synodical organization; so Pastor Mitcham led the organization of the South Carolina program on a synod-committee/district-council arrangement. The synod committee was composed of one youth and one adult from each district; there was an equal number of adult and youth participants on the district youth councils. Members of the synod committee were included on the district councils, thus ideas were shared "through people, not paper."

Another weakness which was really felt by the congregational youth groups was the absence of any program materials from the LCA. Since this was a real difficulty for adult leaders, materials were prepared through the Synod office and distributed to the congregations. Adult Youth Ministry Conferences were also held at the beginning of the year from 1972-1977.

Beginning in 1974, there was a program sponsored by the LCA which gave impetus to Youth Ministry. Youth Staffers were sent into the synods,[6] each to work for one year. They were usually college students; some were taking a year out, and others were devoting their first year after graduation to church service. Thirteen young people served the synod as Youth Staffers.

Each year two district rallies were held. They focused on issues, projects, and worship. Among the programs enjoyed by the youth were an all-day sock hop, a Thanksgiving contemporary worship service, and a walk-a-thon to raise money for Meals-on-Wheels. Synodwide events also boosted the interest in congregational youth groups. These events took the form of both all-day mass rallies and smaller weekend retreats. One rally held at Newberry College featured districts challenging each other with whimsical contests based on the television show "Anything Goes." There were weekend retreats held at Camp Kinard for grades 7 through 9 and for grades 10 through 12. The activities of these conferences revolved around a theme, such as "New Religions," "God Don't Make No Junk," and "Death and Dying." There were also two-week camps at John's Island which involved the youth in migrant ministry.

One youth project in the early 1970's was raising money for a swimming pool at Camp Kinard.[7] It was dedicated on September 8, 1974. Beginning in 1972 and continuing to the present, youth have worked with the camp for Mentally Retarded at Camp Kinard. There are two one-week sessions where the youth work as counselors on a one-to-one basis, planning and leading activities ranging from Bible study to boat rides, from trips to the shopping malls to painting with pudding.

Governor Riley presents Youth Volunteer Award to LCY President, D'Etta Price.

From 1972 to 1978 the campers were clients from the Coastal Center, and in more recent years from the Midland's Center. From their experience as counselors at these camps, a number of youth have decided to go into careers in the field of special education therapy. In 1986, the LCY received the Governor's Youth Volunteer Award for its work with the MR camps.[8]

In 1974, memorials were presented at the LCA convention to re-establish a national youth organization, and the 1976

LCA convention voted to instruct the Division for Parish Services to assist synods that wished to develop their own youth organizations. Newberry District proposed a state youth organization for the South Carolina Synod, and in 1977 the synod convention adopted the proposal, the structure to be implemented by the synodical Youth Ministry Committee.[9]

First Lutheran Church Youth Officers: front row, Sara Moeller, President; Lori Shull, Secretary; and back row, Andy Massey, Vice-President; and John Greenwold, Treasurer.

Pastor Mitcham, Cindy Roof, Reedy Hopkins, Dottie Park, Sara Moeller, Jim Riser, Ginny Aull, Jenny Lanning, and Pastors Al Potter and Bob Coon began work immediately to put together a structure for the statewide youth organization.[10] By August 1978, Lutheran Church Youth (LCY) was ready to hold a constituting convention. One hundred and fifty delegates and twenty-nine staff members met at Newberry College August 3-5 to adopt a constitution and elect officers.[11] Congregational constitutions were to be based on the synod document.

The stated purpose was "to express their Christian faith in terms of worship, learning, witness, service, fellowship, and support ... develop leadership that is responsible and visible ... find a common identity as the younger members of the church, the Body of Christ." [12] For a congregational group to become an official member of the synod organization, it must "make a list of officers and enablers and make a pledge of financial support." Each district was required to have four elected officers and four adult enablers. The presidents of the district organizations were included on the Executive Board of the LCY, along with the synodical officers, to carry on business between annual conferences.

The new LCY worked closely with the synod Youth Ministry Committee, focusing on local youth groups and district assemblies, looking at broader ministries where youth could develop leadership, involve themselves in the life of the church, sponsor service projects, and cooperate with the LCA Division for Parish Services. LCY continued the MR camps, made PAL kits for migrant workers, carried out programs at the Lowman Home and Franke Home, and held leadership conferences. Annual convention/conferences were held to conduct the business of the organization as well as to provide new ideas for the congregational organizations and fellowship for the youth.

South Carolina youth have also participated in events which have brought them in contact with other synods of the LCA. In 1981, there was an international youth gathering at Purdue University; another was held in 1985; and regional events were held in 1980 at Furman University, in 1983 and 1986. South Carolina youth also took part in the Global Mission event in 1982 at Wittenberg University.

In 1985, the Rev. Robert L. Dasher was called as assistant to the Bishop upon the resignation of Pastor Mitcham. His work included responsibility for the Youth Ministry program. On July 27, 1987, LCY observed its tenth anniversary at Newberry College with the theme "Reaching Back, Looking Forward." [13] In 1987, Mrs. Nancy Padgett was hired on a part-time basis as the synod's youth ministry coordinator. (See page 51.)

PRESIDENTS OF THE LUTHERAN CHURCH YOUTH

1978-79 .... Sara Moeller
1979-80 .... Debbie Haigler
1980-81 .... Teresa Martin
1981-82 .... Donna Haigler
1982-83 .... Eric Wells
1983-84 .... Catherine Ficken
1984-85......................... Bryan Counts
1985-86.......................... D'Etta Price
1986-87 .... Tom Henderson
1987-88......................... Derek Counts

Lutheran Men

Making gifts and loans to mission congregations continued to be the primary purpose of the Lutheran Men. In 1963, the Loan and Gift Fund was divided into two separate funds, the Mission Gift Fund and the Lutheran Men Loan Fund. In 1971, the goal for the Mission Gift Fund was raised from $7,500 to $12,000, and by 1987 had increased to $15,000. From 1971 to 1987, the Lutheran Men gave 26 different mission congregations over $233,000. These gifts were:

1971 $12,000 Redeemer, Greer ($5,000); Our Shepherd, Hartsville ($2,000); Trinity, Columbia ($2,000); St. Paul, Gaffney ($1,000); Augsburg, Union ($1,000); St. John, Beaufort ($500); and Holy Cross, Charleston ($500).

1972 $12,000 Trinity, Georgetown ($3,000); St. Paul, Gaffney ($3,000); Augsburg, Union ($3,000); Redeemer, Greer ($1,500); Our Shepherd, Hartsville ($1,000); and Holy Cross, Charleston ($500).

1973 $12,000 Trinity, Columbia ($3,000); Augsburg, Union ($3,000); St. Matthias, Easley ($1,000); Christ, Hilton Head ($1,000); St. Mark, Sullivan's Island ($1,000); Redeemer, Greer ($1,000), St. Paul, Gaffney ($1,000); Holy Cross, Charleston ($500); and Our Shepherd, Hartsville ($500).

1974 $12,000 Trinity, Columbia ($2,000); Augsburg, Union ($2,000); St. Paul, Gaffney ($2,000); Peace, Ladson ($1,000); Redeemer, Greer ($1,000); St. Mark, Isle of Palms ($1,000); Christ, Hilton Head ($1,000); St. Matthias, Easley ($1,000); Our Shepherd, Hartsville ($500); Holy Cross, Charleston ($500).

1975 $12,000 St. Mark, Isle of Palms ($4,000); St. Paul, Gaffney ($3,000); Redeemer, Greer ($2,000); St. Matthias, Easley ($1,500); Christ, Hilton Head ($1,500).

1976 $12,000 St. Paul, Gaffney ($4,000); Redeemer, Greer ($3,000); Christ, Hilton Head ($2,000); St. Mark, Isle of Palms ($1,500); St. Matthias, Easley ($1,500).

1977 $13,000 Peace, Ladson ($4,334); All Saints, Mt. Pleasant ($3,250); St. Matthias, Easley ($2,166); Christ, Hilton Head ($1,625); Redeemer, Greer ($1,625).

1978 $12,000 All Saints, Mt. Pleasant ($4,000); Peace, Ladson ($3,000); St. Matthias, Easley ($2,000); Shepherd of the Sea, Garden City ($1,500); King of Glory, North Myrtle Beach ($1,500).

1979 $13,000 Shepherd of the Sea ($5,000); All Saints, Mt. Pleasant ($3,000); King of Glory, North Myrtle Beach ($2,000); Peace, Ladson ($1,500); St. Matthias, Easley ($1,500).

1980 $14,000 King of Glory, North Myrtle Beach ($5,384.60); Shepherd of the Sea, Garden City ($3,230.80); All Saints, Mt. Pleasant ($2,153.80); Lord of Life, Harbison ($1,615.40); A Mighty Fortress, Sangaree ($1,615.40).

1981 $14,000 A Mighty Fortress, Sangaree ($5,384.40); King of Glory, North Myrtle Beach ($3,231.20); St. Matthias, Easley ($2,153.20); Lord of Life, Harbison ($1,615.60); All Saints, Mt. Pleasant ($1,615.60).

1982 $13,000 Cross and Crown, Florence ($5,000); A Mighty Fortress, Sangaree ($3,000); Lord of Life, Harbison ($2,000); All Saints, Mt. Pleasant ($1,500); St. Matthias, Easley ($1,500).

1983 $14,000 A Mighty Fortress, Sangaree ($3,230); King of Glory, North Myrtle Beach ($3,230); All Saints, Mt. Pleasant ($3,230); St. Peter, Pawleys Island ($2,155); Cross and Crown, Florence ($2,155).

1984 $15,000 Augsburg, Union ($3,462); St. Mark, Isle of Palms ($3,462); St. Peter, Pawleys Island ($3,462); Abiding Presence, York (2,307); Our Shepherd, Hartsville ($2,307).

LM Treasurer presents Mission Gift Fund checks to representatives of Augsburg, Union; St. Mark, Isle of Palms; St. Peter, Litchfield Beach; Abiding Presence, York; and Our Shepherd, Hartsville.

1985 $17,000 Cross and Crown, Florence ($3,966.67); St. Peter, Pawleys Island ($3,966.67); Christ the Servant, Conway ($3,966.67); Christus Victor, Columbia ($2,550); Ministry with the Deaf, Columbia (2,550).

1986 $17,500 A Mighty Fortress, Summerville ($4,083); Christus Victor, Columbia ($4,083); Our Shepherd, Hartsville ($4,083); St. Peter, Pawleys Island ($2,625); and Ministry with the Deaf, Columbia ($2,625).

1987 $19,000 Cross and Crown, Florence ($3,750); St. Peter, Pawleys Island ($3,750); Abiding Presence, York ($3,750); St. Mark, Blythewood ($3,750); Ministry with the Deaf, Columbia ($1,000); Living Springs, Columbia ($1,000); Christ the Servant, Conway ($1,000); Christ the King, Greenville ($500); Lake Wylie, Fort Mill ($500).[14]

From 1968 until 1976, the Honorary Life and Memorial Membership fee was the only designated money for the Lutheran Men's Loan Fund. Since 1968 over 1,250 Honorary Life and over 300 Memorial memberships have been received for the Loan Fund. This fund also received a gift of $40,557.09 through the will of a Lutheran layman, Mr. Walter Henry Proescholdt.[15] In 1976, the Committee of One Hundred was established to encourage at least 100 men of the synod to give $100 each to the Loan Fund every year. The Loan Fund has assets of $726,171.63[16] with a goal of $1,000,000. There are 12 churches with loans in the amount of $200,539.55,[17] and since 1971, 19 churches have received loans totalling over $777,000.[18]

In 1966, the Lutheran Men began thinking about building a retreat center. They appointed a committee and were hard at work when the synod decided to develop a Camp and Conference Center. During the year 1970-71, Camp Kinard was constructed, and in 1970 the Lutheran Men constructed the first cottage at Camp Kinard. They also constructed an additional lake and raised the dam of the existing lake by four feet. The mortgage on the cottage was burned at the State LM Convention in 1973. The Lutheran Men also spearheaded the construction of a shelter for the camp, and since the opening of the camp, have used its facilities regularly for retreats. In 1980, Lutheran Men adopted a $20,000 project for paving, sidewalks, landscaping, and a sprinkler system at the Coastal Retreat Center. By 1983, the funds were in hand, and the project was completed.

The Rev. James Fox addresses an LM Breakfast at synod convention.

Throughout the synod, the fourth Sunday in September is observed as Lutheran Men Sunday. At this time, all members of the congregations are encouraged to support the mission work of Lutheran Men. The synod organization has provided many programs, films, and cassette tapes for the local units to use. It has also published a regular newsletter, "The Epistle," to keep congregational units informed about the happenings of Lutheran Men. An annual convention in the fall provides men with the opportunity to review the work of the synodical LM organization, elect officers, conduct other business, and present the annual gifts to mission congregations. Since 1979, a special LM award has been given to men who have served their synod, their congregation, and the auxiliary in an exemplary manner. No more than two awards are made each year. Recipients of the awards have been:

1979	Roy Seay
	Dr. Herman W. Cauble
1980	Harry Stoudenmire
	Raymond S. Caughman
1981	Howard Cook, Jr.
	Dr. Karl W. Kinard
1982	Jim Brittingham
	Reid Wingard
1983	James Hallman
	Phillip T. Kelly, Jr.
1984	Dr. Fred E. Dufford
	B. O. Derrick

LM officers are installed (left to right): Keith Hutto, president; the Rev. Gene Beck (hidden), pastoral advisor; Wayne Caughman, treasurer; Heber Rast, vice-president; Miller Shealy, secretary; Wayne Sease, promotional secretary; by previous pastoral advisor, the Rev. Olin Chassereau.

1985	W. Archie Dodgen
	The Rev. John Koch
1986	Cecil H. Bowers
	The Rev. Charles E. Bernhardt
1987	Raymond Boozer
	The Rev. Dr. James S. Aull[19]

Through the years the Lutheran Men have had excellent leadership from their officers and members. Presidents of the Lutheran Men since 1971 have been:

1971-2	Raymond S. Caughman
1973-4	Reid S. Wingard
1975	Robert N. Hubbs
1976	Louis H. Martens, Jr.
1977	Lawrence D. Chapman
1978	R. Paul Richardson
1979	William B. Drake
1980	Carol O. Ulmer
1981-2	James N. Hallman
1983	Larry Kyzer
1984	Keith Hutto
1985	Heber Rast, Jr.
1986	Miller W. Shealy, Sr.
1987	Wayne E. Caughman

Chapter Four—Institutions and Agencies

The institutions of the synod provide great opportunities for unique ministry programs not only for Lutherans, but all people of the state. From camping, to college and seminary education, to a home for the aged and infirm, the South Carolina Synod has provided financial and volunteer support for these institutions, which in turn fulfill many ministry goals of the synod.

Lowman Home

By 1970, the Lowman Home had served the people of South Carolina in a very special ministry for sixty years. Having received an estate consisting of over 950 acres of land and some money, Lowman Home was established by the synod for the care of the aged and helpless.[1] The 1970's brought new leadership to the Board of Trustees when Mr. Deems Haltiwanger became chairman in 1970, only the fourth person to hold that position. He served until 1972, when Dr. Robert L. Hock was elected chairman. Elected in May 1972, Dr. Hock had to resign in October 1972, when he accepted a call to the Florida Synod. Dr. William F. Austin succeeded Dr. Hock and continues to serve as Chairman of the Board.

Under the leadership of the Rev. Dr. J. Kenneth Webb as President, the Lowman Home, with the infirmary, changed from a home for the aged to a geriatric center, beginning in 1964. The home was fully accredited and appropriately licensed to provide all three levels of nursing care—residential, intermediate, and skilled nursing, including Medicare. A fourth level of care, self-sustaining residency, was later added. The home has been and continues to be open to any person who is over 18 years of age and needs the services offered by Lowman Home.

Skilled nursing care is for those guests who need total or considerable nursing care during the entire day, including those who may be bedridden or up part of the day in a

Lowman Home President, Dr. Kenneth Webb.

wheel-chair. Intermediate care is for guests who are able to be up and around their rooms and can care for their daily personal hygiene, but who need some assistance with walking and may require assistance with dressing and bathing. Boarding-home guests are capable of caring for themselves, walking the covered walkways without assistance to the central dining area and requiring only a small amount of supervision. The self-sustaining residents are those who live in either a cottage or an efficiency apartment located on Lowman Home grounds. These residents are at least 62 years old and can sustain themselves under normal living conditions.

The 1970's brought changes and opportunities to the Lowman Home. For instance, on July 1, 1974, the Southeastern Synod withdrew from the ownership and operation of Lowman Home, making it the sole property and responsibility of the South Carolina Synod.[2] Also, in that same year, four cottages were completed, bringing the number of units in the self-sustaining residency program to 21.

In October 1975, the Home completed a new 29-bed addition to the Boliek Infirmary at a cost of $840,000 financed again by gifts and bequests plus a Hill-Burton grant. This addition, known as Memorial Wing, brought the number of beds in the Boliek Infirmary to 85.[3]

Later, in 1977, the Bernice H. Moose Activities Center was dedicated with no debt on the $90,000 building.[4] With its completion, the Home's physical plant topped the $4.5 million mark.

An important event for Lowman Home took place in 1978 when the Wynne C. Boliek Infirmary was approved as a

The Activities Center building.

dually certified facility by the State Board of Health, making it possible for all beds to be used interchangeably for either skilled nursing or intermediate care.[5] The Lowman Home family also grew. The staff included 155 employees, and there were well over 200 guests.

The Home's friends have also increased in number over the years. Volunteer groups have come to the Home regularly to work, to entertain, or merely to visit with guests. Additionally, there has been a long list of business and professional people who have shared their time and talents toward the ongoing of Lowman Home. Church groups throughout the South and particularly in South Carolina have played a major part in helping make Lowman Home what it is today, a leader in the nursing home field with a caring heart.

In order for the members of the South Carolina Synod to have one of the finest total-care nursing centers of its kind anywhere, the Home's trustees, administration, and staff have always been alert to improving the facility. In August 1981, the Deems Haltiwanger Building was dedicated. The building at completion cost $1,543,125, and it provided 40 private rooms with private baths as a unit in the Residential Care (Boarding Home) section.[6]

Lowman Home depends on others' benevolence in many

The Haltiwanger building.

ways. The quality of life of Lowman Home guests has been enhanced from the very beginning with the volunteers. In 1981, nearly 500 volunteers gave unselfishly of themselves to the Home and its guests. Visiting, sewing, luncheons, trips and help from loving volunteers have made life much better for guests since the early days. Christmas at Lowman Home that year (1981) was blessed with 175 groups assisting with gifts for the residents.

As the Home progressed into the 1980's, many good things continued to happen, but the burden of economic restraints in the area of indigent care began to be felt. Shrinking federal money placed a hardship on Lowman Home's activities. Indigent-care guests were subsidized by nearly $500,000 in 1983 from the Home's reserves.[7] Some of this subsidy was offset by contributions from the synods, individuals, and churches, but the Home had to bear over $240,000 that year. The synod's budgeted support for the Home has grown from $49,000 in 1981 to $100,000 in 1987.[8] During this time the funds from the Home's Mother's Day Appeal and generous gifts at Christmas and during other times of the year have reduced the shortfall caused by indigent care.

In January of 1984, the Board of Trustees was forced to take a dramatic step in an effort to reduce the rising indigent-care costs. The Home's admission policies were amended so that for each three guests admitted to the Home, two have to demonstrate the ability to pay the full rate, until the roster of indigent-care recipients does not exceed one-third of the available beds or available space, or until the Indigent-Care Fund exceeds the cost of one-third of available beds or space. This action was necessary to insure the continued operation of the Home. Moreover, the Indigent-Care Fund mentioned above was established and comprised of synodical apportionment, one-half of the investment income from the Houck Trusts and all other contributions specifically designated for indigent care.[9]

Along with the problem of indigent care, the 1980's have brought blessings, also. Services to the Home and to the community have been expanded with the Education and Training Center under the direction of Dr. J. Obert Kempson. The center has provided a learning setting for student nurses at the University of South Carolina, students in the licensed practical nursing program at Baptist Medical Center, and Master's Degree Candidates in Social Work at USC. Also, Lutheran Theological Southern Seminary and Newberry College students come to the Home to learn through the Education and Training Center. In 1986, the Home expanded its caring hands to the operation of an adult day-

Residents participate in an exercise program at Lowman Home.

care center in Columbia in leased space at Ebenezer Lutheran Church. If this pilot project is successful, the Home plans to investigate further expansion in other areas.

Earlier Mrs. Bessie Black and her daughter, Sara, made a substantial contribution to the Home. In 1983, Lowman Home again received a gift in the form of revenue from a trust fund valued at $369,912 from Miss Sara Black.[10]

Lowman Home received one of its larger gifts, $1,128,163, from the estate of Mrs. Fannie A. Roesel of Augusta, Georgia. The gift is to be paid in increments over a 25-year period. Lowman Home has received special gifts amounting to millions of dollars over her 75-year history.[11] A bequest from the estate of Herman Langford in Newberry was made in 1986.

The year 1986 marked a significant time in the Lowman Home's life, seventy-five years of service to God and to a special segment of His people. As its gift of celebration, the Home refurbished the Wynne C. Boliek Infirmary.[12] A Service of Celebration and Thanksgiving with over 450 people in attendance was held on September 21, 1986, at St. Thomas, Chapin, followed by a reception in the Home's Activities Center. Visitors were also invited to view the refurbished and renovated infirmary. The $75,000 goal as an anniversary offering for the Indigent-Care Fund was exceeded.[13]

Another Home anniversary was celebrated in 1986. Dr. Webb celebrated his 25th anniversary as President of the Lowman Home. He was honored in the celebration service, and the Home's annual Employee Appreciation Day was named for him in honor of his 25 years of service.[14]

Dr. Webb retired in 1987, and he was honored with a retirement dinner in Columbia where over 400 people

Newly elected Lowman Home President, the Rev. Boyd F. Cook.

enjoyed the "roasting" and "toasting" of Dr. Webb and his wife. The Rev. Boyd F. Cook, a member of the Board of Trustees, was elected President.[15]

Lowman Home is operated in 1987, just as it was founded seventy-five years ago, on the strong belief in and reliance upon the benevolence of God's people. Although run by the South Carolina Synod, Lowman Home's 1986-87 budget of $4.8 million is not totally contributed by the synod. Rather, the Home's operation is the result of seventy-five years of gifts, both big and small, from hundreds of caring people who see the need for the services of Lowman Home and have a strong faith in the Home to provide those services in the name of God.

Lutheran Theological Southern Seminary

During the past seventeen years, Southern Seminary has experienced steady growth and has faced significant challenges. It has seen an increase in enrollment and in numbers of faculty and staff. Its budget has risen from $340,000 to $1.8 million. It has been through two changes of curriculum and adjustments in degree programs. It has added a major building in its award-winning Lineberger Library and has undertaken extensive renovations and improvements on other facilities. Its community has become more diverse, more inclusive, and more ecumenical. It has prepared itself to enter the Evangelical Lutheran Church in America, facing new opportunities and offering leadership. These years—in the midst of which the Seminary celebrated its sesquicentennial year—have been marked both by a certain maturity as an academic institution and as a community of faith and by an engagement with new realities, new possibilities for ministry.

When Hugh George Anderson became president of the seminary in the fall of 1970, the institution was poised for an era of energy and progress.[16] In many ways, the administration of F. Eppling Reinartz had stabilized the seminary for such an advance: at the end of his tenure, Dr. Reinartz had worked with the Board of Trustees on a planning proj-

The Lineberger Memorial Library at LTSS.

ect entitled "The Next Phase of This Seminary's Develop-ment." [17] Those plans would begin to take shape early in the 1970's under the seminary's new president. Respected as a teacher by a generation of students, widely known as a speaker and preacher, Dr. Anderson brought to his office a vision of academic development and a commitment to ser-vice of the church.

Central to the changes that would occur was the cultiva-tion of financial resources. The Outreach Appeal, a major effort to build endowment, was initiated in 1972 and even-tually drew over $2.7 million in gifts.[18] The Rev. Curtis E. Derrick was called to assist Dr. Kenneth Hewitt with this appeal and then was named full-time Director of Develop-ment upon Dr. Hewitt's retirement in 1973.[19] This campaign would lead to the first endowed chair, the Dewey F. Beam Professorship of Pastoral Care, to the renovation of three buildings, to expanded programs in continuing education, to student scholarships, and to the endowment fund passing the half-million dollar mark.[20] The creation of the Columbia Advisory Council would bring additional local support to the work of the seminary.[21] By the middle of the decade major grants had been received from the Cannon Trust and the Cannon Foundation, from the Lilly Foundation, and from the Lineberger Foundation. Throughout the seventeen-year period, two benevolent insurance companies, Aid Association for Lutherans and Lutheran Brotherhood, provided annual support for continuing education, student aid, and faculty development.[22]

Early in the new administration adjustments were made in the areas of the president's responsibility: new staff configurations added flexibility and broadened resources to the school's leadership. The strengthening of the development office, of course, would aid the president in his fund-raising efforts. To provide assistance with both business and academic matters, James S. Aull, Professor of Old Testament since 1962, became the Administrative Assistant to the President.[23] In order to extend its programs for pastors, other church workers and members of congregations, the seminary in 1972 called a Director of Continuing Education, the Rev. Martin F. Saarinen, who in addition to creating and guiding continuing education events would develop, by 1974, the Doctor of Ministry degree program.[24] With the calling of Robert C. Schultz as Director of Internship and Professor of Pastoral Care a full administrative team was in place by the fall of 1975.[25]

The heart of the seminary's task remained the preparation of people for ministries in the church. A new curriculum, initiated in 1974, gave students a larger role in the shaping of their own education: the core of required courses was reduced and more elective hours became possible.[26] The Master of Religious Education degree became the Master of Arts in Religion in 1973, also reflecting a broadening of concept and an additional freedom for the student to shape a program suited to his or her professional needs.[27] An evaluation by the American Association of Theological Schools was conducted in 1972; Southern Seminary again received accreditation and remained the only accredited theological school in South Carolina.[28] Within the academic program, opportunities were expanding. More serious attention was given to the presence of Methodist students on the campus, and negotiations began with the United Methodist Church in the hope of adding an adjunct professor with responsibility for courses in Methodist polity, history and theology.[29] The first woman with a Master of Divinity degree graduated in 1974;[30] there would be increasing numbers of women in the student population in all degree programs. Following a trend in other theological schools and with encouragement from the professional leadership committees of the supporting synods, the seminary in 1976 began granting credit for Clinical Pastoral Education.[31] A gift from anonymous donors in North Carolina established an endowed lectureship in memory of Jacob L. Morgan, former president of the North Carolina Synod. As a result of this gift, distinguished theologians would add another dimension to the academic program for the seminary community and for pastors and church members in the area.[32]

In the second half of President Anderson's term, there were significant developments within the Board of Trustees and among the faculty. A series of Trustee Development seminars, supported by the Lilly Endowment, brought deeper levels of involvement among the Trustees and fostered a new relationship between Trustees, faculty and administration.[33] One such meeting led to the reformulation of the seminary's statement of purpose, a statement thought through and written by faculty and trustees and signaling a sense of partnership in the mission of the seminary.

> The purpose of Lutheran Theological Southern Seminary is to educate men and women for the church's ministry, primarily in the Lutheran Church in America, including theological preparation for ordained and lay ministry and continuing theological education of laity and clergy. This theological education seeks to be evangelical in content, relevant to contemporary society, and ecumenical in scope with the intent of developing persons to become spiritually mature, theologically competent, and ethically sensitive within an inclusive and caring community.[34]

New faculty appointments were made necessary by the resignation of men who had played prominent roles in the seminary's life over many years: Arnold E. Carlson in Contemporary Theology, Gordon A. Beaver in Church Music, Richard M. Bland in Old Testament, James S. Aull in Old Testament, George Frederick Schott in Systematic Theology and J. Obert Kempson in Pastoral Care.[35]

One new faculty position in the field of New Testament was created during this time and was filled by Charles P. Sigel.[36] Other faculty members to join the staff during the Anderson administration were Scott H. Hendrix in Church History, Carl F. W. Ficken in Theology and Culture, L. David Miller in Church Music, Michael J. Root in Systematic Theology, and Robert J. Marshall in Old Testament.[37] Mack C. Branham, Jr., became adminstrative assistant and registrar following the resignation of Professor Aull in 1979.[38] In the midst of these changes in its composition, the faculty was also coming to a different stance within the institution. This occurred in its relationship to the Board of Trustees, through the opportunities offered by the Trustee Development seminars, and in having a representative attend Board meetings beginning in 1974.[39] The faculty also prepared a faculty handbook, accepted a larger function in the search for new faculty members and in its own governance, and began participation in an enriched sabbatical program.[40] A curriculum review process which began in 1976 involved the faculty in examination of the objectives for the seminary's educational tasks and of the expectations for its graduates.[41]

With the completion of the Lineberger Library in 1975, the physical plant of the campus seemed adequate for the seminary's program. What had to be done next was to maintain and improve the existing buildings. Extensive and long-needed renovation was begun for the dormitory, the Voigt classroom building, and the Price House which had formerly housed the library.[42] The oldest structure on campus was renovated and named the Beam Dormitory following a substantial gift by Dewey F. Beam of Cherryville, North Carolina.[43] A major landscaping project was carried out in 1976. Needlepoint cushions were provided for the chapel's altar rail under the leadership of Sunny Anderson, wife of the president, through the artistic design of student Michael Knudson, and by the hand work of people in the supporting synods.[44] The undercroft of Christ Chapel was renamed Reinartz Hall in 1978 following the death of former president F. Eppling Reinartz.[45]

By the end of President Anderson's term in 1981, Southern Seminary had experienced a decade of growth and change. Largely through the addition of the Doctor of Ministry program, the student enrollment had increased from 120 to 160; over 750 persons were served in continuing education.[46] The budget passed the one million dollar mark. The library was housed in an exciting new building and had grown to 74,000 volumes.[47] At the time of its one hundred and fiftieth anniversary, the seminary seemed to have reached one of its healthiest moments. A new 16mm film, "So Send I You," was circulating throughout the Southeast, giving to congregations the picture of a modern campus and a vibrant community.[48] As part of the sesquicentennial celebration, lectures were presented on the school's history: each lecture was given on one of the former locations of the seminary and thus brought together analysis of the school's past and recollection and acknowledgment of other places of importance to the life of the institution.

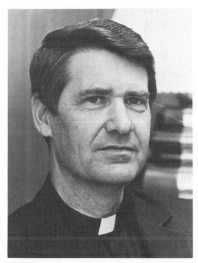

LTSS President, Dr. Mack C. Branham.

Upon the resignation of Dr. Anderson to become president of Luther College in Decorah, Iowa, the Board of Trustees appointed a search committee and named Mack C. Branham to serve as Acting President, effective in January of 1982.[49] The search committee worked for a year before choosing a person already involved in the school's leadership.[50] A native of Columbia and a graduate of Southern, Dr. Branham held a doctorate in Education, Administration and Communication and was familiar with the business operation of the seminary. At a time when the costs of theological education were rising dramatically and when student enrollment seemed about to decline, the Board found a person close at hand who could lead the seminary through what were perceived to be some difficult years ahead. The Inauguration was held on January 28, 1983, with Bishop James Crumley as preacher.[51] The Seminary under Dr. Branham's leadership prepared to face the challenges and opportunities of the 1980's.

With a new president, once again adjustments in administrative responsibilities were desirable. A business manager and registrar was hired in 1982; and three years later, the registrar's duties were moved to another office.[52] By 1984, for the first time in nearly forty years, the Seminary returned to the pattern of president-and-dean: Paul T. Jersild, formerly dean at Wartburg Seminary, assumed the position of academic dean and was named also Professor of Theology and Ethics.[53] Relieved of primary tasks in both the business and academic operations, President Branham was free to play a larger role in institutional development. The sudden death of Dr. Curtis Derrick in February of 1985 was a serious blow to the seminary.[54] Dr. Derrick's many friendships in the Southeast, his deep spirituality and his intense commitment to Southern Seminary had been one of the school's great strengths. During his thirteen years in the development office, the endowment had grown from $338,000 to almost $4 million.[55] By the fall of 1985, a new development officer, Dr. Clyde Kaminska, had begun his work, and within the next two years, he would be assisted by Pastor John Largen, who held responsibility for church relations and student recruitment, and by Ellen Stallworth, who managed media relations.[56] The presence of these two full-time additional staff members marked a commitment by the Board of Trustees to the whole development program of the seminary. Thus in 1987, Dr. Branham headed an administrative team which included an enlarged development staff, an academic dean, a registrar, and a business manager.

Early in Dr. Branham's administration, several major gifts to the seminary were to have a significant impact on the future direction of the institution. One of these gifts was the new Flentrop Organ for Christ Chapel.[57] Long a dream of the seminary, the organ became a reality through the generosity of Anna Barbara Fisher of Winston-Salem,

North Carolina, and her mother, Mrs. Loula Schaeffer Fisher of Concord, North Carolina. Presented in memory of Miss Fisher's father, the Arthur William Fisher Memorial Organ was dedicated on Reformation Day 1985. Additional gifts by Miss Fisher provided for maintenance of the organ, recitals, and music and worship workshops. The second gift came to establish the Lineberger Library Endowment Fund, a continuation of the long-time support of the seminary and especially its library by J. Harold Lineberger.[58] The third gift, considered at the time to be the largest single gift by an individual donor, was received in the fall of 1984 from Seminary Trustee and Atlanta, Georgia executive, Richard C. Kessler.[59] The designation of this gift would be determined after study of the seminary's needs. In addition to these large contributions, hundreds of individuals across the country contributed to the school's second endowed professorship: initiated in 1980, the campaign to fund a Hugh George Anderson Chair exceeded its goal of $300,000 in November of 1982 and was designated by the Board as the Chair in Church History.[60] In 1981, the North Carolina Synod had begun designating monies from its Michael Peeler Endowment for the eventual establishment of another endowed professorship; throughout the 1980's, the synod continued to make annual gifts from the Peeler Funds, aiming toward $250,000 in accumulated contributions—with earnings, a $300,000 endowment.[61]

Following Mr. Kessler's gift, the Board established a Long-Range Planning Committee which would draw on the expertise of people in varied fields across the Southeast in order to evaluate key areas of the seminary's program and to make recommendations to the Board about the future of the school.[62] The whole committee of some thirty-five people met with the Board and faculty in August of 1985; then, working in subcommittees over the next nine months, they prepared a report entitled *Vision 21* for consideration by the Board.[63] Numerous recommendations would be acted on by appropriate committees in the following months. One of the major recommendations—and the one responded to most quickly by the Board—had to do with the increased effort in the area of development: it was this action by the

Board that led to additional staffing in the development office and an energetic program to raise funds, to extend awareness of the school to potential students and benefactors, to enhance the seminary's image, and generally to strengthen the institution for its missions in the church.

A significant issue explored during the period of this long-range study was the question of location. Among the task groups of the Long-Range Planning Committee, attention had been given to the values and liabilities of the Columbia campus and to the possible advantages of relocation to another site, most notably Atlanta. As this conversation was occurring within the seminary's own structures, the Consultation on Theological Education of the Commission on the New Lutheran Church was also re-evaluating the location and mission of seminaries across the church: in its final report, the Consultation advised that Southern Seminary study relocating in Atlanta.[65] Both the Consultation's report and *Vision 21* thus had placed this issue before the Board of Trustees in the spring of 1986; the Board agreed to further study of the issue but asked that the committee appointed for that study also consider other locations, and that it examine the benefits of staying in Columbia.[66] When that committee reported to the Board in October of 1986, the Board reaffirmed its commitment to the Columbia location but agreed to give further consideration to the possible establishment of a Lutheran House of Studies in Atlanta.[67]

Another major development during the middle of this decade lay in the composition of the faculty. In 1985, Mary B. Havens became an Assistant Professor of Church History and the first woman on the faculty; she replaced Scott H. Hendrix.[68] In 1986, after seeing the seminary through the dedication of the Fisher Organ, L. David Miller retired; Robert D. Hawkins became Assistant Professor of Worship and Music in the fall of 1986.[69] The 1986-1987 academic year brought more changes. The Board called Daryl S. Everett to become Dewey F. Beam Professor of Pastoral Care, and Professor Austin F. Shell became Director of Contextual Education which included supervision of the internship program.[70] Two professors also announced their retirement: Harold F. Park, who had taught Christian Education and

Church Administration since 1961, and W. Richard Fritz, who had served as Librarian since 1947[71] and had seen the library's collection grow from 13,500 to 95,000 volumes.[72] In April 1987, the Board of Trustees named Luther E. Lindberg Professor of Educational Ministry and Mitzi Jarrett Derrick Director of the Library and Assistant Professor of Bibliography.[73] In the spring of 1987, Dr. Robert J. Marshall announced his retirement, and Dr. Lamontte M. Luker was called in October to be Assistant Professor of Old Testament. The seminary also announced that former Bishop of the Lutheran Church in America, James R. Cumley, Jr., would join the faculty and administration of the school as Distinguished Visiting Professor of Ecumenism.[74]

Through this period Southern's faculty persisted in providing leadership to the church, as authors, speakers, board members, and workshop leaders. In the summer of 1986, the faculty issued its first theological journal, TAP-ROOT, an annual publication by which seminary faculty, students and guest lecturers would present essays, sermons and book reviews to encourage reflection and conversation on the campus and in the church.[75]

In September 1987, Pope John Paul, II visited Columbia. In coordination with this visit, Southern Seminary, the LCA, and the National Conference of Catholic Bishops hosted a colloquy titled "Day of Dialogue" the day following the Pope's visit. Johannes Cardinal Willebrands, President of the Vatican Secretariat for Promoting Christian Unity, was the principal speaker, and LCA Bishop James R. Crumley gave the response. This event was attended by over 300 church leaders, pastors, and laity. Medals were struck for the event by the LCA and were given to the sponsors and to Cardinal Willebrands. Miniature medals were given to each person in attendance.[76]

The academic program of the seminary was also undergoing expansion. A new curriculum, introduced in 1982, placed more emphasis on a strong core of coursework and yet allowed opportunity for elective studies; the curriculum was clearly related to the expectations of the church for its ministers.[77] A perception was growing that Southern Seminary was becoming more demanding in its academic program. The program was reviewed again in the early 1980's and won accreditation from both the Association of Theological Schools and from the Southern Association of Colleges and Universities.[78] The internship program was widely recognized as one of the finest among Lutheran seminaries.[79] In 1982, the faculty approved an ambitious program designed to enable bivocational black pastors to receive a Master of Divinity degree over an expanded period of years as they continued their secular employment and their pastoral duties.[80] Other black students were enrolled in the regular Master of Divinity studies. A relationship with the Dominican Order brought Roman Catholic students into certain courses. The number of women students increased steadily, reaching a high of 50 in 1986, 29.6% of the student population.[81] More students entered the seminary after having worked in other careers and begun raising a family; the average age of seminarians rose, and diversity within the student community was a key characteristic and a stimulus for the whole campus. The seminary began offering off-campus opportunities through the Urban Training Organization of Atlanta, the Appalachian Ministries Educational Resource Center in Berea, Kentucky, and the National Capital Semester for Seminarians at Wesley Seminary as well as the Lutheran House of Studies, both in Washington, D. C.[82] New continuing education programs, such as the Summer Institute for Leadership in Ministry and the Academy of Bible and Theology, initiated in 1980 and 1986 respectively, provided varied schedules of courses for pastors and other church members.

Maintenance of the campus buildings became a major item on the school's agenda during the 1980's. Various types of improvement had to be undertaken for the president's home, for student apartments and for faculty housing; substantial grants from the Lineberger Foundation and the Cannon Trust as well as other gifts and grants made this work possible.[83] The chapel windows, which because of loosened and falling glass had for some years been of concern, evolved into a rather dangerous problem: the Board finally had to authorize replacement of the windows, and that work was carried out in the summer of 1987.[84] Rising costs,

Replacing the stained-glass windows in Christ Chapel, LTSS.

inflation, and the necessity of dealing with long-delayed maintenance problems forced the seminary for the first time in recent decades to operate at a deficit in the middle years of the 1980's and to borrow money for extensive projects such as the replacement of the chapel windows.[85] The increased efforts of the development office, a Columbia-area capital funds appeal under the sponsorship of the Columbia Advisory Council, and participation in the One in Mission campaign of the new Evangelical Lutheran Church in America were seen as avenues for a return to financial stability.

This history of Southern Seminary during the 1970's and 1980's is not complete without acknowledgement of the leadership and devotion of members of the Board of Trustees, Alumni/ae, Auxiliary members, and benefactors. The story of a theological school is a story of God's people exercising ministry; administrators, faculty, staff, students, trustees, constituents, benefactors. Students stand at the heart of the institution, engaged each year in reflection and in activities of both preparation and ministry. Those students become pastors and church workers, the new leaders of the church. It is no accident that Southern Seminary graduates have provided notable service to the church in the offices, for example, of Bishop of the Lutheran Church in America, James Crumley, or Editor of *The Lutheran*, Edgar Trexler;[86] nor is it accident that Southern Seminary graduates serve and are members of congregations, large and small, across the country and in Japan, New Guinea, India, Liberia, Namibia, Tanzania, Austria, England, and Germany. Such service is entirely consistent with the school's stated purpose. To make this ministry possible, many people must perform the often thankless tasks of seminary life. Devotion to the school and to their ministries is evident from the long tenure of members of the seminary's staff in all areas. Southern Seminary has come to be known as a community because of the people—students, staff, administrators, faculty, trustees, constituents, benefactors—who come together under the call and presence of God and who join in the proclamation of the Gospel.

Lutheridge

Located in Arden, North Carolina, Lutheridge celebrated its 25th anniversary of camping ministry for the Lutheran Church in 1975. Celebrations included an anniversary banquet, a special worship service, memorabilia display, and the renaming of Leadership Hall to Thornburg Hall, in honor of the Rev. Dr. J. Lewis Thornburg, the first Executive Director. A much-needed endowment fund was begun by a gift from the Lutheran Church of the Ascension, Savannah, Georgia.[87] Throughout the years, the camp's operations have been funded by contributions from the supporting synods and individuals and from campers' fees. Special camping appeals in each supporting synod allowed

Senior High Drama in Chapel at Lutheridge.

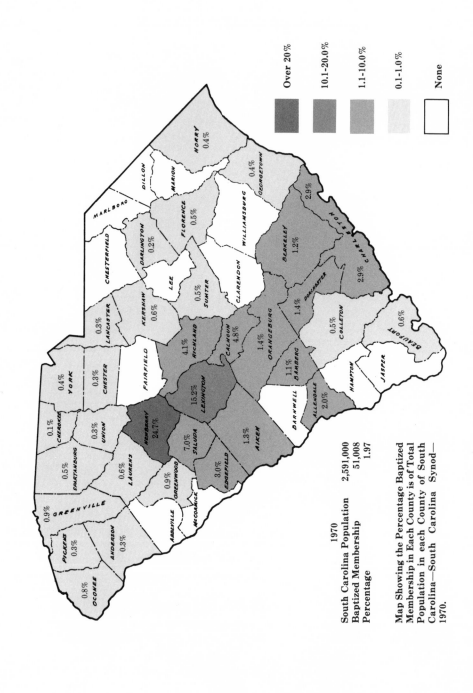

Over 20%

10.1-20.0%

1.1-10.0%

0.1-1.0%

None

1970
South Carolina Population   2,591,000
Baptized Membership   51,008
Percentage   1.97

Map Showing the Percentage Baptized
Membership in Each County is of Total
Population in each County of South
Carolina—South Carolina Synod—
1970.

HORRY
0.4%

MARION

DILLON

MARLBORO

CHESTERFIELD

DARLINGTON
0.2%

FLORENCE
0.5%

WILLIAMSBURG

GEORGETOWN
0.4%

CHARLESTON
2.9%

BERKELEY
1.2%

DORCHESTER
1.4%

ORANGEBURG
1.4%

2.9%

LEE

SUMTER
0.5%

CLARENDON

KERSHAW
0.6%

COLLETON
0.5%

RICHLAND
4.1%

CALHOUN
4.8%

BAMBERG
1.1%

HAMPTON

JASPER

BEAUFORT
0.6%

FAIRFIELD

LANCASTER
0.3%

CHESTER
0.3%

YORK
0.4%

LEXINGTON
15.2%

ALLENDALE
2.0%

BARNWELL

AIKEN
1.3%

CHEROKEE
0.1%

UNION
0.3%

NEWBERRY
24.7%

SALUDA
7.0%

EDGEFIELD
3.0%

SPARTANBURG
0.5%

LAURENS
0.6%

GREENWOOD
0.9%

MCCORMICK

ABBEVILLE
0.9%

GREENVILLE
0.9%

PICKENS
0.3%

ANDERSON
0.3%

OCONEE
0.8%

Lutheridge to undertake major renovation to several buildings, upgrading them to year-round capability. In 1980, a
budget item called "Funded Depreciation" was established
to be used for the replacement, renovation and renewal of
its facilities. Monies are added to the fund each year by
every registrant at Lutheridge. In 1985, a generous gift
from the Lineberger Foundation enabled the establishment
of the Lineberger Hall Endowment Fund, the income from
which will be used for the maintenance and upkeep of Lineberger Dining Hall.[88] This building had been completely
renovated and the kitchen re-equipped in 1982.[89] In 1983, the
Rev. Donald R. Fauble became the new Director of Development and Promotion;[90] his appointment has resulted in a
greatly increased level of financial support by friends of the
camp.

Campers enjoy the swimming pool at Lutheridge.

Major renovations and expansions of Lutheridge's facilities during these years have included work on Efird Hall in
1974 and 1982;[91] a three-phase renovation of the swimming
pool: solar collectors were installed for heating water, the
electrical system was replaced, and the pool itself was rebuilt with a new concrete shell and deck in 1980;[92] Thornburg Hall was expanded with a lounge and meeting rooms,
a new heating system installed, and the building completely
redecorated and refurnished in 1982-3;[93] the Hill Cabins and

Mission Hall were renovated in 1987;[94] a carillon was installed in Whisnant Chapel in 1974;[95] and computers were purchased for the office in 1983.[96] In 1976, the property owned by Mr. and Mrs. Walter R. Bacot was acquired and converted the next year from a private residence to a high-comfort-level housing facility.[97] A much needed maintenance building was built in 1980.[98]

As facilities became usable year round, Lutheridge was able to expand its program offerings, especially for adults, in the non-summer months. The first of these was "An Autumn Weekend for Families" in October 1974 with 113 persons representing 41 families in attendance.[99] The next year twenty-seven persons attended the first non-summer senior citizen program.[100] Other non-summer programs have included ones for remarried couples, singles, singles again, and continuing education events for pastors. Lutheridge has become particularly popular during the fall "color" season. Summer camping programs have also been expanded. In 1970, the minimum age for campers was lowered to those having completed the third grade.[101] They join fourth and fifth grades as Junior Campers; Intermediate Campers are from grades seven through eight; and Senior Campers are from grades nine through twelve. These summer youth campers, who participate in a wide variety of camping experiences, account for about 15% (over 2,200) of the total persons (over 15,000) involved in activities at Lutheridge.[102] Camping weeks have been consistently full throughout Lutheridge's history, with Music Week being one of the most popular, and the newly organized "half-weeks" proving to be very popular. The use of clergy was also expanded, making them an integral part of the camper program as the primary leader of Christian Education and as counselors for campers and staff. College students continue to serve ably as summer counselors augmenting an ever growing and important year-round staff. A camp for the mentally retarded has also been an important part of Lutheridge's ministry.

Two of the most exciting new programs for Lutheridge have been the Satellite Camps and Confirmation Camps. In 1972, four Lutheridge counselors traveled to Nashville, Tennessee, to conduct two one-week camping sessions for campers from the Southeastern Synod, thus beginning Lutheridge's Satellite Camps.[103] This program continued at Rau Wood Retreat Center in Nashville, and was expanded with Satellite Camps at New Ebenezer Family Retreat Center, Rincon, Georgia, in 1980; Lenoir-Rhyne College in North Carolina, Kinard Conference Center in South Carolina, and Camp Dixie in Alabama in 1983; and Gulf State Park in Alabama and Biblia Village in Florida in 1985.[104] The first Confirmation Camp was held in the summer of 1971 and by 1987 had expanded to 15 clusters. During these weeks, Confirmation Campers spend part of their day in confirmation ministry programs and part of their day in the regular Lutheridge activities. Another program just in the planning stages is the development of a retirement community on Lutheridge property. In 1987, the Board of Trustees agreed to lease a portion of the Lutheridge property to Lutheran Services for the Aging in North Carolina for the establishment of such a community.[105]

Throughout these years, leadership for the camp's ministry has been provided by a Board of Trustees elected by the supporting Synods. Day-to-day operations have been the responsibility of the Executive Director, the Rev. Robert L. Troutman. He has been assisted through the years by John S. Cline, Assistant Director, 1974-1979; Mr. Compton H. Usina, Business Manager until his retirement in 1974, and Mr. Fred Park since 1985; Maintenance Manager, Mr. Herbert J. Volkert until 1981, and Mr. Jonathan W. Frock since 1982; Dietitian, Mrs. Minnie M. Combs, 1970-1976; Food Service Managers, Mr. Fred J. Laube, 1977; Mrs. Ruby R. Safrit, 1978-1979; Mrs. Barbara J. Strickland, 1979-1981; Miss Leanne Carpenter, 1982; Mr. F. J. "Don" Benoway, 1983-1985; and Mrs. Annette H. Jacobson since 1985; Mrs. Sarah B. Frey, Resident Manager of Kohnjoy Inn and Retreat/Conference Registrar, 1972-1980; Registrars, Mr. Larry W. Jones, 1981-1983; Mrs. Nancy Richburg, 1983-1984; and Mrs. Renee M. Park since 1985; Mrs. Nellie H. Robertson, Bookkeeper-Secretary, 1974-1980 and Administrative Assistant, 1980 to 1984; and several other full-time persons in maintenance and kitchen staff.

With excellent facilities, an expanded year-round program schedule, quality leadership and support staff, and a growing financial-support basis, Lutheridge has provided the synod with an excellent camping ministry and promises to continue in that tradition for years to come.

Newberry College

Change and purpose were emphasized by Dr. Fredric B. Irvin in his remarks to the student body of Newberry College in September 1971 in his first public appearance as president. "We need to know where we stand and what our particular goals are as we try to educate our students," he emphasized; "we want to pursue excellence in everything we do, and we willingly accept the challenge of change in our society." Dr. Irvin concluded his charge to the students by saying, "And I ask this morning, particularly of the students, that you help me to work through many of the difficult problems facing all of us in our colleges these days. These are the problems of curriculum, evaluation of faculty members, our philosophy of education in a changing society, campus morals, and all those things that always affect communities, wherever they are or in whatever period of history they exist." [106]

Dr. Irvin's remarks on "change and purpose" set the tone for his four-year tenure as president and the terms of the presidents who followed him. Dr. Irvin was elected the college's 12th president in 1971 to succeed Dr. A. G. D. Wiles, who guided the college through the 1960's. Prior to assuming the presidency, Dr. Irvin was a foreign service officer for eleven years. He was no newcomer to teaching and college administration, having begun his academic career as a Special Teacher of English and German in the schools of Puerto Rico during the thirties. He served as President of Thiel College from 1952-60 and as Professor of English and Vice-President of the Andhra Christian College, Guntur, India, from 1947-52.

The veteran educator retired in 1975; in announcing his retirement to the Board of Trustees he stated that his administration had successfully come to grips with serious problems facing all independent colleges in the rapidly changing circumstances of the mid-1970's. Enrollment reached a high of 863 students in 1974; the college surpassed the goals of its annual funds and added around $500,000 in plant improvements to complete the Alumni Music Center and to improve other facilities.

Newberry College President, Dr. Glenn Whitesides.

The Trustees looked to the Newberry administration to find a successor to Dr. Irvin; they elected Dr. Glenn E. Whitesides, the vice-president for academic affairs, to the college's top position. When elected, Dr. Whitesides had served as academic dean for three years. He came to Newberry from Lenoir-Rhyne College, where he was Assistant Professor and Chairman of the English-Honors Program from 1963-69 and Associate Professor and Chairman of the Department of English until he came to Newberry in 1972.

President Whitesides led the College for nine years. He took the opportunity whenever he could to speak on the "Newberry Experience." "I maintain that Newberry is special, distinctive, worthy of support, does provide a need— something that the large state system cannot—is relevant, and does indeed emphasize Christian values in many and various ways. Part of the key educational task at Newberry is to help students recognize problems and to confront them with questions and help them find the answers. The students begin to think; the students begin to question. And to find some of the answers, the students begin to participate. It's not real life yet—but it is real to them—and they do it in their way—and we let them—they make mistakes, but we help them to learn from those mistakes. The Newberry

Experience is in the classroom, on the baseball diamond, with friends, with professors and counselors. The Newberry Experience is in the laboratory and the library, on the campus quadrangle, on the basketball court—and it's putting together a student newspaper and writing an editorial that upsets the administration and alumni and parents." [107]

Dr. Whitesides would conclude his remarks by emphasizing, "There is a need for Newberry College in the present and in the future just as there has been a need in the past. As Lutherans, we can and we must answer that need— through our church college—through a curriculum and program that prepare the student for life and to earn a living." [108]

He announced his resignation in 1984 to the Board of Trustees by declaring, "We need a Newberry renewal. We need fresh ideas and perhaps a different style of leadership and direction." [109]

Veteran member of the Board of Trustees, John S. Ammarell was named the Interim President in 1984 until the Presidential Search Committee could recommend and the Board of Trustees could elect a new president to succeed President Whitesides.[110] The new Interim President had been a member of the Newberry Board of Trustees since 1970 and vice-chairman of the Board and chairman of the finance committee since 1983. The chairman of the executive committee and senior consultant of the Wackenhut Corp., Ammarell retired from the Miami-based security firm in 1983 after serving for 25 years as the company's Executive Vice President.

The board elected as president Dr. Paul Tillquist, a Senior Development Associate at Gustavus Adolphus College, where he was the coordinator for deferred giving and long range planning and director of marketing.[111] He took over the reins of office from Interim President Ammarell on January 1, 1985, but he resigned the presidency after only three weeks on the job. "In our discussion with Dr. Tillquist," Porter Kinard, chairman of the 35-member Board, said, "differences in our management philosophy and style made it apparent that the relationship could not continue." [112]

Newberry College President, Dr. John Ammarell.

The Trustees turned to John Ammarell for the second time and elected him president after the sudden resignation of Dr. Tillquist. "We are very fortunate indeed to have someone of Mr. Ammarell's experience and background to assume the college presidency. He is familiar with the college operations and personnel through his membership on the Board and his tenure as Interim President," Kinard said.[113]

At his inauguration, President Ammarell declared, "I accept the Presidency of Newberry College because I believe that it is for me the path of Christian ministry and stewardship. As a graduate of a Lutheran liberal arts college, I continue to believe that we should preserve and strengthen colleges like Newberry which have produced so many men and women who have acquired knowledge and skills that have helped our state and nation develop. As a result of my own education and varied career pursuits, I believe in the importance of a liberal arts education." [114]

One of the major goals of his tenure as the college's 15th president was to reduce the college's operating deficit that had grown to $918,000.[115] The college ended the 1985-86 fiscal year in the black. The budget surplus of $86,100, the first since the 1979-80 fiscal year, reduced the college's current fund deficit to $731,500.[116]

In addition to special fund-raising campaigns to reduce the deficit, "a concentrated effort was made to hold down expenditures; academic departments and administrative offices cut spending to a minimum; a mild winter decreased utilities; and the installation of Line One long-distance service cut the cost of communications," according to Eric Farmer, treasurer and chief financial officer. "Too, a general drop in interest rates, coupled with better management of cash, resulted in a savings of interest expense," he said.[117]

Newberry College President, Dr. Hubert Setzler.

When he accepted the presidency, Ammarell indicated that he planned to serve only until a permanent president could be elected. So the Board of Trustees began the search again. This time they chose a 1962 graduate, Dr. Hubert H. Setzler, Jr.[118] The new president followed a family tradition established by his grandfather and continued by his father—a tradition of service to Newberry College that encompassed nearly 75 years.

Dr. Setzler is the former Director of Training Systems Development for the International Division of National Educational Corporation. He was responsible for developing the educational and training needs in the United States, Western democracies, and lesser developed countries.

When elected, Dr. Setzler declared, "Newberry College is more than a school, it is a way of life; it continues in the traditions established by past leaders, distinctive, not elitist. What we have here is not merely an alternative, but a superior way of life. Newberry College is in business—the business of building better lives, the business of helping young people realize that they have the skills and the training they need to become leaders in their communities, their churches, and their professions. We will stress leadership at Newberry College. We will help young people develop and understand what it is that will bring them joy . . . then we will give them the knowledge and skills they need to accomplish that. In sharing their successes, we will multiply our own," he concluded.[119]

One of Dr. Setzler's innovative programs is the Service Internship Program (SIP), a service-oriented program intended to train students in basic life skills, basic organizational skills, and principles of leadership. The program was introduced in the 1986-87 academic year. It will be fully operational in three years, linking campus and community in volunteers, work sites, and service projects. It involves students at the sophomore, junior, and senior levels. The SIP balances training and specific skill building at each level with service and experience in the arenas of college, community, church, and business and industry. The sophomore level focuses on basic training and practical exercises. The junior level focuses on team participation and skill building. The senior level focuses on leadership development, responsibility, service, and stewardship. Having equal importance with the academic program, the SIP is a life-laboratory for applying Christian values, academic knowledge, and social and interpersonal skills in service and leadership.[120]

In 1987, The Rev. Dr. Raymond Bost became Dean of the College with responsibilities in both the areas of Academics and Student Affairs. An Associate Dean of Men and an Associate Dean of Women work with him in the daily operational functions of student affairs, while he oversees the academic programs of the college.[121]

An innovative program which seeks to ensure that qualified students who wish to attend Newberry will not have to compromise their plans because of financial resources was begun. Incoming students are guaranteed that 100% of their financial need will be met through a package of scholarships and loans.[122] The Founders and Presidential Scholarship programs successfully attract more academically talented students to the campus. For the third straight year enrollment was up in 1986-87 with an increase in the average Scholastic Aptitude Test scores of entering freshmen.

ACADEMIC PROGRAM

As stated in its objectives, the college "continually reappraises its total program in order to meet the challenges of a changing world." Nowhere is this "continual change" more apparent than in the curriculum. The faculty made sweeping changes in the course of study in 1972 when it approved a Core Curriculum that required 42 semester hours for all students; it replaced the old 59 hours of required courses.[123]

After the faculty voted to discontinue the Interim in 1980, it amended the Core Curriculum to what it is today. All students must take 3-6 hours of communications skills, 6 hours of religion, 9 hours of humanities, 8 hours of natural sciences, 12 hours of social sciences, and one hour of physical education.[124] A faculty committee began another study of the curriculum and expects to make recommendations for a "curriculum for the 1990's."

Since the 1970's, academic majors have been added in art, arts management, computer science (either in combination with business administration or mathematics), early childhood education, industrial safety, and physical education. Dual-degree programs were also negotiated with Clemson and Georgia Tech in computer science, engineering, industrial management, management science and physics. Army ROTC was also added to the curriculum. The Music Department added two professional degree programs: Bachelor of Music and Bachelor of Music Education.

Newberry College has been fully accredited by the Southern Association of Colleges and Schools since the 1930's. The college will be reviewed for reaccreditation in 1991-92. In addition, Newberry's teacher education programs are accredited by the National Council of Accreditation for Teacher Education (NCATE) and by the South Carolina Department of Education. Newberry programs accredited by NCATE include early childhood education, elementary education and secondary school programs in biology, chemistry, economics, English, history, mathematics, political science, and sociology. Kindergarten-12th grade (K-12) programs accredited are music and physical education. The NCATE accreditation is valid until the 1989-90 school year.

The College's Music Department also received full accreditation in 1984 from the National Association of Schools of Music (NASM). Only a select 500 colleges and universities in the nation are accredited by NASM.

During the past few years accrediting agencies have

adopted new standards concerning the "Value-Added Dimension" of higher education. "This approach to institutional evaluation means that all colleges must begin to measure change in students' skills, knowledge, and attitudes from the start to the completion of their college careers," President Hubert H. Setzler, Jr. said.

As a part of Newberry's effort to comply with the new academic assessment requirements established in 1985 by the Southern Association of Colleges and Schools, all seniors take a three-part examination in reading, vocabulary, and writing. "From the moment an individual enrolls at Newberry College, he or she begins to accumulate a variety of ideas, skills, and experiences, which are the essence of higher education. What we are planning to do," noted President Setzler, "is to measure as accurately as possible those changes which occur in each student from the freshman through the senior years." The testing of seniors on basic reading, writing, and vocabulary skills is simply the first step in the creation of a comprehensive, systematic program of value-added assessments of the Newberry College experience.

Newberry students who have difficulty in reading, writing, study, and mathematical skills have a new home on campus—the Academic Skills Center—to assist them in their studies. The Center is a laboratory established to help students improve their performance in those basic skills which are necessary for successful college work: reading, writing, mathematics, and effective study techniques. Each student who visits the Center is given individualized attention which should greatly enhance the opportunity for academic success.[125]

It is staffed with skilled and experienced instructors and is fully equipped with reading machines, cassette-tape players, slide-tape viewers, and current teaching materials. The Center's program is designed not only to help students improve their academic skills but also to help them gain more pleasure from their studies. The Academic Skills Center was established in 1976; it is located in Wright Hall behind Wessels Library.

PHYSICAL PLANT

During the 1970's, the rapid growth in the physical plant that the campus had seen during the previous 15 years slowed down. The $600,000 Alumni Music Center that was completed in 1972 was the only new building constructed during the decade.[126] However, major renovations were made on Holland and Smeltzer Halls as well as minor renovations and routine maintenance projects on most of the other buildings. The remodeling of Holland Hall in 1972 brought all of the administrative offices under one roof. For the first time in the structure's 70-year history, there were no classes taught in the building.[127]

The first plans to remodel Smeltzer Hall, the freshman women's dormitory and the oldest building on campus, were revealed in 1973. After much study and debate, the Board of Trustees endorsed a loan for the renovation of Smeltzer in the spring of 1976. That fall, the college received a $500,000 federal loan for the work and, with the loan, the "green light" to go ahead with plans that called for the complete renovation of the building to include new wiring, heating, plumbing, air-conditioning, and roof.[128] Although the "new" Smeltzer was to be completely new on the inside, the architects were to leave the exterior of the 100-year-old building and the lobby and the public areas similar to what they were to remind Newberrians of the century of history that Smeltzer had helped to make. The contractors moved into the building as soon as the 1976-77 school year was over, and it remained closed during the 1977-78 school year. The renovation was completed just in time for classes in September 1978. The historic heritage of Smeltzer was recognized in 1976 when the National Park Service created the Newberry College Historic District that includes the College's four oldest buildings: Smeltzer, Keller, Holland, and Derrick.[129]

While Smeltzer was being renovated, the College went ahead with its plans for a new physical education complex to replace the outmoded MacLean Gymnasium. In 1977, fund-raising plans for the proposed unit were, according to President Whitesides, "to be quiet and low-keyed." He was

Physical Education Building at Newberry College.

optimistic about its success, because, he said, "we think no college ever had a more obvious need than we have for a decent facility, not just for athletics, but for the academic programs as well. In health and physical education, we have a fast-growing program which demands special classrooms and laboratory area. And, of course, the college badly needs more recreational outlets for the students." [130] The fundraising efforts for the $1.5 million unit finally bore fruit but only after delays that forced the elimination of the proposed swimming pool from the plans because of high costs. Groundbreaking ceremonies for the new complex were in August 1980;[131] the first basketball game in Eleazer Arena inaugurated the 1981-82 cage season.[132]

The physical-education facility contains a field house, handball courts, classrooms, and office space. It has also become a convention center during the summer months for church-wide groups and youth camps. The basement of MacLean Gymnasium was also remodeled to provide locker room and dressing facilities for the football and baseball teams.

The newest addition to campus facilities, a 35' x 75' outdoor swimming pool, was completed in April 1987.[133] The pool is the first phase of a planned Student Life Center that will contain a book store, canteen, game room, and televi-

Mrs. Casey breaks ground for Student Life Center with Dr. Setzler look-ing on.

sion lounge. Ground was broken for the O. L. Casey Student Center on December 9, 1987, after a gift of $225,000 was received from Mrs. Casey in memory of her husband.[134]

The Physical Education Complex, which adjoins MacLean Gymnasium, brought about two other changes to the campus: new tennis courts and the relocation of Wright Hall. In 1979, six tennis courts were built just north of the Alumni Music Center; the old courts were razed when the construction on the Physical Education Complex began. Wright Hall was moved for the third time to make room for the new building. Located next to Cromer Hall and Wessels Library, it now houses the Academic Skills Center.

Other remodeling projects of the 1970's included the completion of the basement of the Science and Mathematics Building for the new and growing Department of Art, a new basketball court in MacLean Gymnasium to replace the original floor, new bleachers for Setzler Field, and a Special Collections Room in Wessels Library. Funding for these projects came from the Newberry College Women's League, the Lutheran Brotherhood, and several foundations.

Major renovation in five buildings (Derrick and Brokaw residence halls, Kaufmann Hall, Holland Hall, and Wessels

Library) and campus landscaping were a result of IQE gifts in the early 1980's. Sixty-two-year-old Derrick Hall received the most attention in the renovation projects that began in 1984. The work included new carpeting in the hallways and tile in the 39-room women's residence hall, new lounge and study-parlor furniture, and new bathrooms on each floor. The plumbing and electrical wiring were also brought up-to-date. Renovations to the exterior of the building included new windows, paint, and roof.

Returning students in September 1984 also found major changes in Kaufmann Hall, particularly in the dining rooms. The renovations included the rearrangement of the serving lines to make them more functional, attractive, and eye appealing and the redecorating of the main student dining room, the Presidential and the Faculty Dining Rooms, and the hallways.[135] The long-needed air conditioning unit in Brokaw Hall was installed in the early summer of 1984; student rooms and the corridors were also painted that summer.[136]

Renovation work in the 83-year-old Holland Hall was done in two phases in 1984 and 1985. The first phase was the renovation of the old chapel-auditorium into a Board of Trustees Room and theatre. The theatre area of the renovated auditorium has seating for 150. Actors can perform from the stage or in the center of the auditorium area with seating on three sides of the acting area. The funds for the renovation of the chapel-auditorium were donated by Mrs. Catherine Bates Rast in memory of her husband, George Rast, who served as a trustee for 14 years.[137]

The second phase of the Holland Hall renovation was completed in 1985; it included repainting and carpeting of all administrative offices, lobby, and stairs.

The remodeling of Wessels Library was completed in 1985; it was the last major project to be funded with IQE gifts. The emphasis of this remodeling was in the public service and student service areas. The remodeled reference room on the ground floor has 25 individual study carrels; another 16 carrels, five study rooms, and a student typing room are on the lower level. The library renovation included new lighting, carpeting, ceiling and wall treatment for noise reduction, and structural changes to improve the work-flow efficiency of the Technical Services and Media Services Department. New library furniture was also purchased.[138]

Other IQE funded projects included painting in the Classroom Building and new roofs for Kinard Hall, Brokaw Hall, and the Classroom Building.

FUND RAISING

Pledge payments for the college's Second Century Campaign were completed in 1972; the three-year campaign raised funds to complete payment on Wiles Chapel and the Science and Mathematics Building and to assist in the construction of the Alumni Music Center.

During the past 15 years, the college has raised over $15 million dollars in volunteer giving from alumni, friends, the synods, churches, businesses and industries, and foundations for restricted and unrestricted giving. Newberry College seeks special contributions through three different channels: the Annual Fund, Capital or Building Funds, and Estate Planning Programs. Each fundamentally benefits a different phase of the college's operations: the current budget, the physical plant, and the endowment, and supplements regular benevolence gifts from the supporting synods.

The college has conducted three major capital gifts campaigns since 1971: the Smeltzer Hall renovation campaign in 1976-77;[139] the Marathon Campaign for the new Physical Education Complex;[140] the major Investment in Quality Education (IQE) Campaign from 1981-86.[141] The IQE funds were used for additions to and renovations of the physical plant, strengthening the college's academic program and financial aids program, and adding to the endowment for campus maintenance needs. A low-key campaign was also conducted in 1986-87 to raise funds for the swimming pool and Student Life Center.[142]

The college's first million-dollar fund-raising year was 1977-78 when $1,017,389 was received through volunteer giving.[143] Since then, the million-dollar plateau has been reached six times, including a record $2,000,000 during the

1986-87 fiscal year that ended June 30, 1987.[144] By that time the current fund deficit had been reduced to $306,715.[145]

PURPOSE AND OBJECTIVES

Lutherans in Newberry College's three supporting synods discussed and voted on the purpose and objectives of the college and on the mutual responsibilities of the college and of the synods to each other in 1985. The LCA required the church-supported colleges to prepare a Covenant Statement and to update it periodically. The last statement was approved in 1977. The purpose of Newberry College is to provide students with opportunities for liberal and culturally relevant education enriched by a clear consciousness of Christian values. This purpose underlies an academic program which endeavors to combine the broad base of the liberal arts with preparation for vocation in a number of specialized fields.

While always mindful of its heritage and traditions, the college continually reappraises its total program in order to meet the challenges of a changing world. The objectives of the program are to provide an environment and the resources through which each student may:

- Explore a portion of the accumulation of human knowledge and relate to it as person, as citizen, as worker, and as a creature of God.
- Develop skills of critical analysis in order to solve problems in both a humane and a scientific context.
- Refine a system of values and priorities consistent with the heritage of the Christian faith so as to influence in a positive way the standards of American society.
- Identify and accept the qualities and characteristics that contribute to individual uniqueness.
- Establish satisfactory relationships with other persons.
- Acquire basic preparation for a profession/vocation.
- Develop skills and attitudes related to the fulfilling use of leisure.

Newberry College has continued to be a vital part of the total Lutheran ministry in South Carolina.[146]

Agencies

The congregations and members of the synod have consistently demonstrated their desire to provide care for people with special needs in their communities. In most cases this work is done through social ministry groups of the local congregations or in cooperation with ecumenical and/or community agencies. In several cases, Lutheran congregations have come together to facilitate their programs for this ministry.

LUTHERAN SOCIAL SERVICES OF GREATER CHARLESTON

Lutheran Social Services of Greater Charleston.

The idea for initiating a program to serve the less fortunate and others with special needs in the greater Charleston area evolved from the concern of the Social Ministry Committee of the Lutheran Churches of the Coastal District. In 1982, two Lutheran pastors, L. E. Cumbee and Matthew Moye, began to interest Lutheran laity of Charleston in the need for raising the level of social services, and by late 1984, a formal organization was structured as the Lutheran Social Services of Greater Charleston (LSSGC). As organized, its purpose was broadly stated: to provide a framework for cooperative voluntary action by the Lutheran churches of Charleston in a more active and effective ministry to persons with special needs. More specifically, LSSGC helps those in need—the hungry and those who require clothing and other emergency needs, as well as providing other ministries as needed. The general goal of helping the needy has been extended to lead those in whatever need they may be to a lifestyle which will enable them to become more self-supporting and potential servers of other needy individuals. LSSGC operates Monday, Wednesday, and Friday from a two-story building on Rivers Avenue provided by Advent Lutheran Church, serving people's needs through the distribution of packaged food and clothing, a hot mid-day meal, and Christian counseling. In 1987, over 7,000 pieces of clothing were distributed; over 16,000 meals were served; and over 1,800 families were assisted by LSSGC. Clients are referred to LSSGC by area ministers and other social service groups, although many of the clients are self-referred. Financial support for this ministry comes primarily from the Lutheran churches of Charleston, although through the years the support of other denominations has grown to be sizeable and important to the ministry. Many volunteers have contributed thousands of hours in labor at the center as well as through the management and operation of the agency through the board. In February 1984, the board hired the first employee, Mrs. Adlay Tapp, who now serves as director. She participates in the training and supervising of volunteers, maintains files, and manages the operations of LSSGC.

THE FRANKE HOME

Having been established in 1892 as a result of a bequest from the estate of Mr. C. D. Franke, the Franke Home in Charleston had grown to a capacity of housing 42 persons in 1959. In 1970, because there was a need to provide even more accommodations for the growing older population, another building was constructed. This construction was financed by a bond issue subscribed to by the Lutherans and their friends in the Charleston area and was paid off in ten years. The new facility enabled the home to expand its capacity to 77 guests, and the original building which was built in the 1850's was demolished. While not an official institution of the synod, the home is owned and operated by the Evangelical Lutheran Charities Society of Charleston, which consists of twelve Lutheran congregations in the Charleston area. Each member church provides three representatives to constitute the Board of Directors which governs the home. The Franke Home is largely dependent upon the fees charged its guests for its financial support. In 1987, approximately 4% of the financial support comes from the Lutheran churches of the Charleston area and less than 1% from endowment income.

During 1986, there was a change in the administrator, and the position is now filled by George H. Keil, a member of St. Andrew Lutheran Church. That year saw a continuation of efforts to enhance the comfort and safety of the residents at the home. The improvements included the installation of storm windows throughout the entire facility and smoke/heat detector alarms to supplement the sprinkler system.

The Franke Home Auxiliary continues its contribution to and support of the Home and residents. A major contribution was the furnishing of new drapes for the entire home. A special project has been the making of Chrismon ornaments to decorate the main-lobby Christmas tree.

The Franke Home operates as a residential care facility for the aged and infirm without regard to religious affiliation, race, sex, or national origin.

LUTHERAN SOCIAL SERVICES OF CENTRAL SOUTH CAROLINA

The decades of the 1970's and 80's brought great changes to the programs and direction of the coordinated social ministry agency in the midlands of South Carolina. On January 1, 1971, the Lutheran Social Missions Society of Greater Columbia became the Lutheran Social Ministry Agency of Greater Columbia. Having originally been organized in 1938 as the Lutheran Inner Missions Society of Columbia with an immediate objective of distributing Christian literature to the patients and inmates of hospitals and other institutions in the city and county, it was operated by a committee composed of the pastor and one lay representative from each cooperating church with financial support coming dirctly to the agency from individuals. The Rev. Dr. P. D. Brown was elected as the first president, and the committee's work continued in this manner until 1943 when the South Carolina Synod Board of Social Missions was formed. With the call of the Rev. Carl B. Caughman as the first Social Missions Pastor, the Society began working closely with him and the board. During World War II the Society provided a variety of ministries through the Lutheran Service Center in Columbia. Services were provided at Fort Jackson, the Veterans Hospital, and the tubercular hospital.

On October 1, 1947, Sister Miriam Shirey became the Society's first full-time worker. Under her leadership the work was organized on a congregational level with congregational responsibilities. Several churches sponsored special programs at various institutions. On January 15, 1960, the Lutheran Social Missions Society of Greater Columbia was incorporated for the purpose of religious work. Three deaconesses, Sister Bertha Schwanewede, Sister Delphine Dasher, and Sister Edna McVickers, followed Sister Miriam in providing leadership for the Society until 1969. During this time the ministry to shut-ins and patients of hospitals and institutions was particularly emphasized. Sunday School was also taught at several institutions.

With the change to the Lutheran Social Ministry Agency of Greater Columbia in 1971, a new structure provided for the coordination of the social ministry programs of the cooperating congregations. The Rev. J. Harry Crout began his work as Executive Director on December 1, 1970, and served in that capacity until November 1984. During that time the 21 cooperating congregations offered ministries that were indicative of the needs of the community. Services by the agency included emergency funds, food, clothing, and other items for individuals and families. A camp program for underprivileged and retarded children was held at Camp Kinard, nearly 30 congregations were assisted in sponsoring Vietnamese refugees, and child-care ministry was provided for Lutheran families. The greatest increase in demand for ministry came in the area of counseling. This included family, marriage and divorce, alcohol and substance abuse, etc.

A reorganization in late 1984 resulted in a new name and direction for the agency. Lutheran Social Services of Central South Carolina (LSS/CSC) was organized with members being Lutheran congregations. Each congregation sent representatives to an annual meeting which elected a 15-member Board of Directors to govern the work of the agency. The Rev. Dr. Henry M. McKay was called as Executive Director in 1985. LSS/CSC is available to serve others without regard to church affiliation, origin, or background. Its programs include advocacy, education, counseling, and emergency services. It has also developed programs aimed at prevention and enrichment through retreats, leadership training, and workshops designed to strengthen individual and family wellness. A Coordinator of Volunteers was added to the staff in 1986 to direct the important ministry programs and activities of the agency. This provided the other staff with more time for the ever increasing caseload in family therapy and counseling. LSS/CSC continues to provide coordinated and planned social ministry programs for Central South Carolina from its new headquarters at Southern Seminary.[147]

Chapter Five

Congregational Histories

1. List of Congregations
2. Congregational Histories
   a. Active Congregations
   b. Mission Congregation
   c. Disbanded Congregation

Most of the information for this chapter has been provided by the pastor and members of the congregations. It is intended to reflect the scope of the ministry of the congregation within the community it serves. Congregations are listed in alphabetical order, and statistical information for each as of December 31, 1971, and December 31, 1987 is included in Appendix 3. The earlier history of those congregations organized prior to 1971 is found in A History of the Lutheran Church in South Carolina, *1971, referred to as HLCSC with page numbers. Pictures are included of those congregations that have experienced significant changes in their buildings since 1971.*

List of Congregations

Abiding Presence . . . . 323 N. Congress St., York
Advent . . . . 3347 Rivers Ave., North Charleston
All Saints . . . . 1901 Hwy 17 N., Mt. Pleasant
A Mighty Fortress . . . . 1737 N. Main St., Summerville
Ascension . . . . 827 Wildwood Ave., Columbia
Atonement . . . . 415 Farley Ave., Laurens
Augsburg . . . . 176 By-Pass N., Union
Bachman Chapel . . . . Rt. 3, Prosperity
Bethany . . . . 8 Mi. SE Hwy 6, Rt. 4, Lexington
Bethany . . . . 3rd and Nance Streets, Newberry
Beth-Eden . . . . 5 Mi. NW/Hwy 81, Newberry
Bethel . . . . Hwy 76, White Rock
Bethlehem . . . . 10,000 Broad River Rd, Irmo
Bethlehem . . . . 7 Mi. SE Pond Branch Rd., Leesville
Bethlehem . . . . 2 Mi. NW/Rt. 1, Pomaria
Cedar Grove . . . . Rt. 5, Leesville
Christ . . . . 1323 Winyah Dr., Columbia
Christ . . . . Hwy 278, Hilton Head
Christ the King . . . . 7239 Patterson Dr., Columbia
Christ the Servant . . . . Conway
Christus Victor . . . . Harbison, Columbia
Colony . . . . 5 Mi. E Hwy 76, Newberry
Corinth . . . . 10 Mi. E Saluda/Hwy 194, Prosperity
Cross and Crown . . . . 906-A S. Cashua Dr., Florence
Ebenezer . . . . 1301 Richland St., Columbia
Ehrhardt Memorial . . . . . . Franklin and Washington, Ehrhardt
Emmanuel . . . . 2491 Emmanuel Church Rd., West Columbia
Enon . . . . 3 Mi. SE Pond Branch Rd., Leesville
Epiphany . . . . Pou and Carlisle, St. Matthews
Faith . . . . 102 S. Oak St., Batesburg
Faith . . . . 374 Maybank Hwy., John's Island
Faith . . . . 1505 Wilson Rd., Newberry
Faith . . . . 1717 Platt Springs Rd., West Columbia
Gethsemane . . . . 5400 Two Notch Rd., Columbia
Good Hope . . . . 4 Mi. NE Ward, Saluda
Good Shepherd . . . . 3909 Forest Dr., Columbia
Good Shepherd . . . . Lady Street, Swansea
Good Shepherd . . . . 106 May St., Walterboro
Grace . . . . Main at Church, Gilbert
Grace . . . . Hwy 76, Prosperity
Grace . . . . 508 Aiken Ave., Rock Hill

Holy Comforter .... 2152 Savannah Hwy, Charleston
Holy Communion .... 1430 Reidville Rd., Spartanburg
Holy Cross .... 5300 Dorchester Rd., Charleston
Holy Trinity .... 209 Broad St., Anderson
Holy Trinity .... Church Street, Little Mountain
Holy Trinity .... 1002 Carolina Ave., North Augusta
Holy Trinity .... 168 Main St., Pelion
Immanuel .... E. Creswell & McLees, Greenwood
Incarnation .... 3005 Devine St., Columbia
King of Glory .... 814 Jordan Rd., North Myrtle Beach
Macedonia .... 11 Mi. SE, Prosperity
Martin Luther .... 1605 Harbor View Rd., Charleston
Mayer Memorial .... Drayton and Cromer, Newberry
Messiah .... 1106 Yeamans Hall Rd., Hanahan
Messiah .... Log Shoal and Old Laurens Rd., Mauldin
Ministry with the Deaf .... 1715 Bull St., Columbia
Mt. Calvary .... Rt. 2, 9 Mi. SE, Johnston
Mt. Hebron .... 8 Mi. N. Hwy 391, Leesville
Mt. Hermon .... River St., Peak
Mt. Hermon .... 3011 Leaphardt Rd., West Columbia
Mt. Horeb .... Columbia Ave., Chapin
Mt. Olivet .... Rt. 2, Hwy 176, Chapin
Mt. Olivet .... 7 Mi. SE, Prosperity
Mt. Pilgrim .... 3 Mi. E, Prosperity
Mt. Pleasant .... 1¼ Mi. SW, Ehrhardt
Mt. Pleasant .... 101 N. Calhoun St., Saluda
Mt. Tabor .... 1 Mi. W. Hwy 76, Little Mountain
Mt. Tabor .... 1000 B Ave., West Columbia
Nativity .... 1530 Asheville Hwy, Spartanburg
Nazareth .... 1800 Nazareth Church Rd., Lexington
Orangeburg .... 610 Ellis Ave. NE, Orangeburg
Our Saviour .... 2600 Wade Hampton Blvd., Greenville
Our Saviour .... 1500 Sunset Blvd., West Columbia
Our Shepherd .... Hwy 151 By-Pass, Hartsville
Peace .... 8015 Dorchester Rd., Charleston Heights
Pilgrim .... 3 Mi. N Hwy 6, Lexington
Pine Grove .... 1 Mi. NW, Hwy 267, Lone Star
Pisgah .... 1350 Pisgah Church Rd., Lexington
Pomaria .... Peak Rd., Pomaria
Prince of Peace .... 126 York St., Chester
Providence .... 840 Old Chapin Rd., Lexington
Redeemer .... Avondale and Riverdale, Charleston
Redeemer .... 525 St. Andrews Rd., Columbia

Redeemer .... Hwy 101 N., Greer
Redeemer .... Johnstone and Wilson, Newberry
Reformation .... 1118 Union St., Columbia
Reformation .... N. French St., Lancaster
Resurrection .... Old State Rd., Cameron
Resurrection .... 3706 Moss Ave., Columbia
St. Andrew .... 5 Mi. NE Hwy 21, Blythewood
St. Andrew .... 37-43 Wentworth St., Charleston
St. Andrew .... 1416 Broad River Rd., Columbia
St. Barnabas .... 45 Moultrie St., Charleston
St. David .... St. David's Church Rd., West Columbia
St. Jacob .... Rt. 2 Hwy 48, Chapin
St. James .... 200 Laurel Dr., Graniteville
St. James .... Rt. 3 Church St., Leesville
St. James .... 4 Mi. SE Rt. 6, Lexington
St. James .... 7 Mi. NW Hwy 76, Newberry
St. James .... 1137 Alice Dr., Sumter
St. Johannes .... 48 Hasell St., Charleston
St. John .... 108 Ribaut Rd., Beaufort
St. John .... Archdale and Clifford, Charleston
St. John .... Greenwood Hwy, Clinton
St. John .... Off Kennerly Rd., Irmo
St. John .... Calhoun and Jackson, Johnston
St. John .... 8 Mi. W Rt. 2, Lexington
St. John .... 6 Mi. NW, Pelion
St. John .... Rt. 2—1 Mi. off Hwy 176, Pomaria
St. John .... 415 S. Pine St., Spartanburg
St. John .... 301 W. Main St., Walhalla
St. Luke .... 1127 Olympia Ave., Columbia
St. Luke .... 800 King Ave., Florence
St. Luke .... 4 Mi. SW Stoney Hill Section, Prosperity
St. Luke .... 206 Central Ave., Summerville
St. Mark .... Hwy 21, Blythewood
St. Mark .... Palm Blvd, Isle of Palms
St. Mark .... 10 Mi. N Leesville/Hwy 391, Prosperity
St. Matthew .... 7 Mi. NW Hwy 6, Cameron
St. Matthew .... 405 King St., Charleston
St. Matthew .... 7 Mi. SW Rt. 3, Lexington
St. Matthew .... Rt. 2 10 Mi. NW, Pomaria
St. Matthias .... 501 Powdersville Rd., Easley
St. Michael .... 15 Mi. W. River Rd., Columbia
St. Michael .... 2619 Augusta Rd., Greenville
St. Michael .... W. Main St., Moncks Corner

St. Nicholas .... 10 Mi. NE, Fairfax
St. Paul .... 353 Laurens St., Aiken
St. Paul .... 1715 Bull St., Columbia
St. Paul .... 1600 W. Baker Blvd., Gaffney
St. Paul .... 6 Mi. N, Gilbert
St. Paul .... 604 Pitt St., Mt. Pleasant
St. Paul .... Hwy 773 N of I-26, Pomaria
St. Peter .... 2 Mi. S, Batesburg
St. Peter .... Billy Dreher Island Rd., Chapin
St. Peter .... 5 Mi. W—Hwy 378, Lexington
St. Peter .... Litchfield Beach
St. Philip .... 6200 N. Kings Hwy, Myrtle Beach
St. Philip .... 7 Mi. N, Newberry
St. Stephen .... 119 N. Church St., Lexington
St. Thomas .... St. Thomas Church Rd., Chapin
St. Timothy .... 1301 Mill St., Camden
St. Timothy .... Hwy 52 at Camelot, Goose Creek
St. Timothy .... 309 S. Main St., Whitmire
Sandy Run .... Swansea
Shepherd of the Sea .... Hwy 17/Pine Rd., Garden City
Silverstreet .... Railroad Ave., Silverstreet
Summer Memorial .... Player and Milligan, Newberry
Transfiguration .... 1301 12th St., Cayce
Trinity .... 7900 Nell St., Columbia
Trinity .... Hampton and Lexington, Elloree
Trinity .... Hampton and 4th St., Fairfax
Trinity .... Shopwall and Oak, Georgetown
Trinity .... 421 N. Main St., Greenville
Trinity .... 5 Mi. NW, Saluda
Union .... Rt. 2, Hwy 378, Leesville
University .... 120 Sloan St., Clemson
Wittenberg .... N. Lee St., Leesville
Zion .... Corley Mill Rd., Lexington

MISSION CONGREGATION

Living Springs ..... Clemson and Hard Scrabble Rd., Columbia

DISBANDED CONGREGATION

Immanuel .... Ridge Spring

Congregations

ABIDING PRESENCE, YORK
Organized 1957
(HLCSC, pg. 554)

Vigorous efforts by the small membership of this congregation in the years following 1971 have resulted in steady growth. Following the pastorate of the Rev. Lewis B. Doggett, Jr., which extended from 1972 to 1975, the Rev. Edward H. Wiediger served from 1976 to 1979.

During the term of the Rev. D. Timothy Robinson, who became pastor in 1980, a Baldwin organ was given and dedicated in 1983. After Pastor Robinson left, in 1983, the Rev. Robert E. McCollum became the pastor in 1984. In 1986, the metal folding chairs in the nave were replaced with permanent padded pews.

The congregation participates in P.A.T.H. (People Attempting to Help) and in the work of the Yorkville Literacy Council, providing facilities for the use of the tutors. The congregation looks forward to increasing its membership and to the renovation and expansion of its facilities.

ADVENT, CHARLESTON HEIGHTS
Organized 1936
(HLCSC, pp. 555-556)

In 1972, Advent served as the host for the convention of synod. In that same year, the Rev. J. Cantey Nye became assistant pastor, and a fifteen-foot wooden cross was dedicated. Pastor Earl H. Loadholt, who had served since 1969, resigned in 1973, and Pastor Nye accepted the call to become pastor, and continues in that position.

In 1975, Advent marked its 40th anniversary. The occasion was celebrated with a special program involving former pastors and charter members. That same year, the congregation began its participation in the seminary's internship program.

There have been many changes in the worship life and activities of Advent during this period. A Wednesday morning Bible class has been formed, and an adult fellowship group has been established. The use of ashes on Ash Wednesday and an Easter sunrise service have been instituted. A joint Thanksgiving service with Cherokee Place United Methodist Church, St. Thomas the Apostle Catholic Church, St. John Catholic Church, First Baptist Church, and the Korean Methodist Church is held annually. The "Live Wires," a singing group, takes programs to the elderly and shut-ins; and a senior citizens group, "Prime of Life," meets twice a month. A birthday party honoring Martin Luther's 500th birthday was held in 1983.

Much has been done to improve the church's facilities. A chair lift has been installed to the gymnatorium. In 1978, a Zimmer 24-rank tracker organ was installed, and the choir was re-located in the rear gallery of the church. Ramps and handrails for the handicapped, a new church sign, an eternal light, and lexon covering for the windows have been installed. In 1982, the church mortgage was burned, and in 1985, a 15-passenger van was purchased.

In 1986, Advent celebrated its 50th anniversary. The occasion was marked with special services and programs throughout the year involving former pastors, charter members, summer students, and past interns.

Mr. Richard A. Frederick has been Director of Christian Education since 1984; and Mr. W. Lawrence Miller joined the staff as Organist-Choir Director in 1986. A son of the congregation, John W. Withrock, Jr., was ordained in 1975.

ALL SAINTS, MT. PLEASANT
Organized 1975

With the completion of Interstate 26 into Charleston, the construction of the second Cooper River Bridge, and the expansion of Highway 17, Mt. Pleasant, by the late 1960's, became a city destined for major population growth and economic development. Aware of the potential for ministry in this area, the Division for Mission in North America, LCA, purchased 2½ acres of land on Highway 17 about six miles north of Charleston. In 1974, the Executive Board of synod called the Rev. William E. Stone as the pastor/developer for the area. After several months of visiting and planning, the first worship service for All Saints was held

at Wando High School on June 9, 1974. Approximately ninety persons, including many visitors from neighboring congregations, attended the service. In September, Sunday School classes were begun; Charter Sunday was July 27, 1975; and the congregation was organized on September 7, 1975 with 102 baptized members on roll. Pastor Stone was called by the congregation as its first pastor.

In December 1977, ground was broken for the construction of the first unit. This building was completed in 1978 and dedicated in January 1979. In June of that year, Pastor Stone resigned, and in September, the Rev. Matthew O. Moye, Jr. began his ministry as pastor.

Since its organization, the congregation has continued to grow, reflecting the growth and the profile of Mt. Pleasant. The congregation is basically composed of young professionals and executives who work outside of Mt. Pleasant in the surrounding metropolitan Charleston area. Although there had been a great deal of mobility in the early years, the community and the congregation are beginning to stabilize, and the character of the congregation has remained very much the same since its organization.

With a full range of ministry programs, All Saints also has an active Lutheran Church Women auxiliary that has provided the major volunteer core for the congregation's ministry programs. Altar guild, teachers, secretarial support, social ministry programs, and evangelism efforts have been primarily organized and implemented through the LCW. The Lutheran Men has also been active with regular programs for the men, work projects for the church building and grounds, and financial support for the youth programs. The Lutheran Church Youth meets regularly for programs and enjoys special retreats, field trips, and social outings. They also coordinate the collection of food for needy people in the community.

The congregation has been very active in social ministry outreach programs. Food, clothing, and volunteers support the Charleston Interfaith Crisis Ministry, the Lutheran Social Services of Greater Charleston, the Open Door Ministries for homeless women and children, and the East Cooper Helping Others programs. Ecumenical services and programs have included an Easter Sunrise Service, Lenten worship services, Bible studies, and shared services of the Eucharist with the local Episcopal church.

All Saints is particularly challenged in the area of evangelism because of the rapid growth of the area. Having doubled in size since its organization, the congregation has begun to solidify and, with continued growth in the area expected, looks forward to more fully developing its mission opportunities. The expansion of ministry and service programs as well as the construction of a new sanctuary are primary goals for All Saints.

A MIGHTY FORTRESS, SUMMERVILLE
Organized 1981

The population of the Summerville area has more than tripled in recent years. Just one development, Sangaree, is adding over 900 homes. This rapid growth led to the decision to place a new Lutheran congregation there.

On November 25, 1979, the Rev. Tommy K. Beaver was commissioned as Pastor/Developer at St. Luke, Summerville. The first service was held on May 18, 1980 in a double-wide building on Main Street at Sangaree; there were 18 persons in attendance.

The congregation was organized on April 26, 1981, with Rev. Beaver as its first pastor. Worship space was added

later that year. Pastor Beaver resigned in 1985, and the Rev. Carl L. Ritchie has been pastor since 1986.

The membership of the congregation is young, with over half being children and youth. It is also highly transient, since many members are associated with the armed forces. A large number are from non-Lutheran backgrounds.

An important goal of A Mighty Fortress is growth in stewardship so that it can become self-supporting and build its permanent home by 1988.

ASCENSION, COLUMBIA
Organized 1912
(HLCSC, pp. 556-557)

Ascension Lutheran Church is located in an area that has seen considerable change in the characteristics of its population since 1970, but has begun to stabilize. As a result of these changes the congregation attempts to serve a widely scattered membership, consisting of persons having a wide range of occupations and educational backgrounds.

The Rev. Frank E. Lyerly was pastor of the church until 1972. During his term of service, in 1971, repairs were made to the physical facilities, including a new roof for the parish building.

The Rev. John L. Setzler was pastor from 1973 to 1979. During this time the organ was rebuilt and enlarged.

The Rev. Joseph Huntley assumed leadership of the congregation in 1980 and remained at that post until 1984. He was succeeded by the Rev. Craig Versprille, who has been pastor from 1985 to the present.

Ascension enjoys active LCW and LCY programs. It was involved in a Word and Witness pilot project and in PLMD. The congregation has contributed generously to such causes as the Lowman Home Appeal, Seminary Outreach, and Strength for Mission. It gives regular missionary support.

The following sons of the church have been ordained into the ministry: James Dickert, Richard Fritz, Charles Fritz, Fred Schott III, and Tommy Hamm.

As it faces the future in a changed situation, Ascension hopes to reverse declining membership trends and to involve itself more heavily in ministry to its community.

ATONEMENT, LAURENS
Organized 1945
(HLCSC, pp. 558-559)

The later 1970's and 80's were years of development and growth for the congregation of Atonement. Among the accomplishments were the renovation of the first floor of the church building, making it more attractive and useful for the church program, and the addition of a new roof on the church building.

In 1980, many things were accomplished in relation to the physical facilities of the church. The pews were refinished and upholstered, adding beauty and comfort to the nave. This was undertaken as a 35th anniversary project. A funeral pall, leather-bound chancel Bible, processional cross, and two processional torches were given. Another project was the construction of a cabinet for the storage of paraments, linens, and the funeral pall.

A Lutheran Men's Group was organized in February 1980. They undertook as their first project the erection of a new sign in front of the church. That same year floodlights were placed so that the exterior of the church building could be lighted.

In 1981, a new Baldwin piano was purchased, and in 1982, a portable addition was located adjacent to the church building, to be used as a church office and Sunday School classroom. The program of the congregation was enhanced with the gift of a 16mm sound projector as well as the equipment to establish a tape ministry for shut-ins.

In 1973, the Rev. Fred E. Dufford resigned as pastor of Atonement, and the Rev. J. Marion Rhoden, Jr. became pastor in 1975. He resigned in 1984, and the next year a call was extended to the Rev. R. Cecil Warren.

In 1986, construction was begun on a second floor to the parsonage. Other additions included a new sanctuary lamp, white paraments, liturgical banners, and a two-octave set of handbells. In May 1987, a new altar was constructed and dedicated.

AUGSBURG, UNION
Organized 1930
(HLCSC, pp. 559-560)

The congregation sold its building on South Mountain (not "Main" as stated in HLCSC) Street in 1972. Pastor Ralph Riddle and the congregation held services in the Welcome Grill until June 1974, when they moved into the newly-constructed facility on the Duncan By-pass.

When Pastor Riddle resigned in 1976, he was succeeded by the Rev. Ronald Roscoe, who served until 1979. The Rev. W. Earl Jernigan became pastor the following year and

served until 1983. At this time the congregation terminated its association in a two-church parish with St. Timothy, Whitmire.

Since that time Augsburg has been served by part-time pastors, the Rev. Fred Ramseur (1983-84) and the Rev. Jasper J. Smith, who continues in that capacity. Several problems have combined to prevent growth in membership. High unemployment due to closing of textile mills, the movement of youth from the area, and the lack of a resident ministry have made progress difficult.

However, the members, largely non-Lutheran in background and in the over-fifty age bracket, have continued to maintain viable programs and service projects in the community. The LCW provides regular care and maintenance of the church building, fellowship opportunities for the congregation, and services in the Lowman Home and the local county home. Both the LM and the LCY are also active. In 1987, the mortgage was burned.

The congregation's goals are to increase in membership, become self-supporting, and have a full-time pastor with a parsonage for the pastor and family.

BACHMAN CHAPEL, PROSPERITY
Organized 1886
(HLCSC, pp. 560-561)

The Rev. William H. Link continued to serve as pastor until he resigned in 1973. That same year the Rev. James F. Shealy accepted the call to become the pastor and continues to serve. The congregation continues to grow and witness in the community.

Through the Interfaith Community Services of Newberry County the church assists in the chaplaincy ministry at the Newberry County Memorial Hospital, the ministry to transients, and the jail complex ministry. The LCW, LM, and LCY are very active. In addition to their monthly educational programs, these organizations sponsor congregational activities which promote fellowship.

A fellowship hall, completed in 1982, has been added to the facilities. An additional 2.25 acres of land adjacent to

the parsonage property were purchased for $2,250. A gift of 2.75 acres was given to the church by John Ernest Kinard, Sr., and his wife, Blanche L. Kinard.

In 1986, Bachman Chapel celebrated 100 years of service with special services from April through December. The Rev. Dr. James S. Aull preached the sermon for the 28th Anniversary of the first worship service in the brick structure; Homecoming/Golden Age Sunday in August included a sermon by former pastor, the Rev. J. A. Keisler; Bishop Herman W. Cauble preached in October; and a Birthday Party was held in December.

Also during 1986, the congregation completed a number of improvement projects for the 100-year celebration. The church roof was replaced, a celotex ceiling was installed, the nave walls were painted and the floor was refinished, and the sanctuary area and nave aisles were carpeted. Pew cushions were also purchased.

BETHANY, LEXINGTON
Organized 1871
(HLCSC, pp. 561-562)

As Bethany approached the celebration of its centennial anniversary on October 3, 1971, the congregation found itself confronted with pressing practical concerns in light of the need for additional building space. Shortly after the

arrival of the Rev. Dermon A. Sox, Sr. as Bethany's pastor in September 1970, a congregational meeting was held to discuss the possibility of either building a new sanctuary or renovating the current facility. Renovation was determined to be the more prudent course of action, and by 1974 work was completed to brick veneer the exterior of the building, to build a narthex, and to add stained glass windows and a spire. Ground was also broken in 1974 for a new educational annex, a project completed in June 1976.

Pastor Sox retired in 1971 and continued to serve until June 1974. He was succeeded by the Rev. James E. Short, who served until 1978. Both Pastor Sox and Pastor Short had also respectively served Nazareth in Lexington while at Bethany, but each of the two congregations decided to call its own pastor after Pastor Short resigned. The Rev. Ronald E. Roscoe accepted the call to Bethany in 1979. When declining health led to Pastor Roscoe's resignation in 1983, the Rev. G. Baylis Corley became Bethany's pastor.

Like many of the Lutheran churches in the Lexington area, Bethany is a traditional and established congregation in a growing community. One way in which it serves the community is through participation in Lexington Interfaith Community Services. Bethany also serves the church around the world by helping to support a missionary family in Indonesia and Malaysia.

BETHANY, NEWBERRY
Organized 1936
(HLCSC, pp. 562-564)

The Rev. John A. Sanders continued his service as the pastor until his retirement in 1976. In 1973, the mortgage on the parish building was burned as the congregation celebrated its debt-free status. The Rev. Sidney W. Roden became the pastor in November of 1976 and served until his resignation in 1979.

Later the same year the Rev. Michael K. Olson began his work as pastor of the church. During his term of service the church acquired an Allen digital organ and a bus to facilitate fellowship activities. The Lutheran Men received a charter in 1980.

After Pastor Olson resigned in 1981, the pulpit was vacant until the arrival of the Rev. William Flowers in the spring of 1983, and he continues to serve.

New cushions were installed in the pews in 1985. In 1986, Bethany celebrated its 50th anniversary and opened the cornerstone of the nave, which had been erected in 1938. It was found to contain a Bible, a catechism, a list of charter members, a list of monetary and labor contributions to the erection of the building, and a variety of other interesting items. In 1986, a three-octave set of handbells and a piano were given as memorials.

BETH EDEN, NEWBERRY
Organized 1843
(HLCSC, pp. 564-565)

The Rev. Paul Hatch resigned as pastor in 1973 and was succeeded the following year by the Rev. Lester H. Cutter, Jr., who served until 1985. The congregation, which is part of the parish with nearby St. James, has not grown in recent years, and there are few children and young persons in its membership. Under its current pastor, the Rev. Herbert L. Wood, Jr., who arrived in late 1985, it continues the worship ministry and has an active LCW.

It maintains well its large cemetery and one building, to which washrooms have been added, and air conditioning installed. Every year a homecoming service and picnic dinner attract large numbers of former members and friends.

BETHEL, WHITE ROCK
Organized 1762
(HLCSC, pp. 565-568)

In 1979, the cornerstone laid fifty years earlier at the site of the new building for the merged Mount Vernon and Bethel parishes was opened, reminding the congregation of its immediate past. Shortly thereafter, the congregation began work on a new building, a Christian education center, that helped prepare the way for its future. The center, consisting of educational and administrative space, was completed in February 1984.

Like other Lutheran congregations in the Dutch Fork, especially those around Lake Murray, Bethel is also preparing for the steady and rapid growth that began to take place in the late 1970's. With an average age per person of 50 years, ministry with older members has continued to be a priority. However, with younger families, many from non-Lutheran backgrounds, more diverse forms of ministry and outreach will become increasingly important.

The 225th Anniversary was observed with a year-long celebration in 1986-87. An anniversary banquet, an historical pageant, and a worship service were significant events in this celebration. An historical marker at the site of the old Mount Vernon church was erected, and an anniversary gift was given to the Evangelical Lutheran Church in America in thanksgiving for God's blessings. To share with future generations, a time capsule was buried and an investment fund was established. The capsule is to be opened, and the fund is to be used in fifty years.

The Rev. Guy C. Cruse has been Bethel's pastor since 1959. In 1981, Pastor Cruse's son, Guy Reginald Cruse, was ordained into the ministry.

BETHLEHEM, IRMO
Organized 1788
(HLCSC, pp. 568-570)

In September 1972, the Rev. Ronald L. Diegel joined the pastoral staff of Bethlehem in a team-ministry arrangement with the Rev. H. B. Watson, who had been the pastor of the congregation since 1967. When Pastor Watson retired in 1974, Pastor Diegel became the sole pastor of the congregation.

The years immediately following Pastor Diegel's arrival brought other changes as well. From 1970 to 1985, the congregation almost doubled in size as more and more people began to move into the Irmo area; the character of Bethlehem changed from a rural to a semi-rural to an almost suburban congregation in a short period of time. As a result, changes to the building quickly became necessary to accommodate the new growth. A new educational facility was under construction from 1975 to 1977. The sanctuary also underwent renovation during the same time.

As the need for increased building space became apparent, the ministry of the congregation also expanded. More people from varied backgrounds increased the possibilities for new forms of ministry to take root and grow. However, forms of ministry that had been a traditional part of Bethlehem continued, such as support of the nearby Lowman Home, Newberry College, and churchwide causes such as the World Hunger Appeal. The ministry programs of the auxiliaries, Lutheran Church Women, Youth, and Men, have also been strengthened and have benefited from the influx of new people.

Growth in the Irmo area should bring expansion to Bethlehem and further development to its ministry programs.

BETHLEHEM, LEESVILLE
Organized 1829
(HLCSC, pp. 570-571)

From 1947 until 1974 Bethlehem existed in a two congregation parish with Enon, having been served since 1957 by the Rev. Oliver M. Morgan. Pastor Morgan continued to serve Bethlehem, and when he resigned in 1975, the Rev. Jeffrey K. Lageman was called as pastor. He resigned in 1986.

Since 1974 Bethlehem has continued to grow in numbers and in ministry as slow but steady residential growth has brought new potential members into the area. The congregation has expanded its ministry by adding a senior citizens group, reviving a Lutheran Men's group, and strengthening the Lutheran Church Women's organization. Fellowship and study groups have developed in the congregation, along with the addition of several Sunday Church School classes.

Among the major property improvements was the completion of a new parsonage in March 1982.

One of the important aspects of Bethlehem's ministry has been its ability to attract persons of all ages, including a surprising number of young persons for a congregation in a rural area. Many long-standing families continue to provide a stable nucleus for the congregation, with many new families joining the congregation from various occupational and educational backgrounds. The Rev. Randall M. Conley became pastor in 1987.

BETHLEHEM, POMARIA
Organized 1816
(HLCSC, pp. 572-573)

After the retirement of Rev. Charles J. Shealy, Jr., who had served the congregation since 1969, the Rev. Steven D. Jackson was called to be its leader. Pastor Jackson began his ministry at Bethlehem in 1983 and continues as its pastor.

Composed largely of many generations of a few families of Lutheran heritage, the congregation numbers farmers, loggers, construction workers, teachers, and state employees among its membership. With more of its members having to work outside the community and on different shifts, the church has had to adapt its program to meet their changing needs. Since there is little growth in the immediate neighborhood of the church, it has begun to focus attention on the inactive members while continuing to serve the needs of the active ones.

The property has been improved in a variety of ways. In 1983, the congregation installed new carpet and refinished the pews in the nave. In 1984, a picnic shelter and tables were built on church grounds, a new roof was placed on the parish building, and a new piano was given for use in the nave. In 1985, a new heating and air conditioning unit was installed in the sanctuary.

Beyond the congregation's own needs, help was given the Department of Social Services in distributing food and supplies to the victims of the 1984 tornado.

CEDAR GROVE, LEESVILLE
Organized 1852
(HLCSC, pp. 576-578)

With a membership of over 800 baptized persons, Cedar Grove remains the largest congregation in the Western District. To accommodate the needs of its members, an educational building was completed in 1977. The Rev. Miles T. Cullum, who began his ministry at Cedar Grove in 1959, resigned in 1977, and was succeeded by the Rev. J. Hilton Roof, who continues to serve.

Additional land joining the church property has been purchased, and an Eldorado Bus for use by the congregation has also been purchased. Numerous building improvements to the sanctuary, educational building and parsonage have been made. A new Carillon System has also been installed.

CHRIST, COLUMBIA
Organized 1944
(HLCSC, pp. 573-575)

Christ Church has had three pastors since 1970. The Rev. Harold A. Wolff continued his service until 1978. In 1979, Pastor George Karres assumed leadership of the congregation and remained until 1983. The Rev. Timothy A. Haas has been pastor since 1984.

In 1973, groundbreaking ceremonies were held for a new sanctuary, which was dedicated on September 30, 1973.

During the last two decades the community around the church has become integrated, and many members have left the area. Most members are now residing at a distance from the church, with very few coming from its immediate vicinity. Many members are from non-Lutheran backgrounds, and most are blue-collar workers. The average age is rising, while the number of baptized members has declined.

The congregation has given support to the Sudan Interior Mission.

Christ Church faces an important challenge for the future: ministry in an interracial community.

CHRIST, HILTON HEAD
Organized 1973

Christ Lutheran Church was established at Hilton Head in response to the needs and opportunities presented by the substantial real estate and resort development in the area. Its first services were held on October 15, 1972, in the Sea Pines Montessori School, and were led by Mission Developer, the Rev. Boyd Cook. Twenty-six persons were in attendance.

The congregation was organized on October 28, 1973, with 96 charter members. Rev. Cook was its first pastor, serving until 1982. The Rev. Howard Sale became pastor in 1983 and continues to lead the congregation.

Christ Church has grown rapidly in the period since its founding, having 441 baptized members. A sanctuary and fellowship hall were constructed and occupied in 1976. Ad-

ditional growth and an emphasis on Christian education have led to plans for a substantial new addition to the church facilities and for an education and fellowship wing.

One member of the congregation, the Rev. David B. Hunter, has entered the ministry. He was ordained in 1984.

Christ Church continues in its efforts to serve a diverse, growing, and basically young congregation.

CHRIST THE KING, COLUMBIA
Organized 1963
(HLCSC, pp. 575-576)

Christ the King is located in East Columbia, a growing edge of the city, and the congregation's ministry has developed to meet the constantly developing situation.

The Rev. D. Luther Swicegood ended his ministry at the church in 1973, and was succeeded by the Rev. W. Richard Albert in 1974. He served as pastor until 1983. During his ministry the congregation undertook several important projects. Education facilities and a fellowship area were completed in 1979 at a cost of $95,000. The mortgage was burned in 1982.

Christ the King also began resettling Vietnamese families. The first family was sponsored in 1976, the second in 1978. This work has continued under the present pastor, the Rev. George L. Sims, who has served the church since 1984. A third family was resettled in 1986.

In 1983, the congregation opened the Respite Center, funded by the Triangle Fund, part of which provides community service ministry. The center gives the elderly and other adults with special needs a weekly opportunity to interact with other people while being involved in enriching growth experiences and fellowship. Two salaried persons and a corps of volunteers provide programs, meals, and transportation to the church facilities.

One daughter of the congregation, Cathy J. Quinton, was ordained in 1986.

CHRIST THE SERVANT, CONWAY
Organized 1986

The rapid growth of the Conway area, and the fact that the nearest Lutheran church is about 12 miles away, led the Lutheran Church in America and the South Carolina Synod to begin mission work there.

Pastor/Developer Marion C. Brazell began door-to-door visitation in October 1984, seeking to interest persons in the mission. An interest meeting was held in the Conway Motor Inn on March 3, 1985. Seventy people were present.

The first worship service was held on March 24, 1985 in a 2,500-square-foot rented room in a large store building on Highway 544 in Conway. Pastor Brazell presided at the service. The number of persons attending was 121.

The congregation was officially organized on February 16, 1986. Plans are being developed to build the first unit on property which has been purchased along highway 501.

The primary challenge to the church is to so witness in the community that it is able to grow as a congregation.

CHRISTUS VICTOR, COLUMBIA
Organized 1986

With the development of a new community northwest of Columbia called Harbison, the South Carolina Synod began working with an ecumenical group to plan for the religious needs and facilities of the community. After much preliminary work, a site for the location of several churches was chosen, and the ministry aspect began. The Rev. James B. Park was called in May 1979 as Pastor/Developer of

Lord of Life Lutheran Church. Services were held at the Masonic Lodge outside of Harbison in November 1979 and continued there for several months until the community center was completed in Harbison. However, after three years of work, it was determined that the work in Harbison was premature because of the slow development of the community due to the building depression and extremely high interest rates. Pastor Park resigned in 1982, and the mission development was closed for an interim period.

The field was re-entered in October 1984 with the Rev. George W. Eiwen as the Pastor/Developer, and the name of the mission was changed to Christus Victor. A parsonage had already been purchased, and the Board of American Missions of the LCA had purchased a tract of land in the Interdenominational Park. With recovery of the economy and renewed growth in the entire area, worship services began on May 12, 1985 in the recently completed Harbison West Elementary School where the congregation still worships. Over 60 people attended this first service, and the congregation grew so that on October 5, 1986, the Service of Organization was held, with 115 members on the Charter Roll. Pastor/Developer Eiwen became their first pastor.

The congregation, like the community, is comprised of young professional people with a good blend of local people and persons who have been transferred to the area. Soon after organization, the congregation was able to become self-supporting, and with continued growth in the area and the congregation, a building program is projected for 1989.

COLONY, NEWBERRY
Organized 1845
(HLCSC, pp. 578-580)

Following the retirement of the Rev. J. Virgil Long in 1977 the congregation called the Rev. Woodrow F. Frick to become its pastor. Pastor Frick served until 1981, when he responded to a call from another synod. That same year the Rev. Clarence H. Stucke became the pastor of Colony, and he continues to serve in that capacity.

As early as 1975 the congregation was an active member

of the Newberry Interfaith Community Services, and in 1984, Pastor Stucke played a vital role in ministering to the victims of the tornado that hit Newberry County. An LM was organized in 1984, and the LCW continues to be active. One of its members, Mrs. Bernice Shealy, served as synodical LCW president from 1981 to 1983.

The church was reroofed in 1978, and in 1984, the congregation received a gift of 1.4 acres of land adjoining the church property. Although there are a few new members from the community, most of the members are from families who have been connected with the church for several generations. The congregation has also recently purchased a 15 passenger van and built a picnic shelter.

CORINTH, PROSPERITY
Organized 1842
(HLCSC, pp. 580-582)

Having formed a two-point parish in 1936 with St. Mark, Corinth continues to be aligned with that congregation in a mutual ministry. There was some change, however, when in 1983, Corinth called the Rev. Frank Anderson to serve the congregation solely, while the Rev. Mary Anderson was called to serve St. Mark. The arrangement was primarily a financial one, in that neither congregation felt it could support a full-time ministry alone. With the use of a clergy couple, their expenses could be reduced considerably, and they could benefit from two full-time pastors. Previous to the Andersons' arrival, the Corinth-St. Mark Parish had been served by the Rev. Rudolf Ludwig (1969-1976), the Rev. Eddie Miller (1977-1979), and the Rev. Milas Sease (1981-1983).

The composition of the Corinth membership has remained almost unchanged since the 1970's. Many of the members are involved in farming, and have been little affected by the farm crisis which has plagued others in agriculture. A stable family network and low debt levels due to land owned for years by family farmers have contributed to this stability. One problem with this stability is the lack of available land for development and new homes. Corinth has not, as have other congregations, had any influx of new families into the community, in spite of its proximity to Lake Murray. The congregation is almost completely made up of families who have worshiped there for the past one hundred years.

With its own pastoral ministry, Corinth has been able to grow inwardly in its abilities and ministries. Lay leadership has been enhanced, committees organized and functioning, and active auxiliaries for men, women, and youth have all benefited from the additional time and energy offered by a full-time pastor in their midst. In 1987, Corinth was one of only a dozen congregations in the LCA to be asked to participate in a survey on "Ministry in Daily Life," and two lay persons and the pastor attended a conference in Chicago on the subject.

Pastor Anderson resigned in December 1987.

CROSS AND CROWN, FLORENCE
Organized 1981

Florence is a growing community and, because of this population growth, the need was felt for another Lutheran congregation. In August 1977, Pastor/Developer Gary Lyerly arrived on the field and began initial calling. The first worship service was held on December 4, 1977, at the

Windy Hill Fire Station, with 26 persons in attendance. Pastor Lyerly presided at the service and continued to serve until March 1980. The Rev. Joseph L. Griffin arrived in June of that year. The congregation was organized on April 26, 1981, with 87 charter members. Pastor Griffin became their first pastor, serving until 1982.

The next year and a half, the Rev. Luther Ballentine was the interim supply until the Rev. Joseph Holt came to lead the congregation in October 1984. He has continued to serve until the present.

In the years since its first service, Cross and Crown has worshiped at the Fire Station and the South Florence High School, and presently uses rented facilities in a shopping center. In 1984, three acres of land on West Palmetto Street were purchased as a building site, and in October 1987, ground was broken for its first unit.

Cross and Crown has had an active LCW since the congregation's organization. A Lutheran Men's group was organized in 1984.

The major challenges faced by the congregation are to reach out with the Gospel into the southwest area of Florence and to become strong enough to be financially self-supporting.

EBENEZER, COLUMBIA
Organized 1840
(HLCSC, pp. 584-586)

An issue of major importance to Ebenezer is growth and ministry in an urban setting. To fulfill this ministry, the congregation has developed programs and opened its facilities for use by people living in the community. It offers a community after school, a summer day camp, and recently began working with the Lowman Home to provide an adult day care facility. The congregation has also been supporting missionaries, and has paid for a cabin at Camp Kinard.

The Rev. Robert L. Hock served as pastor from 1964 to 1972, and the Rev. Robert F. Sims, who currently serves as pastor, began his ministry in 1973. During this time the congregation has also been served by several assistant pastors: the Rev. Richard R. Campbell (1971-1974), the Rev. Robert E. Van Deusen (1975-1977), the Rev. Darrell Golnitz (1977-1978), the Rev. Earl T. Knaus (1979-1982), the Rev. Derald H. Edwards (1983-1986), the Rev. Mark Bredholt (1986-   ), and the Rev. Robert Harris (1986-   ). Other persons have also contributed to the work of Ebenezer. Cindy C. Honeycutt was Director of Christian Education from 1981 to 1983; and June K. Metts served in that position in 1983 and 1984. The Rev. L. David Miller served as Precentor/Director of Music from 1978 to 1984, and Phyllis B. Sloan Bowden was Assistant Director of Music from 1967 to 1984. Marty Cloninger has been Organist/Director of Music since 1984.

Some landmark accomplishments in recent years include the celebration of the church's 150th Anniversary in 1980 and the retirement of the debt on the gym during that same year. In 1985, two lots next to the church were purchased, and a cross was placed on the steeple. Since 1980, numerous accommodations have been added for handicapped persons, and over $150,000 is contributed annually for benevolent purposes. A special service of this congregation has been the annual broadcast on television of its Christmas Eve Candlelight Service.

Major goals for Ebenezer include an even greater benevolence response, outreach projects, and expanded use of the media. Since the 20-40 age group makes up a significant portion of the congregation, special staff and ministry for that age group is another important goal.

EHRHARDT MEMORIAL, EHRHARDT
Organized 1904
(HLCSC, pp. 586-588)

Ehrhardt Memorial has had four pastors since 1970. The Rev. Edwin Andrews served until 1972; the Rev. James C. Dickert was pastor from 1972 to 1980; the Rev. Edwin H. Wicks ministered during the period 1981-1982; and the Rev. James N. Cobb was pastor in 1983 and 1984. Pastor Fred E. Dufford has been vice pastor and regular pulpit supply since 1984.

The congregation does what it can in a situation of declining membership. It loyally supports the programs and institutions of the synod, giving generously to the World Hunger Appeal and to Newberry College.

EMMANUEL, WEST COLUMBIA
Organized 1853
(HLCSC, pp. 582-583)

As the rural area of West Columbia changes rapidly to a suburban setting, so has the ministry of Emmanuel changed and grown through the years. Although a number of generations of several families continue to be active in this congregation, many new families have also found their

church home here. The Rev. Voigt K. Kleckley served as pastor from 1967 to 1974, having seen before he left the completion of the Christian Development Center in 1973. This large building houses a large fellowship hall/basketball court, classrooms and offices. Emmanuel also participated with two other congregations in building a cabin at the Kinard Conference Center in 1973.

Under the leadership of the Rev. James B. Park, from 1975 to 1979, the congregation grew and expanded its ministry programs. A van was purchased and the Lutheran Men of the church led in the funding and construction of a garage and storage shed. Eleven acres adjacent to the church's property were purchased in 1975. The congregation celebrated its 125th Anniversary in 1978 with several special services and the publication of a cookbook, sponsored by the LCW, that has been reprinted four times. A sterling silver communion set was added to the congregation's worship appointments for this anniversary.

The Rev. Kay Eugene Overcash began his ministry with the congregation in 1980, and has seen the changes in the community reflected in the congregation. With the average age of the congregation about 33, there are 50 households with at least one retired person. In 1985, a twelve-rank pipe organ was installed, and a two-bay van garage/storage shed was built. In 1986, a 107 space, curbed, guttered, and lighted parking area was completed at a cost of $38,500. In 1987, the congregation burned the mortgage on the Christian Development Center and began renovations to the parish building.

One son, the Rev. G. Stanley Steele, has come from this congregation during these years, and many of the lay people of the congregation serve in leadership roles in the district and the synod. Mr. James Hallman served two terms as president of the Synodical Lutheran Men. The congregation also participates in ecumenical community Thanksgiving and Easter Sunrise Services.

Challenges for the future include dealing with a congregation that is in the midst of changing from a rural setting to a suburban setting with goals of providing a new worship center and educational facilities.

ENON, LEESVILLE
Organized 1901
(HLCSC, pp. 588-589)

In 1974, the Bethlehem-Enon Parish was dissolved, and the Rev. Oliver M. Morgan, who had served the parish since 1957, became the pastor of Bethlehem. In 1976, the Rev. Voigt K. Kleckley began his ministry as pastor of this small rural congregation. Over the last 20 years, the membership has remained about the same, and the ministry activities center around the family atmosphere of the church. The major challenge for this congregation is to maintain its

viable presence in this quiet community. Several renovation and improvement projects have been completed for the parish building; carpeting was installed in the parish building and sanctuary in 1976; a new Hammond organ was purchased in 1980; and the steeple was added to the church sanctuary in 1983.

EPIPHANY, ST. MATTHEWS
Organized 1912
(HLCSC, pp. 589-591)

Epiphany continues to maintain itself as a small congregation with dedicated people. The Rev. G. B. Corley continued to serve the church as supply pastor until 1983. Since that time the pulpit has been supplied by students from the seminary in Columbia.

FAITH, BATESBURG
Organized 1926
(HLCSC, pp. 591-592)

In recent years, Faith has made several important improvements to its property. A ramp entrance for handicapped was constructed in 1978, and a steeple was added in 1982. An electronic computer organ was dedicated in November 1983, and the former organ given to a mission congregation in North Carolina. In 1984, a house and lot adjacent to the church property was purchased. The house was subsequently sold and moved off the lot.

Most of the people of Faith have roots that run deep in the Batesburg area. However, more recently persons not native to the area have made their way through the church doors, although the majority of the congregation comes

from Lutheran backgrounds. Within the congregation, there is a nice blend of different ages, and a wide number of educational and occupational fields are represented.

Recent pastors of the congregation include the Rev. Hubert A. Dunlap (1965-1977), the Rev. William C. Ebener (1978-1980), and the Rev. James W. Addy since 1981.

As Faith looks forward to the future, the congregation anticipates further membership growth and the maintenance of active programs in worship, education, and fellowship.

FAITH, JOHNS ISLAND
Organized 1952
(HLCSC, pp. 592-593)

Through many years of a diverse ministry, Faith has provided an important Christian witness for the people of Johns Island. In June 1973, the Rev. Marion C. Brazell accepted the call to lead this congregation. Soon after his arrival, the parsonage debt was retired. Later air conditioning was installed in the church, chimes were given, and the mortgage on the church was burned. In 1977, the congregation celebrated the 25th anniversary of its organization with a special service. That same year, the congregation became the beneficiary of the "Peterson Fund," an endowment provided through the estate of a member. Several youth groups, such as a boxing club and girl scouts, were organized.

After Pastor Brazell's resignation in 1977, the Rev. Kenneth O. Burke accepted the call to serve as pastor in July 1977. He served through 1981, continuing and expanding the ministry programs. The Rev. Paul B. Williams was called in July 1982 and served through August 1984.

Throughout this time, Faith examined different ways to reach out into the community of Johns Island and tried to build programs that would witness to the Christian faith. It also sought ways to express the Lutheran theology in a diverse community.

After a vacancy of almost eighteen months, the Rev. Frederick L. Glazier was called in December 1985. He resigned in 1986, and the congregation has been without a pastor since that time.

Faith has continued to participate in the activities of Rural Missions, Inc., providing a special ministry for migrant workers on Johns Island. Rural missions, Inc. has received several grants through the LCA for its work.

FAITH, NEWBERRY
Organized 1961
(HLCSC, pp. 593-595)

The Rev. William E. Stone served the congregation as its third pastor from 1969 until 1974. He was succeeded by the Rev. James K. Cobb, who served until his retirement in 1982. Following an eight month vacancy the congregation called the Rev. J. Gordon Peery to become its pastor, and he continues to serve.

In recent years, the nave was carpeted and the chancel chairs were re-upholstered. In 1983, stained glass windows, given as memorials, were installed and dedicated. The LCW, besides carrying on a regular educational program, has contributed such appointments to the church as draperies and silverware. The mortgage on the church building was burned in December of 1978.

The slowly growing membership has not been able to provide financial support for the type of community ministry which the congregation aspires to provide, but it is working hard to change this.

FAITH, WEST COLUMBIA
Organized 1941
(HLCSC, pp. 595-596)

One of the key factors which has played an important role in shaping the direction of Faith has been an emerging diversity in its membership. Faith has remained a congregation composed primarily of families of life-long Lutherans and workers employed in blue-collar occupations. But the congregation has also seen a growing number of families from non-Lutheran backgrounds, as well as singles and professional people, added to its membership roster.

The ministry of the congregation has become more diverse as well through Faith's participation in a number of community service projects, including Meals-on-Wheels and involvement in God's Helping Hands, an ecumenical social ministry agency serving West Columbia. Another important project was the sponsorship of a Vietnamese refugee family in the late 1970's. Faith has also had a particularly strong scouting program, and its other organizations, such as Lutheran Church Women and Lutheran Church Youth, have proved significant for the congregation and for the synod. In 1985, a Faith member, D'Etta Price, was elected president of the synod's Lutheran Church Youth organization. The Lutheran Church Men's organization was re-activated in 1982.

In 1981, the mortgage on the church property was paid in full. This enabled Faith to turn its attention to other building concerns, including the installation of a new organ in 1983 and the completion of stained glass windows in the nave in 1984.

In 1981, when Faith celebrated its 40th anniversary, the Rev. E. Bryan Keisler, D.D. was invited to preach the sermon. Pastor Keisler had also preached the first sermon in the newly organized congregation in 1941 and the sermon at the 25th anniversary service in 1966.

Since 1970, Faith has been served by the Rev. J. Marion Rhoden, Jr. (1965-1975), the Rev. Karl G. Bernsdorff (1975-1982), the Rev. Robert Swygert (1982-1984), and the Rev. Everett R. Price since March 1985.

The congregation is currently involved in planning for an addition to the present facilities that would include a multi-purpose building and a narthex for the sanctuary. Groundbreaking is planned for Easter 1988.

GETHSEMANE, COLUMBIA
Organized 1958
(HLCSC, pp. 601-602)

The 70's and 80's were years of change for Gethsemane. The community to which it ministers had stopped growing in the 60's and had begun a socio-economic decline in the 70's. Pastor H. Wyndham Burriss served the congregation until 1976.

At the end of 1976, the Rev. Dermon A. Sox, Jr. became pastor, and has led the church to the present time. In the mid-70's, racial change began to take place in the congregation's service area. In 1977, the first black couple joined the congregation, and the members of the congregation, under Pastor Sox's leadership, developed a spirit of openness and acceptance of all with whom they could share their faith. Within two years Lubin Pickwood was elected to the church council, and in 1981, he became the first black delegate to a convention of the South Carolina Synod. Two black persons seeking ordination in the LCA have become members of the congregation, receiving guidance and experience in leading liturgical worship and in Lutheran polity and practice. Church council membership has reflected the inclusive nature of the congregation. A Korean Seventh Day Adventist congregation has been allowed to use the congregation's facilities on Fridays and Saturdays since 1984.

Because of his advocacy for racial inclusiveness in the church, Pastor Sox was chosen to be the first chairman of the synod's Minority Ministry Task Force, and was also appointed to the LCA's Consulting Committee for Minority Group Interest.

A second major area of change for Gethsemane has been in financial stewardship. Prior to 1977, it failed regularly to meet its benevolence apportionment and was often unable to make its monthly mortgage payments. However, since that time it has always met its benevolence in full, and in a number of years have overpaid by as much as 10%. The mortgage on the church building was burned in 1980. Since 1977, at the end of each year, significant gifts are given to several local social service agencies from surplus funds, and only enough is carried over for itself to begin the new year.

The third area of change is the challenge. Since 1970, the membership of the congregation has declined by 53%, and prospects for growth are not encouraging. The congregation is small and the membership is aging to the extent that educational programs, youth activities, and auxiliaries are difficult to maintain.

One addition has been made to the sanctuary furnishings: in 1982, a baptismal font was designed, built, and hand carved by Pastor Sox.

GOOD HOPE, SALUDA
Organized 1839
(HLCSC, pp. 602-603)

The membership of this small Lutheran Church, near the community of Ward, has continued to decline over the past two decades. Although ably ministered unto by several supply pastors, the church has not been able to sustain its membership because of the declining population of this rural area. However, a ministry for the members and the community continues to be an effective goal for this small band of Lutherans. In 1983, a new heating and air conditioning unit was installed, and in 1985, a new Allen digital organ was purchased. Mr. A. B. Chapman has served as treasurer of this congregation for 50 years.

GOOD SHEPHERD, COLUMBIA
Organized 1950
(HLCSC, pp. 604-605)

The Rev. Larry S. Long became pastor of Good Shepherd in 1975 following the resignation of the Rev. Alton C. Clark who had served since 1958. During this period the congregation has strengthened its ability in ministry through the enlargement of its staff. In 1977, the Rev. Henry M. Moody was called as the first associate pastor and served until 1980. The Rev. George L. Sims served as associate pastor from 1981 to 1984; the Rev. K. Frederick Suhr, Jr. served from 1984 to 1986; and the Rev. Ronald W. Feltman became associate pastor in 1987. With the exception of one year, Dr. Edmund Shay has been organist and choirmaster since 1975, and Mrs. Nancy Hyatt has been administrative assistant since 1981.

Many of the church's former members have moved away since 1975 and, although the congregation is still basically composed of white-collar members, it is now younger than previously, and has far fewer members with traditional Lutheran backgrounds.

To keep pace with its growing and changing membership, Good Shepherd has made many improvements and additions to its physical facilities. In 1976, the balcony was extended, and the parking lot was paved. An addition to the church office complex was completed in 1977. A fellowship activities building was constructed in 1980 and 1981, and a church van was purchased in 1985. During this period, the amount pledged by members has more than quadrupled. A conference room/library was added in 1987.

The congregation has been involved in many ecumenical and community activities including an ecumenical Thanksgiving service, a community blood drive, and an uptown soup kitchen. It has provided resources for Palmetto Place, the Council on Child Abuse and Neglect, and the Oliver Gospel Mission. Space has been provided for a Junior League nursery, neighboring condo associations, and Alcoholics Anonymous. Good Shepherd has also been active in the wider ministry of the church, supporting a missionary since 1978, and supplying district presidents for each auxiliary, a Synodical LCW Treasurer, and a Synod Youth Ministry Committee Chairperson.

The church has become increasingly aware of its responsibilities to the diverse needs of its people. It has developed a program for senior citizens, and is providing a ministry to singles. The adult Sunday Church School program has doubled; ministry to the community has been enlarged, including participation in the Food Pantry and Clothes Closet; and the youth have begun a clown ministry, with visits to churches, hospitals, and homes. The Shepherd's Visitors group makes caring visits to individuals; a community German Easter Service is held; athletic teams and fellowship groups have been established.

Two members of the congregation have entered the ministry: the Rev. Marion Clark in 1966 and the Rev. Roy Riley, Jr. in 1974. Mrs. Anne Riley Merritt became a Certified Lay Professional in 1976.

As it looks to the future, Good Shepherd plans to increase its efforts in ministering to mobile people, many of whom are without family connections in this area.

GOOD SHEPHERD, SWANSEA
Organized 1912
(HLCSC, pp. 605-606)

When Good Shepherd called the Rev. Tony A. Metze on July 1, 1985, it was anticipating having its first full-time pastor since the congregation was organized in 1912. The call of a full-time pastor was made possible by an almost doubling in baptized membership to 91 persons between 1970 and 1985. Such growth, in turn, was made possible by the growth in the Swansea area as new industry began moving into the community. Previously, the Rev. E. K. Counts had served Good Shepherd on an interim basis at the beginning of the 1970's. Good Shepherd shared a pastor with Sandy Run from 1973 to 1979. The Rev. D. Rodney Gunter served both congregations from 1973 to 1977, followed by the Rev. James C. Butt from 1978 to 1979. Between 1979 and 1985, Sandy Run was served by seminary students under the direction of the Rev. Dr. Robert C. Schultz, Director of Internship at Southern Seminary.

Even without a full-time pastor Good Shepherd was able to move forward. For example, an educational building, begun in 1974, was dedicated in 1975. During 1977, a passageway between the church and the educational building was constructed, a two-manual organ was purchased, and a baptismal font was obtained. A public address system was installed in 1978, and the sanctuary and educational building underwent extensive renovation in 1981.

Having a full-time pastor has allowed Good Shepherd to strengthen its existing ministries and to become actively involved in community service. In October 1987, Good Shepherd dedicated its two manual, six rank pipe organ which was donated by the First Baptist Church of Batesburg and was installed by members of Good Shepherd. A new Good Shepherd stained glass window was also dedicated.

The Lutheran Men of Good Shepherd began a cemetery project in 1984. Land was purchased, cleared, and surveyed. Plots are now being sold to interested members.

GOOD SHEPHERD, WALTERBORO
Organized 1940
(HLCSC, pp. 606-608)

When Pastor Virgil Cameron ended his ministry at Walterboro in 1974, the congregation called the Rev. Arthur Greenwalt to be its pastor. He served from 1974 to 1978. During this period the church was able to complete payment on its parsonage, burning the mortgage in 1976.

In 1978, the Rev. Don Nolt became pastor and served until 1981. With his leadership Good Shepherd began its support of two Vietnamese families. One family of eight received church support beginning in 1979, and a second family was added in 1981.

The Rev. B. Gene Baker has been pastor from 1981 to the present. New industry is now bringing new people into the community, and the church is attempting to minister to them.

Plans for the future include the construction of a new church building.

GRACE, GILBERT
Organized 1893
(HLCSC, pp. 596-597)

Growth at Grace Church has been steady both in membership and in program development. Located in the heart of downtown Gilbert, the congregation continues to serve the community through its programs and members. Since 1970, the outside appearance of the church building has not changed; however, several interior changes have been made. A carillon/chime system has been installed, storm windows have been hung, the pastor's study and the parsonage have been renovated, a piano and handbells have been purchased, and the roofs on both the church and the parsonage have been replaced. Additional land has been acquired so that the cemetery could be enlarged, and an endowment fund for the cemetery upkeep has been established.

Ministry programs have continued to grow as the membership has increased by fifty percent since 1970. Most notable among these has been the liturgical development of the congregation's worship. Lectors, cantors, worship and communion assistants, and a crucifer have all become a part of the congregation's worship. The service is often intoned, and a funeral pall was added for use recently.

A "penny fund" was begun in 1980 to provide Lutheridge Music Week scholarships and has been augmented by the establishment of a memorial endowment to provide scholarships for young people to attend Lutheridge each year. A program is now under way to provide financial assistance for young people to attend retreats and training opportunities at Camp Kinard.

The Rev. Andrew Eargle resigned as pastor in 1978, and the Rev. William Stone began his work in 1979, continuing to the present.

GRACE, PROSPERITY
Organized 1859
(HLCSC, pp. 598-599)

The Rev. G. Alvin Fulmer continued to serve as pastor of
the congregation until 1979. One of the major events during
his ministry was the construction of a new nave of contemporary design. Begun in 1973, it was completed in 1974 and
dedicated in March of that year.

In 1975, Grace began a ministry of special education in
the Sunday Church School and has continued it in the Vacation Church School. It conducted a pilot project in 1975 of
Parish Life and Ministry Development for the South Carolina Synod, and has provided leaders for the synod and the
synodical LCW.

The Rev. George T. Moore accepted the call to become the
pastor in 1980 and served until the end of 1985. Since 1980,
the congregation has contributed more than $15,000 to the
World Hunger Appeal. Each fall an Advent devotional
booklet, written by the members, is prepared and distributed. The congregation participates in the Newberry
County Interfaith Community Services and entertains
Lowman Home guests at a special dinner each year. A unit
of the LM was reorganized in 1981.

The Rev. Gary Loadholdt began his ministry in May 1987.

GRACE, ROCK HILL
Organized 1923
(HLCSC, pp. 600-601)

The congregation installed a Zimmer pipe organ the same year in which Pastor John E. Boyd, Jr. resigned, 1975. He had served since 1970 and was succeeded by the Rev. Hollis A. Miller, who was installed in 1976. The following year the congregation purchased a house and lot adjacent to the church building, and in 1979, dedicated its new office and educational building. The previous year it had raised $325,000 with church bonds to finance these projects.

A Lutheran-Catholic dialogue was inaugurated in 1979 and continues to function. Joint Lenten services with the Catholic and Episcopal churches were held from 1981 through 1984. Grace participates annually in an ecumenical Thanksgiving service. In 1980, it sponsored and helped relocate a Vietnamese family.

After Pastor Miller left in 1981, the Rev. Rufus E. Lybrand, Jr. accepted the congregation's call and began his ministry in 1982. Grace has begun participating in the Seminary's Intern program. The church extended its ministry to the less fortunate by contributing to the aid of tornado victims and participating in the Meals-on-Wheels program. Its members have also ministered to prisoners at a pre-release center, raised money for World Hunger, distributed Easter baskets to senior citizens, and provided Christmas gifts for the home-bound. The LCY annually collects and distributes canned goods for HOPE, a community project to help the needy.

Although the membership averages 35 years of age and sponsors a Saturday program for children, the congregation also sponsors a senior citizens group and owns a van for their and others' use. With many college graduates and professional persons on its roll the church continues to grow both in size and in spirituality. The two Sunday services are part of the congregation's attempt to meet the needs of all its members and to welcome new persons into its fellowship. A Folk Worship is used at the early service to offer a variety of worship styles.

HOLY COMFORTER, CHARLESTON
Organized 1959
(HLCSC, pp. 609-610)

On January 27, 1974, Holy Comforter celebrated its fifteenth anniversary. Presiding at the ceremonies was the Rev. H. Wyman Dowd, who had been installed as pastor of the congregation in 1971. Bishop Herman W. Cauble, the Rev. Paulwyn Boliek, and the Rev. Dr. Karl W. Kinard also participated in the celebration. Charter members were honored; and a plaque was hung in the narthex, honoring Kenneth E. Powers, Sr., who had first urged the founding of a Lutheran mission congregation in the area.

Pews with kneelers were installed in early 1976. Later that year organ repairs and the installation of a carillonette were made possible through a bequest from the estate of Cranworth D. Coleman.

In 1978, the congregation embarked on an "Every Member Response Growth Program," which proved to be an excellent incentive to renewed giving. Holy Comforter also began using the *Lutheran Book of Worship* in 1978.

Memorial funds for Mrs. Leila P. Lindenberg and the Coleman fund made it possible to develop a conference room and library in 1980. The Word and Witness program was initiated during that same year. In 1984, an Allen organ was installed.

Since 1984, the church has participated in the Lutheran Social Services of Charleston, and since 1985, it has hosted and provided volunteers for Home Delivered Meals, an interfaith project in which meals are delivered to the homes of aged people.

Holy Comforter looks forward to serving the Lord in the West Ashley area for many years to come.

HOLY COMMUNION, SPARTANBURG
Organized 1960
(HLCSC, pp. 608-609)

The Rev. D. Murray Shull, Jr. became the third pastor of the congregation in 1971 and continues to serve in that capacity. This rapidly growing church is located on the west side section of the city, near the intersection of I-26 and I-85, and attracts many new members from industries moving management personnel into the area. An educational and administration building was added in 1974, an Allen organ was installed in 1983, and new pews with kneelers were added the following year.

Holy Communion helped organize the Greater Spartanburg Ministries in 1974, and Pastor Shull became its second president. It welcomed a Roman Catholic mission to use its sanctuary in 1981-82. It continues to pay partial support for the Rev. William Peery, missionary to India, and provides an annual stipend to Mobile Meals.

A Director of Music, Ms. Frankie W. Deal, B.Mus., was added to the staff in 1987. A significant feature of its 25th anniversary celebration was the making of a $2,500 gift to the mission, Augsburg Lutheran Church in Union, S. C. Since 1980, the Family Enrichment Committee has sponsored retreats and seminars on marriage enrichment, single and step family parenting, positive parenting, and sexual wholeness in children, youth, and married couples. Holy Communion has built a new sanctuary, renovating and enlarging the educational, music and office facilities at a cost of $600,000, to be dedicated in early 1988.

HOLY CROSS, CHARLESTON HEIGHTS
Organized 1960
(HLCSC, pp. 610-612)

Pastor Edwin McKinley served at Holy Cross until 1975. During the later years of his ministry, in 1974-75, the congregation became self-supporting. This financial burden was difficult for the church, and it was a time of testing for the people.

In 1975, the Rev. Carl O. Isaacson was installed as pastor, and he served until 1979. During this period money was raised by selling portions of the church's property. In September 1978, Holy Cross received the gift of pews (old trolley car seats) from Faith, Johns Island.

In 1979, the Rev. G. Alvin Fulmer became the fifth pastor of Holy Cross and has served to the present. Under his leadership renovation and major improvements were made to the nave. The rededication of the building was held on February 27, 1983. Bishop Herman W. Cauble presided at the Service. Important improvements at the parsonage were completed during 1984.

The women of the church have contributed robes for the adult and youth choirs.

The congregation has instituted an annual Lowman Home Sunday. Home residents are invited to attend services and a fellowship dinner.

In 1984, Holy Cross participated in the formation of the Lutheran Social Services Agency of Charleston. In 1985, it celebrated its 25th Anniversary with a series of services that included former pastors.

HOLY TRINITY, ANDERSON
Organized 1936
(HLCSC, pp. 612-613)

Despite several difficulties this half-century-old congregation continues to provide a valuable ministry under the leadership of the Rev. Paul O. Slice. Although a significant number of its members left Holy Trinity to affiliate with the newly-formed congregation of the Lutheran Church-Missouri Synod or with another fundamentalist group, the total membership remains virtually what it was in 1970.

The proportion of older members has risen as that of youth, ages 12-18, has decreased. The membership—made up of long-time Lutherans, transfers from other denominations, and persons of no previous church connection—includes an unusually high percentage of college graduates. The LCW and LM continue to provide important support for the congregation's programs. A very active senior citizens group has been formed and welcomes non-Lutherans into its activities.

Lots adjacent to the original church property were purchased in 1974 and 1976. In 1982, at a cost of $80,000, the sanctuary and one of the educational facilities were refurbished, and the old parsonage was renovated for use as offices, lounge, and conference room. Holy Trinity cooperates with four neighboring churches in an annual community Thanksgiving Service. The congregation is in the midst of a long-range planning study, which it hopes will result in the formation of future goals and a more effective outreach to the community.

Laura Jo Terry, a certified lay professional, serves as part-time organist and music director. One of the congregation's former members, Cindy Honeycutt, attained certified status as a lay professional.

HOLY TRINITY, LITTLE MOUNTAIN
Organized 1891
(HLCSC, pp. 613-615)

Holy Trinity has been served by three pastors since 1970. The Rev. Charles Dawkins came in 1970 and remained until February 1977. He was followed by the Rev. Leon Rawl, who served from 1977 to 1983. The Rev. John E. Pless has been Holy Trinity's pastor since November 1, 1984. Other staff persons have also contributed significantly to Holy Trinity. Betsy Guice has served as parish secretary since 1963. Ted Arnold served as sexton for approximately fifteen years. Louise Derrick was choir director from 1975 to 1985, followed by Benji Ricard.

Over the years Holy Trinity has adapted its ministry to meet the needs of a changing community. Youth programs have been expanded, including a newly opened pre-school program. A single-parents-ministry program has been established to assist parents and families affected by divorce and separation. In 1975, the congregation sponsored 2 Vietnamese refugee families. Organizations within the church have remained active in supporting community and synodwide causes. A tape ministry for shut-ins has also been organized, along with the formation of a new senior citizens group.

The church building has also undergone change to keep up with the times. The parking lot was paved in 1971. A new organ was also obtained that same year. Additional Sunday school rooms were installed in 1974. Three years later an elevator was added. Both the exterior and the interior of the building underwent a major renovation in 1982-83.

In 1984, renovations were completed for the balcony, new pews were installed, and a new front entrance to the church was completed. In 1985, a new 30-passenger church bus was purchased; a bus garage was built in 1986; and in 1987, renovations to the parish building (painting, new carpet, kitchen remodeling) were made. A Meals-on-Wheels program for the community was begun in 1987.

A son of the congregation, John M. Stoudemayer, was ordained into the ministry in 1987.

HOLY TRINITY, NORTH AUGUSTA
Organized 1952
(HLCSC, pp. 615-616)

Having been organized in 1952, Holy Trinity is the youngest congregation in the Western District. Its relative youth is also reflected by an average age of 34 among its baptized membership. Not only is Holy Trinity the newest congregation in the district, it also seems to show a greater diversity among its membership. Approximately three out of every four new persons who join come from non-Lutheran backgrounds.

Among the recent ministry programs undertaken by the congregation has been a 4-year old kindergarten begun in 1973. This was in addition to a 3 and 5-year old program begun a decade earlier. In 1980, Holy Trinity began participating in a Meals-on-Wheels program, and in 1983, joined a downtown soup kitchen project. In 1985, a com-

bined effort with five other churches of other denominations resulted in the organization of the North Augusta
Thrift Shop for the sale of used clothing and household
items at a minimal price to the needy of the community. All
of these are programs which operate alongside Holy Trinity's active auxiliaries, Lutheran Church Women, Lutheran
Men, and Lutheran Church Youth. Holy Trinity has also
sponsored two refugee families for resettlement in North
Augusta.

To support an active program of ministry, Stephanie
Meynardie was hired as Holy Trinity's first Director of
Christian Education from 1984 to 1985. Pastoral leadership
has been provided by the Rev. Larry S. Long (1970-1975),
the Rev. John E. Boyd, Jr. (1976-1985), and the Rev. Stephen
T. Gragg (1986-present).

Recent improvements to the property have included the
construction of an educational building and office complex,
completed in 1973, the addition of a parking lot in 1974, and
the renovation of the sanctuary in 1981.

HOLY TRINITY, PELION
Organized 1913
(HLCSC, pp. 616-618)

The splitting of a tri-church parish in 1964 brought many
changes and a dependency on Southern Seminary to provide
worship leadership for Holy Trinity. For several years,
many familiar faces have returned to the church for Sunday

services, and several served during the summer months. Near-by pastors augmented the work of these seminarians through the years. In 1973, the Rev. J. Harry Crout began a twelve year tenure as a "permanent supply." In 1985, the Rev. Otto J. Reenstjerna became vice pastor and, with the assistance of seminary students, continued to provide pastoral leadership for the congregation. Since 1986, the participation of the youth has added much new life to the congregation. Although it has been without the services of a full-time pastor for 23 years, this congregation has continued to provide the ministry needed for its members and the community.

The congregation also participates in several activities throughout each year. Participation in the community Thanksgiving Service with three other churches, a live outdoor nativity scene for the community presented by the youth, an Easter Sunrise Service followed by breakfast, and a summer service with dinner on Lake Murray, have all become annual parts of the congregation's program.

The parsonage was renovated and converted into a parish house, which also provides a place for outreach ministry for the community. Part of the building is rented to the Lexington County Circulating Library and serves as the permanent home for the Library in Pelion. The building also serves as a meeting place for service clubs and town government groups.

Although small in numbers with a baptized membership of 82 and a confirmed membership of 62, Holy Trinity, Pelion, is big at heart. A letter from the Division for Parish Services, LCA, points this out when it says: "Your congregation is among the relatively few LCA congregations whose per capita benevolent giving was $51 or more for 1985. The median for the LCA was $35. Only one out of five congregations reached or exceeded the $51 figure. Your congregation is one of the 35 high per capita benevolence congregations selected to participate in the research study for benevolence support."

IMMANUEL, GREENWOOD
Organized 1902
(HLCSC, pp. 618-620)

Major improvements to the church building marked the latter years of the pastorate of the Rev. Frank L. Roof. During 1974-75, a parlor was added, the kitchen was renovated, and the nave and classrooms were recarpeted. The entire interior was repainted, the bathrooms were done over, and new lighting fixtures were installed. At this time chancel furnishings which had been part of the original building were presented to a mission congregation, Shepherd of the Sea, Surfside Beach, S. C.

A new pipe organ was installed in 1974, the dedication of which featured a recital by Mr. Karl Kinard, Jr., grandson of Immanuel's first resident pastor. In 1975, the congregation had a part in sponsoring a Vietnamese family in Greenwood. After Pastor Roof retired at the end of 1975, he was honored by being named Pastor Emeritus.

The following year the Rev. William B. Trexler became pastor and served until 1979. During his ministry the Sunday School was reorganized, teacher-training sessions were begun, and five lay assistants were trained to participate in leading the worship services. The use of banners and processional torches was introduced, and a Christmas Eve candlelight communion was initiated. Mrs. Helen Rudy became the first Director of Parish Music (1976-77), a position filled by Mrs. Judy Tolbert from 1977 until 1985, and now occupied by Ms. Rosie Gable.

In 1977, Immanuel celebrated its 75th anniversary of organization, at the same time renewing its commitment to community service, to support of churchwide causes, and to renewal in worship.

The Rev. R. Earl McCombs accepted the call to become Immanuel's pastor in 1980 and continues to provide leadership. The church underwent a major renovation in 1982, including the installation of an elevator. A new position, Coordinator of Educational Ministry, was added in 1986, and is occupied by Mrs. Susan Lorick.

INCARNATION, COLUMBIA
Organized 1921
(HLCSC, pp. 621-623)

The Lutheran Church of the Incarnation is a congregation consisting largely of traditional Lutheran families, including all age groups, with a high percentage of white collar workers and college graduates. The congregation has increased its outreach in recent years through several community projects, including participation in the Shandon Interfaith Council, Community Care, Inc., and Lutheran Social Services of Central South Carolina. It began missionary support in 1970 and established a Child Care Ministry in 1980. Incarnation has funded a cottage unit at Camp Kinard and supplied initial funding for a Director of Volunteer Services at Baptist Medical Center's Hospice. It has also been involved with the Washington Street soup kitchen, and Meals-on-Wheels. In 1984-85, the Sims Avenue building was renovated into a complete administrative and activity center.

Since 1970, a number of clergy have ministered to the congregation. The Rev. Dr. George E. Meetze served as pastor until 1972, and he was assisted by the Rev. William R. Cobb (1968-1972), and the Rev. John Harold Wolff who served until 1974. The Rev. Paul L. Morgan served as pastor from 1974 to 1977. The Rev. Bill B. Mims, Jr. was assistant pastor during that time, along with the Rev. E. Carl Zimmerman. Pastor Mims and Pastor Zimmerman served as co-pastors from 1977 to 1979. The Rev. David A. Donges served as pastor from 1980 to December 1987 when he resigned to join the Synod staff of the ELCA; and the Rev. George L. Onstad served as associate pastor from 1983 to 1987. During the past 17 years, Incarnation has also made use of a number of staff persons, including an organist, Director of Music, Visitation Director, Educational Assistant, Director of Christian Education, Hostess, and Director of Child Care. Two members of the congregation, the Rev. Eugene H. Kern, and the Rev. Ronald W. Feltman were ordained during this period.

The goals of the congregation include a growth in membership, an increase in worship attendance, and becoming more oriented toward service and outreach.

KING OF GLORY, NORTH MYRTLE BEACH
Organized 1976

By the mid-1970's, the upper South Carolina coast had experienced sufficient growth to begin an LCA mission congregation in North Myrtle Beach.

Under the guidance of the Rev. Richard E. Webber as Mission Developer, the fledgling congregation held its first worship service on February 1, 1976, for 120 people. Its meeting place was a brick storefront on Highway 17 South in the Crescent Beach section.

On November 21, 1976, King of Glory organized with 119 charter members, becoming the 155th official congregation of the S. C. Synod. Pastor Webber served as the church's first pastor until 1981, followed by the Rev. Palmer D. Clemmer, who continued pastoral leadership until July 1987.

With the rapid growth of the congregation came new landmarks. After King of Glory became self-supporting in 1979, it built its first unit, including a sanctuary to seat 180, in Tilghman Estates. The church family began services in its new home on February 17, 1980, and added a new Baldwin organ in 1981.

By the early 1980's, the north Strand area (including N. C.'s South Brunswick area) had become one of the fastest growing areas in the country, and King of Glory grew even faster, more than tripling its membership to 396 by the end of 1986. Its membership remains diverse—a healthy blend of ages, regional origins, and denominational or nonchurch backgrounds. A congregational son, the Rev. Jeffrey Wallace, entered the ministry in 1984.

By its tenth anniversary in 1986, the congregation had added a 2,550-square-foot multi-purpose building and remodeled its former fellowship space. Three outdoor showers assist the church in hosting beach-going youth groups each summer from Pennsylvania to Indiana to the Carolinas.

King of Glory and its members continue to be active community participants. Congregational activities have included sponsoring quarterly blood drives since 1978, which have collected more than 2,000 pints for the American Red Cross, helping initiate a Mobile Meals program that since 1984 has become a community-wide effort, giving Christmas health/gift bags to more than 90 needy primary school children each year, and donating handmade quilts to every boy at the Tara Hall Boys' Home in Georgetown.

As the coastal area continues to grow, so will the church family of King of Glory, empowered by the Holy Spirit and committed to both community and worldwide ministry.

MACEDONIA, PROSPERITY
Organized 1847
(HLCSC, pp. 623-624)

Macedonia has seen a steadily increasing amount of activity in and around the congregation in the past 15 years. Much of this increase is due to its location on the shores of Lake Murray. In 1970, Macedonia began having a Sunday morning interfaith worship during the summer to reach the abundant population. This Lakeside Service which has grown very popular is now held at 8:30 a.m. Worshippers come by car or boat, the setting is casual, and the service generally lasts an hour or less. Holy Communion and baptism are sometimes administered at these services.

The ministry of Macedonia has also grown inside the walls of the congregation as well. To accommodate its

growth in activity, construction began on a new Sunday School building in 1972 and was completed in 1973, greatly adding to Macedonia's ability to teach the gospel and to provide ministry and fellowship to the congregation and community. Much of the ministry is provided through the Lutheran Church Women, the Lutheran Men, reorganized in 1984, and the Lutheran Church Youth, which twice in recent years has hosted the Dutch Fork District rally. A Parish Life and Ministry Development study conducted in the early 1970's helped determine the direction of Macedonia's ministry throughout the following years.

In 1978 and 1979, the property lines and boundaries, which had been in dispute for many years, were all clearly surveyed, defined, and recorded. A closer relationship with South Carolina Electric and Gas Co., which owns the lakefront property it has authorized Macedonia to control, was established. Several later improvements include vinyl siding and insulation added to the Sanctuary; a new porch and handicapped ramp; a new roof on the parish building; and a new chain link fence which has greatly improved supervision of the lakefront park and picnic area. In 1986, the mortgage on the educational building was burned. In 1987, a summer internship program was begun with the cooperation of Southern Seminary to provide a ministry primarily for Billy Dreher Island State Park.

The Rev. Clarence Richardson, pastor of Macedonia since 1969, resigned in November 1977. He was followed by the Rev. Randall S. Derrick, who has served since June 1978.

MARTIN LUTHER, CHARLESTON
Organized 1961
(HLCSC, pp. 624-625)

The Rev. Paulwyn L. Boliek served the Martin Luther congregation until 1971. He was followed by the Rev. M. Thomas Sublett, who remained at the church until 1974. In 1975, the Rev. Charles E. Bernhardt was called as pastor and led the congregation until 1984. During his pastorate, pews were installed and dedicated in 1976, and a Vietnamese family was sponsored the same year.

With the departure of the Rev. Bernhardt, Martin Luther went for approximately one and a half years without pastoral leadership until the Rev. James Leon Lingle, Jr. was called as pastor in 1985.

In 1986, Martin Luther paid in full the debt incurred when building the first unit and educational wing. Major renovation that included replacing the roof of the educational building and putting a copper roof on the sanctuary were also completed at a cost of $65,000.

The area around the church is mostly residential, but more businesses are moving in. Members of the congregation are primarily well-educated-white collar workers with traditional Lutheran backgrounds.

Martin Luther has active auxiliaries which contribute to the congregation and to the wider church. It is involved with the Lutheran Social Services Center of Greater Charleston.

One son of the congregation, Steven Douglas Jackson, was ordained during this period.

Martin Luther is a growing church, but faces continual competition from the many beaches and other resort activities in the area.

MAYER MEMORIAL, NEWBERRY
Organized 1899
(HLCSC, pp. 626-627)

The Rev. John H. Koch continued his service as pastor until his retirement in 1974. He was succeeded later that year by the Rev. Floyd E. Sides, who continues as the pas-

tor. The congregation claims as a son in the ministry, the Rev. Eddie C. Miller, Jr., and has provided missionary support to Donald Poole, Louis Bowers, Gary Miller, and Pastor and Mrs. James Brady.

A major event in the recent life of the congregation was the tornado of March 28, 1984. Not only were the homes of fifty of its member families damaged but the church building suffered significant damage. The bell tower was broken off, several windows were broken, and the bell and chimes system were destroyed.

By the end of 1985, a new bell tower had been constructed, faceted glass windows had been installed, and a Schulmerich carillon had been provided. The membership of the congregation, located in an area which has ceased to grow, remains stable.

MESSIAH, HANAHAN
Organized 1955
(HLCSC, pp. 628-629)

Messiah serves a stable resident community and a large number of military personnel. Its members represent a cross-section of the community and have diverse backgrounds.

The Rev. Guy H. Shealy continued to serve the congregation until 1973.

The Rev. F. Adolf Kleindt was pastor from 1974 to 1980. Under his leadership important additions and improvements were made to the church's physical facilities. In 1975, the chancel was redesigned and renovated, and pews were installed in the nave. In 1978 and 1979, a parish hall, rest rooms and a classroom were constructed by the men of the congregation.

The Rev. L. E. Cumbee, Jr. has led Messiah since 1981. During this period the congregation has experienced continued growth, and has been involved in many activities. A steeple was erected in 1981. The church was involved in the formation of Lutheran Social Services of Greater Charleston in 1984, and continues to support it. In 1984, Messiah became one of the "owner" churches of the Franke Home, and has members on the Board. In 1986, the congregation began the installation of stained-glass windows, which were dedicated in November 1987.

The auxiliaries of the church are all active. The LCW supports congregational needs and outreach to the community.

The continuing growth of Messiah presents its people with the need for an ongoing development of its physical plant as they face the future.

MESSIAH, MAULDIN
Organized 1967
(HLCSC, pp. 627-628)

The baptized membership of the congregation in 1970 was 309. Fifteen years later it had reached 426, but this does not tell the story of the many members transferring in and out of the fellowship of this young congregation. The Rev. Rodney W. Parrott, who began his ministry in 1971, resigned in 1982. Just prior to his leaving, a church and community study had led the congregation to start planning for new facilities to serve the rapidly growing Mauldin/Simpsonville area. When the Rev. John L. Yost III arrived in 1983, the group was ready to move forward with the plans.

A new Allen organ was purchased in 1984 and a year later construction was begun on a new sanctuary and administration wing. This new structure was completed and dedicated in 1986. The church's growth is evidenced by the addition of a paid organist and choir director to the staff, as well as by the fact that, in the past two years, worship attendance has increased by 50% and offerings by 90%.

The congregation, which includes very few natives of the area among its members, has many young couples and children, as well as a vital group of retired persons, which calls itself J.O.Y. Many of the members are engaged in engineering, data processing, and manufacturing. The LCY has hosted several district rallies and has provided a district president. The LCW is also active in the congregation and the district. Messiah has set itself the goal of a continuing outreach to the community.

MINISTRY WITH THE DEAF, COLUMBIA
Organized 1985

In the 1970's, the S. C. Synod and the DMNA began exploring the possibility of a deaf ministry. Columbia was chosen as the site for this ministry because of its large number of Lutheran churches, many of which include deaf members, the number of institutions in the area which deal with deaf persons, the location of the Seminary, and the growing population of the region.

The Rev. Dr. Larry W. Bost and his family arrived in Columbia in September 1979, and began contacting deaf persons and building support in the area for a deaf ministry. St. Paul made facilities available for the new work. The first service was conducted in the chapel of St. Paul in March of 1980. Seventy-five persons attended this worship service, which was led by Pastor Bost.

The congregation was organized on April 28, 1985, with 41 charter members. Bishop Cauble presided at the service. The Rev. Dr. Bost was the first pastor of the church and remains in that position.

This congregation has a unique role! Many deaf persons drop out of Lutheran churches and many others are simply unchurched. To provide worship opportunities for the deaf, signing is used throughout the services, as well as the traditional verbal liturgy for the hearing members. The ministry of the congregation also extends to the deaf throughout the Midlands in private homes, institutions, prisons and hospitals. A sign language counseling ministry is provided. The unique nature of the congregation's ministry is reflected in the fact that the majority of persons it serves are not members.

A large part of this church's efforts are devoted to deaf awareness and helping hearing persons understand the needs, challenges, and culture of people who are deaf. Sign language classes are held for medical and other professionals who work with the deaf. Programs on deafness are presented to congregations and other groups. In cooperation with DMNA and DPS, resources are developed for use with hearing-impaired persons.

The name of the congregation was carefully chosen to reflect its special mission. The word "Deaf" was included to give identity to the focal group. The most important word in the name is "With." It was chosen to indicate a team ministry of hearing and deaf people working together in Christ's church. The deaf are equal *with* all persons before the cross.

MT. CALVARY, JOHNSTON
Organized 1830
(HLCSC, pp. 629-631)

In 1980, Mt. Calvary marked a year long celebration of its 150th anniversary, beginning with a birthday party on February 21. The celebration ended in December with the removal and resetting of the cornerstone from the present church building and the burial of a time capsule containing materials relating to Mt. Calvary's history. On December 21, a final anniversary service was held, with the sermon preached by the Rev. Dr. Karl W. Kinard. Dr. Kinard's father, the Rev. J. D. Kinard, had preached at the first service of the then new sanctuary in October 1927.

But more has happened at Mt. Calvary than celebrating its past. Several major improvements have been made to the church property, including a renovation of the parsonage in 1983. The congregation has also been active in its wider ministry to the community and synod. A radio ministry was begun in September 1984. Also, several members of the Lutheran Church Women and the Lutheran Church Youth have held offices on the district level.

While the membership of the congregation has remained steady since 1970, the needs of the members have shifted to reflect the needs of the different age groups within the congregation. Overall, the average age has been lowered resulting in a greater ministry to young married couples and middle age persons. Nevertheless, a significant ministry remains among senior citizens and shut-ins.

In 1987, the congregation authorized the expenditure of over $40,000 for the purchase and installation of a new digital computer organ.

Since 1966, Mt. Calvary has been served by the Rev. C. Louis Shealy.

MT. HEBRON, LEESVILLE
Organized 1898
(HLCSC, pp. 631-632)

On August 26, 1973, the congregation of Mt. Hebron accepted plans for the construction of a new sanctuary with a seating capacity of 225. On April 6, 1975, the newly completed $150,000 structure was dedicated debt-free. A decade later, in September 1985, a similar event took place when Mt. Hebron dedicated a new $70,000 parsonage, also debt-free.

Between building projects the congregation was also busy in other important areas of ministry. In 1978, the joint parish arrangement with Union was terminated. In April of that same year, Mt. Hebron installed the Rev. James E.

Short as its first full-time pastor. Previously, both Mt. Hebron and Union had been served by the Rev. F. Lavaughn Keisler. Pastor Short resigned in 1979 and was succeeded by the Rev. Barry T. Antley from 1980 to 1985. On October 21, 1985, the Rev. William E. Jeffcoat began work as Mt. Hebron's third full-time pastor.

MT. HERMON, PEAK
Organized 1889
(HLCSC, pp. 632-634)

With the decline of the population growth in Peak, this congregation has seen little growth in membership over the last two decades, but continues to provide a vital ministry for the members and the community. With a membership average age of over 60, most families in the congregation have several generations still active in the ministry of this church. A community-centered congregation, its leadership has been provided by the Rev. Larry W. Smith from 1970 to 1983, and the Rev. Richard G. Ballard since 1983. Participation in the Word and Witness Program, as well as fellowship and learning activities, have provided ministry to these members. Mt. Hermon continues to be part of a parish with Mt. Olivet, Chapin.

MT. HERMON, WEST COLUMBIA
Organized 1910
(HLCSC, pp. 634-635)

By the mid-1980's, signs were evident that Mt. Hermon was at the threshold of a new period in the congregation's life and ministry. In 1984, the death of the two remaining signers of the congregation's 1910 charter signalled the end of one period, while the 75th anniversary celebration and a renewed commitment to witness and evangelism by the church council in 1985 seemed to announce the arrival of a new phase for Mt. Hermon. The new age into which Mt. Hermon seems to be entering coincides with a projected influx of new arrivals within its parish as developments in housing and industry continue to transform the surrounding community from rural area to suburban neighborhood.

The transformation was already becoming apparent within the congregation as new names were interspersed on the membership roll among the several traditional family names that had statistically dominated the roster previously in the congregation's history.

Changes were also being noticed in the physical appearance of the building. In 1980, the nave was renovated, followed by a renovation of the church office in 1984. Improvements were made to the cemetery in 1985, and a new heating and air conditioning system was installed. Also during 1985, Mt. Hermon obtained several worship aids, such as banners, a new piano, and pew cushions, to name a few.

Pastoral leadership was provided by the Rev. Ruben H. Olawsky from 1970 to 1979, and by the Rev. Wayne C. Kannaday since 1979.

MT. HOREB, CHAPIN
Organized 1891
(HLCSC, pp. 636-637)

The rapid recent growth of the Chapin area that includes the development of the Lake Murray area has brought growth and diversity to the congregation of Mt. Horeb. While the Rev. Everett A. Dasher served this congregation, the membership consisted mainly of generations of several families who had been in the community and the congregation for years. About the time of his departure in 1973, the changes in the make-up of the community began, and the congregation, reflecting the community, also became more diverse in its membership. The Rev. Earl H. Loadholdt served as pastor of Mt. Horeb from 1973 until his sudden death in March 1981. In October of that year, the Rev. E. Armand Shealy became the pastor.

All three synodical auxiliaries play an active role in the life of this congregation, and programs of fellowship have also been developed for young adults, middle age persons, and senior members. A pre-school serves the community-at-large. Strong educational ministry and music programs have been a strength of this congregation. Several people have worked in these areas, with Mrs. Sylvia Trimmier currently serving as Music/Education Director. The music program includes adult, youth and children's choirs as well as adult and youth handbell choirs. Additional property has been acquired for the church and the cemetery. In 1987, a 15-rank Schantz pipe organ with chimes was installed; other improvements made to the facilities were the addition of a library and family room, the installation of an elevator, and the use of the former parsonage as offices and additional classrooms.

A major goal of this congregation is reaching out and meeting the needs of the people who will be moving into this fast-growing area.

MT. OLIVET, CHAPIN
Organized 1873
(HLCSC, pp. 637-639)

In 1975, with the Rev. Larry W. Smith as pastor, Mt. Olivet completed a new church building that includes worship space and educational ministry areas. In 1983, Pastor Smith resigned, and the Rev. Richard G. Ballard became

the pastor. The change of the rural environment of the Chapin area into a more suburban community has affected the make-up of the congregation. Although most of the members are still from old Dutch Fork families, a number of new families have been received into the congregation, adding a new dimension to the congregation's ministry.

Employment for these members is in farming and in industry located in Columbia. The congregation has completed the Word and Witness program, and continues to have active fellowship, Christian education, and social ministry programs. A new parish building is needed to meet the growing needs of the congregation, and an intentional reaching out to the unchurched of the community must be a priority in this growing area. Mt. Olivet continues to be part of a parish with Mt. Hermon, Peak.

MT. OLIVET, PROSPERITY
Organized 1882
(HLCSC, pp. 639-640)

This tiny congregation continues to worship and provide a ministry for its members and the community despite the fact that it depends entirely upon supply pastors for pastoral leadership. When Pastor Link accepted a call to another synod in 1972, the Rev. J. Pierce Evans held services until 1975. In that year, the Rev. H. A. McCullough, Jr., began to serve as supply pastor. In 1978, the Rev. J. Virgil Long became his associate, and the two held services alternately until 1981.

Physical improvements completed in 1975 were the sanding of floors, carpeting the chancel and aisle, and replacing the old pews with ones purchased from Mt. Olivet, Chapin.

In 1979, the congregation, with help from the South Carolina Synod, erected a fellowship/educational building behind the sanctuary and named it the Moore Fellowship Building in honor of Mr. and Mrs. W. Wyche Moore, faithful, hard-working, and dedicated members for many years. The floor was tiled in 1982.

After the retirement of the associate pastors Long and McCullough in 1981, the Rev. Clarence Richardson took up the work. The congregation marked its 100th anniversary in 1982 with special services. The Rev. Ernest Felker became the supply pastor at the beginning of 1984 and served until March of the following year. Since that time the Rev. James K. Cobb has been serving in that capacity.

MT. PILGRIM, PROSPERITY
Organized 1880
(HLCSC, pp. 640-641)

Although not served by a full-time pastor, the congregation has experienced a 31% growth in baptized membership since 1970. The Rev. Edwin D. Zeigler was vice-pastor from 1970 to 1977. At the beginning of his pastorate a new heating and air conditioning system was installed.

Since 1977, the Rev. Alton C. Clark has been the vice-pastor. In 1978, new pews were installed in the nave of the church.

MT. PLEASANT, EHRHARDT
Organized 1750
(HLCSC, pp. 641-643)

The Rev. Ronald E. Miller served the Mount Pleasant congregation until 1977. During his tenure the church was able to upgrade its physical facilities by giving a brick veneer to the church building in 1974.

In 1975, the congregation celebrated its 225th anniversary. Bishop Cauble preached at the anniversary service, and in the afternoon an original drama was presented, depicting German migration to the Ehrhardt area. Over 500 people attended.

In 1977, the Rev. Ernest Burns was called to serve as pastor, and led the church until 1982. During his ministry extensive renovations of the church building were undertaken. Pews and floors were refinished and stained-glass windows were installed.

Pastor Burns resigned in 1982, and the Rev. Paul B. Williams became pastor in 1984.

The challenges facing Mount Pleasant are considerable. A decrease in agricultural activity is bringing changes to the area and the congregation. Yet the church has managed to show a small growth in the period since 1970, and intends to continue serving its community.

MT. PLEASANT, SALUDA
Organized 1903
(HLCSC, pp. 644-645)

Although the membership of this congregation has declined since 1970, new, younger members have been received into the congregation, bringing new life and direction to the ministry of the church. A strong outreach ministry into the community includes participation in devotional and recreational activities at the Saluda Nursing Center, where the congregation furnished a semi-private room in 1979; work with the literacy and AA programs; and the re-activation of a Cub Scout program. In 1979, an addition was made to the pipe organ, and additional property was purchased in 1984. Serving this congregation as pastor have been the Rev. Robert L. Tutas, 1968 to 1972; the Rev. David L. Lohr, 1972 to 1978; the Rev. Harry Weber, 1979 to 1985, and the Rev. Derald Edwards, 1986 to the present.

This congregation helps fund the Saluda Food Bank, Toys for Tots, The Literacy Council, and the Saluda Ministerial Association, which has programs for the needy. A new program for young adults and strong interest in evangelism have enhanced the ministry and spirit within Mt. Pleasant. A paid secretary has been added to the staff, and a new van was given to the congregation in December 1986, to enhance the ministry of all groups within the congregation.

MT. TABOR, LITTLE MOUNTAIN
Organized 1880
(HLCSC, pp. 645-646)

The period of Mt. Tabor's history since 1970 has brought steady growth to the Little Mountain area and to the membership roll of the congregation, resulting in a 25% increase in baptized members. With the flow of new persons into the community expected to continue, Mt. Tabor anticipates further potential for growth and an increasingly diverse character in the composition of its membership.

Among the more recent ministries of the congregation have been the development of a senior citizens group and the formation of a Word and Witness class in 1978-1979. The year 1980 was significant as the congregation celebrated its 100th anniversary.

The Rev. James C. Taylor was pastor of Mt. Tabor from 1969 to 1977, followed by the Rev. W. Osborne Herlong, Jr. since 1977.

MT. TABOR, WEST COLUMBIA
Organized 1886
(HLCSC, pp. 646-648)

The Rev. Charles E. Bernhardt began his ministry with Mt. Tabor in 1968 and through the next seven years shepherded the congregation through much growth. In July 1972, the Rev. David L. Misenheimer began his ministry as associate pastor and served until 1974. The Rev. Raymond E. Harley, II served as associate pastor and organist from 1978 to 1982. In 1973, two sons of the congregation, Ralph D. Stilwell and Marion C. Brazell, were ordained in a service held at Mt. Tabor. In that same year, adult classes were added to the Vacation Church School program, children's sermons were introduced in the worship service, and the "Coffee House" program which had been started in 1969 became an "After the Game" program for high school youth. This program proved to be not only important for the youth of the congregation, but also a meaningful witness in the community.

A closed-circuit video system was installed in the church

in 1974 to provide wider coverage for worship services and recording facilities for ministry to the shut-ins. The church's sound system was significantly improved and chimes were added to the ranks of the organ. Pastor Bernhardt submitted his resignation in 1975 and about six months later the Rev. Charles W. Easley began his ministry at Mt. Tabor. Pastor Easley arrived on the eve of the congregation's ninetieth anniversary, and plans were made for the celebration of this anniversary that happily coincided with the Bicentennial celebration of our nation. Several special services and events that included sons of the congregation and former pastors were held throughout the year. An Anniversary Cookbook was printed under the leadership of the LCW and a perpetual care fund was established for the Mt. Tabor Cemetery. Enhancement of the music program in the late 1970's included the addition of two children's choirs and three handbell choirs. Construction on the Youth Center/Administrative Unit was completed and dedicated in 1980.

A significant event for Mt. Tabor and all of South Carolina Lutheranism occurred in 1981, when a daughter of the congregation, Beverly Dennis Alexander, became the first woman to be ordained by the South Carolina Synod. After the resignation of Pastor Harley in 1982, Mr. Mark Glaeser was employed in 1983 as Director of Special Ministries. He served until 1984, and Edie Hockspeier began her work in that capacity.

Plans for the 100th Anniversary Celebration began shortly after the 90th Anniversary celebrations and came to fruition in 1986. Again services included the return of sons and daughters of the congregation, as well as former pastors. Bishop Cauble participated in the programs, as did a special member of the congregation, Mrs. Nellie H. Cuthbertson, who was born the same year in which the congregation was organized, 1886. In that same year, Newberry College awarded an honorary Doctor of Divinity degree to Pastor Easley, who later that year resigned to accept a call in Virginia. The Rev. James R. Connelly, Jr. began his ministry with Mt. Tabor in May 1987, and later that year the Rev. Pam M. Hix became Assistant Pastor.

NATIVITY, SPARTANBURG
Organized 1937
(HLCSC, pp. 648-649)

The Rev. Melvin Amundson continued to serve as pastor until 1973, and was succeeded by the Rev. Ralph D. Stilwell. A changing neighborhood has caused the congregation to adopt new emphases and programs. The growth of businesses in the area, together with the influx of transients and migrant workers, has provided opportunities for ministry to persons who frequently do not become permanent members of the church. LCW and LCY have been active in this type of ministry.

The year following the resignation of Pastor Stilwell in 1981 saw the arrival of the Rev. John F. Fischer, who continues to serve as the pastor of Nativity. In 1983, the educational facilities were reroofed, with the same treatment applied to the sanctuary the following year. Joint services with Roman Catholics and Episcopalians in 1984 and 1985 provided an exciting ecumenical dimension to the congregation's life. Dedication of new worship furnishings and structures and celebration of debt retirement were held in May 1986.

Vigorous evangelism efforts have resulted in the addition of several persons of non-Lutheran background to the congregation's membership, which has an average age of forty-five. The congregation and its auxiliaries have attempted to make life more palatable for nursing home residents, sponsored a Laotian family, and begun the delivering of food to the elderly and shut-ins. One of its sons, Tony Allen Metze, was ordained as a Lutheran pastor in 1985.

NAZARETH, LEXINGTON
Organized 1810
(HLCSC, pp. 649-651)

Nazareth shared a pastor with Bethany, Lexington until 1978, when Nazareth called the Rev. Louis T. Bowers as its pastor, and Bethany also sought out its own pastoral leadership. Both Nazareth and Bethany had previously been served by the Rev. Dermon A. Sox, Sr. from 1970 until 1971, when he retired. He continued his service until 1974, when the Rev. James E. Short was called and served until 1978. Pastor Bowers remained at Nazareth until 1980, and the Rev. Ralph D. Stilwell was called in 1981.

In 1978, the congregation dedicated its Parish Education building which was begun two years earlier. A Lutheran Men's group was reactivated in 1983 and has worked to improve the grounds and facilities. The Lutheran Church Women made an important contribution by replacing the full set of paraments. The Lutheran Church Youth group has emphasized ministry among the senior high youth.

Nazareth has remained active in other areas as well. A group has completed the Word and Witness study, and in 1983, the Friendship Group, a senior members' organization, was formed. Nazareth is also a member of the Lexington Interfaith Community Services. Development of active committees within the congregation has been a major project in recent years.

Like other congregations in the Lexington community, Nazareth is experiencing the change from an isolated rural community to a suburban community. A changing ministry for this changing community will provide a great challenge for the years ahead.

ORANGEBURG, ORANGEBURG
Organized 1855
(HLCSC, pp. 651-653)

In the period since 1970, Orangeburg Lutheran Church has continued to develop in many meaningful ways.

In 1970, Mrs. Anna Wertz willed the majority of her estate to the congregation. This has allowed it to make sizeable contributions to Camp Kinard, Epiphany Church in St. Matthews, and Newberry College. Scholarships have been funded for members attending Newberry, the Seminary, and Lutheridge.

When Pastor E. A. Shealy completed his years of ministry in Orangeburg in 1972, the Rev. Robert Tutas was called as pastor and served until 1974. He was followed by Rev. Olin Chassereau, who led the congregation from 1975 until 1978. The Rev. Bill B. Mims, Jr. became pastor in 1979 and served until 1987.

In the decades of the 70's and 80's, the city of Orangeburg has grown, bringing a variety of new members into the congregation from other areas and denominations, supplying the church with new ideas and commitment. Of particular significance was the reception of Mrs. Julia Murph as its first black member in 1980.

This congregation has continued to contribute to the ministry of the church as a whole, supporting missionaries and supplying officers and dedicated members to synod committees and auxiliaries. One son of Orangeburg Lutheran, the Rev. Barry Antley, was ordained in 1980.

In 1983-84, an extensive renovation project was undertaken on the church building. A new roof was added, the exterior was treated, new stained-glass windows were added, and the chancel area was completely remodeled. A new pipe organ was also installed.

OUR SAVIOUR, GREENVILLE
Organized 1956
(HLCSC, pp. 653-654)

In the year following the resignation of Pastor John Heyer in 1971, the Rev. Gary L. Safrit accepted the call to become the pastor and continues to serve. From 1982 to 1987 the congregation participated in the internship program with several students from Southern Seminary.

The rapidly growing congregation has been involved in a series of building projects. In 1971, the original nave was converted into classrooms and offices. In 1974, the parsonage was sold and removed from the land, which was reserved for later use. Memorial windows were installed in the nave in 1977 and a 14-rank Schantz organ in 1979. The same year a new office-fellowship-classroom wing was added at a cost of $300,000. In June 1980, fire destroyed a section of the original building and damaged the new wing. By September of the same year, the plant was restored and dedicated, at a cost of approximately $200,000.

With a median age of 45, the congregation is composed mostly of persons of the upper middle class coming from all sections of the country. Most of the adults are college graduates and have come into the church from a variety of denominational backgrounds, with Lutheran and Baptist predominating.

The congregation exhibits a keen awareness of the community's needs and cooperates with other churches in meeting those needs. Such cooperative efforts include Meals-on-Wheels, support of Taylors Day Care Center, United Ministries, emergency chaplain service for juveniles at the Greenville Law Enforcement Center, the Food Bank, and Pendleton Place, a home for abused and neglected girls. The congregation also maintains a Blood Assurance Bank to serve its members and persons of the community, a Hypertension Clinic, and a supper club to promote fellowship among the members.

The auxiliaries continue to carry on strong programs. The LCW has supplied leaders for district and synodical units. The LCY includes nearly 100 participants, divided into three groups. The first president of the synodical LCY, Sarah Moeller, came from this congregation. The LM has also provided district and state leadership, and is proud of the fact that a gift of $41,000 to the LM Loan Fund came from the estate of one of its life-long members, Mr. Walter Proescholdt.

As the congregation looks to the future, it has suspended its participation in the Seminary Intern program in order to add a second pastor to its staff. This action grew out of an extensive staff feasibility study conducted in 1986. The church seeks to continue a strong Lutheran emphasis in the community by working with the other Lutheran congregations in the area. One goal is to complete the Proescholdt Memorial Garden, situated between the nave and the office wing; another is to provide an additional parking lot.

OUR SAVIOUR, WEST COLUMBIA
Organized 1957
(HLCSC, pp. 654-655)

Rapid growth of the community around our Savior as a result of its geographic location close to the state capital, resulted in rapid growth of a congregation that was

organized in 1957 with 152 baptized members. The need for a new sanctuary was met with its dedication in 1974. Eight stained-glass windows were added in 1979. Few two generation families make up the membership of this congregation, although a strong Lutheran heritage is present, with persons from other denominations brought in mainly through marriage. Through the years the congregation has participated in community ecumenical services, and has regularly supported the outreach ministry of the church, including support for Elizabeth Huddle, missionary to Japan. It also participated in the construction of a cottage at Camp Kinard with three other congregations.

The Lutheran Men, Women and Youth of the church all add special dynamics to the congregation's overall ministry. A special Silver Anniversary celebration in 1983 included an Anniversary Service with charter members as guests and a 25th Anniversary Pageant entitled "God in this Place." In 1978, the Education Building was dedicated to the memory of the first pastor of Our Saviour, the Rev. Virgil A. Cameron. The congregation has participated in the Word and Witness program, and annually has a summer worship service at Lutheridge. The Rev. John L. Satterwhite III served as pastor of this congregation from 1970 until his retirement in 1986. The Rev. Gerald P. Wallace became its pastor in March 1987. The Rev. Amaretta Onstad served as assistant pastor from 1982 to 1983.

OUR SHEPHERD, HARTSVILLE
Organized 1968
(HLCSC, pp. 655-656)

Having dedicated its first unit in 1971, the congregation of Our Shepherd continued to grow and serve the community of Hartsville. However, by the mid 1970's, economic depression hit the area hard, and the church was severely affected. The next ten years were a time of struggle, economically, socially, and spiritually. Meeting its regular operating expenses was a constant concern for the congregation, and the vision of being self-supporting seemed out-of-sight. In spite of all the difficulties, the congregation, through the leadership of its mission developer and first pastor, the Rev. Everett R. Price, was able to survive.

In March 1975, Pastor Price resigned, and in June of that year, the congregation issued a call to its second pastor, the Rev. David T. Birnbaum. Under his new leadership, committees and the auxiliaries for women, men, and youth were re-organized. A new mission statement was written, and the congregation adopted a three-year plan to become self-supporting by the 20th anniversary of organization.

Since 1985, Our Shepherd has experienced steady growth both in membership and in stewardship, and is meeting the goals of the three-year plan. It looks forward to celebrating its 20th anniversary in 1988 as a self-supporting congregation with a vision of mission for the future.

Over the past several years, growth has been experienced in many different areas. Congregational family life has expanded, and at least a dozen family events are held each year, providing fellowship opportunities for the congregation. The youth, women, and men are involved actively in the congregation and in the synodical organizations. The congregation is also involved in local community programs, ministering to the needs of the people.

Major renovations of the facilities have been accomplished through the re-organization of its classrooms, fellowship hall, and storage space; the addition of carpet and pews in the sanctuary; the renovation of the chancel area to accommodate a free-standing altar, pulpit, and lectern; and the re-landscaping of the property.

Although Our Shepherd is geographically isolated from other Lutheran congregations, it continues to be a viable and strong witness to Lutheranism and the Gospel in its community.

PEACE, LADSON
Organized 1974

Because of population growth in Charleston Heights, a decision was made to begin work in that area. Pastor/Developer Jack D. Deal arrived in June of 1973, did survey work, and met with interested families.

The first service was held at the Alice-Birney Elementary School in August of 1973, with 17 persons in attendance. Pastor Deal led the worship. The place of worship was moved to the Pepperhill Shopping Center in November of that year. The congregation was organized on October 31, 1974, with 100 charter members. Deal has been its pastor since that time.

Peace has experienced considerable growth since its organization, now having a baptized membership of over 300. In October 1976, it became self-supporting. The congregation continued to worship at the shopping center until October of 1977, when it celebrated its third anniversary by moving to its present location on Dorchester Road.

PILGRIM, LEXINGTON
Organized 1899
(HLCSC, pp. 656-658)

In the early 1970's, Pilgrim began looking forward to its future in the Lexington/Lake Murray area. On April 25, 1971, the Church Council authorized the purchase of two acres of land adjoining the church property. An additional acre was donated by the seller, bringing the total property area of the congregation to almost nine acres.

A decade later in 1981, the congregation decided to add to its building space with the construction of a multi-level

addition. Dedicated on February 14, 1982, the first floor of the addition includes a kitchen and pantry, a large assembly room with a half-court for basketball, a shuffle board, a disappearing stage, storage room for tables and chairs, and rest rooms. The upper level contains a lobby, pastor's study, secretary's office and workroom, conference room, three class rooms, rest rooms, and a storage closet.

Other changes in the physical plant reflect the other important aspects of Pilgrim's ministry. With the needs of youth in mind, a tennis court was built in 1976. In 1985, the youth building was changed into a recreation building, containing weight training equipment, a wrestling/exercise mat, as well as other equipment.

When the Fellowship Hall building was completed, the basement area of the church building was converted from an assembly room to choir and handbell rooms, a small chapel, and a acolyte robing room. In 1974, a digital computer organ was purchased, and a carillon was installed in 1980. The music program was further enhanced in 1983 by the donation of a four octave handbell set.

The Rev. Elford Roof, Sr. served as pastor of Pilgrim from 1970 to 1983. The Rev. J. Marion Rhoden has served since being called in 1984. One member of the congregation, Howard H. Sale, was ordained and entered the ministry in 1983.

PINE GROVE, LONE STAR
Organized 1847
(HLCSC, pp. 658-660)

During the period since 1970, Pine Grove church has continued to minister to a largely rural population, but the development of the Santee-Cooper area has added some new members to the congregation. The Rev. Robert Swygert was called as pastor in 1971. Under his leadership, a new office wing was added to the church building in 1972-1973.

The congregation celebrated its 125th anniversary in 1972 with services at which the Rev. Fred Dufford was the preacher. An anniversary booklet was published to commemorate the occasion.

Pastor Swygert resigned in 1982, and Pastor Dufford served as interim supply in 1983. The Rev. Charles Bernhardt led the congregation from 1984 to 1986; and the Rev. Olin W. Chassereau became Pastor in 1987.

In 1984 and 1985, extensive projects were undertaken to improve the physical facilities: the parsonage was renovated; repairs and improvements were made to the church building; the grounds were improved; the cemetery was enlarged and supplied with a new fence; the parish building was air conditioned. A trust fund was also established.

Pine Grove is strong in its auxiliaries, providing district leaders, and in its support of the world-wide ministry of the church. Its goal is to keep alive the witness to Jesus Christ in its community.

One son of the congregation, James Carroll Butt, was ordained into the ministry during this period.

PISGAH, LEXINGTON
Organized 1878
(HLCSC, pp. 660-661)

On November 21, 1971, a new sanctuary was dedicated by the Pisgah congregation. This unit is contemporary in design with free-standing altar and extensive use of brick, wood, and wrought iron. It will accommodate over 300 worshipers and was built at a cost of approximately $130,000. This new and larger sanctuary is reflective of the changes that the community has experienced over the past 20 years. Industrial growth, the location of Lexington High School and the Lexington Vocation Center within a mile and a half of the church, and the construction of six housing developments in the area, have drastically changed the complexion of the community and the congregation. What was once a predominately agricultural and Lutheran area has now become more heavily industrial and a "bedroom" community for Columbia, resulting in a younger population with much more varied religious background. Pisgah, which was at one time a congregation made up of several generations of a few families, many of whom were of "Old German Lutheran" stock, now reflects the changes that the community has experienced. A younger and better educated population has brought the development of new and diverse programs within the congregation's ministry. Outreach to youth and young adults is a high priority, along with an emphasis on relating to a population that is more transitory and un-churched.

The Rev. Dermont F. Swicegood served as pastor of Pisgah from 1969 to 1979. On August 9, 1980, while the congregation was without the leadership of a pastor, fire destroyed the educational wing of the church. Shortly thereafter the Rev. Henry M. Moody, Jr., was called as pastor, and with his leadership and that of Vice-chairman George W. Roof, ground was broken in February 1981 for a reconstructed education/administrative wing. This wing was dedicated on August 9, 1981, not only debt free, but with a surplus of $120,000. From this surplus $40,000 was used to purchase a new Thomas International bus and to construct a building to shelter it. The remaining $80,000 was used to establish the Pisgah Endowment Fund which has aided mission congregations, various service agencies, and ministries of the Synod, in addition to helping families in crises and providing scholarships for members attending Newberry College. A gymnatorium had been built in 1977.

In addition to their emphasis on youth work, which has resulted in participation in CROP walks, the Lutheran Men have sponsored athletic and Scouting programs, and the Lutheran Church Women have been very active in support-ing the congregation, especially working with craft groups for senior citizens. The Golden Hearts have also become an active part of Pisgah's ministry program. Pisgah was a founding member of the Lexington Interfaith Community Services and for two years served as the contact for provid-ing services through this agency. It has also sponsored a Mother's Morning Out program.

The future presents Pisgah with the challenge of main-taining its ministry for the members, but at the same time developing a ministry profile that will meet the needs of a community changing from agricultural to suburban. Spe-cific program goals include the establishment of an inter-generational day care, more outreach into the community, and an increased level of participation in the wider work of the Church.

Leon A. Rawl, a son of the congregation, was ordained in 1977.

POMARIA, POMARIA
Organized 1910
(HLCSC, pp. 663-665)

The Rev. B. Fulmer Shealy continued to serve the congregation as its pastor until 1978. The following year the Rev. James L. Brady became the pastor and led the congregation until he resigned in 1986 so that he and his wife, Lynne, could become missionaries to Malaysia.

A project begun in 1981 by the LCW, the installation of an elevator for the use of the many disabled members of the congregation, was completed in 1984 at a cost of $10,000. It was dedicated debt-free in honor of an LCW member who had worked hard for the project.

A storage building/picnic shelter was completed in 1982, and in the same year the nave was recarpeted and the pews upholstered. The congregation, with a medium age of 58, is community-oriented and homogeneous. Most of the members are traditional Lutherans but there are some of other denominational backgrounds.

PRINCE OF PEACE, CHESTER
Organized 1957
(HLCSC, pp. 661-662)

The congregation, which together with Abiding Presence, York, forms a parish, has experienced no net growth since 1970. After the Rev. Marion W. Clark resigned in 1971, pastoral leadership was provided by the Rev. Lewis B. Doggett, Jr., who served from 1972 to 1975. The Rev. Edward H. Wiediger succeeded him in 1976 and served until 1979. The parish became self-supporting in 1980, shortly after the arrival of the Rev. Timothy Robinson.

When Pastor Robinson left in 1983, a son of the congregation, the Rev. Robert E. McCollum, was called to become pastor of the York-Chester parish. He began his work in

1984 and continues to serve as Prince of Peace grows in membership and contemplates the expansion of its facilities, which were erected in 1963. A new organ was dedicated in July 1987, and ground was broken in November 1987 for a new parish building. Members of the church participate in the local Meals-on-Wheels program in cooperation with the Chester County Council on Aging.

PROVIDENCE, LEXINGTON
Organized 1866
(HLCSC, pp. 662-663)

In 1974, when the St. John-Providence parish separated to form two independent parishes, Providence, for the first time since at least 1942 when the Providence-Pilgrim-Zion parish was formed, became a parish in its own right. The Rev. James D. Bayne, who had previously served as pastor of both Providence and St. John, remained as pastor of St. John, while Providence in 1975, called the Rev. Otto F. Reenstjerna as its pastor. Pastor Reenstjerna had also served as pastor of Providence from 1960 to 1965, during which time Providence had been joined in a parish with Nazareth Lutheran Church. Pastor Reenstjerna's second period of service ended with his retirement in 1980. The Rev. W. Wayne Young was called as pastor in 1981 and remained until 1984. He was succeeded by the Rev. Robert W. Hawkins, who began his ministry at Providence in 1985.

During the decade of the 70's and the first half of the 80's, Providence experienced a moderate, but important, growth in membership. In 1970, the baptized membership of the congregation had been 125. By the mid-1980's, the baptized membership had increased to over 200. The educational building of the church was extended in February of 1979, and the sanctuary underwent a renovation in the fall of the same year.

REDEEMER, CHARLESTON
Organized 1943
(HLCSC, pp. 665-666)

The neighborhood served by Redeemer is in a process of change. The average resident is older, and there is a shift in the racial make-up of the area. The composition of the congregation is also changing. Despite the increased age of the local population, many young families are joining, as are professionals and people from other areas of the country and from non-Lutheran backgrounds.

Pastor R. M. Van Horne continued to serve Redeemer until 1981. During his pastorate the fellowship hall was enlarged and a kitchen, air conditioning system, and new roof were added. New paraments were purchased. In 1973, an Allen digital computer organ was installed and stained glass windows were completed. In 1975, a house was purchased for use as an office. From 1975 to 1978, the church sponsored Vietnamese refugees.

The Rev. Herman R. Yoos became pastor of the congregation in 1982 and serves to the present time. William F. Hogan has been ministry assistant since 1984.

Redeemer is concentrating much of its efforts on serving the young couples who are moving in. The Sunday Church School is growing, and in 1985, an additional house was purchased for Church School classrooms. There is also increased ministry to older people.

The congregation has been involved in ecumenical activities, including joint communion services with St. Peter Episcopal Church, a joint choir cantata with John Wesley Methodist Church, and participation in the Spoleto Children's Festival Choir.

Redeemer contributes clothing and health kits to migrant workers. It has established a monthly fellowship group for retired members, a weekly Bible study series, a Renewing course, a children's choir, and intercession services. It has supported the Camping Appeal, Strength for Mission, World Hunger Appeal, and a missionary to Liberia.

The youth of the church sponsored a congregational blood drive in 1984 and the World Hunger Appeal in 1985. The

LCW participated in prayer breakfasts with Methodist and Episcopal women. The women have held Head Start Christmas parties, sponsored families, and have supplied district and synodical leaders.

Two members of the congregation have entered full-time ministries during this period: James Short was ordained and Nan Hull became a certified lay professional.

Redeemer looks to the future with the goals of involving more members in the leadership and planning of its ministry, placing more emphasis on servanthood to the community and the world, and reaching out to minority families.

REDEEMER, COLUMBIA
Organized 1965
(HLCSC, pp. 666-667)

Located on St. Andrews Road just off I-26, Redeemer has been one of the fastest growing congregations in the synod. Although the baptized membership in 1970 was 424 persons, that figure had risen to over 1,200 by 1985. Such rapid

growth has resulted in changes in the congregation's building, program, and staff. In March 1971, the congregation approved a study committee's recommendation for additional classroom and office space. The addition was dedicated in November of that same year. In 1975, a study was again conducted to determine facility needs. This time the study resulted in yet another administrative unit and a new sanctuary dedicated on October 14, 1979.

Program areas of ministry have expanded as well. The Lutheran Church Women, for example, have regularly expanded the numbers of circles the congregation supports. The areas of music (with choirs for children as well as adults), youth ministry, and Christian education have also been high priorities. The early 1980's have seen a rejuvenated interest in the Lutheran Men's organization.

The pastoral and professional staff has also changed as the congregation has grown. When the Rev. Alvin Haigler, the mission developer and first pastor of the congregation, resigned in 1972, Redeemer moved the next year to call the Rev. Melvin E. Amundson as its pastor. Beginning in 1976, Redeemer became involved in the intern program with Southern Seminary and hosted a series of interns until 1982. The last of the interns, Vicar Chuck Schwarz, remained as a pastoral assistant while completing his last year at the seminary. In 1983, Redeemer called its first assistant pastor, the Rev. Russell C. Kleckley, who served until 1986. The Rev. Marguerite M. Rourk was called as associate pastor in 1987.

REDEEMER, GREER
Organized 1972
(HLCSC, pp. 667-668)

The Rev. James Addy, developer of the congregation, continued to serve as its pastor until 1976. During his ministry

the congregation was organized on March 26, 1972; the first building was completed; ground having been broken May 25,

1975; and first worship service held therein on March 14, 1976. A new parsonage was purchased the same year. The Rev. John W. Withrock became the pastor in 1977 and served for three years. He was succeeded in 1980 by the Rev. George B. Shealy, whose ministry was shortened by serious illness. He resigned in May 1982.

The Rev. William R. Camlin was the pastor from 1983 to 1985. The current pastor is the Rev. Jeffrey K. Lageman, who began his ministry in 1986. Continuing growth of the area served by the church provides a fertile field for church growth. All ages are well represented in the membership, with a majority employed as skilled laborers. The congregation anticipates a more vigorous evangelism effort and broader scope of service to the community.

REDEEMER, NEWBERRY
Organized 1853
(HLCSC, pp. 668-669)

Under the leadership of the Rev. Dr. H. A. McCullough, Jr. the congregation cooperated with the Lutheran Theological Southern Seminary in its internship program. From 1970 until his retirement in 1974, he supervised the parish training of four interns.

In 1975, the Rev. Teddy P. Dominick, Jr. assumed his duties as pastor of Redeemer. With his energetic encouragement the congregation undertook the resettlement of a large Vietnamese family, which has become an integral part of the community. The success of this venture enabled the congregation to sponsor another Vietnamese family in 1983, long after Pastor Dominick had resigned in 1977.

In 1978, under the guidance of vice-pastor Dr. Francis I. Fesperman, the congregation celebrated its 125th Anniversary. One of the guest preachers for the occasion was a son of the congregation, the Rev. James B. Park, who was ordained in 1975.

The Rev. Hugh E. Baumgartner, Jr. became the pastor in 1979 and served until his retirement in 1986. A Director of Christian Education and Youth Activities was added to the staff in 1981, a move which has helped to revive the LCY into an active group. The first person to fill this position was Mrs. Pam Hix, who was succeeded by Miss Katherine A. Crowell in 1982. After Miss Crowell's resignation in 1984, Mrs. Amy Kinard assumed the post in 1985 and continues to serve. In 1984, Redeemer contributed to the tornado-stricken churches in Newberry: Mayer Memorial Lutheran and St. Luke Episcopal.

A completely new sound system has been installed in the nave, and the Service is broadcast each third Sunday over a local radio station. New communion rail kneelers, a prie dieu, and seasonal banners have been made for the enhancement of worship services. In late 1986, the Rev. R. M. Van Horne became pastor of the congregation. Groundbreaking for a Family Life Center, designed to make possible recreational and fellowship activities which are not possible in the present facilities, was held on May 17, 1987.

In recent years Redeemer has contributed to the support of overseas missionaries, has given generously to relieve world hunger, and has supported the projects of the Newberry County Interfaith Community Services. Extra apportionment monies were also given to the Lowman Home and Newberry College.

The LCW is very active and has four circles. Its projects include a monthly service visit to the Lowman Home. Several members of the congregation regularly deliver Meals-on-Wheels in the city of Newberry. A group, calling itself the Fifty Plus Club, has been organized and enjoys frequent social events, trips, and service projects. Another son of the congregation in the ministry, the Rev. Jeffrey D. Marble, was ordained in 1986.

REFORMATION, COLUMBIA
Organized 1926
(HLCSC, pp. 669-671)

Since 1970, Reformation has dedicated itself to new kinds of ministry in a changing community. Its neighborhood is characterized by transitions in the racial, cultural, socioeconomic, and age balance of the people. Deterioration and renewal, crime increase and crime watch compete for dominance.

The Rev. Stafford L. Swing continued to minister to the congregation until his death in 1980. During his tenure the Rev. William S. Ketchie served as assistant pastor from 1975 to 1977. The Rev. Dr. James H. Nichols has been pastor since 1981. Several interns have also served the congregation. The church also notes the long and dedicated service of its members: in 1982, Mrs. Lera Mae Wingard retired after more than 50 years as organist, and Dr. Milton Moore has completed 22 years as director of music. Heber P. Buff served 28 years as treasurer, retiring in 1982.

The Rev. William R. Albert was ordained in 1971, the ninth son of the congregation to enter the ministry.

With its changing neighborhood and a shrinking and aging membership, Reformation has broadened its ministry, becoming deeply involved in ecumenical and community activities. It has cooperated with community joint Thanksgiving Services and the Oliver Gospel Mission since 1981. A soup kitchen at Washington Street United Methodist Church has been supported since 1983. The congregation has been involved with Cooperative Ministry since 1984, and with Lutheran Social Services since 1985. The church has served as a meeting place for Alcoholics Anonymous, Narcotics Anonymous, the Neighborhood Community Club, a dance group, and a Department of Social Services Parenting Class.

Special projects of the congregation include the Half-Century Club, a monthly community senior citizens group, founded in 1971, and a swing band that entertains at nursing homes and other places. A child care center was established in 1983; a senior citizens daytime group, which meets weekly, began in 1984; and a healing ministry began in 1985. All of these activities are open to everyone, regardless of church membership.

In 1978, chancel rails and clergy stalls were installed, and stained-glass windows were added to the sanctuary in 1983. The church parlor was refurbished that same year. In 1984, the annex was renovated as a child-care center, and in 1985, the sanctuary was repainted. In 1986, a new fellowship hall and kitchen were fashioned from a renovation of the educational wing. The former nave which had been used as a fellowship hall was razed. A new lawn and landscaping completed the renovation project.

The congregation faces the challenges of increasing its membership and ministering to its members as well as continuing its community involvement. Its mood is one of cautious optimism.

REFORMATION, LANCASTER
Organized 1953
(HLCSC, pp. 671-672)

In the last year of Pastor James C. Dickert's ministry, the church and parsonage were renovated. Following his resignation in 1972, the congregation called the Rev. Thomas W. Corbell to become its pastor. He began his ministry in 1973 and served until his resignation in 1979. His period of service saw the construction of a new parish building, the installation of a new Allen organ, and the beginning of the tradition of holding joint Lenten and Epiphany services with Christ Episcopal Church. The congregation also assumed sponsorship of Ernest and Gladys Zellmer, who were commissioned to overseas lay ministry by Lutheran Bible Translators and Wycliffe Bible Translators in 1975. During this period the membership of the church doubled, and one of its sons, Edward Dukes, was ordained as a pastor.

During the ministry of the Rev. James L. Dougherty, 1980-81, a new furnace was installed in the church and a covered walkway between the parish hall and the sanctuary was constructed. In 1982, the Rev. Karl G. Bernsdorff became the pastor and continues to serve. Shortly before his arrival the original parsonage was sold and a new one purchased. The congregation participated with other area churches in the establishment of Hope of Lancaster, Inc., an emergency assistance ministry, in 1983; opened its facilities to the Lancaster County Literacy Association, and in 1984, joined other community agencies in aiding the tornado victims in neighboring counties.

The Lancaster area has experienced considerable change, seen especially in the decline of the textile industry and the arrival of new industries. This has contributed to the congregation's growth, even in an area in which non-Lutherans dominate the population. The congregation has increased its ministry to the community. With very few senior citizens among its membership, the church has a high percentage of young families and a very diverse character in terms of occupation and educational level.

The LCY maintains a full program of events for the youth, while the LCW sponsors a variety of service projects for the congregation and the community. An LM Unit was chartered in 1987.

RESURRECTION, CAMERON
Organized 1844
(HLCSC, pp. 673-674)

Although Resurrection serves a rural area that is presently experiencing a farm crisis, the congregation continues to grow in its worship life and its ministry.

The church is involved in numerous ecumenical and community activities, such as Easter sunrise and Thanksgiving services, a joint Christmas giving fund, food pantry and clothes closet. Help is given to area residents for utility bills and other needs. Resurrection awards two Seminary scholarships and gives generous support to World Hunger, Lowman Home, and local persons in need.

The LCW is very active in supporting church work. Gloria Rast, Synodical LCW president, and her husband, Heber Rast, past president of the Synodical LM, are members of Resurrection. The LCY is being revived after a dormant period.

The Rev. G. B. Corley served as pastor until 1983, and the Rev. David B. Hunter began his ministry in 1984.

RESURRECTION, COLUMBIA
Organized 1948
(HLCSC, pp. 674-676)

In 1974, Resurrection completed contruction of a new educational building with a fellowship hall, kitchen, classrooms, and offices. It was named in honor of the church's longtime pastor, the Rev. Joseph C. Derrick. In 1977, a marble baptismal font was dedicated in memory of Mrs. Julia Derrick.

With the death of Pastor Derrick in 1978, the Rev. Rufus E. Lybrand became pastor. He served the church until 1982. The Rev. Milas Y. Sease III has led the congregation since 1983.

In 1983, a complete renovation of the sanctuary was accomplished adding a new narthex, chancel area, choir loft and additional seating. In 1985, a renovated Möller pipe organ was installed. It had previously been housed in two different Episcopal churches.

During the past ten years the Rosewood-Shandon area has witnessed a revitalization which has attracted many young families and single persons into the older area and the congregation. Many of these younger members are from non-Lutheran backgrounds and are well-educated. A large number of retired persons also remains in the area. The church is thus challenged to develop ministries for both groups.

Resurrection is also increasing its presence in the community and striving to become more inclusive of those who live in its neighborhood, especially one-parent families. The LCW provides ministries to bereaved families. The LCY sponsors an annual Halloween party for the congregation and the community, and was active in leading congregational support for the CROP WALK for World Hunger. The Witness and Service Committee sponsors parties for a cottage at the Midlands Center for the Mentally Retarded.

Clothing and Christmas presents are also provided for some residents of the cottage.

A son of the congregation, the Rev. Dennis R. Bolton, was ordained in 1979.

As Resurrection looks to the future, it plans to work toward the development and use of the ministry of the laity, the implementation of new fellowship and learning programs, and the expansion of its ministry within the community.

ST. ANDREW, BLYTHEWOOD
Organized 1878
(HLCSC, pp. 676-677)

The membership of St. Andrew consists largely of persons with traditional Lutheran backgrounds, but new members, coming from other traditions, have recently been added.

The congregation went for many years without full-time pastoral services. From 1965 to 1975, students supplied the pulpit. From 1975 to 1984, the Rev. John N. Slice, a retired pastor, supplied. In 1985, through early 1986, students were again used. But in March of 1986, the Rev. Cathy J. Quinton became the first regularly called pastor in many years. She continues to serve at St. Andrew.

In 1986, parsonage renovation was begun, with vinyl trim work and plumbing replacement being completed.

The church's goals for the future are to be able to continue maintaining a full-time pastor, to establish a youth group and a children's choir, to broaden the scope of its outreach ministry, and to establish functioning congregational committees.

ST. ANDREW, CHARLESTON
Organized 1853
(HLCSC, pp. 677-680)

Since 1970, St. Andrew has faced the challenge of a changing neighborhood, with an accompanying decline in the number of its members and an increase in their average age. However, in the late 1980's, membership has begun to grow.

Pastor Charles S. Wessinger served the congregation during the first part of this period, continuing his ministry from 1956 to 1976. During this period a number of improvements were made to church properties, such as painting, the installation of lighting and the addition of air conditioning. Chimes with loud speakers were also installed, and improvements were made to the grounds. Property was purchased for additional parking.

Beginning in 1970, the church housed and supported the Lutheran Service Center. During Pastor Wessinger's service St. Andrew hosted a community concert, began to house the Senior Citizens Group of Charleston, the Historic Ansonborough Neighborhood Association, and the Garden Club of Charleston.

The Rev. James W. Addy became pastor in 1976 and remained until 1981. Under his leadership a Neighborhood Plan was started, senior citizen events were held, and a Vacation Church School with downtown churches was begun. The church initiated its Word and Witness program, published an Advent devotional book, and a pictorial directory, held Lenten Services with St. Johannes, and revised its constitution.

In 1978, St. Andrew celebrated its 125th anniversary, updated its historical book, and published a cookbook.

The Rev. Rodney W. Parrott began his service as pastor in 1982. Much of the work during his pastorate has been devoted to extensive renovation, repair, and modernizing of the church, the parish building, and the parsonage. Many individual gifts and memorials have played a significant part in these efforts. The organ has had major revisions and additions.

In recent years the Lutheran Book of Worship has been adopted, and lay communion assistants have been added. The LCY has been re-activated as has the Confirmation Ministry program. An additional adult Sunday School class and a young adult fellowship have been established. Intensive visitation of non-active members has been carried out. Committees of the church have set 3-5 year goals. The congregation has been cooperating with the Lutheran Reformation Worship Service and the Lutheran School of

Religion. The Round Dancers Group, softball, volleyball, and basketball teams have also been organized.

Since 1970, St. Andrew has given significant support to such special projects as missionary support, the Franke Home and church wide appeals. Special gifts have also been regularly given to synodical institutions and needy congregations through extra giving to the benevolence work of the congregation. St. Andrew also joined in the formation of the Lutheran Social Services of Charleston.

In 1986, an additional parking lot was purchased and beautified; a Spoleto Concert was held at the church, and the church participated in the Fall Ansonborough Candlelight Tour. In 1987, a Ministry with the Aging Committee was added and an Adult Literacy Workshop was held, training 40 people to teach adults to read. A ramp and two wheelchairs were given to aid members; and a sound system was installed in the church and the auditorium.

Plans are being made for the 135th Anniversary, to be held in 1988. The congregation's goals also include more extensive long-range planning, the rekindling of inactive members, and increased efforts to attract and minister to young adults.

ST. ANDREW, COLUMBIA
Organized 1835
(HLCSC, pp. 680-682)

Throughout the 1950's and 1960's, St. Andrew enjoyed a period of steady and significant growth. By the time the decade of the 1970's arrived, the need for a new and larger sanctuary was already apparent. In 1974, the church council appointed a building committee, and work was begun. The project, dedicated on December 4, 1977, includes a thirty-three rank Schantz pipe organ and faceted glass windows. The sanctuary has a seating capacity of 500.

Numerical growth of the congregation began to decline as the surrounding area became highly commercial. As it had in the past, the congregation once again had to adjust its style of ministry. Its focus became community-wide, providing ministries to reach the needs of a broad spectrum of

society. Facilities were made available for many groups. Musical concerts were sponsored. Various levels of Boy and Girl Scout programs remain strong. In the meantime, strong stewardship developed. The budget more than doubled between 1970 and 1980. Landscaping was completed and the pride of upkeep became evident as the congregation made a concerted effort to preserve the appearance of the buildings and grounds, all the while contributing more and more to the greater ministries of the synod and the community.

In 1978, the congregation began the sponsorship of a pastoral counseling service, the first of its kind among Lutheran churches in the Columbia area. Currently under study are plans for relocating the offices and refurbishing other parts of the education facilities. In 1987, the mortgage on the new sanctuary was burned.

During this time the congregation has been under the pastoral leadership of the Rev. Robert W. Carswell (1966-1973) and, since 1973, the Rev. Donald E. Woolly. From 1973 to 1975, St. Andrew was involved in the internship program with Southern Seminary. Other full-time professional staff have included Robert Barrett, Director of Youth and Music (1975-1979); Frances Whitener, Director of

Music and Educational Ministry (1980-1982); Nancy Padgett, Director of Education and Youth (1984-1986), and Carolyn Gardner, Organist and Director of Music (1982-   ). The Rev. John C. Peery served the congregation as pastoral associate from 1976 to 1984.

Three members of St. Andrew have entered the ordained ministry since 1970, Fulmer Shealy (1971), George Sims (1975), and Paul Summer (1985).

ST. BARNABAS, CHARLESTON
Organized 1912
(HLCSC, pp. 682-683)

Pastor Wilford Pascal Hendrix, Jr. has served St. Barnabas since 1969. The Rev. E. G. Runge, a retired pastor of the Lutheran Church-Missouri Synod, has been associate pastor since 1979.

The neighborhood of the church has changed over the years, and St. Barnabas is beginning to build viable relations with the black residents of the community. Most of the members are traditional middle class Lutherans.

The congregation has a strong ministry to students, particularly those at The Citadel. Every year Parents Sunday is celebrated in conjunction with Parents Weekend at The Citadel. Parents worship at the church and take part in a dinner after the service.

World Hunger is a top priority for the congregation. Over $10,000 has been raised for this need. St. Barnabas also participates in HELP, an interdenominational agency which helps indigents with food, clothing, and emergency funds.

In 1971, plexiglass was installed to protect stained-glass windows in the parish hall and church. The choir loft was enlarged in 1979, and the same year a new roof was installed on the parish building.

The men's group has a positive influence in bringing the congregation together. They plan the annual picnic and the Easter breakfast.

St. Barnabas celebrated its 100th anniversary in 1983. The Rev. George E. Meetze, a former pastor, helped in the celebration. Many events were held throughout the year. The theme was "Debt Free in '83." This goal was realized.

One son of the congregation has been ordained, Matthew Moye, Jr. in 1972.

In 1986, the church was renovated and restored inside and out, along with the outside of the parish hall. All of this was accomplished without borrowing any funds because of gifts from the congregation.

St. Barnabas faces the future with two major challenges: relating to its neighborhood and enhancing its program of campus ministry.

ST. DAVID, WEST COLUMBIA
Organized 1845
(HLCSC, pp. 683-685)

In 1970, St. David remembered its past as well as began looking forward to its future. Not only did the congregation celebrate its 125th anniversary that year; it also began building an educational and office building on the site of the nave built in 1930. The congregation also increased its staff that year by securing the services of the Rev. D. M. Shull, Sr., as Emeritus Pastoral Assistant. The pastor of St. David during this period of its history was the Rev. R. Earl Mc-Combs, Jr.

When Dr. Shull retired from his position in 1974, St. David moved to enter into the intern program through Southern Seminary. The congregation welcomed a new intern each year until Pastor McCombs' resignation in 1980, and resumed its participation in it after the arrival of the Rev. Richard Webber as pastor in 1981. The intern program was again temporarily discontinued in 1983 when the Rev. David Vaughan was called as St. David's associate pastor in September, 1983. Pastor Vaughan served until September, 1986.

In 1978, Dr. A. K. Roberts became organist/choir director. Shortly after he was hired, a new Zimmer pipe organ was installed, and a renovation of the balcony and chancel area was begun.

In September 1986, Dr. Wayne Earnest became the congregation's first full time Director of Music Ministries. Dr. Earnest came to St. David from Newberry College, where he was serving as college organist and associate Professor of Music. Under his leadership the music program has grown dramatically.

In 1979, the congregation began preparing for the future by engaging in a Parish Life and Ministry Development self-study. A mission statement was subsequently developed to describe the life and purpose of the congregation as a whole. As a result, St. David began to expand in the program areas of its ministry. A Word and Witness program was started in that same year and two groups have completed instruction. A refugee family was adopted and arrived in May 1980, and was baptized the following year.

Under the direction of Pastor Webber, a Long Range Planning Committee was appointed to explore the ways in which the congregation could better serve the community. As a result, St. David has become active in Lexington Interfaith Community Services, Columbia's "Soup Kitchen," quarterly Red Cross drives, a day school for three and four year olds, and is a member congregation of the Midlands Lutheran Council. St. David is also involved in developing a three-phase renovation/building program, which began in 1986 under the leadership of a Planning, Design and Building Committee.

St. David has re-entered the Intern Program for 1987-88 and has secured the part-time service of Pastor George Moore in assisting with congregational pastoral visitation.

As they move toward their 150th Anniversary in 1995 the members continue to plan for ways in which they can be a servant community.

Other congregational ministries are the "Young At Heart" group for 55 years of age and older, a Grief Support group that meets monthly, a Junior and Senior High LCY group, and an active Scouting program for girls and boys.

ST. JACOB, CHAPIN
Organized 1776
(HLCSC, pp. 685-687)

At the end of the 1980's, St. Jacob, like other Lutheran churches in the Chapin area, is a congregation preparing itself for a new era in its long history which will be characterized by youth and renewed energy. Once a congregation with an emphasis toward ministry to a large population of senior citizens, St. Jacob is now preparing for an expanded

ministry to a growing number of younger persons and families as well, especially as the surrounding population grows with newer families moving into the area. What was once a congregation ministering to a largely agricultural community of traditional Lutheran families is now finding itself surrounded more and more by persons employed in other fields of work who have moved to the area to escape the congestion of nearby Columbia. A new fellowship building was dedicated in 1984 in anticipation of the developing new trend. The future direction of the ministry of the congregation will largely be determined by the changing needs of the community St. Jacob serves.

John W. Wessinger served as St. Jacob's pastor for seventeen years until his retirement in 1978. He was followed by the Rev. Andrew D. Eargle, who came in February 1979.

ST. JAMES, GRANITEVILLE
Organized 1860
(HLCSC, pp. 687-689)

Throughout the 1970's and 1980's, St. James has been blessed by strong pastoral leadership and an active congregation that has been growing increasingly diverse. An even representation is present among most of the age groups of the congregation, with a growing number of people from non-Lutheran backgrounds being added to the membership.

Not only has St. James been a strong supporter of the synod, it has also been involved in ecumenical efforts in the Graniteville community by participating in world hunger drives, annual community Thanksgiving services and World Day of Prayer services, and since 1974, an annual area School of Religion. Recent closings in the textile industry have made St. James increasingly aware of its role in ministering to the community.

In August 1978, a new fellowship wing was completed consisting of a large fellowship hall, a multi-purpose room, kitchen, church office, secretary's office and workroom, pastor's study, rest rooms with showers, and a storage room. The wing was named for the Rev. J. Virgil Addy, pastor of the congregation from 1943 to 1973. He was succeeded by the Rev. Al Potter from 1974 to 1984. The Rev. Barry T. Antley has been St. James' pastor since January 1985.

On March 3, 1985, St. James celebrated its 125th anniversary of ministry in the Graniteville community and in 1987, installed a new organ.

ST. JAMES, LEESVILLE
Organized 1873
(HLCSC, pp. 689-690)

Like many Lutheran congregations in the Lexington/ Leesville area, St. James continues to reflect much of the heritage that has been part of its life since organization. Its membership reflects traditional ties with well-established families in the surrounding area, with all age groups well represented. Most people from non-Lutheran backgrounds who have joined St. James in the past have mostly found their way onto the church roll through marriage, but as the Lexington County area continues to grow with persons from non-Lutheran backgrounds, the evangelism outreach to these new arrivals in the community will be a major challenge.

St. James has already made its presence known in the non-Lutheran circles through its participation in the Gilbert-Summit ecumenical services that are held monthly with Methodists, Baptists, and other Lutherans in the area.

Since 1971, pastoral leadership has been provided by the Rev. W. Richard Albert (1971-1974), the Rev. J. Pierce Evans, Jr. (1975-1982), and the Rev. Keith R. Cook (1983-present). One member of the congregation, E. Arden Hallman, Jr., was ordained into the ministry in 1975.

ST. JAMES, LEXINGTON
Organized 1921
(HLCSC, pp. 691-692)

The seventeen year period from 1971 to 1987 was one in which St. James engaged in making extensive improvements to its facilities. In 1972, air conditioning was installed in the parsonage and a basketball and tennis court was built behind the church. In addition, the Lutheran Church Women had new carpet installed in the sanctuary. The possibility for further improvements became more evident on November 18, 1973, when the indebtedness on the existing church building was paid in full and the mortgage burned, four years ahead of schedule. In 1976, the parsonage was enlarged by adding a dining room and carport and by expanding the laundry room. A new Zimmer pipe organ was installed in the sanctuary in 1979, and the next year an outdoor ramp was installed, making the church building more accessible for the aged and handicapped. In 1982, a sound system was installed in the sanctuary, and a van was purchased. A new hallway to the nursery was built in 1983, and new carpet was installed in the educational building. During the same year new cushions were installed in the pews, and a new kitchen was added to the activities building.

Throughout this phase in the congregation's life, St. James was led by three pastors. After the Rev. H. Wyman Dowd resigned in 1971, the Rev. William R. Cobb was called and served from 1972 to 1979. He was followed in 1980, by the Rev. Olin W. Chassereau, who served until 1987. In 1979, an additional staff position was created when Patricia Hood was hired as a full-time organist/choir director. In 1985, Mr. David Birnbaum, member of St. James, graduated from Southern Seminary and was called as the pastor of Our Shepherd, Hartsville.

As the population in the Red Bank/Lexington area continues to grow, St. James anticipates the opportunity for its own growth and service to the community.

ST. JAMES, NEWBERRY
Organized 1840
(HLCSC, pp. 692-694)

The Rev. Paul Hatch continued to serve as pastor until 1973. An addition to the educational portion of the church plant, providing assembly and fellowship space, was added in 1967. The Rev. Lester H. Cutter, Jr. became the pastor in 1974 and, with his family, moved into the new parsonage near the church. The modern residence was dedicated June 16, 1974 and the mortgage thereon burned in November 1977. Air conditioning was added to the educational/fellowship rooms the same year.

In 1980, a barbecue pit and shed were built on the church grounds to facilitate fellowship activities for the congregation and the community. The parking lot was paved and plexiglass storm windows were installed to protect the stained-glass windows.

New lighting fixtures were placed in the nave as memorial gifts in 1981. The following year a carillon system was installed, also provided by memorial and honorary gifts.

The congregation began to contribute to the support of a missionary in 1976. With an average age of thirty-three, its membership includes many families and a host of children.

Besides a majority from Lutheran background, a large number come from other denominational traditions. The congregation has emphasized Bible study and has participated in a Word and Witness program. Pastor Cutter resigned in 1985 and was succeeded later that year by the Rev. Herbert L. Wood, Jr. St. James continues in a parish alignment with Beth Eden, Newberry.

ST. JAMES, SUMTER
Organized 1890
(HLCSC, pp. 694-696)

Pastor Carl A. Honeycutt led St. James in 1971 and 1972. In 1972, the Rev. Alvin H. Haigler became pastor, and has served to the present time.

A thorough study of the needs of the congregation was made during 1973, and it became evident that the church should move to the five acres of land on Alice Drive that had been purchased in 1971. A building program was launched and ground-breaking ceremonies were held for the new church in August of 1976. The first service was held there on November 20, 1977, with 365 people in attendance. With its new facilities, the membership of the church continues to grow.

St. James is active in the support of a missionary. It also supports the Sumter Christian Charities. One Sunday a month is set aside as Christian Charities Day. It lends support to the Safe House, a home for abused spouses and children, and to The Shepherd's Center, an Interdenominational program for senior citizens.

Two sons of the congregation, the Rev. Lester H. Cutter and the Rev. Harold Benton Lutz, have been ordained since 1970.

ST. JOHANNES, CHARLESTON
Organized 1878
(HLCSC, pp. 696-698)

In 1970, the buildings of this historic church were entered on the National Register of Historic Places, and in 1978, the congregation celebrated its centennial year. The German Girls' Glee Club, Porter-Gaud School Choir, and The Citadel Choir provided special music during the celebration. Former pastors and Bishop Cauble participated in the Centennial Service on April 30th. All of this history points to a congregation that has served in the Charleston area for many years, and to a faithful membership with many generations of several families. Its ministry has been not only to the residents of the city, but to the many people who come to Charleston as tourists. The donations of a Zuckerman harpsichord and handbells have greatly enhanced the music program of the congregation. Installation of a new heating and air conditioning unit, as well as a new roof for the church, and renovations to the parsonage have kept these historic buildings in excellent condition within the heart of the Ansonborough District.

Serving this congregation have been the Rev. Gary L. Safrit from 1968 to 1972; the Rev. Frank E. Lyerly, from 1972 to 1974; and the Rev. Clifford I. Riis from 1974 to the present. Organist-choir directors for this period have been Miss Louise Mathis (1941-1979), Mrs. Ann Hood (1979-1986), and Mrs. Jane Bradley (1986-present). The congregation has been active in the Rural Missions program and in the Greater Charleston Lutheran Social Services Agency. The Lutheran Church Women are involved in many service projects, including work in the Hospice, Franke Home, and Lowman Home. The Lutheran Men are primarily involved in the restoration and maintenance of the church's historic buildings.

This congregation will continue to provide a ministry to the people of its community who are looking for a small inner-city church. A recent growth in the number of young people of the congregation makes the future bright for this historic congregation.

ST. JOHN, BEAUFORT
Organized 1953
(HLCSC, pp. 698-700)

The Rev. Robert Finkbeiner concluded his ministry at St. John in 1972, and was replaced by the Rev. Olin Chassereau, who served as pastor from 1972 to 1975. During this period the congregation began participating in the Cooperative Ministries for Christ, offering a combined witness to the community, in various ways, along with churches of other denominations.

Upon the resignation of Pastor Chassereau, the Rev. Ralph Riddle was called in 1976, and he has served the congregation to the present time.

Due to its proximity to military facilities, the church ministers to a large number of military personnel and their families. Many retired military persons have also chosen to locate in the Beaufort area, and they have also become involved in the work of the congregation. This situation has encouraged the church to expand its horizons: women are taking a greater part in the work of the congregation, and St. John became integrated in 1976.

The physical facilities of the church have been improved in the period since 1970. A new fellowship building was constructed in 1978-79, and a Meditation Garden was also completed in 1979.

St. John continues to grow and faces a bright future.

ST. JOHN, CHARLESTON
Organized 1742
(HLCSC, pp. 700-702)

As an historic downtown church, St. John serves the entire metropolitan area of Charleston. The restoration and redevelopment of the downtown area has led to a revitalization of the congregation. New growth is being experienced due to movement back into the city and an increase in young adults in the area.

The Rev. Heyward W. Epting served the church for 30 years until his death in 1972. At this time the Rev. E. Armand Shealy, who had been serving as associate pastor, was called to lead the congregation and remained in that position until 1981. The Rev. Edward L. Counts began his ministry to the congregation in 1982 and continues to serve as pastor. In 1987, the Rev. C. Phillip Whitener became associate pastor.

On October 7, 1984, St. John celebrated the 250th anniversary of the first Lutheran Communion Service celebrated in South Carolina. The guest preacher and celebrant for the service was the Rev. Larry Llewellyn, pastor of Jerusalem Lutheran Church (Ebenezer), Rincon, Georgia. This was significant, because the celebrant at the service in 1734 had been the Rev. John Martin Bolzius, pastor of The Jerusalem church.

Another significant event took place in September of 1986, when St. John celebrated a joint communion service with St. Michael Episcopal Church. This, too, had historical roots. In the early nineteenth century many Episcopal clergy supplied the pulpit of St. John during pastoral vacancies. The earthquake of 1886 did considerable damage to St. Michael, and the facilities of the Lutheran church were used by the congregation until repairs were completed. Chalices which were given by St. Michael in appreciation were used at the service.

The St. John Ladies Sewing Society has been supporting Lutheran seminarians for over 160 years.

Richard Frederick, a son of the congregation, is a certified lay professional.

ST. JOHN, CLINTON
Organized 1920
(HLCSC, pp. 702-704)

Since Pastor Marion W. Clark began his work as leader of the congregation in 1971, the area in which the church building is located has undergone considerable change. A highway bypass was constructed adjacent to the church, textile employment has decreased but apparently stabilized, and housing construction has slowed. The economy has been spurred by the location of a large Presbyterian Home in Clinton and the building of a huge distribution center for a large chain store.

The congregation's strong educational ministry has been expanded by the tutoring project of its Social Ministry Committee. Besides this project, which helps disadvantaged children as well as adults learn to read, the committee was active in a successful movement to bring running water to an adjacent community. The LCW has also been very active in social ministry. The church is seeking to strengthen its ministry of and with senior citizens and to be more vigorous in its evangelistic outreach.

The median age of the membership has risen, with teenagers and over sixty-fives constituting the largest age groups. A strong cooperative youth ministry with Methodists and Episcopalians was begun in 1973, and it has proven to be a successful ecumenical witness. The congregation purchased a new parsonage in 1973 in which Pastor Clark lived until his resignation at the end of 1987.

ST. JOHN, IRMO
Organized 1914
(HLCSC, pp. 704-706)

The community that has surrounded St. John has for years been rural, but recently many new residents have moved into the community. Farms have been sold and divided into smaller tracts of land with many new homes being built. In October 1972, St. John and Bethlehem, Irmo, ended their parish relationship, and St. John became self-supporting in 1973. The Rev. H. B. Watson had served the two church parish from 1967 to 1972, and in 1973 the Rev. J. Virgil Addy began his four years of part-time service to the congregation. The first full-time pastor for St. John was the Rev. Paul B. Williams who served from 1977 to 1982. Later that same year the Rev. Raymond E. Harley II became its pastor.

Since 1970, a number of young families have joined the congregation, diversifying the family base, the age, and occupations of the membership. Throughout the years the LCW has been active with a new group recently started. The Lutheran Men organized in 1986, and the Lutheran Church Youth was re-activated in 1984. The congregation maintains a cemetery providing free burial space for active members, with space available for others upon approval and payment of a fee.

An additional two acres of land was recently purchased, giving the congregation a total of five acres. Initial plans have been completed for the construction of a new fellowship hall, and long range plans include a new educational building and sanctuary.

ST. JOHN, JOHNSTON
Organized 1903
(HLCSC, pp. 706-707)

Although this congregation had two periods of two years each when it was without a pastor, the membership of the congregation is the same size now that it was in 1970. Although the community has not experienced change and growth over the past 20 years, the congregation has seen a great internal growth and response to ministry. This is due in some part to the re-organization of the congregation's committees and program structure. The Rev. J. Cantey Nye, Jr. served for almost eleven years as pastor and, after his resignation in 1972, the Rev. John G. Anderson came to the congregation. He served until 1973, and the congregation experienced a pastoral vacancy of two years until the Rev. Roger E. Lindler began his ministry in 1975. Pastor Lindler resigned in 1978, and another two year pastoral vacancy occurred until the Rev. Voigt M. Sink, who currently serves the congregation, came in 1980.

In that same year, improvements to the church's facilities were made, including air conditioning of the parish building and parsonage, a new heating system in the parsonage, complete repainting, a new roof on the church, and restoration of the stained-glass windows, all at a cost of $40,000, which has been paid in full. Repainting the whole interior of the parish building, equipping the windows with new blinds, and equipping the office with a new copier and typewriter were completed. St. John is among the top churches of the LCA in per capita giving toward benevolence. In 1975, Rufus E. Lybrand, a son of the congregation, was ordained by the South Carolina Synod.

ST. JOHN, LEXINGTON
Organized 1832
(HLCSC, pp. 708-709)

When the Rev. Dr. H. S. Petrea ended his five year service as an interim pastor at St. John in 1972, the St. John-Providence parish called the Rev. James D. Bayne to serve both congregations. In 1974, the alliance, which was formed between the two congregations in 1969, ended as each felt the need and ability to call its own pastor. Pastor Bayne remained with St. John and continued to serve until his death in 1977. The Rev. Dr. J. Milton Frick served from 1978 to 1983, followed by the Rev. E. A. Hallman from 1983 to 1986.

During the early 1980's the physical plant of St. John underwent several significant changes. A recreation center was built in 1980. In 1983, an Allen digital computer organ was given, as well as a Maas-Rowe Symphonic Carillon-Harp. The new was incorporated with the old as a set of VibraChimes given earlier was integrated into the new organ system.

August 16, 1981, was an important date in the life of St. John as the congregation celebrated its 150th anniversary. The congregation still reflects much of its tradition in its membership which is composed to a large degree of several generations of particular families with deep Lutheran roots. But in the 1980's, St. John became increasingly aware of the community at large through its participation in Lexington Interfaith Community Services. The growing Lexington area will continue to provide opportunities and challenges in the future for growth and ministry. The Rev. Ronald Brown became the pastor in 1987.

ST. JOHN, PELION
Organized 1894
(HLCSC, pp. 708-711)

This small parish in the small, rural community of Pelion, continued to be served by the Rev. J. L. Drafts as its supply pastor. Through his ministry, the congregation was able to maintain its programs, even though its numbers diminished over the years. In 1975, construction of the educational building was completed. A part-time call was extended to the Rev. Fred S. Tate, Jr. in 1978, and he continues to serve the congregation in that manner.

ST. JOHN, POMARIA
Organized 1754
(HLCSC, pp. 711-713)

To commemorate its long and rich history, St. John in 1978 was approved for the National Register of Historic Places under the auspices of the South Carolina Department of Archives and History. Six years later, in 1984, the congregation celebrated its 230th anniversary of ministry. Much of the rich tradition is still evident around St. John, as it is preserved through artifacts on display as well as through the collective memories of the members of the congregation. For example, in conjunction with the anniversary celebration the men of the church constructed a model of the former log church building of 1754, that remains in the archives.

However, not all of St. John's attention is on its past. New and continuing programs of ministry are being carried out to meet present day needs. The Lutheran Church Women participate in a monthly volunteer sewing service for the residents of the Lowman Home. Lutheran Men loyally support the mission work of the synodical organization. A highlight of the youth ministry is the gathering of health kits for migrant workers. A tape ministry for the shut-ins of the congregation was begun in 1981. A first ecumenical venture in local ministry was a Spiritual Renewal Mission in 1984 held with Capers Chapel United Methodist Church. A Lutheran Cluster for catechetical instruction was also begun in 1986.

Recently, St. John has been served by the Rev. Austin F. Robertson (1967-1972), the Rev. David E. Kinsler (1973-1979), and the Rev. J. Henri Bishop (1980-present). James F. Kinsler, the son of Pastor Kinsler, was ordained into the ministry in 1981.

As the area around St. John continues to change and the community undergoes a transition from farming community to working class neighborhood, a major emphasis will be on evangelism as new people move into the community. In addition, a unique challenge for the congregation is a special ministry to the retired population.

ST. JOHN, SPARTANBURG
Organized 1902
(HLCSC, pp. 713-715)

A great deal has happened in this strong congregation since the Rev. Everette Lineberger began his ministry in 1963. Its steady growth in membership and programs led it to call an associate pastor in 1979. The first person to fill

this position was the Rev. Charles E. Fritz, who served until 1983. The Rev. Steven F. Marko succeeded him the same year and served until 1987; he was followed by the Rev. Marion W. Clark on January 1, 1988.

To provide for its expanding program the congregation added educational and fellowship space in 1971-2, at the same time renovating existing facilities. It became a charter member of Greater Spartanburg Ministries in 1974 and a founding partner of the Spartanburg Shepherds' Center, a service organization "of, by, and for older adults," in 1980. It continues to provide partial support for the Rev. Dr. William Peery, missionary to India, and has given generously to the LCA Strength for Mission appeal.

The economic growth of the area; the arrival of multinational corporations, bringing French, German, Swiss, Japanese, Italian, and other nationalities; and the resettlement of refugees from Uganda and Indochina have made an impact on the life of the congregation. Each year a Christmas Eve service in German is held, a practice begun in 1972.

The largest age group in the congregation is that of persons between 20 and 30. The membership, more transient than in the past, includes a large number of business and professional persons and many with non-Lutheran backgrounds. The congregation claims the Rev. R. Wayne Wood as one of its sons.

ST. JOHN, WALHALLA
Organized 1853
(HLCSC, pp. 715-717)

Under the continuing leadership of Pastor George B. Shealy the congregation renovated its educational facilities and erected a parish house, completing the project in 1972. The complexion of the congregation has changed significantly since 1970. New residents, many of whom are retirees from other areas of the United States, have enlarged the membership roll and enriched parish life.

At the beginning of 1981, following Pastor Shealy's resignation in 1980, the Rev. Robert H. Thompson II, D.Min., became the pastor. The congregation has developed a genuine concern for persons beyond the parish, as is revealed by its support of Appalachian Ministries and of a local home for battered and abused women.

In 1985, a sprinkler system was added to the church building. The LCW purchased a movie projector, a slide projector, and a speaker-equipped lectern to enhance the educational and fellowship life of the church. Since 1970, a son of the congregation, David H. Miley, has entered the Lutheran ministry.

ST. LUKE, COLUMBIA
Organized 1904
(HLCSC, pp. 717-719)

The community in which St. Luke is located has witnessed drastic changes since the late 1960's. There has been an exodus from the city. As older residents have died or moved away, homes have been turned into apartments, inhabited largely by college students and transients. The congregation has struggled to render faithful service in this situation, with a membership that has declined in numbers and increased in average age.

The Rev. Otto F. Reenstjerna served St. Luke until 1975. The Rev. John W. Withrock, Jr. was pastor from 1975 to 1977. The Rev. William Bryan Kyzer has led the congregation since 1977.

A great deal of effort over the past decade has been put into the upgrading and repair of physical facilities. In 1977, a parking lot was purchased. Heating and air conditioning systems have been replaced. A new Allen organ was purchased in 1983.

The congregation concentrates on a good quality worship service and a good Sunday School. An annual Bible School is offered, as are frequent church family nights, Word and Witness classes, and morning Bible classes. The LCW and LM are active and support synodical projects. Since there are so few young people, there is no LCY, but activities aimed at the youth are offered. Pastor and people remain strongly involved in ecumenical activities in the area.

St. Luke knows that it probably faces decreasing membership for the foreseeable future, but it is also aware that its people must be challenged to live out their individual responsibilities as the People of God. Its goal is to be faithful to the mandate from Christ and to reach people in its immediate community, serving them in the name of God.

ST. LUKE, FLORENCE
Organized 1896
(HLCSC, pp. 719-720)

During the time since 1970, St. Luke has found itself in the midst of a changing neighborhood, but has experienced little change in the type of member that it serves. The Rev. A. W. Howell has been pastor during the entire period.

The congregation continues in its ministry. A senior citizens group has been established, and the men's organization is now affiliated with the Lutheran Men of South Carolina.

Ethel Broadway, a member of the church, was selected as the first Sunday School Teacher of the Year by the South Carolina Synod. The church was renovated in 1978.

The Rev. Wayne Campbell Kannaday, a son of the congregation, was ordained in 1979.

As it faces the future in a changing situation, St. Luke is beginning to make long range plans which will involve making additions to its church building at its present site or moving to a new location.

ST. LUKE, PROSPERITY
Organized 1828
(HLCSC, pp. 720-722)

The Rev. J. Hilton Roof, who had served the congregation as its pastor since 1963, resigned in 1977. In 1978, the Rev. Henry N. Brandt accepted the congregation's call and has been its spiritual leader since. St. Luke, which is composed largely of persons who are members of families which have been in the community for generations, numbers approximately one hundred persons seventy years of age or older in its membership.

The church celebrated its 150th anniversary in 1978, having assumed its organizational year was 1828. The research by Mr. and Mrs. John V. Pugh strongly suggests, however, that the actual organization occurred a year earlier. It also lends credibility to the claim that four other Newberry County churches were established by a St. Luke pastor or as outgrowths of the congregation: Colony, Redeemer, Grace, and Silverstreet.

Recent improvements to the physical plant include the erection of a ramp for the handicapped in 1978, the paving of the parking area in 1984, and the carpeting of the nave floor in 1985.

ST. LUKE, SUMMERVILLE
Organized 1892
(HLCSC, pp. 722-723)

The Rev. T. Parker Dominick, Jr. served St. Luke from 1965 to 1974. During this period, in 1971, the parish education building was renovated, and in 1972 the fellowship hall was completed. That same year a kindergarten program for 4- and 5-year-olds began.

In 1975, the Rev. Hartmut Fege became pastor, and led the congregation until 1982. Under his leadership a Mother's Day Out program was established in 1978. In 1979, the kindergarten was expanded to include 3-year-olds. In 1982, a day care center was established. It is open six days a week. It is housed in the former parsonage, converted for this use. Susan Wilds McArver became Director of Education in 1980 and served in that capacity until 1985. The Rev. Leon A. Rawl has been pastor of St. Luke since 1983, and the Rev. Barry Harte became associate pastor in 1987.

The congregation has been experiencing rapid growth since 1970. Its baptized membership has risen from 460 to over 900. Many of its members are somewhat transient, due to the frequent moving of personnel by industry and the military. Most are well educated business and professional people. The church has had black members since 1970.

St. Luke is involved in many activities. It supports the Migrant Ministry on Johns Island and takes part in World Day of Prayer services. It has sponsored a Vietnamese family and organized a group for senior citizens. It contributes liberally to the World Hunger Appeal. There are four choirs. A church van has been purchased.

The auxiliaries at St. Luke are extremely active. The Lutheran Men sponsor an Easter breakfast and serve congregational dinners to raise money for the chapel of the McDougal Correctional Center. The Lutheran Women have adopted an American Indian girl. Each spring they hold a lunch for Lowman Home residents. They also donate Thanksgiving and Christmas gifts to them. Baskets are furnished to needy families at Christmas. Basic materials are supplied to migrant workers and to Lutheran World Relief. Assistance and support are given to a home for abused wives and children, Meals-on-Wheels, HELP, literacy programs, and other worthwhile projects. A pantry for the needy is maintained at the church.

In recent years, Youth Ministry has grown from only eight members to over 50. Members take an active role in the running of the church and in its worship life. In 1983-84 they raised thousands of dollars for World Hunger and Meals-on-Wheels. In 1985, 18 members attended the Youth Gathering at Purdue University. They participate actively in district and synodical youth programs.

A new sanctuary which will seat 450 people was constructed at a cost of over $1 million, and was dedicated in December 1987. Plans for the future include a building for administrative offices.

ST. MARK, BLYTHEWOOD
Organized 1885
(HLCSC, pp. 723-724)

The Rev. C. K. Derrick served St. Mark from 1967 to 1976. In 1977, the Rev. Rodney Gunter became pastor and remained in that position until 1982. The first year of his ministry saw important changes for the congregation: it returned to mission church status, entering a joint ministry venture with DMNA. This action was based on a decision to remain at its location and to serve the Blythewood community. During the same year the church built a new parsonage.

With the departure of Pastor Gunter, the Rev. Austin F. Robertson was called to serve as pastor, and continues to lead the congregation.

St. Mark's community is beginning to change as the "Northeast Corridor" of Columbia expands, with great growth being expected in the area in the next two decades. The congregation faces the challenge of adapting its ministry to that growth and making that ministry more inclusive.

To enlarge its opportunities to serve, the church purchased 2.9 acres of land adjacent to its property in 1984. Renovations have been made to the church building. St. Mark participates in the Greater Columbia Missionary Strategy Study.

The LCW at the church is small but active. The LM has been reorganized, and the LCY is active and well. They produced a videotape of the oral history of the congregation as part of its centennial celebration in 1985. All groups in the church were involved in preparations for this important event.

St. Mark is involved in services to people. The Word and Witness program is strong. The Social Ministry Committee is active in helping non-Lutheran families who are in need. The Holy Communion service is regularly taken to a predominantly black Community Care Home.

The goals of the congregation for the future are to recognize and meet the opportunities presented by the expected growth in the area and to equip its people to reach out to others.

ST. MARK, ISLE OF PALMS
Organized 1953
(HLCSC, pg. 725)

On April 17, 1973, St. Mark voted to sell its original facilities on Sullivan's Island and to relocate on the Isle of

Palms. Groundbreaking for the new building took place in May 1974. The first worship service was held there on Easter 1975. During the two-year interval, the congregation gathered at the Exchange Club across the street from the new facilities.

In the meantime, Pastor F. Adolph Kleindt had resigned in 1974. He had served the congregation since 1963. He was followed by the Rev. K. Michael Varn in 1975, and he led the congregation until 1979. The Rev. Eugene H. Kern was pastor from 1979-1983, and the Rev. Timothy Robinson served in that position from 1983-1986. The Rev. Russell L. Meyer became pastor on November 30, 1986.

St. Mark has witnessed the rapid transition of its area from one of summer and permanent residents to a resort community. This has led to a membership which is largely transitional and mobile. In this situation the congregation seeks to minister to residents, vacationers, and Coastal Retreat visitors. The congregation voted to become self-supporting in December 1986.

ST. MARK, PROSPERITY
Organized 1827
(HLCSC, pp. 725-727)

When the Rev. Mary W. Anderson became pastor of St. Mark in 1983, several "firsts" were accomplished for the congregation as well as for the South Carolina Synod. For the first time since at least 1870, St. Mark had the exclusive service of a full-time pastor, having been previously aligned with Corinth in a two-congregation parish. Also, since Pastor Anderson's husband, the Rev. Frank Anderson, had accepted a call to Corinth, the synod for the first time had a clergy couple serving on its territory. Pastor Mary Anderson's acceptance of the call to St. Mark also marked the first time a woman had been called to serve as the sole pastor of a congregation in the synod.

Pastors prior to the Andersons who had also served the St. Mark/Corinth Parish during the 1970's and 1980's were the Rev. Rudolph F. Ludwig (1969-1977), the Rev. Eddie C. Miller (1977-1979), and the Rev. Milas Sease (1980-1983).

In 1970, a new heating and air conditioning system was installed in the church, followed in 1973 by major renovations to the parsonage. Additional parsonage renovations were also made in 1985. In 1983, the worship life of the congregation was enhanced through the gift of a new electronic organ.

While St. Mark still maintains its traditional ties, an increased population in the Lake Murray area poses challenges for evangelism in the future, while a growing younger population within the congregation offers the possibility of increased lay leadership, witness, and ministry.

The Rev. Mary Anderson resigned in December 1987 to accept a staff position with the ELCA.

ST. MATTHEW, CAMERON
Organized 1737
(HLCSC, pp. 727-730)

Although it continues to have a very small membership, St. Matthew does remarkably well in supporting itself. Since 1970, it has purchased a new organ and made repairs to its parish building.

The Rev. G. B. Corley served the congregation, along with Resurrection, Cameron, until 1983. The Rev. David Hunter has been the pastor of both churches since 1984.

St. Matthew is the oldest congregation in the South Carolina Synod! It held its 250th anniversary celebration in 1987.

ST. MATTHEW, CHARLESTON
Organized 1840
(HLCSC, pp. 730-732)

During the last twelve years, Charleston has experienced a rebirth of the downtown business area. Tourism has also become a major industry. The redevelopment of the city has brought new downtown residents and given people in the suburbs a more secure feeling with regard to attending a downtown church. St. Matthew during this time has changed from an even membership congregation, to a growing church family. While many third generation families are still active, an ever-increasing number of new residents, military families, young singles, and professionals are joining the congregation. An active evangelism program is drawing many diverse people into the total program of the church. The congregation also reaches out to the community by providing aid to the homeless and poor through the Crisis Assistance Program, and through the Lutheran Social Services of Charleston. The 11:00 a.m. worship service is broadcast through the radio each Sunday.

The Rev. A. James Laughlin, Jr. served as pastor from 1964 to 1974. In 1975, the Rev. Dr. John L. Yost, Jr. began his ministry that continued until his retirement in 1986. Later that year, the Rev. Richard Campbell became the pastor. Serving as assistant pastors during this time have been the Rev. W. Raymond Hollifield (1971-75), the Rev. George T. Moore (1976-80), the Rev. George E. Tilley (1981-82), the Rev. R. Cecil Warren (1983-85), and the Rev. Dwight L. DuBois (since 1986).

LCW, LM, and LCY programs have been strong at St. Matthew, and each adds its unique contribution to the total ministry program of the congregation. Restoration and protection of the stained glass windows, restoration of the chancel organ, carpeting of the Sunday School rooms, and painting have been the major physical improvements completed. Involvement in ecumenical programs and the activities of the Spoleto Festival have broadened the awareness of the members of the congregation and the community to the importance of this downtown church.

ST. MATTHEW, LEXINGTON
Organized 1890
(HLCSC, pp. 732-734)

Much of the history of St. Matthew from 1970 through the 1980's has been marked by expansions in church facilities and staff. During the summer of 1976, ground was broken for a new parish building. A year later the 7,500 square foot building, consisting of eight Sunday School rooms, a conference room, fellowship hall, kitchen, and offices, was dedicated. In 1973, St. Matthew hired its first part-time secretary; organists and custodians were hired for the first time in 1978. In August 1986, the congregation became debt free by paying off the loan on a Rogers organ that was purchased in 1984. In 1987, several items of improvement were completed to the various church buildings.

During this period pastoral leadership was provided by the Rev. William E. Jeffcoat, from 1972 to 1976, the Rev. Marion C. Brazell, from 1977 to 1984, and the Rev. H. Lester Cutter, Jr., since August 1985.

Like other congregations in the rural Lexington area, St. Matthew is experiencing a period of transition as families and individuals of diverse backgrounds find their way into the area. In 1984, St. Matthew became an integrated congregation when a black family joined on April 8. Certain factions of the congregation resisted having the family join, and the congregation as a whole experienced discord while the issue was being resolved. Largely due to the perseverance of Pastor Brazell and the courage of the family members, a successful resolution was reached while a greater appreciation of the diversity of the Body of Christ was gained.

ST. MATTHEW, POMARIA
Organized 1827
(HLCSC, pp. 734-735)

The Rev. C. Alan Sellman continued to serve as pastor of the congregation until 1980. During his tenure it celebrated the 150th anniversary of its organization. The Rev. F. Adolf Kleindt became the pastor in 1980 and continues to serve.

In recent years, the congregation has seen an increase in the number both of retirees and of younger persons in its membership. This enabled it to sponsor an active LCY group as well as a growing LCW, which now has two circles. However, the same trend, together with the fact that the church is located in a slow-growing area, has created some difficulty in reaching its budgetary goals.

On May 17, 1985, the congregation observed the 100th anniversary of its present church building. Three years earlier the building was thoroughly renovated. This renovation included the replacing of wooden siding with steel, re-leading of the stained-glass windows, and installing storm windows. At the same time new lighting fixtures, including a large chandelier and wall sconces, were installed.

ST. MATTHIAS, EASLEY
Organized 1974

On September 9, 1973, a group of seventy persons gathered in the Sitton Buick Building on West Main Street in Easley for the first worship service of what was to become St. Matthias Lutheran Church. This was preceded by months of doorbell ringing and other personal contacts by Mission Developer Rev. Tommy Hamm and a small group of Lutherans living in the area who were hoping for a Lutheran church in their town. Already a building site of 3.5

acres had been acquired in 1972 through the combined efforts of the Division for Mission in North America of the LCA and the South Carolina Synod.

The preparatory work came to fruition on October 6, 1974, when the congregation was organized with 103 charter members, sixty of whom were confirmed. Pastor Hamm accepted the call to become its first pastor. In the early years of its existence, this new congregation underwent a considerable struggle and experienced slow growth in a mostly non-Lutheran environment. When Pastor Hamm resigned in 1976, the Rev. Thomas Steele succeeded him and served for fourteen months. In 1978, the Rev. William Schaeffer accepted the call to lead the church. Under his leadership the first building was erected, being completed in 1980. The congregation became self-supporting in 1982.

When Easley began to grow, spurred on by new industries from northern states relocating in the vicinity, many Lutherans moved to the city. These, together with the non-Lutheran unchurched who were reached by a sustained evangelism effort, produced a rapid increase in membership, which has tripled since its organization.

When Pastor Schaeffer resigned in 1982, he was succeeded by the Rev. Charles Fritz, who began his work in 1983 and continues to serve. The original building was found to be too small for the rapidly growing membership, and a second unit was completed in 1985.

The congregation, two-thirds of whose members are from non-Lutheran backgrounds, is composed mainly of young families and has few elderly members. It occasionally worships with churches of other denominations, its ties with the Episcopalians being especially strong. Good Friday and

Christmas Eve services are held jointly with the Episcopal Church.

St. Matthias has been greatly aided by the active auxiliary organizations: LM, LCW, and LCY. The latter two have participated regularly in community service projects, as well as in activities of the larger church. They have been active in synodical conventions and have provided leaders for district organizations.

ST. MICHAEL, COLUMBIA
Organized 1814
(HLCSC, pp. 735-737)

Although St. Michael is listed as being in Columbia, it is actually located close to the Lake Murray Dam and draws most of its membership from the surrounding area. In the past 15 years its membership has doubled, reflecting the growing population trends of the community as new construction and the migration of people from Columbia are rapidly turning the area into a suburb of the capital city.

With the influx of people coming into the area, evangelism has become a growing priority. The ministry of the congregation is also strengthened by active Lutheran Church Women, Men, and Youth auxiliaries. In order to be better prepared for the ministry opportunities in its changing context, St. Michael participated in the Parish Life and Ministry Development program in the early 1980's. In 1984, the first part-time secretary was hired. Pastors of St. Michael during the 1970's and 1980's have been the Rev. Henry Brandt (1965-1977), and the Rev. Dwight Wessinger (1978-present). Mary Williams Anderson, a member of the congregation, was ordained into the Lutheran ministry in 1983.

Changes in the church's facilities were also made to keep up with the changing situation of St. Michael. A new parsonage was built in 1975. In 1979, the ceiling was renovated and a sound system added. The year 1983 was a busy one as the church exterior was painted, the stained-glass windows restored, and an activity shelter built. Pew cushions were placed in the church in 1984. A study by the church council led to the construction of a 5,000 foot building that includes a large fellowship hall, kitchen, restrooms, six additional Sunday School rooms, and a 2,500 square foot basement for storage. Three acres of land adjoining the church property were given in 1986 to the congregation.

ST. MICHAEL, GREENVILLE
Organized 1948
(HLCSC, pp. 738-739)

In the years following 1970, the congregation continued to prosper under the guidance of Pastor Harold Skinner, who resigned in 1973. A new sanctuary had been completed the year before. Growth in both membership and service to the community have continued under the Rev. D. Luther Swicegood, who began his pastorate in 1973 and continues to serve the congregation.

In the same year (1978) in which the kindergarten was discontinued, a class for Special Christians (the mentally retarded and those with learning disabilities) was formed. The congregation is a vital part of United Ministries, an ecumenical organization serving the needs of all sorts of persons in the community. It is also part of the New Life Alliance, another ecumenical group serving the needy in the Augusta Road area. As a member of this organization St. Michael provides temporary shelter for persons in emergency situations and has sponsored refugee families. The congregation now emphasizes its ministry to the elderly.

Physical improvements include the purchase of the Chaplin House in 1977, the construction of a fellowship hall in 1979, the installation of a pipe organ in 1981, and the addition of a parking lot in 1983. A church administrator was added to the staff in 1982, and an evangelism coordinator the following year. The congregation reports that its members, whose average age is 34, are mostly white-collar workers, are mostly from LCA backgrounds, and include a large number of college graduates.

ST. MICHAEL, MONCKS CORNER
Organized 1964
(HLCSC, pp. 737-738)

St. Michael has had four pastors in the period since 1970. The Rev. John E. Wertz served the congregation from 1971 to 1977. Highlights of this period include the celebration of the church's tenth anniversary in November 1974, and the fact that St. Michael became self-supporting in 1977.

The Rev. B. Fulmer Shealy was pastor from 1978 to 1982. During his ministry the C. E. Wolff Lutheridge Scholarship Fund was established by the members of Mr. Wolff's family in 1980. A picnic shelter was built in 1981.

The Rev. Eddie C. Miller, Jr. led the congregation from 1983 to 1986. In 1984, the twentieth anniversary was celebrated, the by-laws were updated, and St. Michael was able to pay off its loan to the Board of American Missions. The LCW and LM were reorganized during this period.

The Rev. Clarence K. Derrick has been pastor since October 1986. In that year the congregation sold the parsonage to him. The mortgage on the sanctuary was burned on January 25, 1987.

ST. NICHOLAS, FAIRFAX
Organized 1800
(HLCSC, pp. 739-741)

St. Nicholas has attempted to carry out its ministry in the 1970's and 80's despite a shrinking population in the area. After the departure of the Rev. Ernest Burns who had led the congregation since 1968, the Rev. Tommy Hamm served this congregation as well as Trinity, Fairfax from 1976 to 1984. In 1987, the Rev. Eddie C. Miller, Jr. became their pastor.

ST. PAUL, AIKEN
Organized 1907
(HLCSC, pp. 741-743)

One change in pastoral leadership has occurred at St. Paul during the 1970's. In 1979, the Rev. John B. McCullough resigned, having served as St. Paul's pastor since

1948. In the same year that Pastor McCullough resigned, the Rev. William R. Cobb accepted the call to follow him as pastor. In 1983, the congregation entered the intern program of Southern Seminary and has received an intern every year since then.

In 1985, a member of the congregation, Craig W. Versprille, was ordained into the Lutheran ministry.

ST. PAUL, COLUMBIA
Organized 1886
(HLCSC, pp. 743-745)

In the period since 1970, St. Paul has become an inner-city church with all of the problems and opportunities that represents. In response to its situation, the congregation has developed several special programs and activities; midday and afternoon worship services for the downtown community, a weekly radio program, and morning Bible studies. It has sponsored eight Vietnamese refugees, developed a Child Care Ministry program, works with Literacy programs, and houses and helps support the Ministry With the Deaf Congregation.

During its transitional period, the church has been served by a number of pastors. The Rev. Leroy Trexler and the Rev. Raymond E. Harley, II served St. Paul as pastor and associate pastor until 1975. In 1977, the Rev. Ralph J. Wallace was called as pastor and continues in that position to the present. The Rev. Wayne W. Young was assistant pastor from 1979 to 1981, and that position was held by the Rev. Beverly D. Alexander from 1981 to 1985.

St. Paul is proud that it led all synod congregations in giving to Newberry College in the IQE campaign and in support of the Lowman Home. It was also among the leaders in giving to the LCA's World Hunger Appeal. The church also supports a missionary to Japan.

In 1987, St. Paul celebrated its 100th Anniversary. While the celebrations included the traditional banquet, the printing of a church history, "Century Book," a "McCullough Homecoming," and special services, the heart of the 100th Anniversary Celebration was the reaching out by St. Paul to help others. Special gifts of $10,000 each were presented to Southern Seminary, Newberry College, the Lowman Home, and Lutheridge. The Division for World Mission and Ecumenism was given $15,000, and a special $20,000 fund was established to support the work of an evangelism specialist in the congregation for one year.

One son, the Rev. K. Michael Varn, was ordained in 1975.

Although the mean age of the congregation has become lower recently and there is a very active young adult group, the congregation maintains a core of loyal and supportive older members. Its goals for the future include the development of major Youth and Educational Ministry programs.

ST PAUL, GAFFNEY
Organized 1971
(HLCSC, pp. 745-746)

This young congregation has had to face a number of difficulties since its organization in 1971. Located in a non-Lutheran part of South Carolina, its growth has been slow.

Loss of jobs in the textile industry led many of the members to relocate elsewhere. The Rev. William B. Kyzer continued to serve as pastor until 1977. Under his guidance the congregation erected a building, in which the first service was held on November 23, 1975.

When the Rev. Roger E. Lindler began his work as pastor in 1978, he noticed that there was some movement into the area by persons from northern states who found Gaffney a good place to retire. An Allen organ was installed in the church in 1980, with the kitchen renovation, done by the

LCW, following in 1981. A ramp for the use of the handicapped was built in 1983, while the LM constructed a storage shed the following year. The mortgage on the parsonage was liquidated and the congregation became self-supporting in 1984. The position of part-time Secretary, begun in 1978, was changed to Parish Worker in 1985, with increased hours and responsibility in Christian Education and visitation.

About one-half of the members come from non-Lutheran background. All age groups are well represented in the membership, with approximately one-third being of school age. The congregation's concern for others may be noted from such acts as the contribution of $450 to the Lowman Home Indigent Care Fund and $400 to St. Peter, Litchfield Beach as part of St. Paul Self-Support Celebration, and support of the local Meals-on-Wheels program at the rate of $450 per year. For several years it has cooperated with the local Episcopal Church in conducting a vacation Bible school.

Following a survey of members and friends of the congregation in the Spring of 1987, the Stewardship Committee recommended the beginning of a Building Addition Fund Drive for much needed educational space. A Building Committee was appointed in the Summer of 1987, and a fund drive was started.

ST. PAUL, GILBERT
Organized 1803
(HLCSC, pp. 746-748)

The growing ministry of this congregation can be seen in the development of a new LCW Circle called "Joy" in 1985, the organization and charter of an LM Unit in 1985, and the re-organization of the LCY program. Much of this growth in ministry comes from the recent increase in the membership of the congregation as the community of Lexington and the development of the Lake Murray areas nearby continue to grow. This growth should have a significant impact on St. Paul as it moves into the 1990's.

In 1985, the congregation also began regular support of

the Rev. Jerry Livingston, missionary in Japan. "Son-lighters," an organization for members who are 50 plus, was begun in 1983, and they have an active program. The Social Ministry Committee of the congregation has greatly expanded its work to include visiting the sick and shut-in; maintaining a food pantry; sponsoring blood pressure checks once a month; and adopting a family with special needs at Christmas.

The Rev. Roy W. Werner served as pastor from 1966 to 1976, succeeded by the Rev. J. Gordon Peery from 1977 to 1982, and the congregation is currently served by the Rev. Larry W. Smith, who began his ministry there in 1983. Goals of the congregation include equipping the members for evangelism to reach the new residents who move into the area, and providing new facilities to meet the needs of a growing congregation with expanding programs. Construction is underway that will enlarge the assembly room and provide additional classrooms.

ST. PAUL, MOUNT PLEASANT
Organized 1884
(HLCSC, pp. 748-750)

The area served by St. Paul has experienced rapid growth in recent years, and the church has also grown.

The Rev. William C. Ebener continued to serve this congregation until 1974. Under his leadership a nave, educational, and office building were constructed. Ground was broken for the structure in 1971, and the first worship service was held on September 10, 1972.

The Rev. H. Gene Beck has been pastor of St. Paul since 1975.

ST. PAUL, POMARIA
Organized 1761
(HLCSC, pp. 750-752)

The Rev. R. Delano Ricard became the pastor in 1971 and continues to serve in that capacity. He provided leadership for the significant celebration of the congregation's 225th anniversary in 1986, which culminated in a well-attended outdoor pageant depicting the long history of the church. An Allen Digital Organ was dedicated that same year.

The congregation continues to be a stable Lutheran influence in Newberry County. Most of its members come from families whose affiliation with the congregation can be traced back several generations. It has a large, active Golden Age group, with eligibility beginning at age seventy.

Some new members from non-Lutheran backgrounds are being received. Most of the working members are employed in textile and other manufacturing. The congregation has provided important support for the World Hunger Appeal and foreign-mission activities. The auxiliaries (LCW, LM, and LCY) continue to be active locally and synodically. A Word and Witness program provided incentive for broadening the congregation's outreach to the community.

ST. PETER, BATESBURG
Organized 1849
(HLCSC, pp. 752-753)

Although St. Peter is one of the smallest congregations in the South Carolina Synod, it nevertheless has remained an important part of the lives of its members and the families it has served since its organization in 1849. In fact, only since April 1986 has St. Peter had services with preaching on every Sunday. Previously the congregation shared supply pastors with Immanuel, Ridge Spring, and held preaching services on every other Sunday. The Rev. Dr. S. W. Hahn served as supply pastor from 1962 to 1976. The Rev. Hubert Dunlap has served in this capacity since 1977.

Other changes besides weekly worship services have also recently been undertaken. A new electric organ was donated in 1974. A major remodeling effort was undertaken in

1983. Included was the addition of two rooms and a porch, as well as bricking the exterior of the building. Stained-glass windows were installed, along with the renovation of the interior of the sanctuary. Central heating and air conditioning was also included.

St. Peter continues to be a congregation with a few family names extending far into the past. The Lowman family, which was instrumental in the organization of the church in the mid-1840's, is still represented on the roll.

ST. PETER, CHAPIN
Organized 1794
(HLCSC, pp. 753-755)

St. Peter is still sometimes referred to as "Piney Woods" because of its original setting, surrounded by a heavily wooded area of long-leaf pines. But the congregation is traditional in other ways as well. Several generations of the same families still predominate in the membership of St. Peter, and even now some former members who moved to Columbia are moving back to the Chapin area and re-establishing their ties with the congregation. Such a stable setting provides a strong base of support for programs in the congregation and ministry to its members.

For a large portion of St. Peter's recent past, pastoral ministry was provided by the Rev. John D. Zeigler, who retired in October 1981 after thirty-three years of ministry to the congregation. He was followed in September 1982, by the Rev. Boyd F. Cook, who served until July 1987. In 1985, St. Peter became involved in Southern Seminary's Internship program.

Several recent improvements have been made to the church property. In 1983, a new parsonage was dedicated debt-free. The parking lot was also paved and extended that same year. In 1984, the stained glass was restored and protected, while in 1986, the heating system was renovated, the brick exterior of the church remortared, and the addition of a covered porch and ramp to the church entrance were completed. In 1987, the congregation added an additional rank of pipes and revoiced the Zimmer pipe organ that was installed in 1974.

Much growth is anticipated in the Lake Murray area around St. Peter in the near future. A major challenge for the congregation will be to continue its strong ministry among its traditional membership while reaching out and incorporating newcomers to the community.

ST. PETER, LEXINGTON
Organized 1780
(HLCSC, pp. 755-757)

Among the highlights for the St. Peter congregation in recent years was the celebration in 1980 of its bicentennial. The occasion was noted with a special thanksgiving cantata, historical drama, and publication of a congregational history recalling 200 years of ministry in Lexington County. Serving as pastor at the time was the Rev. Charles B. Dawkins, who served the congregation from 1977 to 1987. Prior to his arrival, the congregation was served by the Rev. Dermon A. Sox, Jr. (1965-1977). In 1985, another anniversary was observed as the Lutheran Church Women sponsored a celebration of 50 years of ministry by Pastor and Mrs. Dermont F. Swicegood. Pastor Swicegood had joined the staff as a visitation minister that same year.

Other notable events in the recent life of St. Peter include its role in the organization of Lexington Interfaith Community Services in 1978, and involvement with Methodist, Episcopal, Roman Catholic, and other Lutheran congregations in a Lenten pulpit exchange. A carillon set was installed in 1981, and the church parking lot was improved and expanded in 1985. A new music room was developed in the basement in 1986 as a memorial gift.

In 1975, St. Peter hosted the Synod ordination service as a member of its own ranks, Roger E. Lindler, entered the ministry. In 1979, two of its members, Jerry Bryan Arnold and W. Edward Shealy, were ordained into the Baptist ministry.

ST. PETER, PAWLEYS ISLAND
Organized 1984

The Rev. Hartmut Fege arrived in Pawleys Island in late 1982, and during the early spring of the next year was busy as mission developer. The first worship service of St. Peter was held in the Litchfield Inn on Easter Sunday 1983, with 305 persons in attendance. Pastor Fege led the service. The congregation was organized on October 7, 1984, with 98 charter members.

The present membership of St. Peter reflects the population of its surroundings—a retirement and recreation area. Half of its members are from non-Lutheran backgrounds, and over half are more than 50 years old.

The congregation participates with other churches in joint Good Friday and Thanksgiving services, the Pawleys Island Ministerial Association, and Ecumenical Ministries. Men's and women's groups have been organized and are functioning.

Since 1984, St. Peter has moved its place of worship from the Litchfield Inn to the Waccamaw School. One of its goals is to construct a first unit for its services on property along Highway 17.

ST. PHILIP, MYRTLE BEACH
Organized 1956
(HLCSC, pp. 757-758)

In the period since 1970, St. Philip has grown to over 500 baptized members, but growth is now slowing due to the close proximity of other Lutheran congregations. The population in the immediate area is becoming older and more retirees are joining the church. One of the goals of St. Philip is to develop more fully its retirement ministry. Being in a resort area, the church also seeks to serve the large "snow bird" population that associates with it from January through March.

Much work has been done on the buildings and grounds in the last decade. The period of 1976-77 saw extensive renovation to the nave and the building of a fellowship hall. In 1981, a carillon was installed. Extensive work was done to the grounds in 1982. The offices were renovated in 1983, and a computer system was installed in 1985.

The congregation is involved in ecumenical and community activities. It cooperates in Mobile Meals, Campground Ministry, and Helping Hand. It also participates with the Grand Strand Pastoral Counseling Center, Associated Charities, and Community Volunteer Services. Support is also provided for a missionary.

The Rev. William F. Wingard served as pastor of this congregation from its organization in 1956 until his retirement in 1987. In 1978, he was joined in ministry by Cynthia H. Moore, certified lay professional, and in 1983, by associate pastor W. Richard Albert, who became pastor in 1987.

ST. PHILIP, NEWBERRY
Organized 1881
(HLCSC, pp. 758-760)

The years since 1970 have been a time of growth for the congregation—in membership, in service to the community, and in the quality of its property. The Rev. Clarence G. Walck, Jr. resigned at the end of 1978 and was succeeded by the Rev. Wilbur D. Miller in 1979.

In 1981, an elevator for the handicapped was installed, in 1982 a new parsonage was built next to the church, and in 1984 the fellowship hall was renovated. The purchase of a new activity bus has greatly helped in the activities of the youth and Golden Age groups.

The congregation has offered its facilities for schools of religion for the Newberry District on several occasions. Significant contributions were made by the church to the World Hunger Appeal, to the local tornado relief, and to the Newberry County Department of Social Services.

St. Philip remains a stable, traditional Lutheran body, with its members tending away from farming toward work in neighboring industries and the professions. An increasing number of its members are college graduates.

ST. STEPHEN, LEXINGTON
Organized 1830
(HLCSC, pp. 760-762)

St. Stephen was the first Lutheran church to be organized in the Lexington community, and by 1986 remained the largest Lutheran congregation in the area with a baptized membership of over 800 persons. The growth in the membership of St. Stephen has been accompanied by an equally significant growth in the ministry of the congregation. Especially important has been an expanding ministry to the surrounding community, as evidenced through St. Stephen's role in Lexington Interfaith Community Services, and the congregation's role in establishing a thrift shop for clothing, a food bank, and an emergency fund to help the needy of the Lexington area. Among the more notable ministries of the congregation was its sponsorship of a Vietnamese refugee family in 1984.

Changes in staffing and facilities have run parallel with the increased ministry. The Rev. J. Milton Frick served as pastor from 1967 to 1975. He was followed by the Rev. Leroy Trexler from 1975 to 1978. The Rev. Thomas W. Corbell has served as the pastor of St. Stephen since 1979. In 1983, Ronald Feltman was added to the staff as Director of Christian Education. He was followed in that same year by Ina Berkey. Following Mrs. Berkey's departure, the position was changed to Director of Special Ministries and was filled by Cheryl Brannon in 1985. The Rev. Otto F. Reenstjerna, a retired pastor living in Lexington, joined the staff in 1984 as a visitation pastor, and served through 1986. The Rev. Stephen C. Bailey began his ministry as associate pastor in September 1987. In 1983, St. Stephen gave two sons to the ministry, the Rev. Richard A. Poole and the Rev. Thomas Steele, Jr.

The 1970's and 1980's have also brought many physical changes to St. Stephen. Between the summer of 1972 and October of 1973, a new social hall, kitchen, parlor, music room, and storage space were added. A Moeller organ was installed in 1979. A carillon system was added in 1980. Since that time numerous renovations have been made to the existing physical plant.

With new industry bringing more people into the Lexington community, St. Stephen is finding that its membership is becoming more diverse. Once made up primarily of people with deep Lexington County roots, today around 50 percent of the membership have moved in from outside the Lexington area, many from non-Lutheran backgrounds. As more people become part of the congregation's roster, St. Stephen will place a greater emphasis on lay involvement in its total ministry. An initial step is the congregation's involvement in the national program of Stephen's Ministry which trains lay persons in caregiving to people in need or crisis situations.

ST. THOMAS, CHAPIN
Organized 1876
(HLCSC, pp. 762-763)

The doubling of the membership of this congregation since 1970 has resulted in several building projects, and the development and expansion of ministry programs for the congregation and the community. The 1937 church building

was torn down, and in 1972, groundbreaking was held for the new sanctuary with a fellowship hall, classrooms, and office space. This building, with much of the construction work done by members of the congregation, was dedicated in 1976 at a cost of $100,000. A new 2,400 square foot parsonage was completed in 1978 at a cost of $58,000, and a new heating and air conditioning unit was installed in the church building in 1984 at a cost of $51,000. The Lutheran Men planned and constructed a picnic shelter seating over 200 under cover, and the Lutheran Church Women funded the concrete paving of the shelter area. The LM group has also constructed a playground area for the use of the congregation's and community's young children. All mortgages on these construction projects have been retired with the exception of indebtedness on the heating and air conditioning system.

The rapid influx of new residents on Lake Murray has profoundly changed the community and resulted in the doubling of the congregation's membership. It also led to the establishment of Presbyterian, Episcopal, Baptist and Roman Catholic congregations in a community that had been predominately Lutheran. The congregation is now challenged to minister to a diverse resort community focused on recreation and retirement, yet to minister from a community based in traditional rural values. The worship life has become the central focal point for creating and sustaining the community among the congregation, and has thus become re-vitalized. A paid choir director and organist have been added to the staff. A growing ministry with older persons has developed, and the LCW sponsors a sewing circle at the Lowman Home. The congregation has also recently participated in ecumenical activities with the Episcopal church.

Goals for this congregation include continued integration of new residents into the congregational family; the development of a ministry program that can include both "old" and "new"; and construction of additional facilities for classes, fellowship, and offices.

The Rev. Dwight C. Wessinger is a son of this congregation; the Rev. Matthew O. Moye, Jr. served as pastor from 1972 to 1979, and the Rev. Robert I. Miles, Jr. continues the ministry he began in 1980.

ST. TIMOTHY, CAMDEN
Organized 1951
(HLCSC, pp. 763-764)

The Rev. David H. Herbertson continued to serve St. Timothy until 1972. During this time, the congregation experienced some financial difficulties. They abolished the pledge system they had been using for years and adopted a policy of faith giving that included the congregation's commitment to pay its benevolence apportionment first, before current expenses. Since that time, financial support has been excellent, both for the local work of the congregation and for the wider support of the church's ministry.

After the departure of Pastor Herbertson, the Rev. Everett A. Dasher served as pastor from 1973 to 1981. In 1977, the congregation began participating in a community

Lenten Series that includes the Roman Catholic, Episcopal, Baptist, Presbyterian, and United Methodist churches. In 1984, an interdenominational Lay School of Religion was founded, and they participate in the Community Thanksgiving Service. All of these programs have visibly strengthened the Christian community of Camden. In 1987, shared services of Holy Communion were begun with the Episcopal Church.

The Rev. James B. Park has led the congregation since 1982. A new sanctuary was constructed in that year with the Rev. Dr. James S. Aull, Secretary of Synod and a former pastor of the congregation, leading the Service of Dedication. Eleven stained-glass windows were added in 1986.

Community growth has leveled off recently, but the confirmed membership has increased over 50% since 1970. The membership now represents a broader spectrum of the community than previously, with a wider range of ages and an increased diversity of backgrounds; and it continues to grow.

Through the years, programs have been expanded and strengthened, including the Confirmation Ministry program, an additional adult Sunday School class, the Word and Witness program, a weekly adult Bible study class, the addition of handbell choirs, the establishment of an LM group, a third circle to an already active LCW program, and the upgrading of the Youth Ministry program. Full support continues to be given to Synodical and LCA programs and appeals, and the congregation has been very supportive of the World Hunger Appeal. In 1985, the "In the Name of Christ Fund" was established to help people in Kershaw County with special needs. St. Timothy has also made special gifts to mission congregations in South Carolina. The congregation celebrated its 35th Anniversary in 1986 with a special service honoring the charter members, including the first pastor, the Rev. J. Shelton Moose.

The congregation continues to strengthen its worship and ministry programs, being more responsive to the human needs of the community as well as of its members, and at the same time to upgrade its facilities, especially those needed for educational ministry programs. It will also burn the mortgage on its five-year-old sanctuary in early 1988.

ST. TIMOTHY, GOOSE CREEK
Organized 1964
(HLCSC, pp. 764-766)

St. Timothy is located in a rapidly expanding area. Business, industry and naval facilities have grown in recent years. There is a housing boom in the area. Congregational membership has grown, too. More professionals have joined the church, as have people of diverse backgrounds and callings. In 1970, St. Timothy was 80% military. Now only 25% are involved in active military service.

The Rev. John F. Fischer served as pastor until 1981. During his ministry the congregation almost doubled the size of its facilities: Sunday School, office, and worship spaces were expanded at a cost of $135,000.

The Rev. Earl T. Knaus III led St. Timothy from 1982 to 1984, and the Rev. Albert B. Moravitz has been pastor from 1984 to the present.

The church gives strong support to the Lutheran Social Services Center of the Greater Charleston area. It has fielded a number of athletic teams, and sponsors a Boy Scout troop. The LCW has been very active in supporting benevolence projects. It works with My Sister's House, a shelter for battered women and children, Jenkins Orphanage, the North Charleston Convalescent Center, the John's Island Rural Mission and many other special projects.

The growth and change in its membership present many challenges to St. Timothy as it seeks to incorporate new members into its congregational life. Facilities must be expanded; and growth in stewardship is a significant challenge. Because of the youth of its membership, leadership training has become an important part of the ministry program.

ST. TIMOTHY, WHITMIRE
Organized 1939
(HLCSC, pp. 766-767)

The Rev. Ralph Riddle continued to serve as the pastor until 1975. Improvements to the sanctuary during his ministry include the addition of chimes, a sanctuary lamp, and a white cross, which was installed on the front gable.

Pastor Ronald Roscoe arrived in late 1976 and served until early 1979. He was succeeded by the Rev. W. Earl Jernigan, who began his work in 1980. In that year, stained-glass windows were installed as memorial gifts, providing beauty and symbolism to enhance the worshipful nature of the sanctuary. In 1981, a processional cross, a communion rail, and kneeling pads for the rail were given as memorials. The following year the narthex, the nave, and the chancel were completely renovated. The LCW began the Chrismon Tree tradition in 1982 by making 172 Chrismons, a project coordinated by Mrs. Faye Jenkins Baker.

After Pastor Jernigan resigned in 1983, the Union-Whitmire Parish was dissolved. Since then St. Timothy has been served by the Rev. J. Paul Rimmer on a part-time basis. In 1986, a sound system was added to the nave and a new heating/air conditioning system was installed.

Congregational growth has been slow, due in part to the unfavorable economic situation in the area served by the church. St. Timothy has begun to participate in a Community Vacation Church School with the local Methodist and Presbyterian churches.

SANDY RUN, SWANSEA
Organized 1765
(HLCSC, pp. 767-769)

The biggest challenge faced by Sandy Run in the fifteen years from 1970 to the middle 1980's has been to sustain its membership and ministry, without benefit of full-time pastoral leadership most of that time. The Rev. Rodney Gunter served as pastor of both Sandy Run and Good Shepherd in Swansea from 1973 to 1977, followed by the Rev. James Butt, who also served both congregations from 1978 to 1979. Seminarians and a lay supply, Mr. Earl Smith, provided leadership for the congregation until the Rev. Charles E. Seastrunk, Jr. became a part-time supply in 1984. The congregation has met its challenge, growing in membership from 93 baptized members in 1970 to around 120 by 1985. In 1986, the Rev. Alice D. Klatt became the pastor.

Sandy Run will maintain its ministry in this small community, and hopes that future development in close proximity to Columbia will provide it with opportunities for growth.

SHEPHERD OF THE SEA, GARDEN CITY
Organized 1975

A survey of the Surfside area, which was conducted by the LCA in 1973, revealed the need for a Lutheran congregation. In September of 1974 the Rev. Bob Tutas began his work as mission developer. A small storefront site was rented in Pavilack Square, and a small group of people began planning for the future congregation.

The first service of Shepherd of the Sea was held on February 2, 1975, with 102 persons in attendance. The congregation was officially organized on November 30, 1975.

The church grew quickly and the need for a building was

urgent. Property originally purchased in Surfside for a building site was traded for a lot in Garden City in order to take advantage of projected growth in that area. Groundbreaking for the new church home took place on Palm Sunday, March 19, 1978.

Pastor Tutas resigned in May of 1978, but construction continued. Pastor Darrel D. Golnitz began his work with the congregation in December of 1978 and served until 1986.

In January 1979, Shepherd of the Sea began worshiping in the fellowship hall of its new building and then in the new sanctuary. The women of the church made the paraments. In 1982, a new six-and-a-half-rank organ was built, and its installation was marked with concerts by leading organists.

In the period from 1980 to 1984, the church continued to grow, with many young families joining the congregation, and it became necessary to expand facilities for Christian education and community service. Construction began in August of 1983, and the newly completed building was dedicated on February 5, 1984.

The church continues to minister to its people. A Vacation Church School was begun in 1979, and Word and Witness classes in 1980. Communion has been offered weekly since 1981. The first youth retreat program was held in 1984.

Shepherd of the Sea is involved in many ecumenical and community activities. It helped to organize the Ecumenical Clothes Closet and Mobile Meals of Surfside Beach and Garden City. The congregation has participated in a joint communion service with the Episcopal Church of the Resurrection. The women of the church send items to Lutheran World Relief and to the residents of Lowman Home.

In 1985, Shepherd of the Sea was pleased to celebrate its tenth anniversary. The Rev. Ruben H. Olawsky became its pastor January 1, 1987.

SILVERSTREET, SILVERSTREET
Organized 1908
(HLCSC, pp. 771-772)

In 1974, the Rev. Horace J. C. Lindler, who had been the pastor since 1968, resigned and was succeeded by the Rev. E. Arden Hallman, who began his ministry at Silverstreet in 1975. When he resigned in 1981 to accept a call to special service, the congregation called the Rev. D. Rodney Gunter to become its leader. Pastor Gunter arrived in 1982 and continues to provide pastoral leadership for the congregation.

The members of the congregation are earning a living less and less from farming and more and more from work in industry, businesses, and the professions. Although the over-seventy age group is growing there is also a large number of children in the membership. The congregation benefits from the work and support of the LM, LCW, and LCY. One of its goals is to become more aware of social needs within the congregation and the community.

A major addition to the church building was completed in 1977, providing space for a church office, as well as for educational and fellowship activities. The mortgage on this facility was burned in 1985. The LM led in the construction of the Lutheran Service Shelter of Silverstreet, dedicated in 1983. In 1979, 1.7 acres of land was added to the church property to provide for cemetery growth in the future. A perpetual care policy and fund were established.

SUMMER MEMORIAL, NEWBERRY
Organized 1910
(HLCSC, pp. 769-770)

After the Rev. J. Pierce Evans, who had been the pastor since 1968, resigned in 1975 to accept a call to another synod, the Rev. Robert E. McCollum succeeded him and remained the pastor until 1984. The Rev. John F. Weaver arrived that same year to assume the pastoral leadership of the congregation and continues in that role.

The congregation has survived the closing of two Newberry textile mills in 1977, the tornado of 1984, and the static situation of its community. It focuses upon serving the needs of its growing elderly membership. Closed-circuit TV relays the service in the sanctuary to handicapped/elderly seated in the lounge on the lower level. Video tapes of the worship service are taken to the homes of shut-ins.

The congregation has become involved in the Newberry County Interfaith Community Services and joins nearby Baptist and Methodist congregations in senior citizens' programs as well as for Easter and Thanksgiving programs.

A major addition to the church building was completed in 1980. This included a fellowship hall and kitchen, administrative offices, choir room, lounge, and classrooms. In 1984, a house and lot adjoining the church property was purchased. The LM has been reorganized and has become a very active and productive part of the congregation. The LCW continues its long tradition of service in many areas. The congregation is seeking to develop the ministry of the laity and has begun a Word and Witness program to promote that emphasis.

TRANSFIGURATION, CAYCE
Organized 1954
(HLCSC, PP. 772-773)

By the time the early 1970's arrived, Transfiguration, with a baptized membership of 535 persons, recognized the need for a new sanctuary to accommodate the increased membership. In September 1973, an architect was hired and plans were put on the board for a new worship facility. Ground was broken in August 1975. Construction continued until October 1976 when the sanctuary was completed and dedicated.

From 1962 to 1983, Transfiguration was led by the Rev. C. P. Fisher, the third pastor in the congregation's history. Following his retirement, Pastor Fisher was succeeded by the Rev. William C. Ebener, who began his work at Transfiguration in 1984. Henry M. Moody, Jr., a charter baptized member of the congregation, was ordained as a pastor in the synod on May 5, 1977.

After having experienced rapid growth in the early years of its existence, Transfiguration found that its growth had stabilized by the 1970's, as the Cayce area was becoming more commercial with less room for additional residential development. Also noteworthy is the fact that the average age of the surrounding community has been rising as the number of retired persons has increased while the number of school-aged children and youth has begun to decline. However, in the mid 1980's Transfiguration, with an average age in membership of 40-45 years, remains a relatively young and suburban congregation with a growing ministry as once again young families began to populate the area surrounding the church.

TRINITY, COLUMBIA
Organized 1970
(HLCSC, pg. 773)

As a quickly growing young congregation, Trinity has had to expend a great deal of its time and resources in the building of its physical plant.

The Rev. Edward L. Counts remained as pastor of the church until 1982. Under his leadership the church building, of a contemporary design, was constructed in 1973-74. It was dedicated on September 15, 1974. Its tracker organ was a gift of Trinity Lutheran church (Missouri Synod) of New York City. Members of the congregation went to New York, dismantled the organ and brought it to Columbia. Many of the sanctuary furnishings came from the chapel of the convent of the Little Sisters of the Poor at Savannah, Ga. The altar, pulpit and baptismal font were handcrafted by members of the congregation. In addition to the sanctuary, the new building contained an office, nursery, kitchen, and a large room used for Sunday School classes.

A second and smaller building was constructed debt free in 1975. Most of the labor for this building was supplied by members. A third building, containing classrooms, kitchen and gymnasium was dedicated on September 16, 1979.

From 1977 through 1980, changes were made in the first two buildings. More space was provided for worship by removing the wall separating the sanctuary from the Sunday School room. The narthex was enlarged and two offices and a library were added within the second building.

In 1983, the Rev. Keith A. McDaniel became pastor of Trinity and has continued to serve to the present. The congregation participates in ecumenical Lenten and Thanksgiving services, God's Storehouse, and the Columbia area soup kitchen.

One son of the congregation, Jeffrey Kent Lageman, was ordained in 1976.

TRINITY, ELLOREE
Organized 1849
(HLCSC, pp. 774-775)

Although the membership numbers for Trinity reflect a decline since 1970, the last couple of years have brought growth to the community and to the congregation. The Santee area, seven miles from Elloree, is rapidly becoming a major retirement community, and a major industry recently located in Elloree. Both of these factors have brought new membership into Trinity.

The congregation participates in the Fifth Sunday Night Community Services which is an interdenominational program in Elloree. The congregation has four active LCW circles and an active LCY program. In 1984, an Allen electronic organ was installed. Serving Trinity have been the Rev. J. Luther Ballentine from 1958 to 1980, the Rev. James F. Kinsler from 1981 to 1985, and the Rev. Ronald W. Feltman from 1986 to 1987.

TRINITY, FAIRFAX
Organized 1906
(HLCSC, pp. 775-777)

Trinity church has experienced a small but steady growth since 1970. After the departure of the Rev. Ernest Burns who had served the congregation since 1968, the Rev. Tommy J. Hamm led this congregation as well as St. Nicholas, Fairfax from 1976 to 84. The Rev. Eddie C. Miller, Jr. became their pastor in 1987.

Several projects, important to the congregation, have been undertaken during this period. The parsonage was renovated in 1976, the church in 1977, and stained-glass windows were installed in 1987. A softball field was completed in 1978.

TRINITY, GEORGETOWN
Organized 1945
(HLCSC, pp. 777-778)

Even though a severe economic depression in the Georgetown area has caused much movement out of that part of the state, Trinity has been able to maintain growth in its membership since 1970. The congregation has had four pastors during this time. The Rev. Clifford A. Riis was pastor from 1966 to 1974. In the period from 1975 to 1978, the Rev. Rufus E. Lybrand, Jr. led the church. The Rev. Carl O. Isaacson served from 1979 to 1984, and the Rev. Paul W. Baumgartner served as pastor from 1984 through 1986.

In January 1982, groundbreaking ceremonies were held for a new multi-purpose unit, which includes administration, educational, and fellowship facilities, and is handi-

capped accessible. The new building was dedicated on June 6 of the same year.

Some of the congregation's important programs are Word and Witness, establishment of a day care and pre-school, development of a group for community senior citizens, and a weekly Bible study.

Trinity also participates in ecumenical activities, including a shared communion with Prince George, Winyah Episcopal Church, a community Easter service, funding for ministry to transient persons in the area, and youth activities with other denominations.

The auxiliaries of the church function primarily to provide distinctly Lutheran opportunities for fellowship, education and service in a non-Lutheran community. About half of the members of the LCY are "teen friends," non-members from the community.

Two sons of the congregation, Charles W. Easley and Haco von Hacke, have been ordained into the ministry.

Trinity continues to be faced with a major movement out of the community. In this situation an important challenge to the congregation is to gain the personal commitment of each member to the work of the church. Community relations and evangelism are high priorities as Trinity attempts to continue as an active Lutheran voice of Christianity and to seek out the unchurched in its area.

TRINITY, GREENVILLE
Organized 1909
(HLCSC, pp. 778-780)

When the Rev. Bernard L. Trexler retired at the end of June 1983, he had established an enviable record of 22 years of service as pastor of the congregation. In 1972, an associate pastor was added to the staff in the person of the Rev. Robert G. Coon. Pastor Coon served in that capacity until Pastor Trexler's retirement, whereupon he became the pastor. In 1973, Louise R. Waldrep became Director of Christian Education, a position she held until 1981, when she became Director of the Day School. E. Ray Mohrman joined the staff in 1983 as Director of Parish Ministries.

When the kindergarten area and the church nave were renovated in 1980, a Steiner tracker action organ was installed, all at a cost of $350,000. The physical improvements have been matched by the congregation's community service and outreach. It has been actively involved in United Ministries, an ecumenical social ministry organization, since it began in 1970. It has ministered to Lutheran students attending Furman University; participated in the Meals-on-Wheels program and the tutoring program of the Literacy Association; and provided a ministry to the residents of a neighboring apartment building which houses senior citizens. Extensive renovation of the Pence Educational Building was completed in 1987 at a cost of $500,000.

The diverse membership of the congregation has seen the median age decrease annually to the current age of 35. The rapid growth of the whole Greenville area has enabled Trinity to grow by attracting non-native persons, including many professionals and white collar workers. The leaders are attempting effectively to integrate new members into the life of the congregation. Ninety members of the church, making up seven classes, have completed the Word and Witness program. A son of the congregation, the Rev. William C. Ebener, was ordained in 1970.

In May 1987, Trinity Lutheran Day School was closed, and the Trinity Lutheran Child Development Center was opened to serve the growing need for year round early childhood care in the downtown area. Susan Park is the Director.

TRINITY, SALUDA
Organized 1837
(HLCSC, pp. 780-782)

Throughout the 1970's and early 1980's, Trinity was served by a series of supply pastors who provided leadership for the congregation's worship life. By 1985, however, the people of Trinity felt the need for more sustained pastoral leadership. In January of that year, the congregation decided that, while it was not yet ready to call a full-time pastor, the services of someone who could provide part-time ministry beyond the scope of a supply pastor should be sought. Shortly thereafter the Rev. Elford B. Roof, Jr., was elected to serve in such a part-time position, and in January 1987, was called as its pastor.

Even though Trinity has been without the benefit of a full-time pastoral ministry for much of its life, the congregation has been able to provide service to its members, witness to the community, and support to the church at large. The Lutheran Church Women have played an especially prominent role as the major auxiliary of the congregation.

In 1985, Sunday School classes for all age groups were offered for the first time since 1964. In 1986, again for the first time since 1964, a Vacation Church School was offered. In 1987, the congregation celebrated their 150th anniversary with special events during the year. Bishop Herman W. Cauble was guest preacher on August 16, 1987, and a revised printing of the history of Trinity congregation was accomplished.

UNION, LEESVILLE
Organized 1855
(HLCSC, pp. 782-783)

Like many other Lutheran congregations in rural South Carolina in the 1970's, Union became a parish in its own right, dissolving multi-congregation parishes scattered around the countryside. The break for Union occurred on January 1, 1978 when Union and Mt. Hebron divided on friendly terms, their joint parish in order that each might concentrate on its own congregation and immediate area. The Rev. F. Lavaughn Keisler, who had served both congregations since July 1971, remained as the pastor of Union.

While Union's membership has declined slightly since 1970, opportunities have developed for increased evangelism and growth. While the number of children in the congregation has declined, fewer young people have moved closer to the Columbia area than in the past. Also, the population in the community has seen other persons, especially in the older age groups, moving in. A number of the families in the congregation have connections back to the organization of the church. Yet, at the 1984 election of church council members, three of the four members elected had come into the church during the previous three years and were not originally of Lutheran background.

The ministry of the congregation continues to be supported by strong auxiliaries. Among recent property improvements have been the construction of a parsonage in 1977, and the establishment of a cemetery endowment fund from 1981-1984.

UNIVERSITY, CLEMSON
Organized 1951
(HLCSC, pp. 784-785)

Under the leadership of Pastor W. E. (Gene) Copenhaver the young congregation continued its steady growth in the years following 1970. It celebrated anniversaries of organization in 1976 and 1986, marking 25 and 35 years of service in the Clemson community.

In 1977, Associate Pastor Ronald G. Luckey joined the staff. Pastor Copenhaver resigned in 1982 and plans were begun to develop a co-pastorate team. Plans were activated with the arrival of the Rev. G. Steven Plonk in 1984. Pastor Luckey resigned in 1987, and the call process was begun again to restaff the team ministry.

Additional property was purchased in 1980 to accommodate congregational expansion. A residence was converted to meeting/classroom space and named Stockman House in memory of the church's first pastor. A second property, next door to the church building, was secured in 1983 to allow for future expansion on the current site. Two successful capital fund appeals were held in 1984 and 1987, respectively. Groundbreaking ceremonies are planned for the Spring of 1988 to construct a new worship area and social hall.

The congregation was active in the re-location of two Vietnamese families, one in 1974, a second in 1986. Pastors and lay persons have also taken leadership roles in developing an ecumenical ministry group known as Clemson Congregations In Touch. Other community contacts include involvement in the Council on Aging, Habitat for Humanity, Helping Hands Children's Program, and Clemson Heat Assistance program.

The congregation continues to be closely tied to the Clemson University community but has also experienced growth in members not related to the university. The congregational leadership group of the 1970's and '80's has included university and local industry folk, members and students, men and women, older and younger persons.

Thirteen of its student members have attended seminary: Richard Anderson, John Heyer, Gene Lenk, Walter Shealy, Alfred Rhyne, Cathy Quinton, Hank Moody, Frank Honeycutt, Ron Brown, David Tholstrup, Debbie Wood, and Linda Locklin. LTSS President, Mack Branham, is also a former University Lutheran student member. Through active student participation in parish activities and programs, University Lutheran will continue to prepare future leaders of the church.

WITTENBERG, LEESVILLE
Organized 1870
(HLCSC, pp. 785-787)

Throughout the 1970's and 1980's, Wittenberg has remained a steady congregation in the community, experiencing no major increase or decline in membership. Most of the families on the membership roster have traditional Lutheran ties as well as ties to the community, although expected arrivals in the community could change the picture in the future.

While no significant change has occurred in the context in which the congregation serves, Wittenberg has become involved in outreach efforts through social services provided by the local Good Samaritan Center and Meals-on-Wheels.

The only significant update of the physical plant involved the renovation of the church interior in 1985.

The Rev. H. G. Beck served as pastor at Wittenberg from 1967 to 1973, followed by the Rev. Harold Skinner from 1973 to 1982. The Rev. Leroy C. Trexler came as pastor in 1983 and served until his retirement in 1986. The Rev. David Butler became its pastor in 1987. One member of the congregation, Randall Derrick, has entered the ordained ministry since 1970.

ZION, LEXINGTON
Organized 1745
(HLCSC, pp. 787-789)

Another congregation facing the change from a rural to suburban community is Zion, Lexington. One of the oldest

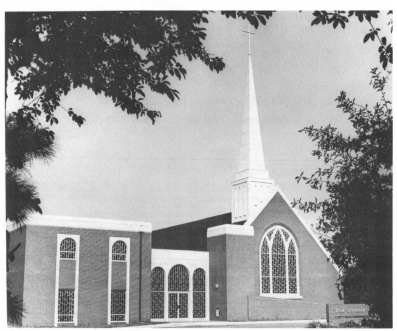

congregations in the Synod, this church has grown through the assimilation of new people in the community into the congregation. A major change for this congregation came in 1979 with the renovation of and additions to the sanctuary and education building at a cost of over $300,000. Additional land and paved parking areas were also added about this time. The Rev. Garth L. Hill served as pastor of this congregation from 1969 until his retirement in 1980. In 1981, the Rev. Dr. Hollis A. Miller began his ministry with Zion.

This congregation will work to meet the needs of the people in the community and to grow as the community grows, with a major 100-store mall scheduled for construction within one-half mile of the church. In addition, the congregation will continue its participation in community ecumenical activities, and support for Jeanette Isaacson Kpissay, a missionary in Liberia, as well as other churchwide activities, as it has done in the past.

MISSION CONGREGATION
LIVING SPRINGS, COLUMBIA
(Under development)

In July 1987, the Rev. Dr. E. Edward Long entered the field of northeast Columbia to begin the development of a new Lutheran Church in that rapidly growing area. Under appointment from the DMNA-LCA and called by the South

Carolina Synod, Pastor Long began visiting with families in the area. The first worship service was held on November 15, 1987 at North Springs Elementary School. Property for

the new congregation has been purchased at the corner of Hard Scrabble and Clemson Roads. The congregation looks forward to organization soon.

DISBANDED CONGREGATION
IMMANUEL, RIDGE SPRING
Organized 1921
(HLCSC, pp. 620-621)

Immanuel struggled for its existence since its organization. Having a baptized membership of only five members in 1970, that figure had risen to only eight by the mid-1980's. However, the congregation has had its own church structure since 1923, and renovated it in 1974-1975. The Rev. Hubert A. Dunlap began serving as a supply pastor in 1970.

On May 4, 1986, the last worship service was held, and the congregation was disbanded. Assets of the congregation were turned over to the synod, which in turn gave the deed to the property to St. Peter, Leesville. After some discussion with members of the Ridge Spring community, the deed to the property was turned over to Ridge Spring, which now uses the building as a community facility.

Chapter Six

Biographical Sketches of Pastors

Data for the sketches in this chapter has been provided by the pastors and obtained through much research. Included in this listing are all pastors who have ever served in the South Carolina Synod. Those whose service in the synod was concluded with the publication of A History of the Lutheran Church in South Carolina, *1971, are listed by name with a reference to the page number of the 1971 volume. Those whose service has continued or resumed in the South Carolina Synod since the publication of 1971, are included with updated information and a page reference to the 1971 volume. Those who have served in the South Carolina Synod since the 1971 volume are included with complete biographical information. Some of the pastors listed were ordained by the synod and transferred to another synod for service; others have been received into the synod after service in other synods or since their retirement. In either case, no attempt has been made to list the specific places of service outside the South Carolina Synod before or after, except to note the synod and dates of service in that synod before coming to South Carolina, or the synod to which the pastor transferred.*

Data included in this chapter includes name, date and place of birth, education and honorary degrees, date and synod of Ordination, locations and dates of ministry, name of spouse, date of retirement, date of death, place of burial, and other special information such as service on national boards and committees. Synodical committee work has not been included. All "B.D." degrees have been changed to "M.Div." though many of the pastors originally received the "B.D." degree.

ABBREVIATIONS

B. .... Born, Buried
Cem. .... Cemetery
Col. .... College
D. .... Died
D.D. .... Doctor of Divinity
DMNA .... Division for Mission in North America
D.Min. .... Doctor of Ministry
DPS .... Division for Parish Services
DWME .... Division for World Missions and Ecumenism
Ed. .... Education
ELCA .... Evangelical Lutheran Church in America
LCA .... Lutheran Church in America
LST .... Lutheran School of Theology
LTS .... Lutheran Theological Seminary
LTSS .... Lutheran Theological Southern Seminary
M.Div. .... Master of Divinity
M.R.E. .... Master of Religious Education
Ret. .... Retired
Sem. .... Seminary
S.T.M. .... Master of Sacred Theology
Theo. .... Theological
Trans. .... Transferred
ULCA .... United Lutheran Church in America
Univ. .... University

ADDY, JAMES VIRGIL: *Served:* In S. C., St. James, Graniteville, 1943-1973. *Ret.* 1973. *Spouse:* Murttie Elese Fulmer Addy (*D.* 1987). *D.* 1985, *B.* Mt. Horeb, Chapin. (*See page 831.*)

ADDY, JAMES WILBUR: *Served:* In S. C., Redeemer, Greer, 1970-1976 (Mission Developer and Pastor); St. Andrew, Charleston, 1976-1981; Faith, Batesburg, 1981—. *Spouse:* Mary Lucile Metz Addy. (*See page 831.*)

ADDY, ROBERT A.: (*See page 831.*)

ALBERT, WILLIAM RICHARD: *Ed.* McCormick Theo. Sem., D.Min., 1982. *Served:* In S. C., St. James, Leesville, 1971-1974; Christ the King, Columbia, 1974-1983; St. Philip, Myrtle Beach, 1983— (Associate Pastor 1983-1987). *Spouse:* Linda Jeannette Fogle Albert. (*See page 831.*)

ALDRICH, NICODEMUS (NICHOLAS): (*See page 831.*)

ALEXANDER, BEVERLY DENNIS: *B.* Oct. 15, 1953, Columbia, S. C. *Ed.* Univ. of S. C., B.S., 1975; Univ. of S. C., M.S., 1977; LTSS, M.Div., 1981. *Ord.* 1981, S. C. Synod. *Served:* In S. C., St. Paul, Columbia, 1981-1985 (Assistant Pastor); Trans. to N. C. Synod, 1985.

ALKSNIS, TALLY: (*See page 831.*)

ALLEN, ROBERT E.: (*See page 831.*)

AMAN, JOHN ANDREW: *Served:* In S. C., Professor of Economics and Business Administration, Newberry College, 1936-1968 (Head of Department, 1946-1968). *Ret.* 1968. *D.* 1972, *B.* Newberry Memorial Gardens. (*See page 831.*)

AMUNDSON, MELVIN EDWARD: *Served:* In S. C., Nativity, Spartanburg, 1969-1973; Redeemer, Columbia, 1973—. LCA Pastor/Evangelist, 1982-1987; LCA Consulting Committee on Stewardship, 1979-1987. *Spouse:* Nancy Trexler Amundson. (*See page 831.*)

ANDERSON, BRUCE PALMER: (*See page 831.*)

ANDERSON, FRANK WILLIAM: *B.* Mar. 8, 1956, Southampton, Bermuda. *Ed.* Newberry Col., B.A., 1978; LTSPhiladelphia, M.Div., 1983. *Ord.* 1983, Florida Synod. *Served:* In S. C., Corinth, Prosperity, 1983-1987; "On Leave From Call," 1988—. *Spouse:* The Rev. Mary Williams Anderson.

ANDERSON, HUGH GEORGE: *Served:* President, LTSS, 1970-1981. Trans. to Iowa Synod, 1982. *Spouse:* Synnöve "Sunny" Anderson (*D.* 1982); Jutta Hermann Anderson. (*See page 831.*)

ANDERSON, JOHN GORDON: *B.* Sept. 10, 1945, Bristol, Virginia. *Ed.* Newberry Col., A.B., 1968; LTSS, M.Div., 1972. *Ord.* 1972, SE Synod. *Served:* In S. C., St. John, Johnston, 1972-73; Trans. to SE Synod, 1973.

ANDERSON, MARY WILLIAMS: *B.* April 2, 1956, Florence, S. C. *Ed.* Newberry Col., B.A., 1978; LTSPhiladelphia, M.Div., 1983. *Ord.* 1983, S. C. Synod. *Served:* In S. C., St. Mark, Prosperity, 1983-1987; Call to Special Service, Commission on Women, ELCA, 1988—. Member, LCA Executive Council, 1987. *Spouse:* The Rev. Frank William Anderson.

ANDERSON, R. HOMER: (*See page 832.*)

ANDREWS, EDWIN WALTER: *Served:* In S. C., Ehrhardt Memorial, Ehrhardt, 1969-1972. *Ret.* 1972. *Spouse:* Margaret Andrews. *D.* 1977, *B.* Beaufort National Cem. (*See page 832.*)

ANGERER, AUGUSTUS: (*See page 832.*)

ANTHONY, JACOB BROWN: (*See page 832.*)

ANTLEY, BARRY THOMAS: *B.* Feb. 12, 1954, Orangeburg, S. C. *Ed.* Clemson Univ., B.S., 1976: LTSS, M.Div., 1980. *Ord.* 1980, S. C. Synod. *Served:* In S. C., Mt. Hebron, Leesville, 1980-1985; St. James, Graniteville, 1985—. *Spouse:* Deborah Tanner Antley.

APPEL, HAROLD AUGUST: *B.* Sept. 21, 1915, Braddock, Pa. *Ed.* Wittenburg Univ., A.B., 1961; Hamma Divinity School, M.Div., 1963. *Ord.* 1963, Ohio Synod. *Served:* In Ohio Synod, 1963-1971; in Central Pa. Synod, 1971-1978. *Ret.* 1978. Trans. to S. C. Synod, 1981. *Spouse:* Thelma Klingelhofer Appel. *D.* 1984, *B.* Cremated.

ARMSTRONG, CHARLES H.: (*See page 832.*)

AULL, J. HERMAN: (*See page 832.*)

AULL, JAMES STROUD: *Ed.* LSTChicago, S.T.M., 1970; Duke Univ., Ph.D., 1971. *Served:* Associate Professor of Old Testament, LTSS, 1962-1979; Registrar, LTSS, 1970-1979; Administrative Assistant, LTSS, 1972-1979; Secretary, S. C. Synod, 1979-1987; Bishop, S. C. Synod, ELCA, 1988—. *Spouse:* Virginia Kloeppel Aull. (*See page 832.*)

AULL, WILLIAM BOWMAN: (*See page 832.*)

AUSTIN, C. D.: (*See page 833.*)

AUSTIN, JACOB: (*See page 833.*)

BACHMAN, JOHN: (*See page 833.*)

BADEN, J. H.: (*See page 833.*)

BAILEY, JAMES H.: (*See page 833.*)

BAILEY, S.: (*See page 833.*)

BAILEY, STEPHEN CARLTON: *B.* Jan. 12, 1947, Long Beach, California. *Ed.* Univ. of Nebraska, B.S., 1970; LTSS, M.Div., 1987. *Ord.* 1987, S. C. Synod. *Served:* In S. C., St. Stephen, Lexington (Associate Pastor), 1987—. *Spouse:* Jane Wescott Bailey.

BAKER, BOBBY GENE: *B.* Nov. 9, 1952, Concord, N. C. *Ed.* Lenoir-Rhyne Col., A.B., 1975; LTSS, M.Div., 1979. *Ord.* 1979, N. C. Synod. *Served:* In N. C. Synod, 1979-1982; in S. C., Good Shepherd, Walterboro, 1982—.

BALLARD, RICHARD GENE: *B.* Jan. 15, 1958, Asheville, N. C. *Ed.* Mars Hill Col., B.A., 1979; LTSS, M.Div., 1983; Univ. of S. C., M.Ed., 1986. *Ord.* 1983, N. C. Synod. *Served:* In S. C., Peak-Springhill Parish (Mt. Olivet, Chapin; Mt. Hermon, Peak) 1983—. *Spouse:* Ruth Holland Ballard.

BALLENTINE, ARTHUR W.: *Spouse:* Anna Elizabeth Derrick Ballentine (D. 1957). *D.* 1973, *B.* Rosemont Cem., Newberry. (*See page 833.*)

BALLENTINE, JACOB LUTHER: *Served:* In S. C., Trinity, Elloree 1958-1980. *Ret.* 1980. *Spouse:* Frances Kickson Ballentine. *D.* 1986, *B.* Trinity Cem., Elloree. (*See page 834.*)

BALLENTINE, JOHN O.: (*See page 834.*)

BALLENTINE, S. C.: (*See page 834.*)

BALSOBER, MR.: *(See page 834.)*

BAMBERG, ISAAC: *(See page 834.)*

BAMBERG, J. G.: *(See page 834.)*

BANGLE, JAMES HENRY: *(See page 834.)*

BANSEMER, C. F.: *(See page 834.)*

BARCLAY, E. E.: *(See page 834.)*

BARGER, GLENN LEROY: *(See page 835.)*

BARNHART, DAVID RALPH: *(See page 835.)*

BATTERMANN, WILLIAM HENRY: *Served:* In S. C., Community of Hope Mission, Columbia, 1970-1973 (Mission Developer); Trans. to Virginia Synod, 1973. *(See page 835.)*

BAUMGARTNER, HUGH EDWARD: *B.* July 12, 1921, Brunswick, Georgia. *Ed.* Lenoir-Rhyne Col., A.B., 1944; LTSS, M.Div., 1945. *Ord.* 1945, Georgia-Alabama Synod. *Served:* In Ga.-Ala. Synod, 1945-1959; in N. C. Synod, 1959-1965; in SE Synod, 1965-1979; in S. C., Redeemer, Newberry, 1979-1986; LCA Pastor/Evangelist, 1976-1986. *Ret.* 1986. *Spouse:* Frances Morris Wisdom Baumgartner.

BAUMGARTNER, PAUL WISDOM: *B.* May 9, 1956, Macon, Georgia. *Ed.* Newberry Col., A.B. 1977; LTSS, M.Div. 1981. *Ord.* 1981, SE Synod. *Served:* In SE Synod, 1981-1984; in S. C., Trinity, Georgetown, 1984-1986. Trans. to SE Synod, 1987. *Spouse:* Debbie Stutler Baumgartner.

BAYNE, JAMES DEOULIA: *Served:* In S. C., Military Chaplain, U. S. Army, 1967-1972; St. John and Providence, Lexington, 1972-1974; St. John, Lexington, 1975-1977. *Spouse:* Katherine Auvil Bayne. *D.* 1977, *B.* St. John Cem., Lexington. *(See page 835.)*

BEAM, KEITH JUNIOUS: Removed from Roll of Ministers, 1971. *(See page 835.)*

BEARDEN, GEORGE STEELE: *(See page 835.)*

BEATTY, HAROLD ELMER: *(See page 835.)*

BEAVER, BEN ROBERT: *B.* June 2, 1945, Charlotte, N. C. *Ed.* Lenoir-Rhyne Col., A.B., 1967; LTSS, M.Div., 1971. *Ord.* 1980, S. C. Synod. *Served:* Trans. to Virginia Synod, 1980.

BEAVER, TOMMY KALE: *B.* Sept. 17, 1942, Concord, N. C. *Ed.* Appalachian State Univ., 1964; LTSS, M.Div., 1969. *Ord.* 1969, N. C. Synod. *Served:* In N. C. Synod, 1969-1979; in S. C., A Mighty Fortress, Summerville, 1979-1985 (Pastor/Developer, 1979-1981). Trans. to N. C. Synod, 1985. *Spouse:* Rosalind Beacer Beaver.

BECK, ALFRED RILEY: *(See page 835.)*

BECK, HAROLD GENE: *Served:* In S. C., Wittenberg, Leesville, 1967-1973; St. Paul, Mt. Pleasant, 1975—. *Spouse:* May Frances Jantzen Beck. *(See page 835.)*

BECK, WALTER HERMAN: *(See page 835.)*

BECKER, F.: *(See page 836.)*

BEDENBAUGH, CLYDE EUGENE: *(See page 836.)*

BEDENBAUGH, JOHN BENJAMIN: *Served:* Professor of New Testament, LTSS, 1961—. (*See page 836.*)

BEDENBAUGH, LEVI: (*See page 836.*)

BEDENBAUGH, S. W.: (*See page 836.*)

BEDENBAUGH, ZACCHEUS WRIGHT: (*See page 836.*)

BELL, HERBERT CHARLES: (*See page 836.*)

BERGMAN, C. F.: (*See page 837.*)

BERGMAN, ERNEST: (*See page 837.*)

BERGMAN, ERNEST JOHN: (*See page 837.*)

BERLY, JOHN EUSEBIUS: (*See page 837.*)

BERLY, WILLIAM: (*See page 837.*)

BERNHARDT, CHARLES EDWARD: *Served:* In S. C., Mt. Tabor, West Columbia, 1968-1975; Martin Luther, Charleston, 1975-1984; Pine Grove, Lone Star, 1984-1986. *Ret.* 1987. *Spouse:* Gladys Irene Boggs Bernhardt. (*See page 837.*)

BERNHARDT, CHRISTIAN EBERHARD: (*See page 837.*)

BERNHARDT, DAVID: (*See page 838.*)

BERNHEIM, CHARLES HERMAN: (*See page 838.*)

BERNHEIM, GOTTHARDT DELLMANN: (*See page 838.*)

BERNSDORFF, KARL GEORGE: *B.* Aug. 10, 1948, Lienz, Austria. *Ed.* Baptist Col., B.A., 1971; LTSS, M.Div. 1975. *Ord.* 1975, S. C. Synod. *Served:* In S. C., Faith, West Columbia 1975-1981; Reformation, Lancaster, 1982—. *Spouse:* Mary Louise Kuhn Bernsdorff.

BERRY, B. F.: (*See page 838.*)

BERRY, SAMUEL WALLACE: (*See page 838.*)

BICKLEY, JOHN JACOB: (*See page 838.*)

BINNICHER (DINNINGER, CHARLES), M. CARL: (*See page 838.*)

BIRNBAUM, DAVID THEODORE: *B.* Sept. 18, 1953, Saginaw, Michigan. *Ed.* Central Michgan Univ., B.A., 1975; LTSS, M.Div. 1985. *Ord.* 1985, S. C. Synod. *Served:* In S. C., Our Shepherd, Hartsville, 1985—. *Spouse:* Mary Rose Birnbaum.

BISCHOFF, WILLIAM: Removed from Roll of Ministers, 1971. (*See page 839.*)

BISHOP, JEROME HENRI: *Ed.* LSTChicago, S.T.M., 1975. *Served:* Missionary to Malaysia/Singapore 1963-1978; in S. C., Missionary-in-Residence, 1979; St. John, Pomaria, 1980—. *Spouse:* Frances Carolyn Crooks Bishop. (*See page 839.*)

BLACK, HENRY JESSE: (*See page 839.*)

BLACKWELDER, DANIEL M.: (*See page 839.*)

BLOMGREN, S. L. (*See page 839.*)

BODIE, EARL KENNAN: (*See page 839.*)

BODIE, NATHAN D.: (*See page 839.*)

BOEHM, J. A.: (*See page 839.*)

BOGGS, JAMES RUSSELL: *Served:* Military Chaplain, U. S. Army, 1957-1977; in S. C., Director of Chaplains and Chaplain to Corps of Cadets, The Citadel, 1977-1980; Director of Church Relations (1980-87) and Director of Planned Giving (1984-87), Newberry College, 1980-1987. *Ret.* 1987. *Spouse:* Mary Cloninger Boggs. (*See page 839.*)

BOINEST, THADEUS STREET: (*See page 839.*)

BOLAND, ARTHUR GLENN: (*See page 840.*)

BOLAND, LAWSON PETTUS: (*See page 840.*)

BOLDT, KARL L. J.: (*See page 840.*)

BOLIEK, PAULWYN LEE: *Served:* In S. C., Secretary, S. C. Synod, 1971-1979; Trans. to SE Synod, 1979. *Spouse:* Betty Boliek. (*See page 840.*)

BOLIEK, WYNNE COLFORD: (*See page 840.*)

BOLLES, EDWIN ABIEL: (*See page 840.*)

BOLLINGER, LAWRENCE HUGH: (*See page 840.*)

BOLTON, DENNIS RUDOLPH: *B.* March 24, 1953, High Point, N. C. *Ed.* Univ. of S. C., B.A., 1975; LTSS, M.Div., 1979. *Ord.* 1979, S. C. Synod. *Served:* Trans. to N. C. Synod, 1979. *Spouse:* Angela Maye Polk Bolton.

BOLZIUS, JOHN MARTIN: (*See page 840.*)

BONHAM, NEHEMIAH: (*See page 840.*)

BOOZER, ALLEN HAYNE: (*See page 841.*)

BOOZER, CORNELIUS PRIOLEAU: (*See page 841.*)

BOOZER, VIRGIL YOUNG: (*See page 841.*)

BOST, LARRY WAYNE: *B.* Dec. 11, 1942, Mooresville, N. C. *Ed.* Catawba Col., A.B., 1964; LTSS, M.Div. 1968; LTSS, D.Min., 1984. *Ord.* 1968, N. C. Synod. *Served:* In N. C. Synod, 1968-1979; in S. C., Ministry with the Deaf, Columbia, 1979— (Pastor/Developer 1979-1985). *Spouse:* Mary Sidler Bost.

BOST, RAYMOND MORRIS: Lenoir-Rhyne Col., D.D., 1976. *Served:* In N. C. Synod, 1966-1976; in New England Synod, 1976-1984; in Southeastern Pennsylvania Synod, 1984-1985; in N. C. Synod, 1985-1987; in S. C., Dean of the College, Newberry College, 1987—. *Spouse:* Margaret Martha Vedder Bost. (*See page 841.*)

BOUKNIGHT, SAMUEL: (*See page 841.*)

BOWDEN, GEORGE STEWART: (*See page 841.*)

BOWERS, ANDREW JACKSON: (*See page 841.*)

BOWERS, LOUIS THORN: *B.* July 14, 1910, Philadelphia, Pa. *Ed.* Gettysburg Col., B.A., 1934; LTSGettysburg, Diploma, 1937. *Ord.* 1937, East Penn. Synod. *Served:* UCLA Missionary to Liberia 1938-1972; in Central Pa. Synod, 1972-1978. *Ret.* 1978; Trans. to S. C. Synod, 1978. *Spouse:* Virginia McQuilkin Bowers.

BOWLES, JOHN D.: *(See page 842.)*

BOWMAN, WILLIAM SPENCER: *(See page 842.)*

BOYD, JOHN EBENEZER, JR.: *Served:* In S. C., Grace, Rock Hill, 1970-1975; in SE Synod, 1975-1976; in S. C., Holy Trinity, North Augusta, 1976-1985; Trans. to N. C. Synod, 1985. *Spouse:* Lynda Dianne Strange Boyd. *(See page 842.)*

BRADY, JAMES LAWRENCE: *B.* Oct. 7, 1950, St. Petersburg, Fla. *Ed.* Emory Univ., B.A., 1973; LTSS, M.Div., 1979. *Ord.* 1979, SE Synod. *Served:* In S. C., Pomaria, Pomaria 1979-1986; Missionary to Malaysia, 1986—. *Spouse:* Mary Lynne Fowlkes Brady.

BRANDT, HENRY NEWTON: *Served:* In S. C., St. Michael, Columbia, 1965-1977; St. Luke, Prosperity, 1978—. *Spouse:* Rose Smith Brandt. *(See page 842.)*

BRANDT, WILLIAM F.: *(See page 842.)*

BRANHAM, MACK CARISON, JR.: *Ed.* LTSS, S.T.M., 1963; George Washington Univ., M.S., 1968; Arizona State Univ., Ph.D., 1974. *Served:* Military Chaplain, U. S. Air Force, 1959-1979; Admin. Asst. and Registrar, LTSS, 1979-1981; Vice Pres. for Administration, LTSS, 1981-1982; Pres., LTSS, 1982—. *Spouse:* Jennie Louise Jones Branham. *(See page 842.)*

BRAZELL, MARION CROMER: *B.* Nov. 7, 1943, Columbia, S. C. *Ed.* Univ. of S. C., B.A., 1966; LTSS, M.Div., 1973. *Ord.* 1973, S. C. Synod. *Served:* In S. C., Faith, Johns Island, 1973-1977; St. Matthew, Lexington, 1977-1984; Christ the Servant, Conway, 1984— (Pastor/Developer 1984-1986). *Spouse:* Valerie Jan Taylor Brazell.

BREDHOLT, MARK STANLEY: *B.* July 20, 1953, Owosso, Michigan. *Ed.* Saginaw Valley State Col., B.A., 1977; LTSS, M.Div., 1984. *Ord.* 1984, Michgan Synod. *Served:* In Fla. Synod, 1984-1986; in S. C., Ebenezer, Columbia, 1986— (Associate Pastor). *Spouse:* Mary Alice Jording Bredholt.

BRODFUEHRER, J. C.: *(See page 842.)*

BROWN, GEORGE H.: *(See page 842.)*

BROWN, HENRY MAXWELL: *(See page 842.)*

BROWN, JAMES ALLEN: *(See page 842.)*

BROWN, JOHN DANIEL: *(See page 843.)*

BROWN, PLEASANT DAVID: *(See page 843.)*

BROWN, RONALD NEIL: *B.* Dec. 3, 1952, Wichita Falls, Texas. *Ed.* Clemson Univ., B.A., 1974; LTSS, M.Div., 1981. *Ord.* 1981, S. C. Synod. *Served:* Trans. to SE Synod, 1981; in S. C., St. John, Lexington, 1986—. *Spouse:* Kathy Chapman Brown.

BROWN, THOMAS SHANNON: *(See page 843.)*

BROWN, WALTER U.: *(See page 843.)*

BRUNK, RICHARD E.: *(See page 843.)*

BRYANT, KENT EMORY: *B.* Nov. 30, 1949, Sacramento, California. *Ed.* Univ. of Mississippi, B.A., 1972; LTSS, M.Div., 1977. *Ord.* 1977, S. C. Synod. *Served:* Trans. to SE Synod, 1977. *Spouse:* Dorothy Virginia Reese Bryant.

BUCK, JAMES LAFAYETTE: (*See page 843.*)

BULOW, JOACHIM: (*See page 843.*)

BURKE, KENNETH OETGEN: *B.* June 5, 1946, Savannah, Georgia. *Ed.* Newberry Col., B.A., 1973; LTSS, M.Div., 1977. *Ord.* 1977, S. C. Synod. *Served:* In S. C., Faith, Johns Island, 1977-1982; Trans. to Texas/La. Synod, 1982. Chaplain, Franke Home, 1978-1981; Chaplain, Rural Mission, Johns Island, 1977-1982. *Spouse:* Josephine Hardy Burke.

BURNS, ERNEST TARVER: *Served:* In S. C., St. Nicholas and Trinity, Fairfax, 1968-1976; Trans. to SE Synod, 1976; in S. C., Mt. Pleasant, Ehrhardt, 1977-1982; Trans. to SE Synod, 1982. (*See page 843.*)

BURRISS, HENRY WYNDHAM: *Served:* In S. C., Gethsemane, Columbia, 1967-1976; Trans. to Florida Synod 1976. (*See page 843.*)

BUSBY, LEVI E.: (*See page 844.*)

BUSHNELL, JOHN EICHELBERGER: (*See page 844.*)

BUTLER, DAVID JOHNSON: *B.* Jan. 18, 1957, Rocky Mount, N. C. *Ed.* Univ. of S. C., B.S., 1979; LTSS, M.Div., 1987. *Ord.* 1987, S. C. Synod. *Served:* In S. C. , Wittenberg, Leesville, 1987—.

BUTLER, JAMES WILLIAM: (*See page 844.*)

BUTT, JAMES CARROLL: *B.* Sept. 11, 1950, Charleston, S. C. *Ed.* Newberry Col., A.B., 1972; LTSS, M.Div., 1977. *Ord.* 1977, S. C. Synod. *Served:* Trans. to SE Synod, 1977; in S. C., Good Shepherd and Sandy Run, Swansea, 1978-1979; "On Leave From Call," 1979-1980; Trans. to N. C. Synod, 1980.

CAMERON, VIRGIL ALONZO: *Served:* In S. C., Good Shepherd, Walterboro, 1967-1974. *Ret.* 1974. *Spouse:* Erie Lee Bauknight Cameron. *D.* 1978, *B.* Greenlawn Cem., Columbia. (*See page 844.*)

CAMLIN, WILLIAM ROLAND: *B.* Jan. 27, 1945, Columbia, S. C. *Ed.* Francis Marion Col., B.S., 1974; LTSS, M.Div., 1978. *Ord.* 1978, S. C. Synod. *Served:* In Ohio Synod, 1978-1983; in S. C., Redeemer, Greer, 1983-1985. Resigned from the Ministry, 1985. *Spouse:* Chris Newman Camlin.

CAMMAN, DIETRICH PETER: (*See page 844.*)

CAMPBELL, RICHARD ROSS: *Served:* In S. C., Ebenezer, Columbia, 1971-1974 (Associate Pastor); Trans. to N. C. Synod, 1974; in S. C., St. Matthew, Charleston, 1986—. *Spouse:* Rebecca Cromer Campbell. (*See page 844.*)

CARPENTER, CECIL WALTER: (*See page 844.*)

CARPENTER, RUBERTUS MELANCHTON: (*See page 844.*)

CARSWELL, ROBERT WAYNE: *Served:* In S. C., St. Andrew, Columbia, 1966-1973; "Awaiting A Call," 1973-1975; Resigned from Ministry, 1975. *Spouse:* Elizabeth Cromer Carswell. (*See page 844.*)

CASSELL, JOSEPH BUCHANAN: (*See page 844.*)

CASTOR, DAVID FREDERICK: (*See page 845.*)

CAUBLE, HERMAN WOODROW: *Served:* Bishop, S. C. Synod, 1971-1987. Member, LCA Board of Pensions, 1973-1980 (Secretary, 1976-1980). *Ret.* 1987. *Spouse:* Anna Elizabeth Petrea Cauble. (*See page 845.*)

278   A HISTORY OF THE LUTHERAN CHURCH IN S. C.

CAUGHMAN, CARL B.: Trans. to SE Synod, 1967. (See page 845.)

CAUGHMAN, EMANUEL: (See page 845.)

CHASSEREAU, OLIN WARREN: B. April 27, 1939, Ehrhardt, S. C. Ed. Univ. of S. C., A.B., 1968; LTSS, M.Div., 1972. Ord. 1972, S. C. Synod. Served: In S. C., St. John, Beaufort, 1972-1975; Orangeburg, Orangeburg, 1975-1978; "On Leave From Call," 1978-1980; St. James, Lexington 1980-1987; Pine Grove, Lone Star, 1987—. Spouse: Claudia Jean Rentz Chassereau.

CHEWNING, JOHN THOMAS, JR.: (See page 845.)

CHRISEMER, EDGAR TROEDER: (See page 845.)

CLARK, ALTON CLAUD: Birthplace: Little Mountain, S. C. Served: In S. C., Good Shepherd, Columbia 1958-1975; Chaplain, Wil Lou Gray Opportunity School, West Columbia, S. C. 1975-1980; Chaplain, S. C. House of Representatives, 1965—; Chaplain, S. C. National Guard (retired). Ret. 1975. Spouse: Alice Marjorie Warner Clark. (See page 845.)

CLARK, BENJAMIN MCLAURIN: (See page 845.)

CLARK, MARION WARNER: Served: In S. C., St. John, Clinton, 1971-1987; St. John, Spartanburg, 1988— (Associate Pastor). Spouse: Edith Roberta Rikard Clark. (See page 845.)

CLEMMER, PALMER DEKALB: B. June 5, 1952, Gastonia, N. C. Ed. Lenoir-Rhyne Col., B.A., 1974; LTSS, M.Div., 1978. Ord. 1978, N. C. Synod. Served: In N. C. Synod, 1978-1981; in S. C., King of Glory, North Myrtle Beach, 1981-1987; Trans. to N. C. Synod, 1987. Spouse: Cynthia Louise Long Clemmer.

CLINE, WILLIAM PINCKNEY: (See page 845.)

CLINE, WILLIAM PRESTON: D. 1978, B. Oakwood Cem., Hickory, N. C. (See page 846.)

CLOY, ROBERT: (See page 846.)

COBB, JAMES KIVETT: Served: In Va. Synod, 1958-1972; in N. C. Synod, 1972-1974; in S. C., Faith, Newberry, 1975-1982. Ret. 1982. Spouse: Ellen Wingard Cobb. (See page 846.)

COBB, JAMES NEAL: B. April 10, 1953, Macon, Georgia. Ed. Oral Roberts University, B.A., 1975; LTSS, M.Div., 1980. Ord. 1984, S. C. Synod. Served: In S. C., Ehrhardt Memorial, Ehrhardt, 1983-84; "On Leave From Call," 1984-1987; Removed from Roll of Ministers, 1987. Spouse: Barbara Rhodes Cobb.

COBB, WILLIAM ROGERS: Served: In S. C., Incarnation, Columbia, 1968-1972 (Assistant Pastor); St. James, Lexington, 1972-1979; St. Paul, Aiken, 1979—. Spouse: Barbara Shearin Knox Cobb. (See page 846.)

CONLEY, RANDALL MARK: B. Oct. 24, 1953, Cincinnati, Ohio. Ed. Univ. of Central Florida, B.A., 1983; LTSS, M.Div., 1987. Ord. 1987, S. C. Synod (for Florida Synod). Served: In S. C., Bethlehem, Leesville, 1987—. Spouse: Deborah Lynn Estes Conley.

CONNELLY, JAMES R., JR.: Served: In SE Synod, 1960-76; LCA Deployed Staff, DPS Southeast Region, 1976-87; in S. C., Mt. Tabor, West Columbia, 1987—. Spouse: Faith Bunger Connelly. (See page 846.)

COOK, BOYD FULMER: *Served:* In SE Synod, 1968-1972; in S. C., Christ, Hilton Head, 1972-1982 (Pastor/Developer, 1972-1973); St. Peter, Chapin, 1982-1987; President, Lowman Home, 1987—. *Spouse:* Margaret Rose Marth Cook. (*See page 846.*)

COOK, KEITH ROGER: *B.* May 18, 1952, Marietta, Ga. *Ed.* West Georgia Col., B.A., 1974; LTSS, M.Div., 1983. *Ord.* 1983, SE Synod. *Served:* In S. C., St. James, Leesville, 1983—. *Spouse:* Margaret Watson Cook.

COON, ROBERT GEORGE: *B.* Aug. 28, 1946, Lincolnton, N. C. *Ed.* Lenoir-Rhyne Col., B.A., 1968; LTSS, M.Div., 1972. *Ord.* 1972, N. C. Synod. *Served:* In S. C., Trinity, Greenville, 1972— (1972-1983, Associate Pastor), Lutheran Chaplain, Furman Univ., 1972—. *Spouse:* Ann Hampton Barker Coon.

COOPER, JOHN CHARLES: (*See page 846.*)

COOPER, LUTHER GRADY: Newberry College, D.D., 1977. *Served:* In S. C., Prof. Philosophy, Religion & Greek, Newberry College, 1957-1973; Professor Emeritus 1973—. *Spouse:* Miriam Roberta Greever Cooper. (*See page 846.*)

COPENHAVER, WILMER EUGENE: *Served:* In S. C., University, Clemson, 1969-1982; Campus Pastor, Clemson Univ., 1969-1982; Trans. to Va. Synod, 1982. (*See page 846.*)

CORBELL, THOMAS WRIGHT: *B.* Feb. 3, 1944, Richmond, Va. *Ed.* Pfeiffer Col., B.A., 1969; LTSS, M.Div., 1973. *Ord.* 1973, N. C. Synod. *Served:* In S. C., Reformation, Lancaster, 1973-1979; St. Stephen, Lexington, 1979—. *Spouse:* Anne Tysinger Corbell.

CORLEY, GEORGE BAYLIS: *Served:* In S. C., St. Matthew and Resurrection, Cameron, 1960-1983; Bethany, Lexington, 1983—. Business/Circulation Manager, *South Carolina Lutheran,* 1957—. *Spouse:* Barbara Ruth Dennis Corley. (*See page 847.*)

COUNTS, EDWARD LUTHER: *Served:* In S. C., Trinity, Columbia, 1969-1982 (1969-1970 Mission Developer); St. John, Charleston, 1982—. *Spouse:* Donna Brittiana Abee Counts. (*See page 847.*)

COUNTS, ERNEST KARL: *Ret.* 1963. *Spouse:* Nellie Derrick Counts. *D.* 1983, *B.* Pomaria Church Cem., Pomaria. (*See page 847.*)

COUNTS, HENRY P.: (*See page 847.*)

COUNTS, PAUL MELANCHTON: *Spouse:* Bertha Dierolf Counts (D. 1983). *D.* 1972, *B.* Southland Memorial Gardens, West Columbia. (*See page 847.*)

CRAUN, WILLIAM ARTHUR: (*See page 847.*)

CRAWFORD, CLAUDE EVERETTE, JR.: (*See page 847.*)

CREAGER, HAROLD LUTHER: *Served:* Professor Emeritus (LTSS), 1969-1984. *Spouse:* Dorothy Clarke Creager (D. 1981). *D.* 1984, *B.* Crescent Hill Memorial Gardens, Columbia. (*See page 847.*)

CRIM, JACOB: (*See page 847.*)

CROMER, JAMES ALBERT: (*See page 848.*)

CROMER, JOSEPH LEE: (*See page 848.*)

CROMER, VOIGT RHODES: *(See page 848.)*

CRONK, BENJAMIN WESLEY: *(See page 848.)*

CRONK, ELI CALVIN: *(See page 848.)*

CROUSE, ANDREW LEONHARDT: *(See page 848.)*

CROUT, JACOB HARRY: *Served:* Executive Director, Greater Columbia Lutheran Social Ministry Agency, 1970-1984; Assistant Administrator, Lowman Home, White Rock, 1985-87; Director of Special Projects and Chaplain, Lowman Home, 1987—. *Spouse:* Joyce Anne Lord Crout. *(See page 848.)*

CRUSE, GUY CALVIN: *Served:* In S. C., Bethel, White Rock, 1959—. *Spouse:* Cary Dowd Cruse. *(See page 849.)*

CRUSE, GUY REGINALD: *B.* Aug. 14, 1955, Columbia, S. C. *Ed.* Newberry Col., A.B., 1977; LTSS, M.Div., 1981. *Ord.* 1981, S. C. Synod. *Served:* Trans. to N. C. Synod, 1981. *Spouse:* Amanda West Cruse.

CULLUM, MILES TIMMERMAN: *Served:* In S. C., Cedar Grove, Leesville, 1959-1977. *Ret.* 1977. *Spouse:* Margaret Clayton Cullum. *D.* 1985, *B.* Elmwood Cem., Columbia. *(See page 849.)*

CUMBEE, LURIA ERASTUS, JR.: *Served:* In N. C. Synod, 1957-1981; in S. C., Messiah, Hanahan, 1981—; USAR Chaplain, 1957-1972; Chaplain, Franke Home, 1982—. *Spouse:* Sylvia Faye Pitts Cumbee. *(See page 849.)*

CUPP, JOHN H.: *(See page 849.)*

CUTTER, LESTER HENRY, JR.: *B.* Nov. 4, 1945, Sumter, S. C. *Ed.* Newberry Col., A.B., 1968; LTSS, M.Div., 1972. *Ord.* 1972, SE Synod. *Served:* In SE Synod, 1972-1974; in S. C., Beth Eden/St. James, Newberry, 1974-1985; St. Matthew, Lexington, 1985—. *Spouse:* Cheryl Jonette Frick Cutter.

DAILY, JOHN S.: *(See page 849.)*

DAILY, LEVI: *(See page 849.)*

DARR, WM. L.: *(See page 849.)*

DASER, FREDERICK AUGUSTINE: *(See page 849.)*

DASHER, BERGMAN S.: *(See page 849.)*

DASHER, EVERETT AUSTIN: *Served:* In S. C., Mt. Horeb, Chapin, 1961-1973; St. Timothy, Camden, 1973-1981. *Ret.* 1982. *Spouse:* Helen Mae Stoudemayer Dasher. *(See page 849.)*

DASHER, LEWIS OTTO: *(See page 849.)*

DASHER, ROBERT LEWIS: *Ed.* Univ. of S. C., M.Ed., 1975. *Served:* In S. C., Lutheran Campus Pastor, Univ. of S. C., Columbia, 1969-1984; Assistant to the Bishop, S. C. Synod, 1985-1987; Assistant to the Bishop, S. C. Synod, ELCA, 1988—. *Spouse:* Ann Secrist Krider Dasher. *(See page 849.)*

DAVIS, RAYMOND EARLE, JR.: *(See page 849.)*

DAVIS, WALTER C.: *(See page 850.)*

DAWKINS, CHARLES BARRYMORE: *Served:* In S. C., Holy Trinity, Little Mountain, 1970-1977; St. Peter, Lexington, 1977-1987; "On Leave

From Call," 1987—. *Spouse:* Betty Louise Frierson Dawkins. (*See page 850.*)

DEAL, JACK D.: *B.* March 8, 1932, Hickory, N. C. *Ed.* Florida Southern Col., B.S., 1959; LTSS, M.Div., 1962; LTSS, S.T.M., 1971. *Ord.* 1962, N. C. Synod. *Served:* In N. C. Synod, 1962-1973; in S. C., Peace, Ladson, 1974— (Mission Developer, 1973-1974). *Spouse:* Carolyn Hollar Deal.

DEAL, JAMES FRANCIS: (*See page 850.*)

DEATON, WILLIS ALEXANDER: (*See page 850.*)

DERRICK, CLARENCE KESLER, JR.: *B.* March 21, 1932, Kings Mountain, N. C. *Ed.* Newberry Col., A.B., 1954; LTSS, M.Div., 1957. *Ord.* 1957, Georgia-Alabama Synod. *Served:* In SE Synod, 1957-1971; in N. C. Synod, 1971-1986; in S. C., St. Michael, Moncks Corner, 1986—. *Spouse:* Mary Ethel Hutto Derrick.

DERRICK, CLARENCE KESLER, SR.: *Ret.* 1967. *Spouse:* Myrtle Ada Davis Derrick. *D.* 1977, *B.* Holy Trinity Cem., Little Mountain. (*See page 850.*)

DERRICK, CURTIS EUGENE: *Served:* In Ala., 1966-1972; in SE Synod, Vice-President for Development, LTSS, 1972-1985. *Spouse:* Rebecca Wise Derrick. *D.* 1985. *B.* Bethel Cem., White Rock. (*See page 850.*)

DERRICK, J. B.: (*See page 850.*)

DERRICK, J. N.: (*See page 850.*)

DERRICK, JOHN PERRY: (*See page 851.*)

DERRICK, JOSEPH CHARLES: *Served:* In S. C., Resurrection, Columbia, 1951-1978. *Ret.* 1978. *Spouse:* Julia Eargle Derrick (D. 1976). *D.* 1981. *B.* St. John Cem., Irmo. (*See page 850.*)

DERRICK, PATRICK HENRY ELMORE: (*See page 851.*)

DERRICK, PAUL: (*See page 851.*)

DERRICK, RANDALL STEVEN: *B.* Sept. 20, 1952, Leesville, S. C. *Ed.* Univ. of S. C., B.A., 1973; LTSS, M.Div., 1978. *Ord.* 1978, S. C. Synod. *Served:* In S. C., Macedonia, Prosperity, 1978—. *Spouse:* Kathy Lynn Addison Derrick.

DICKERT, JAMES CANNON: *Served:* In S. C., Reformation, Lancaster, 1957-1972; Ehrhardt Memorial, Ehrhardt 1972-1980. *Ret.* 1980. *Spouse:* Nell Julia West Dickert. (*See page 851.*)

DIEGEL, RONALD LYELL: *B.* July 3, 1937, Albany, N. Y. *Ed.* Hartwick Col., B.A., 1962; LTSS, M.Div., 1965; Univ. of S. C., M.Ed., 1980. *Ord.* 1965, N. C. Synod. *Served:* In N. C. Synod, 1965-1969; U. S. Army Chaplain, 1969-1972; in S. C., Bethlehem, Irmo, 1972— (Associate Pastor, 1972-1974). Chaplain in S. C. Army National Guard (Retired). *Spouse:* Charlotte Anne Lesemann Diegel.

DIETZ, JOHN CALVIN: (*See page 851.*)

DINNINGER, M. C.: (*See page 851.*)

DOGGETT, LEWIS BELTON, JR.: *B.* Oct. 3, 1946, Charlotte, N. C. *Ed.* Univ. of N. C., A.B., 1968; LTSS, M.Div., 1972. *Ord.* 1972, N. C. Synod. *Served:* In S. C., Prince of Peace, Chester and Abiding Presence, York,

1972-1975; "On Leave From Call," 1975-1978; Resigned from Ministry, 1978; Reinstated to Ministry, 1979; Trans. to N. C. Synod, 1979. *Spouse:* Margo Marie Myers Doggett.

DOMINICK, TEDDY PARKER, JR.: *Served:* In S. C., St. Luke, Summerville, 1965-1974; Redeemer, Newberry, 1974-1978; Resigned from Ministry, 1978. (*See page 851.*)

DONGES, DAVID ALTON: *B.* Dec. 17, 1940, Johnstown, Pa. *Ed.* Gettysburg Col., A.B., 1962; LTSGettysburg, M.Div., 1966. *Ord.* 1967, Central Pa. Synod. *Served:* In SE Synod, 1967-1980; in S. C., Incarnation, Columbia, 1980-1987; Assistant to the Bishop, S. C. Synod, ELCA, 1988—. *Spouse:* Carolyn Shinn Donges.

DOSH, THOMAS WILLIAM LUTHER: (*See page 851.*)

DOUGHERTY, JAMES LIONEL: *B.* Feb. 25, 1955, Norfolk, Va. *Ed.* Newberry Col., A.B., 1976; LTSS, M.Div., 1980; Univ. of N. C., M.Ed., 1985. *Ord.* 1980, S. C. Synod. *Served:* In S. C., Reformation, Lancaster, 1980-1981; Trans. to N. C. Synod, 1981.

DOWD, HUGH WYMAN: *Served:* In S. C., Holy Comforter, Charleston, 1971—. *Spouse:* Edna Earle Fant Dowd. (*See page 851.*)

DRAFTS, DANIEL: (*See page 851.*)

DRAFTS, JEFFERSON L.: *Spouse:* Mary Madden Leitzsey Drafts. (*See page 851.*)

DREHER, DANIEL ISAIAH: (*See page 852.*)

DREHER, GODFREY: (*See page 852.*)

DUBOIS, DWIGHT LEE: *B.* Feb. 18, 1954, Milwaukee, Wi. *Ed.* Newberry Col., B.A., 1977; LTSS, M.Div., 1981. *Ord.* 1981, SE Synod. *Served:* In SE Synod, 1981-1986; in S. C., St. Matthew, Charleston, 1986— (Associate Pastor). *Spouse:* Janice Winkler DuBois.

DUCKER, WILLIAM JOHN: *Ret.* 1970. Trans. to S. C. Synod, 1977. (*See page 852.*)

DUFFORD, EPHRAIM: (*See page 852.*)

DUFFORD, FRED EPHRAIM: *Ord.* 1928, S. C. Synod. *Served:* In S. C., Atonement, Laurens, 1969-1973. *Ret.* 1974. *Spouse:* Mary Emily Martin Dufford. (*See page 852.*)

DUKES, JAMES EDWARD, JR.: *B.* Feb. 28, 1938, Columbia, S. C. *Ed.* Univ. of Florida, B.A.E., 1961; Emory Univ., M.Div., 1965; Univ. of S. C., M.A., 1974; LTSS, Certificate, 1975. *Ord.* 1975, S. C. Synod. *Served:* Trans. to N. C. Synod, 1975. *Spouse:* Gladys Irene Canada Dukes.

DUNLAP, HUBERT AULDRIA: *Served:* In S. C., Faith, Batesburg, 1965-1977. *Ret.* 1977. *Spouse:* Eltryn Angeline Long Dunlap. (*See page 852.*)

DUTTON, WADE HAMPTON: (*See page 852.*)

DUTTON, WILLIAM ADDISON: See page 852.)

DYSINGER, HOLMES: (*See page 853.*)

EARGLE, ANDREW DAVID: *Served:* In S. C., Grace, Gilbert, 1968-1979; St. Jacob, Chapin, 1979—. S. C. Synod, Necrologist, 1982-1987. *Spouse:* Janie Katherine Mayer Eargle. (*See page 853.*)

EARGLE, MARVIN EARLE: (*See page 853.*)

EASLEY, CHARLES WARD: Newberry Col., D.D., 1986. *Served:* In N. C. Synod, 1961-1975; in S. C., Mount Tabor, West Columbia, 1975-1986; Trans. to Va. Synod, 1986. *Spouse:* Emma Lou Bossart Easley. (*See page 853.*)

EBENER, WILLIAM CLARK: *Served:* In S. C., St. Paul, Mount Pleasant, 1971-1974; in N. C. Synod, 1974-1978; in S. C., Faith, Batesburg, 1978-1980; in SE Synod, 1981-1984; in S. C., Transfiguration, Cayce, 1984—. *Spouse:* Margaret Busbee Ebener. (*See page 853.*)

ECKARD, GLENN STINE: *Served:* In N. C. Synod, 1953-1973. *Ret.* 1973. Trans. to S. C. Synod, 1973. *Spouse:* Ruby Sandel Eckard. *D.* 1976, *B.* St. Stephen Cem., Hickory, N. C. (*See page 853.*)

EDWARDS, DERALD HENRY: *B.* March 20, 1954, Columbia, S. C. *Ed.* Newberry Col., B.A., 1979: LTSS, M.Div., 1983. *Ord.* 1983, S. C. Synod. *Served:* In S. C., Ebenezer, Columbia, 1983-1986 (Associate Pastor); Mt. Pleasant, Saluda, 1986—. *Spouse:* Vicky Lindler Edwards.

EDWARDS, FRANCIS REED: (*See page 853.*)

EFIRD, ADAM: (*See page 853.*)

EFIRD, DANIEL: (*See page 853.*)

EFIRD, JACOB KILLIAN: (*See page 853.*)

EICHELBERGER, LEWIS F.: (*See page 854.*)

EICHELBERGER, ROBERT NICHOLAS: *B.* Dec. 20, 1946, Hagerstown, Md. *Ed.* Shenandoah Conservatory of Music, Winchester, Va., B.M.E., 1969; LTSS, M.Div., 1974. *Ord.* 1974, S. C. Synod. *Served:* Trans. to Virginia Synod, 1974.

EICHELBERGER, WEBSTER: (*See page 854.*)

EICHHORN, GARY WAYNE: *B.* March 16, 1953, Camden, New Jersey. *Ed.* Hanover Col., B.A.. 1975; LTSS, M.Div., 1979. *Ord.* 1979, S. C. Synod. *Served:* Trans. to N. C. Synod, 1979. *Spouse:* Deborah Meek Eichhorn.

EISEMANN, RICHARD G.: *B.* June 26, 1927, Mineola, N. Y. *Ed.* Wittenburg Univ., B.A., 1952; Hamma School of Theol., M.Div., 1955. *Ord.* 1955, Ohio Synod. *Served:* In Ohio Synod, 1955-1961; U. S. Military Chaplain, U. S. Air Force, 1961—; in S. C., 1971-1973; Trans. to SE Synod, 1973. *Spouse:* Shirley Hehl Eisemann.

EIWEN, GEORGE WILLIS: *B.* April 7, 1953, Lancaster, Pa. *Ed.* Penn State Univ., A.B., 1974; LTSGettysburg, M.Div., 1978. *Ord.* 1978, Central Pennsylvania Synod. *Served:* In Texas-La. Synod, 1978-1984; in S. C., Christus Victor, Harbison, 1984— (Pastor/Developer, 1984-1986). *Spouse:* Virginia Karvois Eiwen.

ELAM, J. DONALD: (*See page 854.*)

ELLSWORTH, RAYMOND ROBERT: (*See page 854.*)

ELMORE, ELIJAH: (*See page 854.*)

EMANUEL, PHILIP GRANTHAM: *B.* Jan. 10, 1956, Lancaster, S. C. *Ed.* Furman Univ., B.A., 1978; LTSS, M.Div., 1987. *Ord.* 1987, S. C. Synod. *Served:* Trans. to Va. Synod, 1987. *Spouse:* Susan-Marie Sherwin Roper Emanuel.

EPPING, WILHELM: (*See page 854.*)

EPTING, EUGENE L., JR.: (*See page 854.*)

EPTING, HEYWARD WIGGERS: *Served:* In S. C., St. John, Charleston, 1942-1972. *Spouse:* Charlotte Elizabeth Neeley Epting (D. 1973). *D.* 1972, *B.* St. John Cem., Charleston. (*See page 854.*)

EPTING, MONROE JACOB: (*See page 854.*)

EPTING, THADDEUS: (*See page 854.*)

EUBANKS, WILLIAM ALEXANDER: *B.* Sept. 2, 1920, East Point, Ga. *Ed.* Univ. of Ga., B.B.A., 1956; LTSGettysburg, M.Div., 1959; LTSS, D.Min., 1982. *Ord.* 1959, Ga.-Ala. Synod. *Served:* In SE Synod, 1959-1962; in Fla. Synod, 1962-1973; in S. C., Chaplain, Beckman Mental Health Center, Greenwood, 1973-1980; Chaplain, Self Memorial Hospital, Greenwood, 1980—. *Spouse:* Mary Elizabeth Whitehead Eubanks.

EVANS, J. PIERCE, JR.: *Served:* In S. C., Summer Memorial, Newberry, 1968-1975; St. James, Leesville, 1975-1982; Trans. to N. C. Synod, 1983. (*See page 854.*)

EVERETT, DARYL STEPHEN: *B.* June 24, 1942, Salem, Ohio. *Ed.* Youngstown Univ., A.B., 1963; Hamma School of Theology, M.Div., 1966; Boston Univ. School of Theology, Th.D., 1976. *Ord.* 1968, Ohio Synod. *Served:* In Ohio Synod, 1969-1973; in Upper New York Synod, 1973-1977; in Ohio Synod, 1977-1987; in S. C. Synod, Dewey F. Beam, Assoc. Professor of Pastoral Care, LTSS, 1987—. *Spouse:* Judith Ann Schuller Everett.

FABER, JOHN CHARLES (CHRISTOPHER): (*See page 855.*)

FABER, MATTHEW FREDERICK CHARLES: (*See page 855.*)

FARB, ROBERT C.: *Served:* In S. C., Vice-President for Development, Newberry College, 1963-1975; Trans. to Florida Synod, 1975. (*See page 855.*)

FEGE, HARTMUT: *B.* Nov. 8, 1942, Gelnhausen, W. Germany. *Ed.* Middle Tennessee State Univ., B.S., 1961; LTSS, M.Div., 1969; Vanderbilt Univ. Divinity School, D.Min., 1980. *Ord.* 1969, SE Synod. *Served:* In SE Synod, 1969-1976; in S. C., St. Luke, Summerville, 1976-1981; St. Peter, Pawleys Island, 1981— (Pastor/Developer, 1981-1984). *Spouse:* Brigitte Ziesemer Fege.

FELKER, ERNEST ARTHUR: *Served:* In Eastern Canada Synod, 1963-1981. *Ret.* 1981. Trans. to S. C., 1983. *Spouse:* Virginia Felker. (*See page 855.*)

FELTMAN, RONALD WILLIAM: *B.* Sept. 12, 1957, Jacksonville, Florida. *Ed.* Univ. of S. C., B.A., 1980; LTSS, M.Div., 1986. *Ord.* 1986, S. C. Synod. *Served:* In S. C., Trinity, Elloree, 1986-1987; Good Shepherd, Columbia, 1987— (Associate Pastor).

FERNSLER, EUGENE ROBERT: *B.* May 31, 1947, Easton, Pennsylvania. *Ed.* Baldwin-Wallace Col., B.A., 1969; LTSS, M.Div., 1973. *Ord.* 1973, S. C. Synod. *Served:* Trans. to Florida Synod, 1973.

FESPERMAN, FRANCIS IRVING: *Served:* Professor and Head of Religion Department, Newberry College, 1957—. *Spouse:* Ruby Kathleen Castor Fesperman. (*See page 855.*)

FICKEN, CARL FREDERICK WILHELM, JR.: *Ed.* Univ of S. C., Ph.D., 1972. *Served:* In N. C. Synod, 1973— (Associate Professor of Theology and Culture, LTSS, 1976—). *Spouse:* Anne Holderfield Ficken. (*See page 855.*)

FINCK, WILLIAM JOHN: (*See page 855.*)

FINK, WILLIAM H.: (*See page 855.*)

FINKBEINER, ROBERT GLYNN: *Served:* In S. C., St. John, Beaufort, 1971-1972. Trans. to Upper N. Y. Synod, 1972. (*See page 855.*)

FISCHER, JOHN FREDERICK: *Served:* In S. C., St. Timothy, Goose Creek, 1966-1981; Nativity, Spartanburg, 1982—. *Spouse:* June Loretta Pys Fischer. (*See page 855.*)

FISHER, CLIFFORD PAUL, II: *Served:* In S. C., Transfiguration, Cayce, 1962-1983. *Ret.* 1983; Trans. to N. C. Synod, 1983. *Spouse:* Martha Lou Mauney Fisher. (*See page 855.*)

FISHER, EARL H.: (*See page 856.*)

FISHER, HERMAN GEORGE: (*See page 856.*)

FISHER, RAY RICHARD: (*See page 856.*)

FLOWERS, CARROLL WILLIAM: *B.* Jan. 11, 1928, Hickory, N. C. *Ed.* Lenoir-Rhyne Col., B.S., 1966; LTSS, M.Div., 1969. *Ord.* 1969, N. C. Synod. *Served:* In N. C. Synod, 1969-1982; in S. C., Bethany, Newberry, 1983—. *Spouse:* Delorys E. Duncan Flowers.

FOELSCH, CHARLES B.: (*See page 856.*)

FOX, CLARENCE MERKEL: (*See page 856.*)

FOX, JUNIUS BOST: (*See page 856.*)

FRANKLOW (FRANCKLOW), JOHN PHILIP: (*See page 856.*)

FRASER, ROBERT L.: (*See page 856.*)

FRAZIER, VERNON F.: (*See page 856.*)

FREED, CHARLES ABRAM: (*See page 857.*)

FREYSCHMIDT, ALFRED: (*See page 857.*)

FRICK, JOHN MILTON: Newberry Col., D.D., 1970. *Served:* In S. C., St. Stephen, Lexington, 1967-1975. *Ret.* 1975. *Spouse:* Nettie Mae Drafts Frick. (*See page 857.*)

FRICK, VERNON A.: (*See page 857.*)

FRICK, WOODROW FELTON: *B.* Dec. 7, 1946, Newberry, S. C. *Ed.* Univ. of N. C. at Charlotte, B.A., 1969; LTSS, M.Div., 1973. *Ord.* 1973, N. C. Synod. *Served:* In N. C. Synod, 1973-1977; in S. C., Colony, Newberry, 1977-1981; Trans. to N. C. Synod, 1981. *Spouse:* Zelia Fisher Frick.

FRIEDERICHS, JOHN GEORGE: (*See page 857.*)

FRITZ, CHARLES EVERETT: (*See page 857.*)

FRITZ, CHARLES EVERETT II: *B.* Dec. 14, 1951, Columbia S. C. *Ed.* Lenoir-Rhyne Col., B.A., 1974; LSTChicago, M.Div., 1979. *Ord.* 1979, S. C.

Synod. *Served:* In S. C., St. John, Spartanburg, 1979-1983 (Associate Pastor); St. Matthias, Easley, 1983—. *Spouse:* Janice Louise Makin Fritz.

FRITZ, WILLIAM RICHARD, JR.: *B.* Feb. 7, 1949, Columbia, S. C. *Ed.* Yale Univ., A.B., 1972; LTSS, M.Div., 1977. *Ord.* 1977, S. C. Synod. *Served:* Trans. to Virginia Synod, 1977. *Spouse:* Cecilia Carpenter Fritz.

FRITZ, WILLIAM RICHARD, SR.: *Served:* In S. C., Librarian and Professor of Bibliography, LTSS, 1947-1987 (Assistant Librarian, 1947-1952). *Ret.* 1987. *Spouse:* Evelyn Rogers Ackerman Fritz. (*See page 857.*)

FROELICH, CARL FREDERICK: (*See page 857.*)

FULENWIDER, EDWARD: (*See page 857.*)

FULLER, HAROLD F., JR.: (*See page 858.*)

FULMER, GUERRY ALVIN: *Served:* In S. C., Grace, Prosperity, 1970-1979; Holy Cross, Charleston Heights, 1979—. *Spouse:* June Oliva Moore Fulmer. (*See page 858.*)

FULMER, VERLEY LORENZO: (*See page 858.*)

GASSER, JOHN (JOHANN): (*See page 858.*)

GIESSENDANNER, J. ULRICH I: (*See page 858.*)

GIESSENDANNER, JOHN U. II: (*See page 858.*)

GLAZIER, FREDERICK LEROY: *B.* Dec. 8, 1938, Springfield, Ohio. *Ed.* Newberry Col., A.B., 1960; LTSSaskatoon, M.Div., 1965. *Ord.* 1965, Ohio Synod. *Served:* In Canada, 1965-1966; in Central States Synod, 1966-1968; in U.S. Army, 1968-1985; in SE Synod, 1985; in S. C., Faith, Johns Island, 1985-1986; "On Leave From Call," 1986—.

GODFREY, RICHARD: (*See page 858.*)

GOLNITZ, DARRELL DEAN: *B.* April 22, 1949, Alta, Iowa. *Ed.* Concordia Col., B.A., 1971; Christ Seminary, M.Div., 1975. *Ord.* 1976, S. C. Synod. *Served:* In S. C., Ebenezer, Columbia 1975-78 (Associate Pastor); Shepherd of the Sea, Garden City, 1978-1986. Trans. to SE Synod, 1986. *Spouse:* Mary M. Schultz Golnitz.

GONGAWARE, GEORGE JONAS: (*See page 858.*)

GOODMAN, REUBEN ALONZO: (*See page 858.*)

GOTWALD, WILLIAM KURTZ: (*See page 859.*)

GRAFF, JOHN HENRY: (*See page 859.*)

GRAGG, STEPHEN THOMAS: *B.* Nov. 2, 1948, Hickory, N. C. *Ed.* Newberry Col., A.B., 1971; LTSS, M.Div. 1975; Southern Baptist Center for Biblical Studies, Atlanta, D.Min., 1984. *Ord.* 1975, N. C. Synod. *Served:* In N. C. Synod, 1975-1980; in Nebraska Synod, 1980-1986; in S. C., Holy Trinity, North Augusta, 1986—. Chaplain, U.S. Navy Reserves. *Spouse:* Susan Yost Gragg.

GRAICHEN, JOHN GEORGE: (*See page 859.*)

GREEN, GAREY: *B.* Aug. 16, 1935, Jacksonville, Fla. *Ed.* Benedict Col., B.A., 1967; Virginia Union Univ., M.Div., 1970; Univ. of S. C., M.Ed., 1976; Univ. of S. C., Master of Criminal Justice, 1978; Friendship Col., D.D.,

1978; LTSS, D.Min., 1981. *Ord.* 1983, S. C. Synod. *Served:* Trans. to Metro N.Y. Synod, 1983. *Spouse:* Carolyn Davis Green.

GREENWALT, ARTHUR EDWARD, SR.: *B.* July 7, 1925, Shenandoah, Pennsylvania. *Ed.* Muhlenberg Col., A.B., 1945; LTSPhiladelphia, M.Div., 1948. *Ord.* 1948, Ministerium of Pennsylvania. *Served:* In Ministerium of Penn., 1948-1951; in Northeastern Penn. Synod, 1951-1955; Military Chaplain, U.S. Air Force, 1955-1974; in S. C., Good Shepherd, Walterboro, 1974-1978. *Ret.* 1978; Trans. to Florida Synod, 1978. *Spouse:* Helen Carlisle Greenwalt.

GREEVER, WALTON HARLOWE: *(See page 859.)*

GRIFFIN, JOSEPH LEROY: *B.* Oct. 1, 1922, Rural Hall, N. C. *Ed.* Lenoir-Rhyne Col., A.B., 1943; LTSS, M.Div., 1948; Newberry Col., D.D., 1963. *Ord.* 1948, N. C. Synod. *Served:* In N. C. and SE Synods, 1948-1980; in S. C., Cross and Crown, Florence, 1980-1982 (Pastor/Developer, 1980-1981); Trans. to N. C. Synod, 1982. *Spouse:* Rita Wallace Griffin.

GROSECLOSE, DAVID BITTLE: *(See page 859.)*

GROSSMAN, HENRY CLAY: *(See page 859.)*

GRUETZMACHER, ROGER FRANKLIN: *(See page 859.)*

GUEBNER, GEORGE F.: *(See page 859.)*

GUNTER, DENNIS RODNEY: *B.* May 30, 1946, Brunswick, Ga. *Ed.* Newberry Col., A.B. 1968; LTSS, M.Div., 1973. *Ord.* 1973, S. C. Synod. *Served:* In S. C., Good Shepherd & Sandy Run, Swansea, 1973-1977; St. Mark, Blythewood, 1977-1982; Silverstreet, Silverstreet, 1982—. *Spouse:* Dell Merchant Gunter.

HAAS, TIMOTHY ALBERT: *B.* June 18, 1958, Newton, N. C. *Ed.* Lenoir-Rhyne Col., B.A., 1980; LTSS, M.Div., 1984. *Ord.* 1984, N. C. Synod. *Served:* In S. C., Christ, Columbia, 1984—.

HACKMANN, AUGUSTUS: *(See page 859.)*

HAHN, SAMUEL WAIGHTSTILL: *Spouse:* Doris Becker Hahn. (D. 1981). *D.* 1981, *B.* Elmwood Cem., Columbia. *(See page 860.)*

HAHNBAUM, JOHN SEVERIN: *(See page 860.)*

HAIGLER, ALVIN HAYNE, SR.: *Served:* In S. C., Redeemer, Columbia, 1964-1972 (Mission Developer, 1964-1965); St. James, Sumter, 1972—. Military Chaplain, United States Air Force Reserve, 1959—. *Spouse:* Loretta Virginia Herlong Haigler. *(See page 860.)*

HAIGLER, GEORGE R.: *(See page 860.)*

HAIGLER, IRVIN GORDON: *(See page 860.)*

HAIGLER, JESSE BOWMAN: *(See page 860.)*

HALLMAN, ENOCH ARDEN, JR.: *B.* Aug. 21, 1948, Newberry, S. C. *Ed.* Newberry Col., A.B., 1970; LTSS, M.Div., 1975; S. C. Dept. of Mental Health, Clinical Pastoral Education, 1981-1983. *Ord.* 1975, S. C. Synod. *Served:* In S. C., Silverstreet, Silverstreet, 1975-1981; "On Leave From Call," 1981-1983; St. John, Lexington, 1983-1986; Director of Pastoral Family Counseling Services & Treatment, Newberry County Commission on Alcohol & Drug Abuse, 1986—. *Spouse:* Edna Jean Mathias Hallman.

HALLMAN, SAMUEL THOMAS: *(See page 860.)*

HALTIWANGER, GEORGE, JR.: *(See page 860.)*

HALTIWANGER, GEORGE, SR.: *(See page 861.)*

HALTIWANGER, WILLIAM DARR: *(See page 861.)*

HAMM, LUTHER BOYD: Trans. to N. C. Synod, 1965. *(See page 861.)*

HAMM, TOMMY JOE: *B.* Sept. 30, 1947, Newberry, S. C. *Ed.* Univ. of S. C., B.S., 1969; LTSS, M.Div., 1973. *Ord.* 1973, S. C. Synod. *Served:* In S. C., St. Matthias, Easley, 1973-1976 (Mission Developer, 1973-1974); St. Nicholas and Trinity, Fairfax, 1976-1984; Trans. to Florida Synod, 1984. *Spouse:* Gale Hamm.

HARLEY, RAYMOND EUGENE, II: *Served:* In S. C., St. Paul, Columbia, 1969-1975 (Associate Pastor); "On Leave From Call," 1975-1977; Mt. Tabor, West Columbia, 1978-1982 (Assistant Pastor); St. John, Irmo, 1982—. *Spouse:* Iris Cundiff Harley. *(See page 861.)*

HARMAN, JULIAN BACHMAN: *(See page 861.)*

HARMON, FRED: *(See page 861.)*

HARMS, JOHN HENRY: *(See page 861.)*

HARRIS, FREDERICK F.: *(See page 861.)*

HARRIS, ROBERT WARREN: *B.* Oct. 10, 1950, Bloomsburg, Pa. *Ed.* Susquehanna Univ., B.A., 1972; LTSChicago, M.Div., 1976; Univ. of Chicago, Ph.D. Study. *Ord.* 1986, S. C. Synod. *Served:* In S. C., Ebenezer, Columbia, 1986— (Associate Pastor). *Spouse:* Laura Huestis Harris.

HARTE, BARRY JAY: *B.* July 2, 1960, Bethlehem, Pa. *Ed.* William and Mary Univ., B.A., 1982; LTSPhiladelphia, M.Div., 1986. *Ord.* 1986, Northeastern Pa. Synod. *Served:* In S. C., St. Luke, Summerville, 1987— (Associate Pastor).

HARTER, WILLIAM GEORGE: *(See page 861.)*

HARTWIG, T. G.: *(See page 862.)*

HASKELL, JOHN BACHMAN: *(See page 862.)*

HATCH, PAUL: *Served:* In S. C., Beth-Eden and St. James, Newberry, 1966-1973; "Awaiting A Call," 1973-1974; Resigned from Ministry, 1974. *(See page 862.)*

HAVENS, MARY BERNADETTE: *B.* Oct. 1, 1954, Holdrege, Nebraska. *Ed.* Midland Lutheran Col., Fremont, Neb., B.A. 1976; LTSGettysburg, M.Div., 1980; Princeton Theological Sem., Ph.D. Study. *Ord.* 1985, Nebraska Synod. *Served:* In Nebraska Synod, 1980-1983; in S. C., Assistant Professor, Church History, LTSS, 1985—.

HAWKINS, ELIJAH: *(See page 862.)*

HAWKINS, I. P.: *(See page 862.)*

HAWKINS, JACOB H.: *(See page 862.)*

HAWKINS, PETER W.: *(See page 862.)*

HAWKINS, ROBERT WILLIAM: *B.* Jan. 14, 1950, Alamance County, N. C. *Ed.* Lenoir-Rhyne Col., B.A., 1974; LTSS, M.Div., 1981. *Ord.* 1981,

N. C. Synod. *Served:* In N. C. Synod, 1981-4; in S. C., Providence, Lexington, 1985—.

HAZELIUS, ERNEST LEWIS: (*See page 862.*)

HECKEL, JOHANNES: (*See page 863.*)

HEEMSOTH, F. H. W.: (*See page 863.*)

HEGLAR, DEWEY LEE: (*See page 863.*)

HEIDT, EMORY B.: (*See page 863.*)

HEISEY, PAUL HAROLD: (*See page 863.*)

HELMLY, CECIL CALVERT: (*See page 863.*)

HENDRIX, SCOTT HAMPTON: *B.* Dec. 26, 1942, Columbia, S. C. *Ed.* Duke Univ., B.A., 1963; LTSS, M.Div., 1967; Univ. Of Tuebingen, Germany, D.Th., 1971. *Ord.* 1972, S. C. Synod. *Served:* Professor of Church History, LTSS, 1971-1984; Trans. to N. J. Synod 1984. *Spouse:* Emily Frick Hendrix.

HENDRIX, WILFORD PASCAL, JR.: *Served:* In S. C., St. Barnabas, Charleston, 1969—. *Spouse:* Barbara Jean Feldesy Hendrix. (*See page 863.*)

HENKEL, DAVID: (*See page 863.*)

HENKEL, PAUL: (*See page 863.*)

HERBERTSON, DAVID HILLEN: *Served:* In S. C., St. Timothy, Camden, 1967-1972. Trans. to N. C. Synod, 1973. (*See page 864.*)

HERLONG, WALTER OSBORNE, JR.: *Served:* In SE Synod, 1965-1977; in S. C., Mount Tabor, Little Mountain, 1977—. *Spouse:* Virginia Ruth Peery Herlong. (*See page 864.*)

HERSHER, SAMUEL: (*See page 864.*)

HEWITT, ABEL KENNETH, JR.: (*See page 864.*)

HEWITT, ABEL KENNETH, SR.: *Served:* Director of Development and Alumni Affairs, LTSS, 1967-1983. *Spouse:* Bonnie Moore Hewitt; Ruth Owens Hewitt (D. 1976); Lane Dixon Hewitt (D. 1973). *D.* 1983, *B.* Elmwood Cem., Columbia. (*See page 864.*)

HEYER, JOHN LEWIS: *Served:* In S. C., Our Saviour, Greenville, 1965-1971. Trans. to SE Synod, 1971. (*See page 864.*)

HICKERSON, FESTUS: (*See page 864.*)

HICKS, WILLIAM WATKINS: (*See page 864.*)

HIERS, WILLIAM F.: (*See page 864.*)

HILL, GARTH LEE: *Served:* In S. C., Zion, Lexington, 1969-1979. *Ret.* 1979. *Spouse:* Patricia Steadman Hill. (*See page 865.*)

HILLER, WILLIAM HASKELL: (*See page 865.*)

HIMES, JOHN ROBERT: *B.* July 11, 1912, Newark, Ohio. *Ed.* Wittenberg Col., A.B., 1935; Hamma Divinity School, Cert. of Theology, 1938; Duke Univ., M.Div., 1964 and M.S.T., 1965. *Ord.* 1938, Ohio Synod. *Served:* In Ohio Synod, 1938-1942; "On Leave From Call," 1942-1943; U.S. Army

Chaplain, 1943-1963; Graduate Studies, Duke Univ., 1963-1967; in Western Penn.-West Va. Synod, 1967-1968; in N. C. Synod, 1968-1977 (Assistant Professor of New Testament, LTSS, 1968-1977). *Ret.* 1977. Trans. to S. C. Synod, 1977. *Spouse:* Ruth Marie Dickerson Himes.

HITE, ENOCH: (*See page 865.*)

HIX, PAM MITCHAM: *B.* Oct. 9, 1952, Kings Mountain, N. C. *Ed.* Univ. of N. C., B.Mus.Ed., 1974; LTSS, M.Div., 1987. *Ord.* 1987, N. C. Synod. *Served:* In S. C., Mt. Tabor, West Columbia (Associate Pastor), 1987—. *Spouse:* D. Michael Hix.

HOBBS, ROBERT GEORGE: *B.* Nov. 3, 1930. *Ed.* Univ. of Richmond, B.A., 1960; LTSS, M.Div., 1978. *Ord.* 1978, S. C. Synod. *Served:* Trans. to Virginia Synod, 1978. *Spouse:* Cia B. Huston Hobbs.

HOCK, ROBERT LEROY: *Ed.* McCormick Sem., D.Min., 1977; Newberry Col., D.D., 1981. *Served:* In S. C., Ebenezer, Columbia, 1964-72; Trans. to Fla. Synod, 1972. *Spouse:* Mary Quaid McLean Hock. (*See page 865.*)

HOCKHEIMER, LEWIS: (*See page 865.*)

HOFFMEYER, RALPH W.: (*See page 865.*)

HOLLAND, GEORGE WILLIAM: (*See page 865.*)

HOLLAND, ROBERT CHRISTIAN: (*See page 865.*)

HOLLIFIELD, WILLIAM RAYMOND: *Served:* In S. C., St. Matthew, Charleston, 1971-1975 (Assistant Pastor); Trans. to SE Synod, 1975. (*See page 866.*)

HOLLINGER, RICHARD MILLER: *Served:* In S. C., Our Saviour, Greenville, 1962-1965. Trans. to Florida Synod, 1965. (*See page 866.*)

HOLMES, CHARLES ELBERT: (*See page 866.*)

HOLT, JOSEPH WHITSETT: *Ed.* LTSS, S.T.M., 1977. *Served:* In SE Synod, 1963-1984; in S. C., Cross and Crown, Florence, 1984—. *Spouse:* Melba Taylor Holt. (*See page 866.*)

HONEYCUTT, CARL ADAMS: *Spouse:* Mary Elizabeth Honeycutt. *D.* 1983, *B.* Elmwood Cem., Columbia. (*See page 866.*)

HONNEYCUTT, FRANKLIN GAINES: *B.* May 15, 1957, Chattanooga, Tenn. *Ed.* Clemson Univ., B.A., 1979; LTSS, M.Div., 1985. *Ord.* 1985 by Virginia Synod for S. C. Synod. *Served:* Trans. to Virginia Synod, 1985. *Spouse:* Cindy Christmas Honneycutt.

HONOUR, JOHN H.: (*See page 866.*)

HOOK, WADE FRANKLIN: (*See page 866.*)

HOPE, JOHN CHRISTIAN: (*See page 866.*)

HOPKINS, BURRELL N.: (*See page 867.*)

HOPPE, CHARLES FREDERICK WILLIAM: (*See page 867.*)

HORINE, JOHN WINEBRENNER: (*See page 867.*)

HORN, EDWARD TRAILL: (*See page 867.*)

HORT, ELIAS B.: (*See page 867.*)

HOUCK, WILLIAM ALEXANDER: (*See page 867.*)

HOUGEN, JOHN BYRON: *B.* July 14, 1948, Cedar Rapids, Iowa. *Ed.* Luther Col., B.A., 1970; Harvard Divinity School, M.Div., 1975. *Ord.* 1975, Iowa Synod. *Served:* In Virginia Synod, 1975-1986; in S. C., Lutheran Campus Pastor, Univ. of S. C., 1986—. *Spouse:* E. Marcia Boe Hougen.

HOUGH, GEORGE A.: (*See page 867.*)

HOUSEAL, BERNARD MICHAEL: (*See page 867.*)

HOWELL, ALFRED WAYNE, JR.: *Ed.* McCormick Theological Sem., D.Min., 1978. *Served:* In S. C., St. Luke, Florence, 1961—. *Spouse:* Hattie Delores Antley Howell. (*See page 867.*)

HOWELL, CHARLES WILLIAM: (*See page 867.*)

HOY, DANIEL O.: *B.* May 28, 1930, Sunbury, Pa. *Ed.* Susquehanna Univ., A.B., 1955; LTSGettysburg, M.Div., 1968; Penn. State Univ., M.A., 1961. *Ord.* 1968, Central Penn. Synod. *Served:* In Md. Synod, 1968-1977; in Central Penn. Synod, 1977-1979. *Ret.* 1979; Trans. to S. C., 1985. *Spouse:* Judith Hoy.

HUDDLE, M. D.: (*See page 867.*)

HUFFMAN, ARTHUR M.: (*See page 868.*)

HUGHES, S. P.: (*See page 868.*)

HUNGERPELER, DAVID: (*See page 868.*)

HUNGERPELER, R. J.: (*See page 868.*)

HUNTER, DAVID BRYAN: *B.* May 25, 1946, Amherst, Nova Scotia, Canada. *Ed.* Mount Allison Univ., B.Comm., 1969; LTSS, M.Div., 1984. *Ord.* 1984, S. C. Synod. *Served:* In S. C., Resurrection and St. Matthew, Cameron, 1984—. *Spouse:* Kathleen Ruth Hunter.

HUNTLEY, JOSEPH: *B.* July 16, 1920, Reedsburg, Wisconsin. *Ed.* Univ. of Wisconsin, B.A., 1941; LSTChicago, M.Div., 1948. *Ord.* 1948, Wartburg Synod. *Served:* In Illinois Synod, 1948-1950; in Wisconsin Synod, 1950-1955; in Florida Synod, 1955-1980; in S. C., Ascension, Columbia, 1980-1984. *Ret.* 1984; Trans. to Va. Synod, 1984. *Spouse:* Carolyn Jane Harrison Huntley.

ISAACSON, CARL OSCAR: *B.* Jan. 9, 1950, Chicago, Illinois. *Ed.* Augustana Col., A.B., 1971; LTSS, M.Div., 1975. *Ord.* 1975, Illinois Synod. *Served:* In S. C., Holy Cross, Charleston Heights, 1975-1979; Trinity, Georgetown, 1974-1984; Trans. to SE Synod, 1984. *Spouse:* Barbara Ruth Cooper Isaacson.

IUNGHERR (YUNGHERR), THEODORE: (*See page 868.*)

JACKSON, HARRY ADDISON: (*See page 868.*)

JACKSON, STEVEN DOUGLAS: *B.* Feb. 16, 1957, Key West, Florida. *Ed.* Newberry Col., B.A., 1979; LTSS, M.Div., 1983. *Ord.* 1983, S. C. Synod. *Served:* In S. C., Bethlehem, Pomaria, 1983—.

JEFFCOAT, LUTHER HALL: (*See page 868.*)

JEFFCOAT, WILLIAM ERNEST: *Served:* In S. C., St. Matthew, Lexington, 1971-1976; "On Leave From Call," 1976-1977; Resigned from Ministry, 1977; Reinstated to Ministry, 1985; Mt. Hebron, Leesville, 1985—. *Spouse:* Virginia Gaffos Jeffcoat. (*See page 868.*)

JERNIGAN, WALTER DENZEL: *B.* Oct. 13, 1948, Winnsboro, S. C. *Ed.* The Citadel, B.A., 1970; LTSS, M.Div., 1974. *Ord.* 1978, S. C. Synod. *Served:* Trans. to Maryland Synod, 1978. *Spouse:* Linda Jane Hughes Jernigan.

JERNIGAN, WILLIAM EARL: Trans. to S. C. Synod, 1980. *Served:* In S. C., St. Timothy, Whitmire and Augsburg, Union, 1980-1983; Resigned from Ministry, 1983. *Spouse:* Betty Jean Hartman Jernigan. (*See page 868.*)

JERSILD, PAUL THOMAS: *B.* May 28, 1931, Blair, Nebraska. *Ed.* Dana Col., B.A., 1953, Wartburg Seminary, M.Div., 1959; Univ. of Neb., M.A., 1955; Univ. of Muenster (W. Germany), Dr. Theol., 1962. *Ord.* 1962, The American Lutheran Church. *Served:* In ALC 1962-1984; in S. C., Dean of Academic Affairs & Prof. of Theology & Ethics, LTSS, 1984—. Joined LCA Clergy in 1985. *Spouse:* Marilyn Joyce Steffensen Jersild.

JOHNSON, DAVID FRONTIS: *Served:* In N. C. Synod, Regional Secretary BAM—LCA—DMNA, 1962-1981. *D.* 1981, *B.* Kimball Memorial, Kannapolis, N. C. (*See page 868.*)

JOHNSON, DOUGLAS WALTER: *Ed.* Southern Methodist Univ., Ph.D., 1971. *Served:* Professor of Religion and Philosophy and Assistant to the Vice-President for Academic Affairs, Claflin College, Orangeburg, 1968—. *Spouse:* Annette Marie Petersen. (*See page 868.*)

JOHNSON, HARRY WILLIAM, JR.: (*See page 869.*)

JONES, FRANK COLLINS, JR.: (*See page 869.*)

JORDAN, ROGER CALVIN, JR.: (*See page 869.*)

JULIAN, WILLIAM ALEXANDER: (*See page 869.*)

KAHL, GEORGE CALVIN: *Served:* In S. C., Military Chaplain, U.S. Army, 1958-1975. Trans. to N. C. Synod, 1975. (*See page 869.*)

KANNADAY, WAYNE CAMPBELL: *B.* Nov. 24, 1953, Columbia, S. C. *Ed.* Newberry Col., A.B., 1975; LTSS, M.Div., 1979. *Ord.* 1979, S. C. Synod. *Served:* In S. C., Mt. Hermon, West Columbia, 1979—.

KARN, AARON JACOB: (*See page 869.*)

KARRES, GEORGE R.: *B.* May 31, 1952, Tonawanda, N. Y. *Ed.* Univ. of Central Florida, B.A., 1975; LTSS, M.Div., 1979. *Ord.* 1979, Florida Synod. *Served:* In S. C., Christ, Columbia, 1979-1983; Trans. to Florida Synod, 1983. *Spouse:* Elizabeth Harris Karres.

KARSTENS, HEINRICH LUDWIG ADOLF RICHARD: (*See page 869.*)

KAYLOR, RAY BUFORD: (*See page 869.*)

KEIFFER, EPHRAIM: (*See page 869.*)

KEISLER, EFIRD BRYAN: *Spouse:* Mabel Sease Keisler (D. 1985). *D.* 1983, *B.* St. Paul Cem., Gilbert. (*See page 869.*)

KEISLER, FRANK LAVAUGHN, SR.: *Served:* In S. C., Union/Mt. Hebron, Leesville, 1971-1977; Union, Leesville, 1978—. *Spouse:* Elizabeth Jean Haigler Keisler. (*See page 870.*)

KEISLER, JAMES ALBERT, JR.: *Served:* In Va. Synod, 1969-70; in N. C. Synod, 1970-73. Pastor-Emeritus, Mt. Tabor, West Columbia, 1987—. *Ret.* 1973; Trans. to S. C., 1974. *Spouse:* Violet Huffman Keisler. (*See page 870.*)

KEISTER, THURSTON ORVILLE: (*See page 870.*)

KELLER, SAMUEL LUTHER: (*See page 870.*)

KEMPSON, JAMES OBERT: *Served:* In S. C., Assistant Professor of Pastoral Care, LTSS, 1952-1975; Guest Professor of Pastoral Care, LTSS, 1975-1980, 1982, 1984; Interim Director of Internship, 1985-1986; Pastoral Services Consultant, S. C. Department of Mental Health, 1965-1981. Director, Education and Training, Lowman Home, 1982-87. *Ret.* 1981. *Spouse:* Rachel Louisa Muller Kempson. (*See page 870.*)

KERN, EUGENE HENRY: *B.* Aug. 22, 1952, Sumter, S. C. *Ed.* Erskine Col., A.B., 1974; LTSS, M.Div., 1979; Drew Univ., D.Min., 1985. *Ord.* 1979, S. C. Synod. *Served:* In S. C., St. Mark, Isle of Palms, 1979-1982; Trans. to Fla. Synod, 1982. *Spouse:* Jacqueline Brisben Kern.

KESTER, MOSES LEE: (*See page 870.*)

KETCHIE, WILLIAM STEWART: *B.* Feb. 1, 1949, Salisbury, N. C. *Ed.* Lenoir-Rhyne Col., B.A., 1971; LTSS, M.Div., 1975. *Ord.* 1975, N. C. Synod. *Served:* In S. C., Reformation, Columbia, 1975-1977 (Team Pastor); Trans. to N. C. Synod, 1978. *Spouse:* Kathy Marlene Brown Ketchie.

KINARD, JAMES DAVID: (*See page 870.*)

KINARD, KARL WILLIAM: S. C. Synod President Emeritus, 1971-1983. *Spouse:* Esther Ann Osteen Kinard (D. 1983). *D.* 1983, *B.* Greenlawn Cem., Columbia. (*See page 871.*)

KINARD, MICHAEL MIDDLETON: (*See page 871.*)

KING, CARL STANLEY: *Served:* In S. C., Military Chaplain, U.S. Army, 1963-1972; Trans. to Pacific SW Synod, 1972. (*See page 871.*)

KING, WILLIAM HOWARD: *B.* Oct. 5, 1952, New Orleans, La. *Ed.* Furman Univ., B.A., 1974; LTSS, M.Div., 1980; Louisiana State Univ., M.A., 1976. *Ord.* 1980, S. C. Synod. *Served:* Trans. to N. C. Synod, 1980. *Spouse:* Gail Scott King.

KINNEY, JAMES WILLIAM: *B.* Nov. 12, 1937, Winston-Salem, N. C. *Ed.* Univ. of N. C., A.B., 1959; LTSS, M.Div., 1963. *Ord.* 1963, N. C. Synod. *Served:* In SE Synod, 1963-1966; in N. C. Synod, 1966-1968; Military Chaplain, U.S. Air Force, 1968—. Trans. to S. C. Synod, 1981. *Spouse:* Lois Marie Bouknight.

KINPORTS, PAUL MILLER: (*See page 871.*)

KINSLER, DAVID E.: *Served:* In SE Synod, 1964-1973; in S. C., St. John, Pomaria, 1973-1979. *Ret.* 1979. *Spouse:* Ruth Magdalene Voegele Kinsler. (*See page 871.*)

KINSLER, JAMES FREDERICK: *B.* Aug. 6, 1955, Würzburg, Germany. *Ed.* Newberry Col., B.A., 1977; LTSS, M.Div., 1981. *Ord.* 1981, S. C. Synod. *Served:* In S. C., Trinity, Elloree, 1981-1985. Trans. to Western Pennsylvania/West Virginia Synod, 1985. *Spouse:* Martha E. Wallace Kinsler.

KISER, JOHN FRANKLIN: (*See page 871.*)

KISTLER, HENRY ALFRED: (*See page 871.*)

KISTLER, PAUL: (*See page 871.*)

KLATT, ALICE DEFOREST: *B.* July 13, 1933, Houston, Texas. *Ed.* Univ. of S. C., B.A., 1982; LTSS, M.Div., 1986. *Ord.* 1986, S. C. Synod. *Served:* In S. C., Sandy Run, Swansea, 1986—. *Spouse:* Emil H. Klatt, Jr.

KLECKLEY, HENRY D.: (*See page 872.*)

KLECKLEY, JACOB: (*See page 872.*)

KLECKLEY, RUSSELL CLIFTON: *B.* Nov. 11, 1955, Columbia, S. C. *Ed.* Newberry Col., A.B., 1978; LTSS, M.Div., 1982; LTSPhiladelphia, S.T.M., 1984. *Ord.* 1983, S. C. Synod. *Served:* In S. C., Redeemer, Columbia, 1983-1986 (Assistant Pastor); Call to Special Service as Research Assistant at University of Regensburg, West Germany, 1986—. *Spouse:* Julianne Stuck Kleckley.

KLECKLEY, VOIGT KEISLER: *Served:* In S. C., Emmanuel, West Columbia, 1967-1974; Enon, Leesville, 1975—. *Spouse:* Ella Marie Wahlberg Kleckley. (*See page 872.*)

KLEINDT, FRIEDRICH ADOLF: *Served:* In S. C., St. Mark, Isle of Palms, 1964-1975; Messiah, Hanahan, 1975-1980; St. Matthew, Pomaria, 1980—. *Spouse:* Lenora Adell Zeigler Kleindt. (*See page 872.*)

KNAUS, EARL T., III: *B.* Nov. 20, 1948, Richmond, Virginia. *Ed.* Univ. of Miami, B.A., 1971; LTSPhiladelphia, M.Div., 1979. *Ord.* 1979, SE Pa. Synod. *Served:* In S. C., Ebenezer, Columbia, 1979-1982 (Associate Pastor); St. Timothy, Goose Creek, 1982-1984; "On Leave From Call," 1984-1987; Removed from Roll of Ministers, 1987. *Spouse:* Christine Angela Knaus.

KNUDTEN, RICHARD DAVID: (*See page 872.*)

KOCH, JOHN HENRY, JR.: *Served:* In S. C., Mayer Memorial, Newberry, 1967-1974; "On Leave From Call," 1974-1977. *Ret.* 1977. *Spouse:* Dorothy Clare Schaeffer Koch. (*See page 872.*)

KOERNER, CHARLES F.: (*See page 872.*)

KOHN, ERNEST HOUSEAL: (*See page 872.*)

KOINER, JUNIUS SAMUEL: (*See page 872.*)

KOON, LEWIS FULMER: (*See page 873.*)

KOON, SAMUEL PATRICK: (*See page 873.*)

KOONS, WADE HAROLD: *B.* Aug. 24, 1907, Sycamore, Ohio. *Ed.* Wittenberg Univ., A.B., 1932, Hamma Divinity School, M.Div., 1935. *Ord.* 1935, Ohio Synod. *Served:* In Ohio, 1935-1938, 1942-1949; in N. Y. Synod, 1938-1941; in West Va. Synod, 1949-1953; in MS Synod, 1953-1964; in IA Synod, 1964-1973. *Ret.* 1973; Trans. to S. C. Synod, 1975. *Spouse:* Katharine Heiskell Koons (D. 1984).

KREPS, BARNABAS: (*See page 873.*)

KREPS, MULLER OLIVER JAMIESON: (*See page 873.*)

KROGMANN, RICHARD GORDON: (*See page 873.*)

KUHNS, HENRY WELTY: (*See page 873.*)

KYSER, DREWRY: (*See page 873.*)

KYZER, WILLIAM BRYAN, SR.: *Served:* In S. C., St. Paul, Gaffney, 1971-1977; St. Luke, Columbia, 1977—. *Spouse:* Kathryn Doris Mishoe Kyzer. (*See page 874.*)

LAGEMAN, JEFFREY KENT: *B.* Sept. 11, 1950, Quincy, Illinois. *Ed.* Wofford Col., B.A., 1972; LTSS, M.Div., 1976. *Ord.* 1976, S. C. Synod. *Served:* In S. C., Bethlehem, Leesville, 1976-1986; Redeemer, Greer, 1986—. *Spouse:* Linda Siebert Lageman.

LAUGHLIN, ARTHUR JAMES, JR.: *Served:* In S. C., St. Matthew, Charleston, 1964-1974; Trans. to Metro, N. Y., 1974. (*See page 874.*)

LEAVITT, CHARLES EARL: *B.* Oct. 3, 1931, Juliaetta, Idaho. *Ed.* Baptist Col., B.A., 1971; LTSS, M.Div., 1975. *Ord.* 1975, S. C. Synod. *Served:* Trans. to SE Synod, 1975. *Spouse:* Eva Rebecca Priddy Leavitt.

LECKY, HUGH F.: (*See page 874.*)

LEFSTEAD, WALDEMAR HIRAM: (*See page 874.*)

LEPPARD, JOHN F. W.: (*See page 874.*)

LESLIE, ELMER WALSTINE: (*See page 874.*)

LINDLER, A. WILEY: (*See page 874.*)

LINDLER, COLIE EDGAR: (*See page 875.*)

LINDLER, HORACE J. C.: *Served:* In S. C., Silverstreet, Silverstreet, 1968-1974. *Ret.* 1974. *Spouse:* Mary Shealy Lindler (*D.* 1986). *D.* 1985, *B.* Mt. Horeb Cem., Chapin. (*See page 875.*)

LINDLER, JOHN DAVID: (*See page 875.*)

LINDLER, ROGER EUGENE: *B.* Aug. 4, 1947, Lexington, S. C. *Ed.* Univ. of S. C., B.S., 1971; LTSS, M.Div., 1975. *Ord.* 1975, S. C. Synod. *Served:* In S. C., St. John, Johnston, 1975-1978; St. Paul, Gaffney, 1978—. *Spouse:* Melba Rose Stabler Lindler.

LINEBERGER, EVERETTE LEWIS: Served: In S. C., St. John, Spartanburg, 1963—. *Spouse:* Elizabeth Ann Dry Lineberger. (*See page 875.*)

LINEBERGER, FRED LOUIS: (*See page 875.*)

LINGLE, JAMES LEON, JR. (CHIP): *B.* April 22, 1954, Faith, N. C. *Ed.* N. C. State Univ., B.A., 1976; LTSS, M.Div., 1980. *Ord.* 1980, N. C. Synod. *Served:* In N. C. Synod, 1980-1985; in S. C., Martin Luther, Charleston, 1985—. *Spouse:* Ruthie McCombs Lingle.

LINK, WILLIAM HOMER: *Served:* In S. C., Bachman Chapel, Prosperity, 1964-1973; Trans. to N. C. Synod, 1973. *Spouse:* Katherine Cooper Link. (*See page 875.*)

LINN, JOHN KENNETH: (*See page 875.*)

LINN, JOSEPHIUS ADOLPHUS: (*See page 875.*)

LIVINGSTON, JERRY CULCLASURE: *Served:* Missionary in Japan (LCA-DWME), 1958—. *Spouse:* Janice Ann Koon Livingston. (*See page 876.*)

LIVINGSTON, ROBERT ELFORD: (*See page 876.*)

LOADHOLDT, DONALD BRANTLEY: (*See page 876.*)

LOADHOLDT, EARL HOUCK: *Served:* In S. C., Advent, North Charleston, 1969-1973; Mt. Horeb, Chapin, 1973-1981. *Spouse:* Marcia Marth Loadholdt. *D.* 1981, *B.* Mt. Horeb Cem., Chapin. (*See page 876.*)

LOADHOLDT, GARY ALAN: *B.* Nov. 2, 1960, Columbia, S. C. *Ed.* Furman Univ., B.A., 1983; LTSS, M.Div., 1987. *Ord.* 1987, S. C. Synod. *Served:* In S. C., Grace, Prosperity, 1987—. *Spouse:* Nan Neel Loadholdt.

LOHR, DAVID LINDSEY: *B.* Feb. 21, 1941, Lincolnton, N. C. *Ed.* Lenoir-Rhyne Col., B.A., 1963, LSTChicago, M.Div., 1967. *Ord.* 1967, N. C. Synod. *Served:* In N. C. Synod, 1967-1971; in S. C., Mount Pleasant, Saluda, 1972-1978; Trans. to N. C. Synod, 1978. *Spouse:* Betty Pugh Lohr.

LOHR, LUTHER LINDSAY: (*See page 876.*)

LONG, ERNEST EDWARD: *B.* May 28, 1932, Newton, N. C. *Ed.* Lenoir-Rhyne Col., B.A., 1959; LTSS, M.Div. 1962; Lenoir-Rhyne Col., D.D., 1979. *Ord.* 1962, N. C. Synod. *Served:* In N. C. Synod, 1962-1964; Missionary to Liberia, 1964-1971; in N. C. Synod, 1971-1981; in Florida Synod, 1981-1987; in S. C. Synod, Living Springs, Columbia, 1987— (Pastor/Developer). *Spouse:* Jewel Deal Long.

LONG, IRVING ERNEST: (*See page 876.*)

LONG, JOHN JACOB: (*See page 876.*)

LONG, JOHN VIRGIL: *Served:* In S. C., Colony, Newberry, 1966-1977. *Ret.* 1977. *Spouse:* Caroline Witherspoon Long (D. 1982). *D.* 1982, *B.* Rosemont Cem., Newberry. (*See page 876.*)

LONG, LARRY SIMEON: *Ed.* Drew Univ., D.Min., 1987. *Served:* In S. C., Holy Trinity, N. Augusta, 1970-1975; Good Shepherd, Columbia, 1975—. *Spouse:* Bonnie Wylene Roof Long. (*See page 877.*)

LOWMAN, JESSE B.: (*See page 877.*)

LUCKEY, RONALD GRINNELL: *B.* Oct. 3, 1947, Atlanta, Ga. *Ed.* Lenoir-Rhyne Col., A.B., 1969; LTSS, M.Div., 1973. *Ord.* 1973, SE Synod. *Served:* In N. C. Synod, 1973-1977; in S. C., University, Clemson and Campus Pastor, Clemson University, 1977-87; Trans. to Ind.-Ky. Synod, 1987. *Spouse:* Pacita Yvonne Robinson Luckey.

LUDWIG, RUDOLF F.: *Served:* In S. C., Corinth and St. Mark, Prosperity, 1969-1976; Trans. to N. C. 1977. *Ret.* 1976. (*See page 877.*)

LUFT, JOHN G. (HENRY)?: (*See page 877.*)

LUMAN, RALPH I.: (*See page 877.*)

LUTZ, H. BENTON: *B.* Dec. 6, 1946, Sumter, S. C. *Ed.* Presbyterian Col., B.A., 1969; LTSGettysburg, M.Div., 1973. *Ord.* 1973, S. C. Synod. *Served:* Trans. to Va. Synod, 1973. *Spouse:* Maxine Fell Lutz.

LUTZ, WILLIAM ALONZO: (*See page 877.*)

LYBRAND, ELI LOT: (*See page 877.*)

LYBRAND, RUFUS (RAMMY) EDWARD, JR.: *B.* April 23, 1949, Johnston, S. C. *Ed.* Newberry Col., B.A., 1971; LTSS, M.Div., 1975. *Ord.* 1975, S. C. Synod. *Served:* In S. C., Trinity, Georgetown, 1975-1978; Resurrection, Columbia, 1978-1982; Grace, Rock Hill, 1982—. Author of *Home Is A Four Letter Word* and *Holy Communion Is...* *Spouse:* Jacquelyne Wilson Lybrand.

LYERLY, FRANK EDWARD: *Served:* In S. C., Ascension, Columbia, 1966-1974; Trans. to Florida Synod, 1974. (*See page 877.*)

LYERLY, GARY RAY: *B.* June 19, 1943, Rowan County, N. C. *Ed.* Lenoir-Rhyne Col., A.B., 1965; LTSS, M.Div., 1969. *Ord.* 1969, N. C. Synod. *Served:* In N. C. Synod, 1969-1977; in S. C., Cross and Crown, Florence, 1977-1980 (Pastor/Developer); Trans. to SE Synod, 1980. *Spouse:* Dorthea McCarter Lyerly.

MANGUM, JOHN WESLEY: (*See page 877.*)

MARCARD, JOHN NICHOLAS: (*See page 878.*)

MARGART, JOHN PHILLIPS: (*See page 878.*)

MARKO, STEVEN FREDERICK: *B.* May 18, 1951, New Brunswick, N. J. *Ed.* Univ. of Fla., B.S., 1973; LTSS, M.Div., 1983. *Ord.* 1983, Florida Synod. *Served:* In S. C., St. John, Spartanburg, 1983-1987 (Associate Pastor); Trans. to Florida Synod, 1987. *Spouse:* Elaine Luke Marko.

MARKS, CHARLES ALEXANDER: (*See page 878.*)

MARTIN, JOHN NICHOLAS: (*See page 878.*)

MARTINSON, LEROY: (*See page 878.*)

MARTZ, GEORGE J.: (*See page 878.*)

MATHIAS, HENRY JULIAN: (*See page 878.*)

MAUNEY, JOHN DAVID: (*See page 878.*)

MAUNEY, MARSHALL FRANTZ: (*See page 879.*)

MAYER, JACOB LEGRANDE: (*See page 879.*)

McCOLLUM, ROBERT EUGENE: *B.* Dec. 15, 1938, Chester, S. C. *Ed.* Erskine Col., A.B., 1960; LTSS, M.Div., 1975. *Ord.* 1975, S. C. Synod. *Served:* In S. C., Summer Memorial, Newberry, 1975-1984; Prince of Peace, Chester and Abiding Presence, York, 1984—. *Spouse:* Billie Ann Steinkuhler McCollum.

McCOMBS, ROBERT EARL, JR.: *Served:* In S. C., St. David, West Columbia, 1966-1980; Immanuel, Greenwood, 1980—. *Spouse:* Martha Ann Barnhardt McCombs. (*See page 879.*)

McCRAY, WILLIAM V.: (*See page 879.*)

McCULLOUGH, HENRY ANTINE, JR.: *Served:* In S. C., Redeemer, Newberry, 1959-1974. *Ret.* 1974. *Spouse:* Mary Katherine Johnston McCullough. (*See page 879.*)

McCULLOUGH, HENRY ANTINE, SR.: (*See page 879.*)

McCULLOUGH, JOHN B.: *Served:* In S. C., St. Paul, Aiken, 1948-1979. *Ret.* 1979. *Spouse:* Linwold Kibler McCullough. (*See page 879.*)

McCULLOUGH, PAUL GERBERDING: Newberry College, D.D., 1974. Editor, *A History of the Lutheran Church in South Carolina,* 1971. *Spouse:* Mary Rast McCullough (D. 1972). (*See page 879.*)

McDANIEL, KEITH ALEXANDER: *B.* May 15, 1954, Cabarrus County, N. C. *Ed.* Lenoir-Rhyne Col., B.A., 1976; LTSS, M.Div., 1980. *Ord.* 1980, N. C. Synod. *Served:* In SE Synod, 1980-1983; in S. C., Trinity, Columbia, 1983—. *Spouse:* Georganne Daniels McDaniel.

McKAY, HENRY MANN: *B.* April 13, 1937, Macon, Georgia. *Ed.* Lenoir-Rhyne Col., B.A., 1960; LTSS, M.Div., 1964; Univ. of N. C.-Charlotte, M.Ed., 1973; Grad. Theol. Union, Berkley, D.Min., 1981. *Ord.* 1964, SE Synod. *Served:* In SE Synod, 1964-1967; in N. C. Synod, 1967-1973; in PSW Synod, 1973-1985; in S. C., Lutheran Social Services of Central S. C., Executive Director, 1985—. *Spouse:* Judythe Louise Schott McKay.

McKINLEY, EDWIN W.: *Served:* In S. C., Holy Cross, Charleston Heights, 1968-1974; Trans. to N. C. Synod, 1974. (*See page 879.*)

McMACKIN, A. B.: (*See page 880.*)

MEALY, STEPHEN ALBION: (*See page 880.*)

MEETZE, GEORGE ELIAS: *Served:* In S. C., Incarnation, Columbia, 1942-1974. Chaplain, S. C. Senate, 1950—. *Ret.* 1974. *Spouse:* Margaret Allen Meetze. (*See page 880.*)

MEETZE or METZE, JOHN YOST: (*See page 880.*)

MEISTER, P. A.: (*See page 880.*)

METZE, TONY ALLEN: *B.* Oct. 5, 1958, Spartanburg, S. C. *Ed.* Wofford Col., B.A., 1980; LTSS, M.Div., 1985. *Ord.* 1985, S. C. Synod. *Served:* In S. C., Good Shepherd, Swansea, 1985—. *Spouse:* Christina Ann Kepley Metze.

MEYER, RUSSELL LLOYD: *B.* Sept. 19, 1956, Milwaukee, Wisconsin. *Ed.* Baker Univ., B.A., 1978; Yale Divinity School, M.Div., 1981; LTSGettysburg, S.T.M., 1988. *Ord.* 1984, Central States Synod. *Served:* In Maryland Synod, 1984-1986; in S. C. Synod, St. Mark, Isle of Palms, 1987—. *Spouse:* Maria Julia Balmaseda Meyer.

MEYERS, DONALD JUSTIN: (*See page 884.*)

MEYNARDIE, ROBERT E.: Removed from Roll of Ministers, 1971. (*See page 880.*)

MICHAEL, DON M.: *B.* Sept. 16, 1925, Lexington, N. C. *Ed.* Lenoir-Rhyne Col., A.B., 1946; LTSS, M.Div., 1949. *Ord.* 1949, N. C. Synod. *Served:* In N. C. Synod, 1949-1951; Military Chaplain, U.S. Navy, 1951-1978 (In S. C., 1971-1975); Trans. to N. C. Synod, 1978. *Spouse:* Helen Waggoner Michael.

MILES, ROBERT IRVING, JR.: *B.* Sept. 25, 1953, Richmond, Va. *Ed.* Davidson Col., A.B., 1975; LTSS, M.Div., 1980. *Ord.* 1980, Va. Synod. *Served:* In S. C., St. Thomas, Chapin, 1980—. *Spouse:* Deborah Gail Shuler Miles.

MILLER, C. ARMAND: (*See page 880.*)

MILLER, CALVIN LUTHER: (*See page 880.*)

MILLER, DAVID LEANDER: (*See page 880.*)

MILLER, EDDIE C., JR.: *B.* Dec. 5, 1947, Newberry, S. C. *Ed.* Newberry Col., B.A., 1973; LTSS, M.Div., 1977. *Ord.* 1977, S. C. Synod. *Served:* In S. C., Corinth and St. Mark, Saluda, 1977-1979; Military Chaplain, U.S.

Army, 1979-1983; in S. C., St. Michael, Moncks Corner, 1983-1985; "On Leave From Call," 1985-87; Trinity-St. Nicholas Parish, Fairfax, 1987—.

MILLER, HOLLIS ALLEN: *B.* Dec. 29, 1942, Lexington, N. C. *Ed.* Lenoir-Rhyne Col., A.B., 1965; LTSS, M.Div., 1969; Drew Univ., D.Min., 1984. *Ord.* 1969, N. C. Synod. *Served:* In N. C. Synod, 1969-1976; in S. C., Grace, Rock Hill, 1976-1981; Zion, Lexington, 1981—. *Spouse:* Susan Jane Gribble Miller.

MILLER, JEFFERSON POLYCARP: (*See page 881.*)

MILLER, JOSEPH I.: (*See page 881.*)

MILLER, LESTER DAVID: *B.* April 15, 1919, Lenoir, N. C. *Ed.* Lenoir-Rhyne Col., A.B., 1939; LTSS, M.Div., 1942; Union Theological Sem., M.S.M., 1947; Lenoir-Rhyne Col., D.Mus., 1960. *Ord.* 1942, N. C. Synod. *Served:* In N. C. Synod, 1942-1944; in N. Y. Synod, 1944-1947; in Ind. Synod, 1947-1954; in Ohio Synod, 1954-1978; in S. C., Professor of Church Music, LTSS, 1978-1986; Professor Emeritus, 1986—. *Ret.* 1986. *Spouse:* Annie Lytle Miller (dec.)

MILLER, PETER: (*See page 881.*)

MILLER, RICHARD JAMES: *B.* Dec. 15, 1947, Staten Island, N. Y. *Ed.* Wagner Col., B.A., 1973; LTSS, M.Div., 1977. *Ord.* 1977, S. C. Synod. *Served:* Trans. to N. C. Synod, 1977. *Spouse:* Nancy Sue Cowan.

MILLER, ROBERT JOHNSON: (*See page 881.*)

MILLER, RONALD E.: *Served:* In S. C., Mt. Pleasant, Ehrhardt, 1969-1978; Trans. to SE Synod, 1978. (*See page 881.*)

MILLER, WILBUR DEAN: *B.* Feb. 23, 1929, Goshen, Indiana. *Ed.* Goshen Col., B.A., 1973; LTSS, M.Div., 1976. *Ord.* 1976, Ind.-Ky. Synod. *Served:* In Ind.-Ky. Synod, 1976-1979; in S. C., St. Philip, Newberry, 1979—. *Spouse:* Joann Heime Miller.

MIMS, BILLY BURNS, JR.: *B.* June 18, 1946, Greensboro, N.C. *Ed.* Univ. of N. C., A.B., 1968; LTSS, M.Div., 1972; Union Theological Sem., D.Min., 1983. *Ord.* 1972, N. C. Synod. *Served:* In N. C. Synod, 1972-1974; in S. C., Incarnation, 1974-1979 (Associate Pastor, 1974-1976); Orangeburg, Orangeburg, 1979-1987; Trans. to N. C. Synod, 1987. *Spouse:* Sherry L. Foust Mims.

MISENHEIMER, DAVID LENTZ: *B.* March 19, 1946, Salisbury, N. C. *Ed.* Lenoir-Rhyne Col., A.B., 1968, LTSS, M.Div., 1972. *Ord.* 1972, N. C. Synod. *Served:* In S. C., Mt. Tabor, West Columbia, 1972-1974 (Associate Pastor); Trans. to N. C. Synod, 1974. *Spouse:* Jacqualyn Collins Misenheimer.

MITCHAM, LLOYD WILLIAM, JR.: *Ed.* Univ. of S. C., M.Ed., 1974. *Served:* In S. C., Executive Secretary of Christian Education, S. C. Synod, 1968-1984. *Spouse:* Jane Amelia Pope Mitcham. (*See page 881.*)

MIYAISHI, KYUZO (FRANKIE-SAN): *B.* Sept. 17, 1929, Tokyo, Japan. *Ed.* Hosei Univ., B.A., 1961; LTSS, M.R.E., 1966. *Ord.* 1973, S. C. Synod. *Served:* In S. C., Tent-Making Ministry with the S. C. Department of Corrections, Central Correctional Institution, Columbia, 1973—.

MONROE, PAUL EUGENE, JR.: (*See page 881.*)

MONROE, PLEASANT EDGAR: (*See page 881.*)

MOODY, HENRY (HANK) MAHONE, JR.: *B.* July 22, 1950, Moncks Corner, S. C. *Ed.* Clemson Univ., B.A., 1972; LTSS, M.Div., 1977. *Ord.* 1977, S. C. Synod. *Served:* In S. C., Good Shepherd, Columbia, 1977-1980 (Associate Pastor); Pisgah, Lexington, 1980—. *Spouse:* Patricia Russell Moody.

MOORE, GEORGE TRUETT: *B.* Aug. 25, 1920, Greenville County, S. C. *Ed.* Clemson Univ., B.S., 1942; LTSS, M.Div., 1957. *Ord.* 1957, Ga.-Ala. Synod. *Served:* In N. C., 1959-1976; in S. C., St. Matthew, Charleston, 1976-1980 (Assistant Pastor); Grace, Prosperity, 1980-85. Missionary to Liberia, 1953-1959. *Ret.* 1986. *Spouse:* Elizabeth Stevens Moore.

MOOSE, JOHN BAXTER: (*See page 882.*)

MOOSE, JOHN SHELTON: *Served:* In N. C. Synod, 1968-1979. *Ret.* 1979. Trans. to S. C., 1979. *Spouse:* Evelyn Hamilton Wingard Moose. (*See page 882.*)

MORAVITZ, ALBERT BENJAMIN: *B.* Sept. 6, 1953, Washington, D.C. *Ed.* Newberry Col., A.B., 1976; LTSS, M.Div., 1984. *Ord.* 1984, S. C. Synod. *Served:* In S. C., St. Timothy, Goose Creek, 1984—. *Spouse:* Mary Schuette Moravitz.

MORETZ, WALTER JENNINGS, JR.: (*See page 882.*)

MORETZ, WALTER JENNINGS, SR.: (*See page 882.*)

MORGAN, CARROLL IRVING: (*See page 882.*)

MORGAN, FRANCIS GROVER: (*See page 882.*)

MORGAN, OLIVER MARION: *Served:* In S. C., Bethlehem-Enon, Leesville, 1957-1974; Bethlehem, Leesville, 1974-1975. *Ret.* 1975. *Spouse:* Annie Brown Morgan. *D.* 1975, *B.* Bethlehem Cem., Leesville. (*See page 882.*)

MORGAN, PAUL LOWMAN: *B.* March 16, 1923, Troutman, N. C. *Ed.* Lenoir-Rhyne Col., A.B., 1944; LTSS, M.Div., 1945; Lenoir-Rhyne Col., D.D., 1968. *Ord.* 1945, N. C. Synod. *Served:* Missionary to India 1945-1947; in N. C. Synod, 1947-1974; in S. C., Incarnation, Columbia, 1974-1977; Trans. to Va. Synod, 1977. *Spouse:* Bess Silman Morgan.

MORGAN, WILLIAM RANDOLPH: (*See page 882.*)

MORROW, J.: (*See page 883.*)

MOSER, ADAM DAVID LUTHER: (*See page 883.*)

MOSER, JACOB: (*See page 883.*)

MOSER, JACOB SCHAEFFER: (*See page 883.*)

MOULD, WILLIAM JOSEPH: (*See page 883.*)

MOYE, MATTHEW O'NEAL: *B.* May 18, 1946, Charleston, S. C. *Ed.* Newberry Col., B.A., 1968; LTSS, M.Div., 1972. *Ord.* 1972, S. C. Synod. *Served:* In S. C., St. Thomas, Chapin, 1972-1979; All Saints, Mt. Pleasant, 1979—. *Spouse:* Marcia Missel Moye.

MUELLER, LOUIS: (*See page 883.*)

MUELLER, WILLIAM ALBERT CHRISTIAN: (*See page 883.*)

MULLEN, LESTER ALFRED, II: *Served:* Trans. to N. C. Synod, 1972. (*See page 883.*)

MULLER, WASHINGTON: (*See page 883.*)

NEASE, JACOB WERTS: (*See page 884.*)

NEASE, SHADRACK LABAN: (*See page 884.*)

NELSON, GEORGE W.: (*See page 884.*)

NICHOLS, JAMES HEINLEY: *B.* Feb. 9, 1935, Williamsport, Pa. *Ed.* Ohio State Univ., B.S., 1957; Hamma School of Theo., M.Div., 1961; Oberlin Grad. School of Theo., D.Min., 1966. *Ord.* 1961, Ohio Synod. *Served:* In Ohio Synod, 1961-1981; in S. C., Reformation, Columbia, 1981—. *Spouse:* Mary Marguarette Schofer Nichols.

NOLT, DONALD C.: *B.* March 26, 1938, Marshallville, Ohio. *Ed.* Wittenberg Univ., B.A., 1974; Hamma Sch. of Theo., M.Div., 1978. *Ord.* 1978, Ohio Synod. *Served:* In S. C., Good Shepherd, Walterboro, 1978-1981; Trans. to Florida Synod, 1981. *Spouse:* Nancy McBride Nolt.

NORDSTOM, K. DAVID: (*See page 884.*)

NORRIS, RUSSELL BRADNER, JR.: *B.* March 3, 1942, Hackensack, N. J. *Ed.* Mass. Institute of Tech., B.S.E.E., 1964; LSTChicago, M.Div., 1969; Univ. of Strasbourg, France, Th.D., 1972. *Ord.* 1972, N. J. Synod. *Served:* In Central Penn. Synod 1972-1985; in S. C., South Carolina Christian Action Council, Columbia, 1985— (Executive Minister). *Spouse:* Dixie Krouse Norris.

NYE, JOHN CANTEY, JR.: *Served:* In S. C., St. John, Johnston, 1961-1972; Advent, N. Charleston, 1972— (Associate Pastor, 1972-1974). (*See page 884.*)

OBENSCHAIN, ARTHUR BITTLE: (*See page 884.*)

OLAWSKY, RUBEN HERMAN: *Served:* In S. C., Mt. Hermon, West Columbia, 1970-1979; in Central States Synod, 1979; in S. C., Shepherd of the Sea, Garden City, 1987—. *Spouse:* Jane Anne Hart Olawsky. (*See page 884.*)

OLSON, MICHAEL KENNETH: *B.* June 26, 1952, Phoenix, Arizona. *Ed.* Arizona State Univ., B.S., 1974; LTSS, M.Div., 1979. *Ord.* 1979, S. C. Synod. *Served:* In S. C., Bethany, Newberry, 1979-1981; Trans. to Pacific Southwest Synod, 1982. *Spouse:* Patricia Kay Hutcherson Olson.

ONSTAD, AMARETTA JONES: *B.* April 1, 1949, Billings, Montana. *Ed.* Univ. of Montana, B.A., 1970; LTSS, M.Div., 1982. *Ord.* 1982, SE Synod. *Served:* In S. C., Our Saviour, West Columbia, 1982-1983 (Assistant Pastor); "On Leave From Call" 1983-1984; Chaplain, Baptist Hospital, Columbia, 1984—. *Spouse:* The Rev. George L. Onstad.

ONSTAD, GEORGE LOUIS: *B.* Sept. 7, 1949, Williston, North Dakota. *Ed.* Univ. of Mont., B.A., 1971; LTSS, M.Div., 1983. *Ord.* 1983, SE Synod. *Served:* In S. C., Incarnation, Columbia, 1983-1987 (Associate Pastor); Military Chaplain, U. S. Army, 1987—. *Spouse:* The Rev. Amaretta Jones Onstad.

OVERCASH, KAY EUGENE: *B.* July 30, 1943, China Grove, N. C. *Ed.* Univ. of N. C., A.B., 1965; LTSS, M.Div., 1969. *Ord.* 1969, N. C. Synod. *Served:* In Texas-La. Synod, 1969-1980; in S. C., Emmanuel, West Columbia, 1980—. *Spouse:* Glenda Gail Holshouser Overcash.

OWENS, ALBERT DEWEY: (*See page 884.*)

OXNER, JASON WITHERSPOON: (*See page 884.*)

PARK, GEORGE H. C. (*See page 885.*)

PARK, HAROLD FRANKLIN: Newberry Col., D.D., 1975. *Served:* Associate Professor of Christian Education, LTSS, 1961-1987. *Ret.* 1987. *Spouse:* Betty Mae Habenicht Park. (*See page 885.*)

PARK, JAMES BARTON: *B.* March 15, 1944, Port Arthur, Texas. *Ed.* Newberry Col., B.A., 1965; LTSS, M.Div., 1975. *Ord.* 1975, S. C. Synod. *Served:* In S. C., Emmanuel, West Columbia, 1975-1979; Lord of Life, Harbison, 1979-1982 (Pastor/Developer); St. Timothy, Camden, 1982—. *Spouse:* Jennifer Wilson Park.

PARK, KARL MONROE: (*See page 885.*)

PARKER, THEODORE CALVIN: (*See page 885.*)

PARROTT, RODNEY WALTER: *Served:* In S. C., Messiah, Mauldin, 1971-1982; St. Andrew, Charleston, 1982—. *Spouse:* Patricia Ruth Sprawls Parrott. (*See page 885.*)

PATTON, WILLIAM RANKIN: (*See page 885.*)

PEELER, J. L.: (*See page 885.*)

PEERY, JOHN CARNAHAN: (*See page 885.*)

PEERY, JOHN CARNAHAN, JR.: *Served:* In Florida Synod 1961-1974. *Ret.* 1974. Trans. to S. C. Synod, 1974. *Spouse:* Elizabeth Graham Crapps Peery. (*See page 886.*)

PEERY, JOHN GORDON: *Served:* In S. C., St. Paul, Gilbert, 1977-1982; Faith, Newberry, 1983—. *Spouse:* Leah Jacobson Peery. (*See page 886.*)

PEERY, WILLIAM POWLAS: *Served:* Missionary to India, 1945—; Teacher in United Theological College, Bangalore, India, 1971—. *Spouse:* Marinelle Fridy Peery. (*See page 886.*)

PENCE, EDGAR ZIRKLE: (*See page 886.*)

PENCE, MARTIN LUTHER: (*See page 886.*)

PETERSEN, OTTO CARL: (*See page 886.*)

PETREA, HENRY SMITH: *Spouse:* Gaynelle Crapps Petrea. (*D.* 1985). *D.* 1978, *B.* Elmwood Cem., Columbia. (*See page 886.*)

PHILLIPS, CHARLES ARTHUR: (*See page 886.*)

PHILLIPS, GEORGE ARTHUR: (*See page 886.*)

PIERCE, PALMER PHILLIPPI: (*See page 887.*)

PILZ, W.: (*See page 887.*)

PLESS, JOHN EDWARD: *B.* Dec. 20, 1948, Winston-Salem, N. C. *Ed.* Lenoir-Rhyne Col., A.B., 1971; LTSS, M.Div., 1975. *Ord.* 1975, N. C. Synod. *Served:* In N. C. Synod, 1975-1984; in S. C., Holy Trinity, Little Mt., 1984—. *Spouse:* Linda Russell Pless.

PLEXICO, THURMOND CLAUDE: (*See page 887.*)

PLONK, GARY STEVEN: *B.* March 4, 1954, Mecklenberg County, N. C. *Ed.* Lenoir-Rhyne Col., A.B., 1976; LTSS, M.Div., 1980. *Ord.* 1980, N. C.

Synod. *Served:* In N. C. Synod, 1980-1983; in S. C., University Lutheran Church, Lutheran Campus Center, Clemson, 1984—. *Spouse:* Karen Lynn Sparks Plonk.

POND, WALTER EDWARD, JR.: *(See page 887.)*

POOLE, CHARLES CLAYTON, JR.; *(See page 887.)*

POOLE, DONALD R., JR.: *(See page 887.)*

POOLE, DONALD RAYMOND, SR.: *Ret.* 1973. Trans. to S. C. Synod, 1975. Trans. to Maryland Synod, 1985. *Spouse:* Dorothy Marie Hanzlik Poole. *(See page 887.)*

POSEY, MARK: *(See page 887.)*

POTTER, AL: *Served:* In SE Synod, 1970-1974; in S. C., St. James, Graniteville, 1974-1984; Trans. to SE Synod, 1984. *Spouse:* Beverly H. Boland Potter. *(See page 887.)*

PRICE, EVERETT R.: *Served:* In S. C., Our Shepherd, Hartsville, 1968-1985; Faith, West Columbia, 1985—. *Spouse:* Bernice Lee Mathias Price. *(See page 887.)*

PROBST, JOHN FREDERICK: *(See page 887.)*

PROBST, LUTHER KOLB: *(See page 888.)*

PUGH, WILLIAM EDWARD: *(See page 888.)*

QUINTON, CATHY JOANN: *B.* Aug. 30, 1954, Valdosta, Georgia. *Ed.* Clemson Univ., B.A., 1977; Francis Marion Col., M.S., 1981; LTSS, M.Div., 1985. *Ord.* 1986, S. C. Synod. *Served:* In S. C., St. Andrew, Blythewood, 1986—.

RAHN, SHEPPARD SENECA: *(See page 888.)*

RATCLIFFE, HOWARD I.: *B.* June 20, 1938, Lawrence, Mass. *Ed.* Shepherd Col., B.A., 1962; LTSGettysburg, M.Div., 1965; N. Y. Theo. Sem., S.T.M., 1972. *Ord.* 1965, Virginia Synod. *Served:* In Va. Synod, 1965-1967; Military Chaplain, U. S. Marine Corps, 1967-1984 (in S. C. Synod, 1982-1984). Trans. to Va. Synod, 1984. *Spouse:* June McLauchlin Ratcliffe.

RAU, HARRY LEE, JR.: *(See page 888.)*

RAUCH, MICHAEL: *(See page 888.)*

RAWL, LEON ADAIR: *B.* April 11, 1951, Lexington, S. C. *Ed.* Newberry Col., B.A., 1973; LTSS, M.Div., 1977. *Ord.* 1977, S. C. Synod. *Served:* In S. C., Holy Trinity, Little Mountain, 1977-1983; St. Luke, Summerville, 1983—. *Spouse:* Susan Long Rawl.

REENSTJERNA, OTTO FREDERICK: *Served:* In S. C., St. Luke, Columbia, 1969-1975; Providence, Lexington, 1975-1980. *Ret.* 1980. *Spouse:* Swannee Roberts Reenstjerna. *(See page 888.)*

REINARTZ, FREDERICK EPPLING: *Spouse:* Isabella Martin Reinartz (*D.* 1979). *D.* 1978, *B.* Greenlawn Cem., Columbia. *(See page 888.)*

REISER, WALTER ALLEN: *(See page 889.)*

REPASS, BERNARD: *(See page 889.)*

REYNOLDS, MARTI DAVID: *B.* May 2, 1953, Beloit, Wisconsin. *Ed.*

Univ. of S. C., B.A., 1977; LTSS, M.Div., 1981. *Ord.* 1982, S. C. Synod. *Served:* Trans. to Central Canada Synod, 1982.

RHODEN, JAMES MARION, JR.: *Served:* In S. C., Faith, West Columbia, 1965-1975; Atonement, Laurens, 1975-1984; Pilgrim, Lexington, 1984—. (*See page 889.*)

RHODES, CLARENCE KILLIAN: (*See page 889.*)

RHYNE, SIDNEY WHITE: *Spouse:* Ruth Dry Rhyne (D. 1985). *D.* 1981, *B.* Elmwood Cem., Charlotte, N. C. (*See page 889.*)

RICARD, ROOF DELANO: *Served:* In S. C., St. Paul, Pomaria, 1971—. *Spouse:* Evelyn Ruth Seigler Ricard. (*See page 889.*)

RICE, COLLIE JUSTUS: *Spouse:* Lottie Cannon Rice. *D.* 1973, *B.* Elmwood Cem., Columbia. (*See page 889.*)

RICE, FLETCHER A., III: Removed from Roll of Ministers, 1973. (*See page 889.*)

RICHARDSON, CLARENCE LUTHER: *Served:* In S. C., Macedonia, Prosperity, 1969-1977. *Ret.* 1977. *Spouse:* Floy Sorena Haemer Richardson. (*See page 890.*)

RICKS, EDWIN LEE: *Served:* Staff, Division for Parish Services, LCA, Philadelphia, Pa., 1970-1982. *D.* 1982, *B.* Cremated. (*See page 890.*)

RIDDLE, RALPH HOLLEY: *Served:* In S. C., Augsburg, Union and St. Timothy, Whitmire, 1967-1975; St. John, Beaufort, 1976—. *Spouse:* Rosalyn Godshall Riddle. (*See page 890.*)

RIDENHOUR, VICTOR CLARENCE: (*See page 890.*)

RIECHERS, DONALD F.: *Served:* In S. C., Military Chaplain, U. S. Air Force, 1968-1975; Trans. to Michigan Synod, 1975. (*See page 890.*)

RIIS, CLIFFORD ALFRED: *Served:* In S. C., Trinity, Georgetown, 1967-1974; St. Johannes, Charleston, 1974—. *Spouse:* Jean McLean Riis, (*See page 890.*)

RILEY, EBER LEROY, JR.: *B.* March 31, 1948, Columbia, S. C. *Ed.* Lenoir-Rhyne Col., A.B., 1970; LTSS, M.Div., 1974. *Ord.* 1974, S. C. Synod. *Served:* Trans. to N. C. Synod, 1974. *Spouse:* Brenda Amick Riley.

RING, JAMES P.: (*See page 890.*)

RISER, MARION CLAUDE, SR.: (*See page 890.*)

RISER, SIDNEY T. (*See page 890.*)

RISER, WILBUR H.: (*See page 891.*)

RISER, YANCEY VON ALLEN: (*See page 890.*)

RISINGER, PAUL DAVID: (*See page 891.*)

RITCHIE, C. A. (*See page 891.*)

RITCHIE, CARL LEAMMLE: *B.* March 28, 1932, Charlotte, N. C. *Ed.* Lenoir-Rhyne Col., A.B., 1954; LTSS, M.Div., 1957. *Ord.* 1957, N. C. Synod. *Served:* In N. C. Synod, 1957-1962; in Florida Synod, 1962-1970; in N. C. Synod, 1970-1986; in S. C. Synod, A Mighty Fortress, Summerville,

1986-1987. *Ret.* 1987. *Spouse:* Mary Frances Brown Ritchie.

RITCHIE, CLARENCE ROSS, JR.: (*See page 891.*)

RITCHIE, WILEY WASHINGTON JOSEPHUS: (*See page 891.*)

RIZER, PETER: (*See page 891.*)

ROBERTSON, AUSTIN FULTON, JR.: *Ed.* Univ. of S. C., M.Ed., 1972. *Served:* In S. C., St. John, Pomaria, 1967-1972; "On Leave From Call," 1972-1973; Resigned from Ministry, 1974; Reinstated to Roll of Ministers, 1982; St. Mark, Blythewood, 1982—. Counselor, Director of Financial Aid, Midlands Technical College, Columbia, 1973-1982. *Spouse:* Mary Burton Robertson. (*See page 891.*)

ROBINSON, CARROLL LEONARD: *Served:* In S. C., Director of Pastoral Care, C. M. Tucker Human Resources Center, SCDMH, Columbia, 1972-1981; "On Leave From Call," 1981-1983; Chaplain, Tri-County Mental Health Center, 1983—. *Spouse:* Greta Gail Ball Robinson. (*See page 891.*)

ROBINSON, D. TIMOTHY: *B.* July 17, 1927, Hagerstown, Md. *Ed.* Newberry Col., B.S., 1953; LTSGettysburg, M.Div., 1960. *Ord.* 1960, Pa. Synod. *Served:* In Pa. Synod 1960-1980; in S. C., Prince of Peace, Chester and Abiding Presence, York, 1980-1983; St. Mark, Isle of Palms, 1983-1986. "On Leave From Call," 1986—. *Spouse:* Gwen Witt Robinson.

ROBINSON, RALPH CARLETON: *B.* Feb. 10, 1901, Oakland, Maryland. *Ed.* Gettysburg Col., A.B., 1923; LTSGettysburg, M.Div., 1926. LTS Gettysburg, D.D., 1947. *Ord.* 1926, Maryland Synod. *Served:* In Maryland Synod, 1926-1934; in Central-Penn. Synod, 1934-1955 (Chaplain, U. S. Navy, 1942-1945); Secretary, Central-Penn. Synod, 1955-1965. *Ret.* 1965. Trans. to S. C. Synod, 1983. *D.* 1985. *B.* Mountain View Cem., Sharpsburg, MD.

RODEN, SIDNEY WAYNE: *B.* April 22, 1947, Yoakum, Texas. *Ed.* Texas Lutheran Col., B.A., 1969; LTSS, M.Div., 1973. *Ord.* 1973, Texas-La. Synod. *Served:* In Texas-La. Synod, 1973-1976; in S. C., Bethany, Newberry, 1976-1979; Trans. to Fla. Synod, 1979. *Spouse:* Susan Carol Sims Roden.

ROOF, EDWIN F. K.: (*See page 891.*)

ROOF, ELFORD BENNETT, SR.: *Served:* In S. C., Pilgrim, Lexington, 1970-1983; "On Leave From Call," 1983-1986; Trinity, Saluda, 1987—. *Spouse:* Mary J. Patch Roof. (*See page 892.*)

ROOF, FRANCIS KEARNEY: (*See page 892.*)

ROOF, FRANCIS KEITT: (*See page 892.*)

ROOF, FRANK LEVER: *Served:* In S. C., Immanuel, Greenwood, 1954-1975. *Ret.* 1975. *Spouse:* Mary Adeline Crumley Roof. *D.* 1984, *B.* St. David Cem., West Columbia. (*See page 892.*)

ROOF, J. EMMETT: (*See page 892.*)

ROOF, JOHN HILTON: *Served:* In S. C., St. Luke, Prosperity, 1963-1977; Cedar Grove, Leesville, 1977—. *Spouse:* Eleanor Faye Gable Roof. (*See page 892.*)

ROOF, LESTER ODA, SR.: (*See page 892.*)

ROOF, W. K.: (*See page 892.*)

ROOF, WALTER JAMES: *(See page 892.)*

ROOF, WILLIE HARDEE: *(See page 892.)*

ROSCOE, RONALD ELMER: *B.* April 27, 1939, Pittsburgh, Pa. *Ed.* Valparaiso, B.S., 1970; LTSS, M.Div., 1976. *Ord.* 1976, S. C. Synod. *Served:* In S. C., Augsburg, Union and St. Timothy, Whitmire, 1976-1979; Bethany, Lexington, 1979-1983. *Ret.* 1983, Disability. *Spouse:* Virginia Cole Roscoe. *D.* 1985 *B.* St. David Cem., W. Cola.

ROURK, MARGUERITE MIMS: *B.* Oct. 12, 1946, Greenville, S. C. *Ed.* Greensboro Col., B.A., 1968; LTSS, M.Div. 1987. *Ord.* 1987, S. C. Synod. *Served:* In S. C., Redeemer, Columbia, 1987— (Associate Pastor). *Spouse:* David R. Rourk.

RUDE, ANDERS RUDOLPH: *(See page 893.)*

RUDISILL, DORUS PAUL: *(See page 893.)*

RUSHE, GEORGE M: *Served:* In S. C., Military Chaplain, U. S. Air Force, 1960-1981; Trans. to Texas-La. Synod, 1981. *(See page 893.)*

SAFRIT, DONALD LYNN: *(See page 893.)*

SAFRIT, GARY LEE: *Served:* In S. C., St. Johannes, Charleston, 1968-1972; Our Saviour, Greenville, 1972—. *Spouse:* Brenda Ann Arcuri Safrit. *(See page 893.)*

SALE, HOWARD HERBERT, III: *B.* Nov. 19, 1937, Lynchburg, Va. *Ed.* VPI, B.S., M.E., 1960; LTSS, M.Div., 1983. *Ord.* 1983, S. C. Synod. *Served:* In S. C., Christ, Hilton Head, 1983—. *Spouse:* Joan Turner Sale.

SANDERS, JOHN ALONZO: *Served:* In S. C., Bethany, Newberry, 1958-1976. *Ret.* 1976. *Spouse:* Evelyn Halfacre Sanders. *(See page 893.)*

SATTERWHITE, JOHN LLOYD, III: *Served:* In S. C., Our Saviour, West Columbia, 1970-1986. *Ret.* 1986. *Spouse:* Sarah Willette Padget Satterwhite. *(See page 893.)*

SAYLES, HAROLD A. *(See page 893.)*

SCHAACK, EDWARD ROBERT: *(See page 893.)*

SCHAEFFER, HENRY BRENT: *Spouse:* Lois McCartha Schaeffer (D. 1971) *D.* 1975, *B.* Wittenberg Cem., Leesville. *(See page 893.)*

SCHAEFFER, W. C., SR.: *(See page 894.)*

SCHAEFFER, WILLIAM BRENT: *Served:* In Maryland Synod, 1965-1978; in S. C., St. Matthias, Easley, 1978-1982. *Ret.* 1982. *Spouse:* Mary Ethelyn Riser Schaeffer. *(See page 894.)*

SCHAID, J. G. *(See page 894.)*

SCHECK, JOHN D. *(See page 894.)*

SCHEDE, H. F. *(See page 894.)*

SCHEELE (SHEALY), HENRY FRANK: *(See page 894.)*

SCHERER, JAMES AUGUSTIN BROWN: *(See page 894.)*

SCHERER, MELANCHTHON GIDEON GROSECLOSE: *(See page 894.)*

SCHNEIDER, JOHN ALLEN ENGLEBERT: *(See page 895.)*

SCHOENBERG, JOHN C. A. *(See page 895.)*

SCHOTT, GEORGE FREDERICK, JR.: *Served:* In S. C., Associate Professor of Systematic Theology, LTSS, 1952-1981. Professor Emeritus, LTSS, 1981—. *Ret.* 1981. *Spouse:* Ruth Cauble Schott. *(See page 895.)*

SCHOTT, GEORGE FREDERICK, III: *(See page 895.)*

SCHRECKHISE, JAMES MONROE: *(See page 895.)*

SCHRODER, H. A.: *(See page 895.)*

SCHULTZ, ROBERT CHARLES: *B.* Feb. 22, 1928, Fairbault, Minn. *Ed.* Concordia Col., B.A., 1949;. Concordia Sem., M.Div., 1952; Frederick-Alexander Univ., Erlangen, Germany, Dr. Theol., 1956. *Ord.* 1953, Lutheran Church-Missouri Synod. *Served:* In Illinois, Pennsylvania, New Jersey, Indiana, and New York Synods; in S. C., Professor of Pastoral Care and Director of Internship, LTSS, 1974-1987; Trans. to Pacific Northwest Synod, 1987.

SCHUMPERT (SHUMPERT), S. P.: *(See page 895.)*

SCHWARTZ, JOHN G.: *(See page 896.)*

SEABROOK, WILLIAM L.: *(See page 896.)*

SEAGLE, H. L.: *(See page 896.)*

SEASE, MILAS YODER III: *B.* Jan. 31, 1950, Columbia, S. C. *Ed.* Newberry Col., B.A., 1972; LTSS, M.Div., 1978. *Ord.* 1978, S. C. Synod. *Served:* In Florida Synod, 1978-1981; in S. C., Corinth-St. Mark Parish, Prosperity, 1981-1983; Resurrection, Columbia, 1983—. *Spouse:* Merrilyn Richert Sease.

SEASTRUNK, CHARLES ERNEST, JR.: *Ed.* Pepperdine University, M.A. *Served:* Military Chaplain, U. S. Air Force, 1965-1984: (In S. C., 1971-1974). *Ret.* 1984. Trans. to S. C., 1984. *Spouse:* Sarah Truesdell Seastrunk. *(See page 896.)*

SEASTRUNK, CHARLES ERNEST, SR.: *Spouse:* Louise Eargle Seastrunk. *D.* 1975, *B.* St. Andrew Cem., Blythewood. *(See page 896.)*

SECKINGER, EDWIN H.: *(See page 896.)*

SEEGERS, JOHN CONRAD: *(See page 896.)*

SEIBERT, JOHN F.: *(See page 896.)*

SEILER, LLOYD HENDERSON, SR.: *B.* Feb. 5, 1919, Northumberland, Pa. *Ed.* Gettysburg Col, B.A., 1939; LTSGettysburg, M.Div., 1948: LTS Gettysburg, S.T.M., 1977. *Ord.* 1948, Georgia-Alabama Synod. *Served:* In Ga.-Ala. Synod, 1948-1956; in Mississippi Synod, 1956-1958; in Maryland Synod, 1958-1962; in SE Synod, 1962-1968; in Central Penn. Synod, 1968-1984. *Ret.* 1984. Trans. to S. C., 1985. *Spouse:* Flora Lee Seiler.

SELLMAN, CHARLES ALAN: *Served:* In S. C., St. Matthew, Pomaria, 1969-1980. Trans. to Michigan Synod, 1980. *(See page 897.)*

SENTER, JONAS MICHAEL: *(See page 897.)*

SETZLER, JOHN LUCIEN: *Ed.* Princeton Theo. Sem., Th.M., 1972. *Served:* In New Jersey Synod, 1971-1973; in S. C., Ascension, Columbia,

1973-1979; Chaplain (1979-1987), Assistant Professor of Religion (1979—) and Responsible for Church Related Development (1987—), Newberry College. Member, DPS, Management Comm., LCA, 1982-1987 (Vice-Chairman, 1982-1984). *Spouse:* Constance Rose Bugay Setzler. (*See page 897.*)

SHEALY, BERLEY FULMER: *Served:* In S. C., Pomaria, Pomaria, 1971-1978; St. Michael, Moncks Corner, 1978-1982; "On Leave From Call," 1982-1985; Removed from Roll of Ministers, 1985. *Spouse:* S. Joyce Lee Shealy. (*See page 897.*)

SHEALY, CHARLES JACKSON, JR.: *Served:* In S. C., Bethlehem, Pomaria, 1969-1982. *Ret.* 1982. *Spouse:* Sara Helen Paysinger Shealy. (*See page 897.*)

SHEALY, CHARLES JACKSON, SR.: (*See page 897.*)

SHEALY, CHARLES LOUIS: *Served:* In S. C., Mt. Calvary, Johnston, 1966—. *Spouse:* Patricia Lee Massingale Shealy. (*See page 897.*)

SHEALY, DAVID: (*See page 897.*)

SHEALY, ELDRIDGE ARMAND: Newberry Col., D.D., 1983. *Served:* In S. C., Orangeburg, Orangeburg, 1965-1972; St. John, Charleston, 1972-1981; Mt. Horeb, Chapin, 1981—. *Spouse:* Julia Ganell Bennett Shealy. (*See page 897.*)

SHEALY, GEORGE B.: *Served:* In S. C., St. John, Walhalla, 1968-1980; Redeemer, Greer, 1980-1982. *Ret.* 1982, disability. *Spouse:* Gloria Cleo Hawkins Shealy (*See page 897.*)

SHEALY, GUY HUBERT: *Ed.* Winthrop Col., M.Ed., 1980. *Served:* In S. C., Messiah, Hanahan, 1971-1973; "On Leave From Call," 1973-1975; Clinical Chaplain, Catawba Mental Health Center, York, 1975-1986; Trans. to N. C. Synod, 1986. *Spouse:* Linda Smith Shealy. (*See page 898.*)

SHEALY, JAMES FRANKLIN: *Served:* In N. C. Synod, 1965-1973; In S. C., Bachman Chapel, Prosperity, 1973—. *Spouse:* Belva Elizabeth Stuck Shealy. (*See page 898.*)

SHEALY, JAMES LEE: (*See page 898.*)

SHEALY, JEFFERSON DAVIS: (*See page 898.*)

SHEALY, JOSEPH ALONZO: *Spouse:* Ruth Long Shealy. *D.* 1975, *B.* Wittenberg Cem., Leesville. (*See page 898.*)

SHEALY, PERRY EDGAR: (*See page 898.*)

SHEALY, TILLMAN WESLEY: (*See page 898.*)

SHEALY, WALTER WESLEY: (*See page 898.*)

SHEARHOUSE, OSWELL BENJAMIN: (*See page 899.*)

SHELBY, ROBERT FITZHUGH, JR.: (*See page 899.*)

SHEPHERD (SHEPPARD), STANMORE R.: (*See page 899.*)

SHEPPARD, JOHN W. S.: (*See page 899.*)

SHEPPERSON, C. M.: (*See page 899.*)

SHIERENBACH (SCHIERENBECK), JOHN HENRY CONRAD: (*See page 899.*)

SHIREY, J. D.: (*See page 899.*)

SHORT, JAMES EDMUND: *B.* May 26, 1944, Charleston, S. C. *Ed.* Baptist Col., B.A., 1970; LTSS, M.Div. 1974. *Ord.* 1974, S. C. Synod. *Served:* In S. C., Bethany-Nazareth, Lexington, 1974-1978; Mt. Hebron, Leesville, 1978-1979; "On Leave from Call," 1979-1982; Resigned from Ministry, 1982.

SHULL, DANIEL MURRAY, JR.: *Served:* In S. C., Holy Communion, Spartanburg, 1971—. Editor, *South Carolina Lutheran*, 1966—; Correspondent for *The Lutheran* in S. C. Synod, 1977—. *Spouse:* Christine Wessinger Shull. (*See page 899.*)

SHULL, DANIEL MURRAY, SR.: *Spouse:* Mary Gladys Langford Shull. (*See page 899.*)

SIBERT, DAVID: (*See page 900.*)

SIDES, FLOYD EUGENE, SR.: *B.* Aug. 23, 1940, Albemarle, N. C. *Ed.* Lenoir-Rhyne Col., B.A., 1962; LTSS, M.Div., 1966. *Ord.* 1966, N. C. Synod. *Served:* In N. C. Synod, 1966-1974; in S. C., Mayer Memorial, Newberry, 1974—. *Spouse:* Barbara L. Holshouser Sides.

SIGMAN, WALTER AUGUSTUS: (Correction to *History*, 1971). *Served:* In Va. Synod, 1965-1972. *Ret.* 1972. Trans. to S. C. Synod, 1973. *Spouse:* Emma Lee Cathey Sigman. *D.* 1981, *B.* Pinelawn Memorial Gardens, Clinton. (*See page 900.*)

SIGMON, PAUL CROMER: (*See page 900.*)

SIGWALD, GEORGE A. B.: (*See page 900.*)

SIMS, GEORGE LEE: *B.* Mar. 29, 1948, Columbia, S. C. *Ed.* Newberry Col., B.A., 1971; LTSS, M.Div., 1975. *Ord.* 1975, S. C. Synod. *Served:* In N. C. Synod, 1975-1981; in S. C., Good Shepherd, Columbia, 1981-1984 (Associate Pastor); Christ the King, Columbia, 1984—. *Spouse:* Ann Scott Paetzell Sims.

SIMS, ROBERT FREDERICK: *B.* Nov. 6, 1936, Spartanburg, S. C. *Ed.* Lenoir-Rhyne Col., B.A., 1958; LTSS, M.Div., 1961; LTSS, D.Min., 1978. *Ord.* 1961, N. C. Synod. *Served:* In N. C. Synod, 1961-1967; in Va. Synod, 1967-1973; in S. C., Ebenezer, Columbia, 1973—. *Spouse:* Mary Frances Carpenter Sims.

SINGLY, MARTIN: (*See page 900.*)

SINK, VOIGT MOCK: *Served:* Military Chaplain, U. S. Air Force, 1943-1970; in Texas-La. Synod, 1970-1971; in SE Synod, 1971-1980; St. John, Johnston, 1980—. *Spouse:* Waltraut Livia Timmerman Sink. (*See page 900.*)

SKINNER, HAROLD G.: *Served:* In S. C., St. Michael, Greenville, 1962-1973; Wittenberg, Leesville, 1973-1982; Trans. to N. C., 1982. Director, Karl W. Kinard Camp and Conference Center, 1973-1981. (*See page 900.*)

SLICE, JOHN NOAH: *Served:* In Nebraska Synod, 1951-1975. *Ret.* 1975; Trans. to S. C. Synod, 1975. *Spouse:* Virginia Elizabeth Voer Slice. (*See page 900.*)

SLICE, PAUL OWENS: *Served:* In S. C., Holy Trinity, Anderson, 1967—. *Spouse:* Karilyn Louise Slye Slice. (*See page 900.*)

310   A HISTORY OF THE LUTHERAN CHURCH IN S. C.

SLIGH, J. A.: (See page 900.)

SLIGH, WILBER K.: (See page 901.)

SMELTZ, WILLIAM R.: (See page 901.)

SMELTZER, JOSIAH PAUL (PEARCE): (See page 901.)

SMITH, GERALD WESLEY: (See page 901.)

SMITH, JASPER JAY: B. Jan. 13, 1924, Taylorsville, N. C. Ed. Lenoir-
Rhyne Col., A.B., 1948; LTSS, M.Div., 1951. Ord. 1951, N. C. Synod. Served:
In N. C. Synod, 1951-1956; Military Chaplain, U. S. Air Force, 1956—;
Trans. to S. C. Synod, 1980. Spouse: Sarah Ann Smith (D. 1984).

SMITH, JOHN LEWIS: (See page 901.)

SMITH, LARRY WESLEY: Served: In S. C., Mt. Hermon, Peak and Mt.
Olivet, Chapin, 1970-1983; St. Paul, Gilbert, 1983—. Spouse: Nancy Deree
Abrams Smith. (See page 901.)

SMITH, RONALD C.: (See page 901.)

SMITH, WILLIAM H.: (See page 902.)

SMITHDEAL, J. L.: (See page 902.)

SOLLE (CILLY), GEORGE: (See page 902.)

SOWERS, R. R.: (See page 902.)

SOX, CHARLES JASON: (See page 902.)

SOX, DAVID ADAM: (See page 902.)

SOX, DERMON ALBERT, JR.: Served: In S. C., St. Peter, Lexington,
1964-1976; Gethesemane, Columbia, 1976—. Member, Consulting Committee for Minority Group Interest, DMNA, LCA, 1984-1987. Spouse:
Jean Millen Steele Sox. (See page 902.)

SOX, DERMON ALBERT, SR.: Served: In S. C., Bethany-Nazareth,
Lexington, 1970-1971. Ret. 1971. Spouse: Helen Zobel Sox. (See page 902.)

SOX, ENOCH J.: (See page 902.)

SPOHN, ARNOLD PAUL: (See page 902.)

STECK, JACOB: (See page 903.)

STEELE, GEORGE STANLEY: B. Sept. 12, 1952, Columbia, S. C. Ed.
Univ. of S. C., B.A., 1977; LTSPhiladephia, M.Div., 1981. Ord. 1981, S. C.
Synod. Served: Trans. to Metro N. Y. Synod, 1981. Spouse: Stephanie
Andrea Sutter Steele.

STEELE, THOMAS PINCKNEY, JR.: B. Jan. 19, 1947, Columbia, S. C.
Ed. Newberry Col., B.A., 1969; LSTChicago, M.Div., 1973. Ord. 1973, S. C.
Synod. Served: In Illinois Synod, 1973-1976; in S. C., St. Matthias, Easley,
1976-1977; Chaplain, Holmesview Rehabilitation Center, Greenville,
1977-1984; Trans. to SE Synod, 1984. Spouse: Carol E. Ballentine Steele.

STEMMERMANN, ALBERT: Served: Chaplain, Franke Home,
1971-1983. Spouse: Helen Eddielee Wreden Stemmermann (D. 1973). D.
1983, B. Bethany Cem., Charleston. (See page 903.)

STENDER, WILLIAM HAROLD: (See page 903.)

STILWELL, RALPH DUNCAN: *B.* Dec. 13, 1946; Winston-Salem, N. C. *Ed.* Univ. of S. C., B.S., 1969; LTSS, M.Div. 1973. *Ord.* 1973, S. C. Synod. *Served:* In S. C., Nativity, Spartanburg, 1973-1981; Nazareth, Lexington, 1981—. *Spouse:* Barbara Sue Allen Stilwell.

STINGLEY, JAMES D.: *(See page 903.)*

STOCKMAN, ENOCH D.: *(See page 903.)*

STOCKMAN, JAMES EDGAR: *(See page 903.)*

STONE, WILLIAM EARLE: *Served:* In S. C., Faith, Newberry, 1969-1974; All Saints, Mt. Pleasant, 1974-1979 (Pastor/Developer 1974-1975); Grace, Gilbert, 1979—. *Spouse:* Priscilla Stender Stone. *(See page 903.)*

STORCH (STORK), THEOPHILUS: *(See page 903.)*

STOUDEMAYER, GEORGE ABNEY: *(See page 904.)*

STOUDEMAYER, JOHN M.: *B.* Oct. 6, 1950, Chicago, Illinois. *Ed.* Furman, B.A., 1972; LTSS, M.Div., 1987. *Ord.* 1987, S. C. Synod. *Served:* Trans. to N. C. Synod, 1987. *Spouse:* Stephanie Meynardie Stoudemayer.

STOUDENMIRE, HENRY: *(See page 904.)*

STOUDENMIRE, WILLIAM: *(See page 904.)*

STREIT, CHRISTIAN: *(See page 904.)*

STROBEL, PHILIP ARTHUR: *(See page 904.)*

STROBEL, WILLIAM D.: *(See page 904.)*

STROUP, BRADY LEE: *(See page 904.)*

STUCKE, CLARENCE HENTZE: *Served:* In Ga.-Ala. Synod, 1958-1963; in SE Synod, 1963-1981; in S. C., Colony, Newberry, 1981—. National Guard-U. S. Army Reserve, 1947-1972. *Spouse:* Mary Dorothy McLeod Stucke. *(See page 904.)*

SUBER, THOMAS FRANK: *(See page 905.)*

SUBLETT, MARVIN THOMAS: *B.* May 26, 1935, Asheville, N. C. *Ed.* Lenoir-Rhyne Col., A.B., 1957; LTSS, M.Div., 1960; McCormick Theol. Sem., D.Min., 1975. *Ord.* 1960, N. C. Synod. *Served:* In N. C. Synod, 1960-1964; in Fla. Synod, 1964-1971; in S. C., Martin Luther, Charleston, 1971-1974; Trans. to Florida Synod, 1974. *Spouse:* Elizabeth Beck Sink Sublett.

SUHR, KARL FREDERICK, JR.: *B.* April 1, 1957, Atlanta, Ga. *Ed.* The Citadel, B.S., 1980; LTSS, M.Div., 1984. *Ord.* 1984, SE Synod. *Served:* In S. C., Good Shepherd, Columbia, 1984-1986 (Assistant Pastor); Chaplain in the U. S. Army Reserve and National Guard. Trans. to SE Synod, 1986. *Spouse:* Joan Biser Suhr.

SUMMER, PAUL HARE: *B.* May 2, 1958, York County, S. C. *Ed.* Newberry Col., B.A., 1980; LTSS, M.Div., 1984. *Ord.* 1985, S. C. Synod. *Served:* Trans. to Florida Synod, 1985. *Spouse:* Debra Lock Summer.

SUMMER, WILLIAM RAY: *(See page 905.)*

SWICEGOOD, DERMONT FRITZ: *Served:* In S. C., Pisgah, Lexington, 1969-1980. *Ret.* 1980. *Spouse:* Eloise Blanche Efird Swicegood (*D.* 1985); Lois Winemiller Swicegood. *(See page 905.)*

SWICEGOOD, DERMONT LUTHER: *Served:* In S. C., Christ the King, Columbia, 1964-1973; St. Michael, Greenville, 1973—. *Spouse:* Caroline Derrenbacher Swicegood. (*See page 905.*)

SWIFT, ROY ORLANDO, III: *B.* July 15, 1938, Fairfield, Ala. *Ed.* Samford University, B.A., 1961; Southeastern Baptist Theo. Sem., M.Div., 1964. *Ord.* 1970, Pacific Southwest Synod. *Served:* In S.C., Military Chaplain, U. S. Navy, 1972—. *Spouse:* Sue Clements Swift.

SWING, STAFFORD LEROY: *Served:* In S. C., Reformation, Columbia, 1967-1980. *Spouse:* Dorothy Ketner Swing. *D.* 1980, *B.* City Memorial Cem., Salisbury, N. C. (*See page 905.*)

SWYGERT, GEORGE DAVID: (*See page 905.*)

SWYGERT, LUTHER LEGARE: *Spouse:* Louise Addy Swygert. (*See page 905.*)

SWYGERT, ROBERT LEE: *Served:* In S. C., Pine Grove, Lone Star, 1971-1982; Faith, West Columbia, 1982-1984. *Ret.* 1984. *Spouse:* Dolores Arlene Wiley Swygert. (*See page 905.*)

TARRANT, ROBERT BENSON: (*See page 905.*)

TATE, FREDERICK STANLEY, JR.: *B.* May 19, 1947, Bluefield, W.Va. *Ed.* Roanoke Col., B.A., 1969; LTSS, M.Div., 1973. *Ord.* 1973, Virginia Synod. *Served:* In Virginia Synod, 1973-1978; in S. C., St. John, Pelion, 1978—. Chaplain, USAR. *Spouse:* Linda Kaye Lawson Tate.

TAYLOR, ARTHUR RICHARD: (*See page 906.*)

TAYLOR, DICKSON WALTER: (*See page 906.*)

TAYLOR, JAMES CHARLES: *Served:* In S. C., Mt. Tabor, Little Mountain, 1969-1977; Military Chaplain, U. S. Army, 1977—. *Spouse:* Linda Ann Gause Taylor. (*See page 906.*)

TAYLOR, WALTER ALLEN, SR.: (*See page 906.*)

THEUS (THEIS), CHRISTIAN: (*See page 906.*)

THOLSTRUP, DAVID BRUCE: *B.* May 17, 1985, Pensacola, Fla. *Ed.* Kansas State Univ., B.S., 1977; Clemson Univ., M.S., 1980; LTSS, M.Div., 1984. *Ord.* 1984, S. C. Synod. *Served:* Trans. to Va. Synod, 1984. *Spouse:* Janice Dominy Tholstrup.

THOMAS, DAVID EDWIN: *Served:* In S. C., Professor of Sociology, Newberry College, 1969-1981. *Ret.* 1981. *Spouse:* Maree Olson Thomas. (*See page 906.*)

THOMAS, LUTHER ALEXANDER: (*See page 906.*)

THOMPSON, ROBERT HAROLD, II: *B.* Oct. 6, 1944, Elyria, Ohio. *Ed.* Pfeiffer Col., A.B., 1971; LTSS, M.Div., 1975; Union Theo. Sem., D.Min., 1980. *Ord.* 1975, N. C. Synod. *Served:* In N. C. Synod, 1975-1981; in S. C., St. John, Walhalla, 1981—. *Spouse:* Nadine Broome Thompson.

THUEMMEL, CHRISTIAN BERNHARD: (*See page 906.*)

TILLEY, GEORGE EDWARD: *B.* May 17, 1951, Durham, N. C. *Ed.* Concordia Senior Col., Fort Wayne, Indiana, B.A., 1973; Concordia Sem. in Exile, Shovis, Mo., M.Div., 1977. *Ord.* 1979, N. C. Synod. *Served:* In N. C.

Synod, 1979-1981; in S. C., St. Matthew, Charleston, 1981-1982 (Assistant Pastor). Trans. to Metro N. Y. Synod, 1982.

TISE, JACOB MARSHALL: (*See page 906.*)

TOERNE, ALFRED EDWARD: *B.* Aug. 30, 1951, San Antonio, Texas. *Ed.* Trinity Univ., San Antonio, Tx., A.B., 1973; LTSS, M.Div., 1977. *Ord.* 1977, S. C. Synod. *Served:* Trans. to Texas-Louisiana Synod, 1977. *Spouse:* Lisa Anne Sink Toerne.

TRAUGER, JORDAN C.: (*See page 907.*)

TREXLER, BERNARD LITTLETON: *Served:* In S. C., Trinity, Greenville, 1961-1983. *Ret.* 1983. *Spouse:* Dorothy Caughman Trexler. (*See page 907.*)

TREXLER, LEROY CAUBLE: *Served:* In S. C., St. Paul, Columbia, 1965-1976; St. Stephen, Lexington, 1976-1978; in Florida Synod, 1978-1983; in S. C., Wittenberg, Leesville, 1983-1986. Trans. to N. C. Synod, 1986. *Ret.* 1986. *Spouse:* Mabel Shealy Trexler. (*See page 907.*)

TREXLER, WILLIAM BERNARD: *Served:* In Florida Synod, 1970-1975; in S. C., Immanuel, Greenwood, 1976-1979; Trans. to Florida Synod, 1979. *Spouse:* Karla Christa Gnat Trexler. (*See page 907.*)

TROTTI, JOHN MARION: *B.* Oct. 23, 1948, Fort Jackson, S. C. *Ed.* Univ. of S. C., A.B., 1972; LTSS, M.Div., 1978. *Ord.* 1978, S. C. Synod. *Served:* Trans. to New England Synod, 1978. *D.* 1983, *B.* Pittsfield, Mass.

TROUTMAN, ROY TAYS: (*See page 907.*)

TUTAS, ROBERT LEO: *Served:* In S. C., Mt. Pleasant, Saluda, 1968-1972; Orangeburg, Orangeburg, 1972-1974; Shepherd of the Sea, Garden City, 1974-1978 (Mission Developer 1974-1975); Resigned from Ministry, 1978.

UMBERGER, JAMES BROWN: (*See page 907.*)

VAN DEUSEN, DAYTON G.: *B.* May 20, 1914, Claverack, N. Y. *Ed.* Hartwick Col., B.A., 1935; Hartwick Sem., M.Div., 1938; Union Theo. Sem., S.T.M., 1956. *Ord.* 1938, New York Synod. *Served:* In N. Y. Synod, 1938-1946; Military Chaplain—U. S. Army, 1943-1946; in Central States Synod, 1954-1956; in Ill. Synod, 1957-1961; in Wis.-U.M. Synod, 1962-1977; in S. C., Bryan Psychiatric Hospital, Columbia, 1977-1979 (Director of Chaplaincy Services). *Ret.* 1979. Trans. to Florida Synod, 1979. *Spouse:* Margaret Van Raden Van Deusen.

VAN DEUSEN, ROBERT E.: *B.* April 1, 1909, St. Johnsville, N.Y. *Ed.* Hartwick Col, A.B., 1932; Hartwick Sem., M.Div., 1935; Syracuse Univ., M.A., 1953; American Univ. Ph.D., 1968; Hartwick Col., D.D., 1953. *Ord.* 1935, New York Synod. *Served:* In New York Synod, 1935-1941; in Fla. Synod, 1941-1944; in Md. Synod, 1944-1975. *Ret.* 1975. Trans. to S. C. Synod, 1975. *Spouse:* Ruth Sarah Brown Van Deusen.

VAN HORNE, ROBERT MARION: *Served:* In S. C., Redeemer, Charleston, 1970-1981; in Florida Synod, 1981-84; in N. C. Synod, 1984-86; in S. C., Redeemer, Newberry, 1986—. *Spouse:* Mary Stobo Bradham Van Horne. (*See page 907.*)

VARN, KARL MICHAEL: *B.* Oct. 11, 1946, Columbia, S. C. *Ed.* Lenoir-Rhyne Col., A.B., 1971; LTSS, M.Div., 1975. *Ord.* 1975, S. C. Synod. *Served:*

In S. C., St. Mark, Isle of Palms, 1975-1979; Trans. to N. C. Synod, 1979. *Spouse:* Lynette Kuran Varn.

VAUGHAN, DAVID BARRY: *B.* May 2, 1941, Los Angeles, California. *Ed.* Lenoir-Rhyne Col., B.A., 1974; LTSS, M.Div. 1978. *Ord.* 1978, N. C. Synod. *Served:* In N. C. Synod, 1978-1983; in S. C., St. David, West Columbia, 1983-1986 (Associate Pastor); "On Leave From Call," 1986; Resigned from Ministry, 1986.

VERSPRILLE, CRAIG W.: *B.* Dec. 29, 1953, Rochester, New York. *Ed.* Univ. of Rochester, B.S., 1976; LTSS, M.Div., 1985. *Ord.* 1985, S. C. Synod. *Served:* In S. C., Ascension, Columbia, 1985—. *Spouse:* Linda Foy Versprille.

VOIGT, ANDREW GEORGE: (*See page 907.*)

VOIGT, GILBERT P.: (*See page 908.*)

von HACKE, HACO WILHELM RUDOLF DETLOV: (*See page 908.*)

WALCK, CLARENCE G., JR.: *Served:* In S. C., St. Phillip, Prosperity, 1969-1978; Trans. to N. C. Synod, 1979. (*See page 908.*)

WALLACE, GERALD PATRICK: *B.* April 29, 1946, Concord, N. C. *Ed.* Lenoir-Rhyne Col., A.B., 1968; LTSS, M.Div., 1972. *Ord.* 1972, N. C. Synod. *Served:* In N. C. Synod, 1972-1987; in S. C., Our Saviour, West Columbia, 1987—. *Spouse:* Nancy Caughman Wallace.

WALLACE, HUGH JEFFERSON: *B.* Sept. 24, 1956, Albany, Georgia. *Ed.* Lenoir-Rhyne Col, B.A., 1979; LTSS, M.Div., 1984. *Ord.* 1984, S. C. Synod. *Served:* Trans. to SE Synod, 1984. *Spouse:* Stephanie Stout Wallace.

WALLACE, RALPH JUSTIN: *B.* Oct. 12, 1935, Greensboro, N. C. *Ed.* Lenoir-Rhyne Col., A.B., 1958; LTSS, M.Div., 1961. *Ord.* 1961, N. C. Synod. *Served:* In N. C. Synod, 1961-1977; in S. C., St. Paul, Columbia, 1977—. LCA Pastor/Evangelist, 1977-1981; Preacher for the Lutheran Series of the Protestant Hour, 1975. *Spouse:* Sarah Frances Huddle Wallace.

WALLBURG (WALLBERG), FREDERICK AUGUSTUS: (*See page 908.*)

WALLERN, FREDERICK JOSEPH: (*See page 908.*)

WARNER, JACK HUNTINGTON, JR.: (*See page 908.*)

WARNER, J. T.: (*See page 908.*)

WARREN, ROBERT CECIL: *B.* May 20, 1945, Homestead, Fla. *Ed.* Univ. of Miami, B.M., 1970; LTSS, M.Div., 1983. *Ord.* 1983, Florida Synod. *Served:* In S. C., St. Matthew, Charleston, 1983-1985 (Assistant Pastor); Atonement, Laurens, 1985—. *Spouse:* Julie Saunders Warren.

WARTMANN, H. G. B.: (*See page 908.*)

WATSON, HENRY BENJAMIN: *Served:* In S. C., Bethlehem and St. John, Irmo, 1967-1972; Bethlehem, Irmo, 1972-1973. *Ret.* 1974. *Spouse:* Dorothy Gertrude Dale Watson. (*See page 908.*)

WEAVER, JOHN FRANKLIN: *B.* Feb. 4, 1935, Hickory, N. C. *Ed.* Lenoir-Rhyne, A.B., 1958; LTSS, M.Div., 1961. *Ord.* 1961, N. C. Synod. *Served:* In N. C. Synod, 1961-1965; Military Chaplain, U. S. Navy, 1965-1984; in S. C., Summer Memorial, Newberry, 1984—. *Spouse:* Barbara Joan Aull Weaver.

WEBB, JAMES KENNETH: Newberry Col., Sc.S.D., 1973. *Served:* President of Lowman Home, White Rock, 1961-1987. *Ret.* 1987. *Spouse:* Betty Boozer Hair Webb. (*See page 909.*)

WEBBER, RICHARD EDGAR: *B.* Jan. 12, 1947, St. Petersburg, Fla. *Ed.* Newberry Col., B.A., 1969; LTSS, M.Div., 1973. *Ord.* 1973, Florida Synod. *Served:* In Florida Synod, 1973-1975; in S. C., King of Glory, North Myrtle Beach, 1975-1981 (Mission Developer, 1975-1976); St. David, West Columbia, 1981—. *Spouse:* Jeannie Lee Armfield Webber.

WEBER, CARL: (*See page 909.*)

WEBER, HARRY: *Served:* In S. C., Assistant Professor of Religion, 1959-1979; Dean of Students, 1966-1969; Chaplain, 1962-1974, Newberry College; Mt. Pleasant, Saluda, 1979-1985. *Ret.* 1985. *Spouse:* Ruth Virginia Graham Weber. (*See page 909.*)

WEEKS, ROBERT MARTIN: *Ed.* Princeton Sem., Th.D., 1977. *Served:* Military Chaplain, U.S. Navy, 1966-1985; Trans. to N. C. Synod, 1985. *Spouse:* Sylvia Earline Metz Weeks. (*See page 909.*)

WEEKS, THOMAS HARMON: (*See page 909.*)

WEGENER, WILLIAM ERNEST: (*See page 909.*)

WELTNER, CHARLES E.: (*See page 909.*)

WENTZ, FREDERICK K.: (*See page 909.*)

WERNER, ROY WALTER: *Served:* In S. C., St. Paul, Gilbert, 1966-1976. *Spouse:* Johnnie H. Werner. *D.* 1976, *B.* St. Paul Cem., Gilbert. (*See page 909.*)

WERTS, DAY BEDENBAUGH: *Spouse:* Mini Vogel Werts. *D.* 1983, *B.* Prosperity Cem., (*See page 910.*)

WERTZ, J. H. W.: (*See page 910.*)

WERTZ, JOHN E.: *Served:* In S. C., St. Michael, Moncks Corner, 1971-1977; Trans. to N. C. Synod, 1977. (*See page 910.*)

WERTZ, JOSEPH QUINCY: (*See page 910.*)

WERTZ, LESTER ALLEN, JR.: (*See page 910.*)

WERTZ, LESTER A., SR.: (*See page 910.*)

WESSELLS, C. B.: (*See page 910.*)

WESSINGER, BENJAMIN DAVID: (*See page 910.*)

WESSINGER, BERNICE JUSTUS: (*See page 911.*)

WESSINGER, CARROLL LEROY: (*See page 911.*)

WESSINGER, CHARLES SAMUEL: *Served:* In S. C., St. Andrew, Charleston, 1956-1976; Trans. to SE Synod, 1976. (*See page 911.*)

WESSINGER, DWIGHT CANNON: *B.* March 17, 1946, Columbia, S. C. *Ed.* Newberry Col., 1974; LTSS, M.Div., 1978. *Ord.* 1978, S. C. Synod. *Served:* In S. C., St. Michael, Columbia, 1978—. *Spouse:* Bunny Elise Bedenbaugh Wessinger.

WESSINGER, J. CALVIN (JACOB OR JOHN): (*See page 911.*)

WESSINGER, JOHN WINGARD: *Served:* In S. C., St. Jacob, Chapin, 1961-1978. *Ret.* 1978. *Spouse:* Louise Taylor Wessinger. (*See page 911.*)

WESSINGER, JOSEPH SAMUEL: *Spouse:* Jessie Oxner Wessinger (D. 1974). *D.* 1978, *B.* St. Peter Cem., Chapin. (*See page 911.*)

WHITENER, C. PHILLIP: *B.* March 28, 1953, Hickory, N. C. *Ed.* Concordia Col., B.A., 1975; LTSS, M.Div., 1987. *Ord.* 1987, S. C. Synod. *Served:* In S. C., St. John, Charleston (Associate Pastor), 1987—. *Spouse:* Mary Bernthal Whitener.

WHITTLE, M.: (*See page 911.*)

WICKS, EDWIN H.: *B.* Feb. 22, 1953, Orlando, Florida. *Ed.* Fla. Tech. Univ., B.S., 1976; LTSS, M.Div., 1980. *Ord.* 1981, S. C. Synod. *Served:* In S. C., Ehrhardt Memorial, Ehrhardt, 1981-1982; Trans. to N. C. Synod, 1982. *Spouse:* Lucy McHugh Wicks.

WIEDIGER, EDWARD H.: *B.* May 14, 1921, Buffalo, N. Y. *Ed.* Wagner Col., B.A., 1944; LTSPhiladelphia, M.Div., 1946. *Ord.* 1946, New York and New England Synod. *Served:* In New York and New England Synod, 1946-1976; in S. C., Prince of Peace, Chester and Abiding Presence, York, 1976-1979. *Ret.* 1979; Trans. to New England Synod, 1979. *Spouse:* Ruth Moeller Wiediger.

WIKE, JACOB: (*See page 912.*)

WILKEN, J. F.: (*See page 911.*)

WILLIAMS, FREDERICK CHRISTIE: (*See page 912.*)

WILLIAMS, PAUL BARR: *B.* June 8, 1946, Florence, S. C. *Ed.* Augusta Col., B.A., 1973; LTSS, M.Div., 1977. *Ord.* 1977, S. C. Synod. *Served:* In S. C., St. John, Irmo, 1977-1982; Faith, Johns Island, 1982-1984; Mt. Pleasant, Ehrhardt, 1984—. *Spouse:* Patricia C. Aldridge Williams.

WILLIS, GEORGE TILMER: (*See page 912.*)

WILSON, J. F.: *B.* Aug. 22, 1930, Baltimore, Maryland. *Ed.* George Washington University, B.A., 1952; LTSGettysburg, M.Div., 1955. *Ord.* 1955, Maryland Synod. *Served:* In Maryland Synod, 1955-1985. *Ret.* 1985. Trans. to S. C. Synod 1985. *Spouse:* Dorothy Koch Wilson.

WILSON, JAMES HERBERT: (*See page 912.*)

WINGARD, EMANUEL A.: (*See page 912.*)

WINGARD, HENRY S.: (*See page 912.*)

WINGARD, HENRY SAMUEL: (*See page 912.*)

WINGARD, JACOB: (*See page 913.*)

WINGARD, MULLER RAWLS: (*See page 913.*)

WINGARD, WILLIAM FRANKLIN: *Served:* In S. C., St. Philip, Myrtle Beach, 1955-1987; Chaplain, U. S. Air Force Reserves, 1958-1987. *Ret.* 1987. *Spouse:* Marguerite Thompson Wingard. (*See page 913.*)

WINKHOUSE, HARMAN: (*See page 913.*)

WISE, BERNARD F.: (*See page 913.*)

WISE, CURTIS KERR, SR.: (*See page 913.*)

WISE, WALTER DANIEL: (*See page 913.*)

WITHROCK, JOHN WILLIAM, JR.: *B.* Sept. 21, 1948, Trinidad, Colorado. *Ed.* Univ. of S. C., A.B., 1970; LTSS, M.Div., 1975. *Ord.* 1975, S. C. Synod. *Served:* In S. C., St. Luke, Columbia, 1975-1977; Redeemer, Greer, 1977-1980; Resigned from Ministry, 1980; Reinstated to Roll of Ministers, 1984; Trans. to Florida Synod, 1984.

WITT, EDWARD C.: (*See page 913.*)

WOLFF, HAROLD ALBERT: *Served:* In S. C., Christ, Columbia, 1965-1979. *Ret.* 1979. *Spouse:* Erin Eargle Lever Wolff. *D.* 1984, *B.* St. Andrew Cem., Blythewood. (*See page 914.*)

WOLFF, JOHN HAROLD: *B.* July 23, 1945, Geneva, New York. *Ed.* Newberry Col., B.A., 1967; Univ. of S. C., M.A., 1970; LTSS, M.Div., 1972. *Ord.* 1972, S. C. Synod. *Served:* In S. C., Incarnation, Columbia, 1972-1974 (Assistant Pastor); Resigned from Ministry, 1974. *Spouse:* Carolyn Jeanette Havird Wolff.

WOLFF, LARRY KENT: (*See page 914.*)

WOOD, HERBERT LEE, JR.: *B.* April 11, 1946, Savannah Georgia. *Ed.* Newberry Col., B.A., 1968; LTSS, M.Div., 1976. *Ord.* 1976, SE Synod. *Served:* In SE Synod, 1976-1985; in S. C. Synod, Beth-Eden, St. James, Newberry, 1986—. *Spouse:* Clara Ann Meetze Wood.

WOOD, RAYMOND DOUGLAS: (*See page 914.*)

WOOD, WILLIAM COLLINS: (*See page 914.*)

WOOLLY, DONALD EDGAR: *B.* Aug. 12, 1932, High Point, N. C. *Ed.* Lenoir-Rhyne Col., A.B., 1955; LTSS, M.Div., 1958; McCormick Theo. Sem., D. Min., 1981. *Ord.* 1958, N. C. Synod. *Served:* In N. C. Synod, 1958-1973; in S. C., St. Andrew, Columbia, 1973—. *Spouse:* Anne Judith Rumley Woolly.

WORDMANN (WORTMANN, WARTMAN), H. B. G.: (*See page 914.*)

WORTH, JOHN HOWARD: (*See page 914.*)

WUERZ, HENRY JOHN: *B.* May 16, 1948, Brooklyn, New York. *Ed.* Adelphi Univ., New York, B.A., 1970; LTSS, M.Div., 1976. *Ord.* 1976, S. C. Synod. *Served:* Trans. to N. E. Pennsylvania Synod, 1976. *Spouse:* Lorelle Anne Krogmann Wuerz.

WYSE, JOHN HOPE: (*See page 914.*)

YODER, HAROLD MONROE: *B.* Nov. 23, 1922, Hickory, N. C. *Ed.* Lenoir-Rhyne Col, A.B., 1943; LTSGettysburg, M.Div., 1950; LTSS, D.Min., 1983. *Ord.* 1950, N. C. Synod. *Served:* In N. C. Synod, 1950-1957; in Md. Synod, 1957-1972; in S. C., Chaplain, Richland Memorial Hospital, Columbia, 1972—. Certified Supervisor with Association for Clinical Pastoral Education, Inc.; Certified as a Professional Hospital Chaplain and Fellow, American Protestant Hospital Association. *Spouse:* Selena Frances Kime Yoder.

YONCE, JOHN LUTHER: (*See page 914.*)

YOOS, HERMAN ROBERT: *B.* Jan. 1, 1952, Concord, N. C. *Ed.* Univ. of N. C., B.A., 1974; LTSS, M.Div., 1979. *Ord.* 1979, N. C. Synod. *Served:* In N. C. Synod, 1979-1982; in S. C., Redeemer, Charleston, 1982—. *Spouse:* Cindy Parker Yoos.

318   A HISTORY OF THE LUTHERAN CHURCH IN S. C.

YOST, CARL RUSSELL: *B.* April 17, 1955, Salisbury, N. C. *Ed.* Lenoir-Rhyne Col., B.A., 1979; LTSS, M.Div., 1983. *Ord.* 1983, S. C. Synod. *Served:* Trans. to N. C. Synod, 1983. *Spouse:* Debra Query Yost.

YOST, JOHN L., JR.: *B.* April 27, 1921, Bear Poplar, N. C. *Ed.* Newberry Col., A.B., 1943; LTSS, M.Div., 1945; Lenoir-Rhyne Col., D.D., 1963. *Ord.* 1945, Ga.-Ala. Synod. *Served:* In Va. Synod, 1945-1947; in Ga.-Ala. Synod, 1947-1952; Secretary, Board of Foreign Missions, ULCA, New York, N. Y., 1952-1954; in N. C. Synod, 1954-1975; in S. C., St. Matthew, Charleston, 1975-1986. Delegate to LWF Assembly, Tanzania, Africa; Member Executive Council, LCA, 1974-1982. *Ret.* 1986. *Spouse:* Kathryn Sue Caughman Yost.

YOST, JOHN LEWIS, SR.: *B.* March 9, 1893, Rowan County, N. C. *Ed.* Roanoke Col., A.B., 1914; LTSS, M.Div., 1917; Newberry Col., D.D., 1935; Roanoke Col., L.L.D., 1959. *Ord.* 1917, N. C. Synod. *Served:* In Tenn.-Va. Synod, 1917-1919; in N. C. Synod, 1919-1929; in Ga.-Ala. Synod, 1929-1945; President, LTSS, 1945-1961; President Emeritus, LTSS, 1961-1985. *Ret.* 1961; Trans. to S. C. Synod, 1975. *Spouse:* Eva Louise Dunning Yost (D. 1984). *D.* 1985, B. Elmwood Cem., Columbia.

YOST, JOHN L., III: *B.* Sept. 9, 1948, Savannah, Ga. *Ed.* Lenoir-Rhyne Col., A.B., 1970; LTSS, M.Div., 1974. *Ord.* 1974, N. C. Synod. *Served:* In Florida Synod, 1974-1983; in S. C., Messiah, Mauldin, 1983—. *Spouse:* Brenda A. Wyke Yost.

YOUNG, WAYNE WILLIAM: *B.* Dec. 12, 1953, Baltimore, Md. *Ed.* Univ. of Central Florida, B.A., 1975; LTSS, M.Div., 1979. *Ord.* 1979, Florida Synod. *Served:* In S. C., St. Paul, Columbia, 1979-1981 (Assistant Pastor); Providence, Lexington, 1981-1984; Trans. to SE Synod, 1984. *Spouse:* Susan Jackson Young.

YOUNGBLOOD, JAMES ROBBINS: *B.* July 17, 1947, Charlotte, N. C. *Ed.* Clemson Univ., B.S.E.E., 1970; LTSS, M.Div., 1975. *Ord.* 1975, S. C. Synod. *Served:* Trans. to N. C. Synod, 1975. *Spouse:* Linda Ruth Crawford Youngblood.

YOUNT, NOAH DAVID: *(See page 915.)*

ZAUBERBUHLER, BARTHOLOMEW, JR.: *(See page 915.)*

ZAUBERBUHLER, BARTHOLOMEW, SR.: *(See page 915.)*

ZEIGLER, EDWIN DAVID: *Spouse:* Ruby Hawkins Zeigler. *D.* 1982, *B.* Newberry Memorial Gardens. *(See page 915.)*

ZEIGLER, JOHN DAVID, JR.: *Served:* In S. C., St. Peter, Chapin, 1972-1981; Necrologist, S. C. Synod, 1956-1982. *Ret.* 1981. *Spouse:* Evelyn Bush Zeigler. *D.* 1983, *B.* Ebenezer Cem., Jerusalem Lutheran Church, Rincon, Ga. *(See page 915.)*

ZETTNER, S. (J.) C.: *(See page 915.)*

ZIEGLER, EDGAR DAVID: *(See page 915.)*

ZIMMERMANN, EDWARD CARL: *B.* April 29, 1950, Philadelphia, Pa. *Ed.* Villanova Univ., B.A., 1973; LTSS, M.Div., 1977; Temple Univ., M.A., 1982. *Ord.* 1977, Southeast Penn. Synod. *Served:* In S. C., Incarnation, 1977-1979; Trans. to Southeastern Penn. Synod, 1979. *Spouse:* Bonnie Carol Vance Zimmerman.

ZUBLY, JOHN JOACHIM: *(See page 915.)*

Chapter Seven

Certified Lay Professionals

Certified Lay Professionals have been an important part of the ministry team within the South Carolina Synod for many years. However, until recently, an accurate listing of these persons had not been kept. We have, therefore, included in this listing those persons whom we know have served in the synod as Certified Lay Professionals. We apologize for any omissions. Information given includes name, date of certification, places, and dates of service since certification.

CERTIFIED LAY PROFESSIONALS

DERRICK, MITZI MARIE JARRETT:
Certified: 1985. *Served;* Assistant Librarian, LTSS, 1985-1987; Librarian, 1987—.

DOHNER, IRVIN R.:
Certified: 1985, *Served:* In N. C. Synod, 1985-1987; in S. C., Director of Music and Christian Education, St. Philip, Myrtle Beach, 1987—.

FAIRBANKS, BRENDA JOYCE BOITER:
Certified: 1984. *Served:* Associate Organist and Handbell Director, Our Saviour, Greenville, 1984—.

FREDERICK, RICHARD ALLAN:
Certified: 1984. *Served:* Director of Christian Education, Advent, Charleston Heights, 1984—.

GLAESER, MARK WILLIAM:
Certified: 1983. *Served:* Director of Special Ministries, Mt. Tabor, West Columbia, 1983-1984; Trans. to S.E. Synod, 1984.

GOLNITZ, MARY MARGARET SCHULTZ:
Certified: 1986. *Served:* Music Director, Shepherd of the Sea, Garden City, 1986; Trans. to S.E. Synod, 1986.

HOCKSPEIER, EDITH MARY:
Certified: 1982. *Served:* In N. C. Synod, 1982-1984; in S. C., Director of Music and Educational Ministry, Mt. Tabor, West Columbia, 1984—.

HULL, SHERRON RHODES (NAN):
Certified: 1984. *Served:* Director of Christian Education, Redeemer, Charleston, 1984-1985; "On Leave from Appointment," 1985—.

KINARD, AMY FRICK:
Certified: 1986. *Served:* Director of Christian Education and Youth Activities, Redeemer, Newberry, 1986—.

LORICK, SUSAN DETGEN:
Certified: 1986. *Served:* Educational Ministry Coordinator, Immanuel, Greenwood, 1986—.

LUDLUM, W. DOUGLAS:
Certified: 1978. *Served:* In N. C. Synod, 1978-1981; in S. C., Organist/Director of Music, St. Matthew, Charleston, 1981—.

LYBRAND, JACQUIE WILSON:
Certified: 1987. *Served:* Coordinator of P.L.M.D., S. C. Synod, 1987.

McARVER, SUSAN WILDS:
Certified: 1981. *Served:* Director of Christian Education, St. Luke, Summerville, 1981-1985; "On Leave from Appointment," 1985—.

MERRITT, ALICE ANN RILEY:
Certified: 1978. *Served:* In N. C. Synod, 1978-1979; in S. C., Director of Christian Education and Youth Ministry, Incarnation, Columbia, 1981-1985.

MILLER, WILLIAM LAWRENCE, JR.:
Certified: 1979. *Served:* Organist-Choirmaster, Ascension, Columbia, 1979-1981; Resurrection, Columbia, 1981-1985; Advent, Charleston Heights, 1986—.

MOHRMAN, E. RAY:
Certified: 1984. *Served:* Director of Parish Ministries, Trinity, Greenville, 1984—.

MOORE, CYNTHIA HOPE CALLAWAY:
Certified: 1983. *Served:* Parish Worker, St. Philip, Myrtle Beach, 1983—.

O'BRIEN, THOMAS JOSEPH:
Certified: 1981. *Served:* Field Staff for Southeastern Synods for LCA Division for Parish Services, Department for Parish Support, 1981-1987; Field Staff for Congregational Support, Commission for Financial Support, ELCA, for Region IX, 1988—.

PADGETT, NANCY:
Certified: 1986. *Served:* Director of Christian Education and Youth Ministry, St. Andrew, Columbia, 1986-1987; Youth Ministry Coordinator, S. C. Synod, 1987—.

ROOT, MICHAEL JOHN:
Certified: 1983. *Served:* Associate Professor of Systematic Theology, LTSS, 1983—.

SOUTHERN, KATHERINE CROWELL:
Certified: 1982. *Served:* Director of Christian Education, Redeemer, Newberry, 1982-1984; Trans. to N. C. Synod, 1984.

STOUDEMAYER, STEPHANIE MEYNARDIE:
Certified: 1984. *Served:* Director of Christian Education, Holy Trinity, North Augusta, 1984-1985; "On Leave from Appointment," 1985—.

TERRY, LAURA JO SPEARES:
Certified: 1970. *Served:* Music Director/Organist, Holy Trinity, Anderson, 1970—.

TOLBERT, JUDITH KAY KLASEN:
Certified: 1983. *Served:* Director of Parish Music, Immanuel, Greenwood, 1983-1985; Director of Parish Music, Grace, Rock Hill, 1986—.

Appendix

Chronology of Conventions with Officers

Date	Place	Bishop	Secretary	Treasurer
1972 Apr. 24-26	Advent, Charleston Heights	Herman W. Cauble	Paulwyn L. Boliek	James B. Wessinger
1973 Apr. 29-May 1	St. David, West Columbia	Herman W. Cauble	Paulwyn L. Boliek	James B. Wessinger
1974 Apr. 28-30	Ascension and LTSS, Columbia	Herman W. Cauble	Paulwyn L. Boliek	James B. Wessinger
1975 Apr. 27-29	St. John, Spartanburg	Herman W. Cauble	Paulwyn L. Boliek	James B. Wessinger
1976 May 2-4	St. John, Charleston	Herman W. Cauble	Paulwyn L. Boliek	James B. Wessinger
1977 Apr. 24-26	Incarnation, Columbia	Herman W. Cauble	Paulwyn L. Boliek	James B. Wessinger
1978 June 6-8	Newberry College, Newberry	Herman W. Cauble	Paulwyn L. Boliek	James B. Wessinger
1979 Apr. 29-May 1	St. Matthew, Charleston	Herman W. Cauble	Paulwyn L. Boliek	James B. Wessinger
1980 Apr. 27-29	Ebenezer, Columbia	Herman W. Cauble	James S. Aull	James B. Wessinger
1981 May 3-5	St. Stephen, Lexington	Herman W. Cauble	James S. Aull	James B. Wessinger
1982 May 21-23	Newberry College, Newberry	Herman W. Cauble	James S. Aull	Raymond S. Caughman
1983 May 27-29	Newberry College, Newberry	Herman W. Cauble	James S. Aull	Raymond S. Caughman
1984 May 24-26	Newberry College, Newberry	Herman W. Cauble	James S. Aull	Raymond S. Caughman
1985 May 19-21	Newberry College, Newberry	Herman W. Cauble	James S. Aull	Raymond S. Caughman
1986 May 30-June 1	Newberry College, Newberry	Herman W. Cauble	James S. Aull	Raymond S. Caughman

a. The title of Bishop came into use in 1981; prior to that the title was President.
b. There was no convention of the S. C. Synod of the LCA in 1987; a Constituting Convention for the S. C. Synod of the ELCA was held May 29-30, 1987 at Newberry College.

Synod Statistics

Year	Parish Pastors	Number of Congregations	Baptized Members	Confirmed Members	Confirmed, Communing, Contributing Members
1971	120	148	51,606	38,727	32,624
1972	125	149	52,186	39,409	33,007
1973	126	149	53,010	40,142	33,393
1974	120	150	53,960	41,045	34,010
1975	128	152	54,572	41,758	34,319
1976	132	154	55,210	42,597	35,033
1977	132	155	56,148	43,507	35,507
1978	131	155	56,688	44,165	35,946
1979	129	155	57,322	44,780	35,744
1980	129	155	57,961	45,326	35,733
1981	132	157	58,150	45,486	36,027
1982	124	157	58,355	45,788	36,263
1983	138	157	58,758	46,162	36,737
1984	139	157	59,239	46,630	37,333
1985	140	159	60,135	47,312	37,520
1986	141	160	60,658	47,911	38,295
1987	146	160	61,228	48,288	38,481

Year	Total Income	Current Expenditures	Other Expenditures	Synodical Benevolence	Other Benevolence	Total Expenditures
1971	$ 4,874,109	$ 2,212,761	$1,551,994	$ 888,996	$402,363	$ 5,056,114
1972	5,288,244	2,373,877	1,804,793	943,344	328,699	5,450,703
1973	5,986,180	2,613,075	1,935,072	983,024	391,025	5,972,196
1974	6,734,137	2,970,903	2,392,573	1,034,536	317,298	6,715,310
1975	7,266,079	3,278,092	2,005,410	1,097,519	367,690	6,748,711
1976	8,073,678	3,656,142	2,623,095	1,181,029	310,187	7,770,453

Year						
1977	9,876,901	4,119,474	3,120,075	1,218,706	335,141	8,193,596
1978	10,446,708	4,580,909	3,041,953	1,314,120	445,837	9,382,829
1979	11,010,051	5,036,195	3,380,292	1,350,058	625,130	10,391,675
1980	11,568,183	5,713,154	2,664,575	1,423,301	667,282	10,468,312
1981	12,347,746	6,491,731	2,913,430	1,547,070	664,325	11,616,556
1982	12,859,660	7,013,537	3,037,681	1,685,651	612,219	12,349,088
1983	14,495,202	7,622,523	3,700,838	1,838,222	717,995	13,879,578
1984	15,985,589	8,321,196	3,589,219	2,007,674	907,799	14,825,888
1985	16,510,465	9,152,970	3,590,563	2,162,261	960,488	15,866,282
1986	18,220,727	9,919,989	4,016,548	2,326,289	927,571	17,190,397
1987	19,212,821	10,543,189	4,858,520	2,386,120	913,424	18,701,253

Year	Assets of Church Buildings & Lots	Assets of Parish Houses, Parsonages, and Lots	Endowment Assets	Other Assets	Indebtedness
1971	$16,038,348	$ 9,684,844	$ 457,274	$2,504,063	$3,821,238
1972	17,382,756	10,591,653	618,141	2,663,551	4,186,847
1973	19,798,725	11,723,803	866,285	3,585,544	4,511,110
1974	24,067,588	12,428,921	837,347	3,956,773	5,485,297
1975	25,751,671	13,857,803	1,155,592	3,946,919	5,264,586
1976	28,543,672	14,905,923	1,271,935	4,249,887	5,781,420
1977	31,640,495	16,632,778	1,335,308	4,617,662	6,102,715
1978	35,771,051	17,137,993	1,410,378	5,349,686	6,437,361
1979	39,374,174	19,562,820	1,308,739	4,923,105	7,655,892
1980	43,300,100	21,671,755	1,424,872	5,736,544	7,629,531
1981	47,533,377	22,826,661	1,460,340	6,723,728	7,041,212
1982	48,980,709	25,924,318	1,741,008	6,955,035	6,941,283
1983	51,491,131	27,769,618	2,101,493	6,962,094	7,149,760
1984	54,624,588	27,772,164	3,236,108	7,682,852	6,848,841
1985	61,753,715	29,648,070	2,944,078	8,243,246	6,691,641
1986	63,874,531	34,182,042	4,105,597	5,899,342	6,643,147
1987	68,724,643	34,372,842	4,428,022	6,287,560	6,904,847

Congregational Statistics
as of December 31, 1971 and December 31, 1987[1]

Congregation	Baptized 1971	Baptized 1987	Confirmed 1971	Confirmed 1987	Active (CCC) 1971	Active (CCC) 1987	Total Receipts 1971	Total Receipts 1987
1. Abiding Presence, York	51	85	37	62	37	55	5,839	41,015
2. Advent, North Charleston	773	701	608	548	443	318	63,344	142,399
3. All Saints, Mt. Pleasant a.	107	234	64	158	64	137	25,835	98,705
4. A Mighty Fortress, Summerville b.	125	215	74	142	74	115	26,723	38,248
5. Ascension, Columbia	619	432	521	349	439	244	83,790	104,813
6. Atonement, Laurens	125	172	104	165	86	158	17,853	57,932
7. Augusburg, Union	85	67	53	58	42	42	6,412	33,129
8. Bachman Chapel, Prosperity	275	334	213	261	130	196	13,624	60,806
9. Bethany, Lexington	140	163	102	135	93	90	21,404	42,493
10. Bethany, Newberry	235	209	171	145	129	103	16,048	56,132
11. Beth-Eden, Newberry	59	51	57	48	41	38	4,727	16,949
12. Bethel, White Rock	594	592	478	505	446	438	56,469	173,429
13. Bethlehem, Irmo	289	463	230	370	218	320	17,496	141,012
14. Bethlehem, Leesville	126	207	94	170	82	135	8,833	67,886
15. Bethlehem, Pomaria	189	199	162	165	143	130	18,789	57,883
16. Cedar Grove, Leesville	815	796	627	650	496	481	46,005	123,098
17. Christ, Columbia	246	154	162	122	128	106	25,552	53,172
18. Christ, Hilton Head c.	106	503	76	411	76	245	18,225	240,297
19. Christ the King, Columbia	429	422	279	342	184	180	34,456	89,648
20. Christ the Servant, Conway d.	129	145	98	119	91	112	53,851	54,349
21. Christus Victor, Columbia e.	115	156	65	95	65	95	30,192	49,450
22. Colony, Newberry	269	288	218	238	175	180	19,298	207,283
23. Corinth, Prosperity	171	151	132	128	108	128	11,508	40,483
24. Cross and Crown, Florence f.	89	118	75	90	58	89	25,547	88,025
25. Ebenezer, Columbia	1,037	1,191	841	961	704	798	173,704	583,000

No.	Sub	Current Oper. Expenditures 1971	1987	Benevolence Expenditures 1971	1987	Total Expenditures 1971	1987	Total Assets 1971	1987	Indebtedness 1971	1987
1.		2,479	26,882	794	3,277	5,918	30,159	50,000	245,744	29,620	0
2.		28,923	98,095	17,442	28,502	63,473	141,316	415,000	528,260	102,847	1,180
3.		16,791	69,634	0	7,028	21,474	43,208	39,955	328,289	31,000	169,822
4.	a.	16,695	31,119	639	4,844	19,875	38,018	150,000	315,617	65,300	147,747
5.	b.	26,003	77,467	24,912	25,317	78,038	102,784	407,400	1,350,000	24,125	0
6.		8,339	39,601	6,463	7,429	15,776	58,444	96,700	216,346		3,488
7.		3,048	18,193	1,379	2,290	16,689	25,482	15,000	118,916		22,265
8.		7,084	33,359	3,912	10,172	12,496	52,676	105,000	380,930		0
9.		9,783	32,524	3,955	4,262	17,563	37,165	45,000	362,221	15,283	0
10.		9,704	42,424	1,584	9,397	15,750	58,788	176,000	395,000		0
11.		2,676	10,440	1,936	3,244	4,612	16,317	18,450	92,313		0
12.		24,787	79,127	16,112	37,451	77,821	174,277	172,407	903,818	11,248	120,226
13.		9,031	77,112	4,899	25,283	17,012	1,351,695	159,519	1,021,700		6,000
14.		6,591	28,570	2,242	10,087	8,833	58,880	52,500	394,508		617
15.		9,211	40,973	6,151	11,385	15,991	58,533	65,283	452,815		0
16.		18,235	69,344	13,839	35,278	55,037	108,533	184,647	452,815	900	0
17.		12,338	33,662	4,580	7,001	24,516	50,349	81,479	342,300	43,300	50,735
18.	c.	14,544	114,622	0	22,211	17,889	206,651	51,702	725,816	74,000	152,287
19.	d.	17,715	56,952	7,298	10,725	33,037	71,809	170,000	569,436	94,000	0
20.	e.	20,368	40,986	3,419	2,414	35,398	55,074	132,934	136,300		91,000
21.		n.a.	47,497	3,000	2,549	n.a.	61,423	15,060	81,693		72,450
22.		11,306	45,400	5,688	13,784	18,994	90,581	101,793	566,090		9,683
23.		5,687	26,911	4,659	11,096	10,346	39,722	65,000	196,392		0
24.	f.	22,394	49,532	3,152	5,041	25,547	66,107	51,900	179,149	51,900	143,850
25.		54,345	280,000	55,489	150,546	180,304	641,296	1,755,000	2,704,000	280,880	23,000

Congregational Statistics
as of December 31, 1971 and December 31, 1987[1]

Congregation	Baptized 1971	Baptized 1987	Confirmed 1971	Confirmed 1987	Active (CCC) 1971	Active (CCC) 1987	Total Receipts 1971	Total Receipts 1987
26. Ehrhardt Memorial, Ehrhardt	91	37	74	32	73	32	16,034	21,314
27. Emmanuel, West Columbia	427	600	311	471	228	396	40,974	164,536
28. Enon, Leesville	183	126	123	101	84	74	7,768	32,882
29. Epiphany, St. Matthew's	65	29	50	20	45	18	5,458	7,345
30. Faith, Batesburg	249	353	197	288	190	231	27,530	99,696
31. Faith, John's Island	115	133	72	109	72	109	12,351	36,298
32. Faith, Newberry	208	172	146	140	146	123	21,062	52,602
33. Faith, West Columbia	382	361	263	293	248	263	31,057	98,270
34. Gethsemane, Columbia	235	122	156	110	120	100	22,737	60,486
35. Good Hope, Saluda	75	46	72	40	68	35	5,090	15,000
36. Good Shepherd, Columbia	947	990	663	766	494	813	55,997	285,421
37. Good Shepherd, Swansea	36	109	27	88	27	88	2,205	40,906
38. Good Shepherd, Walterboro	132	128	105	122	102	96	17,927	44,469
39. Grace, Gilbert	164	183	132	145	110	96	17,470	50,831
40. Grace, Prosperity	320	291	259	246	225	203	43,194	110,550
41. Grace, Rock Hill	332	693	235	500	212	435	29,990	216,870
42. Holy Comforter, Charleston	431	270	261	212	197	192	38,106	76,495
43. Holy Communion, Spartanburg	195	551	133	418	110	313	25,283	171,137
44. Holy Cross, Charleston	214	124	142	79	137	79	12,674	37,757
45. Holy Trinity, Anderson	346	367	256	262	256	262	53,654	117,410
46. Holy Trinity, Little Mountain	459	579	349	462	319	404	38,250	115,293
47. Holy Trinity, North Augusta	552	580	395	400	300	382	50,324	151,100
48. Holy Trinity, Pelion	64	69	53	55	32	49	5,111	16,257
49. Immanuel, Greenwood	456	368	329	297	256	268	34,435	169,877
50. Incarnation, Columbia	1,157	815	952	666	802	657	162,461	391,694

	Current Oper. Expenditures		Benevolence Expenditures		Total Expenditures		Total Assets		Indebtedness	
	1971	1987	1971	1987	1971	1987	1971	1987	1971	1987
26.	8,773	14,102	3,655	7,378	15,000	21,480	58,557	145,700	0	0
27.	20,619	98,725	13,821	31,694	39,325	163,144	284,009	1,611,408	0	0
28.	5,639	23,312	2,129	6,119	7,768	32,681	28,500	130,751	0	0
29.	1,600	8,311	518	600	5,326	10,284	45,469	72,313	4,000	875
30.	12,233	58,117	6,963	25,663	27,272	95,114	195,755	756,350	16,091	5,850
31.	9,451	28,406	646	2,314	11,609	30,720	120,246	298,942	20,000	0
32.	9,197	36,039	3,336	2,518	18,512	52,348	140,500	9,724	67,603	15,800
33.	18,774	57,662	8,444	12,515	30,117	86,015	181,941	536,590	25,094	6,504
34.	13,557	43,041	7,881	13,645	22,728	60,716	132,500	212,013	71,628	8,622
35.	5,090	6,000	2,982	2,028	4,895	14,928	35,200	123,000	0	0
36.	26,854	141,319	14,646	57,896	55,696	250,348	364,510	990,159	35,237	83,910
37.	2,205	32,787	1,723	6,370	4,443	42,901	8,170	195,534	0	750
38.	10,716	39,513	3,322	5,285	30,119	48,705	110,000	252,310	14,237	0
39.	9,650	30,156	5,058	9,245	17,470	41,701	111,000	261,396	7,840	0
40.	21,578	42,242	8,655	18,939	30,332	81,810	149,000	952,000	0	0
41.	24,715	116,649	6,996	30,807	32,452	196,964	138,741	481,993	20,200	107,500
42.	17,141	50,999	6,404	7,086	38,831	77,374	280,176	1,036,034	141,466	44,430
43.	11,787	99,340	6,338	24,853	25,651	179,249	150,044	1,104,059	84,692	0
44.	8,550	27,706	185	507	12,859	33,665	134,330	449,003	0	92,320
45.	26,371	79,758	16,023	25,143	53,553	113,306	301,821	827,801	23,194	566
46.	15,223	54,659	13,444	30,607	34,474	117,226	203,070	981,500	0	0
47.	21,882	87,752	11,499	27,148	45,362	149,000	158,500	851,500	41,652	40,307
48.	2,857	8,500	747	2,408	3,604	15,750	32,500	124,175	0	0
49.	17,806	115,639	11,273	35,552	33,936	181,776	172,500	816,539	0	101,364
50.	53,606	200,854	64,609	62,716	146,694	379,830	750,767	3,680,910	19,021	100,000

Congregational Statistics
as of December 31, 1971 and December 31, 1987[1]

Congregation	Baptized 1971	Baptized 1987	Confirmed 1971	Confirmed 1987	Active (CCC) 1971	Active (CCC) 1987	Total Receipts 1971	Total Receipts 1987
51. King of Glory, North Myrtle Beach g.	156	374	118	313	118	292	30,142	186,223
52. Macedonia, Prosperity	276	347	198	227	188	227	19,249	99,777
53. Martin Luther, Charleston	939	893	596	657	396	319	53,735	113,090
54. Mayer Memorial, Newberry	413	355	313	313	300	254	41,764	94,231
55. Messiah, Hanahan	310	280	184	186	163	159	21,528	54,586
56. Messiah, Mauldin	269	506	178	366	178	294	21,760	155,668
57. Ministry with the Deaf, Columbia h.	44	43	31	34	31	32	35,682	44,348
58. Mt. Calvary, Johnston	355	353	297	290	267	229	30,176	110,469
59. Mt. Hebron, Leesville	189	228	158	198	111	135	11,120	64,939
60. Mt. Hermon, Peak	84	94	68	82	65	75	9,658	33,826
61. Mt. Hermon, West Columbia	538	494	402	401	333	321	54,851	129,540
62. Mt. Horeb, Chapin	631	741	500	633	425	485	37,463	315,195
63. Mt. Olivet, Peak	185	204	142	161	113	120	14,059	45,960
64. Mt. Olivet, Prosperity	14	12	14	10	7	10	650	6,840
65. Mt. Pilgrim, Prosperity	134	178	119	139	102	139	7,892	30,971
66. Mt. Pleasant, Ehrhardt	80	109	66	86	66	60	11,507	35,394
67. Mt. Pleasant, Saluda	315	241	249	912	191	167	30,070	84,611
68. Mt. Tabor, Little Mountain	319	445	237	359	229	326	20,296	84,901
69. Mt. Tabor, West Columbia	1,295	1,168	979	928	815	780	130,865	292,987
70. Nativity, Spartanburg	132	157	95	126	78	111	14,602	55,710
71. Nazareth, Lexington	192	196	144	167	115	151	15,831	58,789
72. Orangeburg, Orangeburg	721	550	521	447	449	391	49,337	168,774
73. Our Saviour, Greenville	612	959	398	708	339	614	54,276	270,098
74. Our Saviour, West Columbia	375	546	248	421	226	265	55,028	167,788
75. Our Shepherd, Hartsville	130	137	83	104	70	90	15,048	55,400

		Current Oper. Expenditures		Benevolence Expenditures		Total Expenditures		Total Assets		Indebtedness	
		1971	1987	1971	1987	1971	1987	1971	1987	1971	1987
51.	g.	16,942	68,939	3,536	19,205	31,920	189,196	9,612	851,855	0	251,910
52.		10,730	42,461	4,948	19,183	17,178	61,644	125,538	674,234	0	0
53.		28,009	92,384	11,247	21,779	51,032	124,479	226,999	656,307	112,935	59,952
54.		16,947	59,594	15,814	25,519	41,801	116,074	297,500	568,940	0	0
55.		10,339	41,478	2,188	7,975	20,320	57,128	62,000	451,889	3,331	0
56.		12,738	87,027	100	21,798	18,315	152,079	125,900	555,904	119,708	318,258
57.	h.	21,812	44,000	1,509	1,750	30,321	45,750	10,995	7,978	0	0
58.		15,715	55,281	7,020	17,472	28,209	122,779	143,087	699,915	23,363	0
59.		4,259	39,784	4,910	8,174	11,120	56,619	42,289	517,177	0	0
60.		6,153	24,339	3,038	6,063	9,191	33,672	43,000	332,968	0	0
61.		22,917	74,514	13,000	25,569	52,572	121,259	322,280	1,295,929	71,063	0
62.		14,000	101,585	8,857	31,933	36,462	337,632	210,000	1,528,913	0	122,750
63.		7,197	27,077	3,078	7,713	10,275	39,590	32,500	680,987	0	140,000
64.		480	3,580	160	1,154	640	9,251	10,000	56,000	0	0
65.		2,984	8,798	2,303	10,423	5,899	23,228	55,639	320,889	0	0
66.		8,326	26,869	1,000	4,589	11,507	31,458	57,500	314,244	0	0
67.		30,070	73,660	9,880	12,784	30,070	100,156	235,000	654,873	1,200	0
68.		10,012	49,900	5,485	21,101	16,290	83,334	196,800	701,860	0	0
69.		58,049	198,350	42,154	56,120	125,482	270,702	525,000	2,193,345	38,628	0
70.		8,135	45,101	415	7,694	14,436	55,821	132,000	258,919	57,675	3,010
71.		5,435	48,268	3,198	7,806	14,067	58,178	40,000	288,655	0	0
72.		29,159	100,975	55,310	35,314	92,981	165,185	447,928	823,389	0	159,973
73.		28,717	113,819	8,719	49,928	49,881	198,029	184,000	1,795,888	126,630	237,498
74.		19,173	82,960	7,279	31,003	34,472	148,463	119,139	878,316	12,266	40,262
75.		6,650	36,450	2,776	1,900	23,240	55,500	160,000	367,200	129,406	120,000

Congregational Statistics
as of December 31, 1971 and December 31, 1987[1]

Congregation	Baptized 1971	Baptized 1987	Confirmed 1971	Confirmed 1987	Active (CCC) 1971	Active (CCC) 1987	Total Receipts 1971	Total Receipts 1987
76. Peace, Ladson i.	105	264	62	197	62	197	19,951	89,732
77. Pilgrim, Lexington	455	618	341	507	281	385	42,401	181,927
78. Pine Grove, Lone Star	143	116	126	103	102	93	23,646	58,809
79. Pisgah, Lexington	289	468	208	372	186	281	53,630	97,663
80. Pomaria, Pomaria	177	153	144	141	111	97	20,564	45,503
81. Prince of Peace, Chester	242	82	175	71	154	63	22,683	59,195
82. Providence, Lexington	126	176	101	130	84	89	11,985	33,969
83. Redeemer, Charleston	575	813	461	607	394	481	52,244	206,046
84. Redeemer, Columbia	422	1,323	261	920	233	742	38,995	250,390
85. Redeemer, Greer j.	74	232	51	184	49	104	13,547	52,797
86. Redeemer, Newberry	786	681	663	560	583	542	94,984	563,711
87. Reformation, Columbia	896	459	752	420	602	286	86,614	162,310
88. Reformation, Lancaster	120	284	80	227	76	171	12,509	96,093
89. Resurrection, Cameron	203	211	175	168	162	160	28,643	80,276
90. Resurrection, Columbia	344	371	287	304	271	239	30,274	90,702
91. St. Andrew, Blythewood	110	143	82	123	78	94	7,752	31,044
92. St. Andrew, Charleston	497	370	404	307	374	218	71,930	212,536
93. St. Andrew, Columbia	1,028	1,125	695	899	562	483	86,818	214,524
94. St. Barnabas, Charleston	398	433	340	329	260	230	26,781	101,555
95. St. David, West Columbia	815	1,097	560	851	493	658	91,163	284,948
96. St. Jacob, Chapin	378	456	282	368	237	254	21,731	120,937
97. St. James, Graniteville	273	383	227	319	162	256	30,694	123,374
98. St. James, Leesville	394	348	286	258	286	217	18,424	69,337
99. St. James, Lexington	281	372	214	300	153	260	28,449	104,946
100. St. James, Newberry	206	237	157	180	137	150	28,166	74,911

		Current Oper. Expenditures		Benevolence Expenditures		Total Expenditures		Total Assets		Indebtedness	
		1971	1987	1971	1987	1971	1987	1971	1987	1971	1987
76.	i.	12,521	52,393	690	17,117	14,467	89,732	30,500	850,000	30,000	105,000
77.		14,894	87,677	9,668	31,225	42,393	187,225	304,500	1,108,737	49,992	73,226
78.		12,262	39,594	7,594	16,817	22,856	56,381	68,462	308,158	0	0
79.		12,001	69,420	5,457	21,352	134,854	103,383	246,000	827,469	42,000	0
80.		12,802	20,648	5,005	10,318	19,592	31,066	114,938	267,500	3,000	0
81.		8,809	54,231	2,326	7,680	14,801	63,113	70,000	276,164	34,322	0
82.		5,403	33,308	1,716	6,370	11,108	47,451	46,000	577,297	0	19,117
83.		21,845	141,170	9,638	27,906	50,872	176,879	221,130	1,058,117	26,012	41,000
84.		12,270	149,651	7,697	45,358	38,781	236,949	210,000	694,145	142,734	321,722
85.	j.	6,294	40,726	2,259	968	14,047	51,543	44,443	200,891	34,593	49,787
86.		40,080	148,237	29,629	59,937	95,291	583,796	589,374	1,949,205	120,504	180,330
87.		39,050	93,667	22,206	43,715	90,042	204,142	553,366	1,508,334	66,290	0
88.		6,600	54,124	2,902	17,957	12,051	87,832	72,000	287,365	16,822	41,747
89.		14,481	55,006	11,757	16,538	27,238	80,276	167,225	n.a.	0	0
90.		13,359	61,956	8,996	18,151	23,380	91,921	178,484	807,465	0	37,684
91.		2,900	30,300	1,546	25	7,752	31,855	25,760	312,922	0	0
92.		23,544	119,836	31,376	26,203	69,958	210,187	455,471	1,670,811	14,000	0
93.		42,141	114,611	21,342	56,782	82,837	187,114	353,500	1,845,423	35,000	0
94.		15,887	63,119	6,192	16,309	25,269	102,527	215,430	714,900	0	0
95.		32,950	158,420	22,002	64,618	163,985	287,953	516,500	1,204,658	50,000	0
96.		9,570	56,405	7,523	23,466	18,033	145,802	142,330	559,641	0	38,985
97.		11,562	67,151	8,126	25,167	28,471	120,809	174,413	557,224	0	55,000
98.		12,660	48,505	5,764	15,157	18,424	63,662	139,041	572,150	0	0
99.		13,584	53,199	6,546	24,662	27,760	90,348	155,000	404,152	25,463	0
100.		13,518	37,797	5,387	15,514	30,800	68,739	109,600	646,325	5,908	0

Congregational Statistics
as of December 31, 1971 and December 31, 1987[1]

Congregation	Baptized 1971	Baptized 1987	Confirmed 1971	Confirmed 1987	Active (CCC) 1971	Active (CCC) 1987	Total Receipts 1971	Total Receipts 1987
101. St. James, Sumter	410	620	302	457	275	314	42,214	146,567
102. St. Johannes, Charleston	427	326	326	275	263	245	32,907	91,274
103. St. John, Beaufort	264	432	177	316	149	201	19,728	82,461
104. St. John, Charleston	641	684	503	532	369	385	32,907	191,659
105. St. John, Clinton	173	177	137	150	137	113	65,384	50,295
106. St. John, Irmo	111	185	91	149	88	128	7,461	68,857
107. St. John, Johnston	122	131	101	95	82	68	15,134	38,239
108. St. John, Lexington	102	155	86	131	85	118	20,488	62,812
109. St. John, Pelion	70	29	39	25	39	25	4,204	5,832
110. St. John, Pomaria	239	234	202	197	177	167	20,876	75,458
111. St. John, Spartanburg	611	914	455	747	370	607	86,407	267,275
112. St. John, Walhalla	333	457	281	345	281	259	46,790	145,407
113. St. Luke, Columbia	467	320	330	263	260	239	33,586	89,734
114. St. Luke, Florence	420	447	306	358	288	317	28,969	133,034
115. St. Luke, Prosperity	811	710	584	594	489	393	26,882	97,959
116. St. Luke, Summerville	508	1,011	355	723	321	645	45,762	856,947
117. St. Mark, Blythewood	96	162	78	135	53	121	9,515	49,548
118. St. Mark, Isle of Palms	114	122	84	109	84	109	10,270	54,044
119. St. Mark, Prosperity	158	159	135	131	115	119	10,024	40,734
120. St. Matthew, Cameron	36	28	30	24	27	24	4,163	10,269
121. St. Matthew, Charleston	1,640	1,708	1,264	1,376	1,026	947	105,422	444,163
122. St. Matthew, Lexington	336	434	249	338	214	269	19,407	103,427
123. St. Matthew, Pomaria	174	166	145	127	130	126	12,716	46,705
124. St. Matthias, Easley	124	311	80	235	80	217	24,538	106,999
125. St. Michael, Columbia	162	334	137	265	120	151	20,861	193,231

k.

	Current Oper. Expenditures		Benevolence Expenditures		Total Expenditures		Total Assets		Indebtedness	
	1971	1987	1971	1987	1971	1987	1971	1987	1971	1987
101.	17,033	66,886	9,901	24,513	31,145	153,377	228,000	809,252	0	297,624
102.	20,707	60,978	8,273	8,633	32,844	85,167	246,245	825,081	20,227	2,300
103.	14,463	56,523	1,597	18,415	20,351	78,750	101,000	705,800	22,530	16,361
104.	25,388	145,741	14,876	33,952	57,136	190,793	592,000	2,988,839	9,816	0
105.	14,794	41,146	4,796	9,648	27,000	51,316	253,109	445,745	15,098	0
106.	4,413	39,233	2,323	9,130	6,847	54,144	47,500	471,858	0	0
107.	11,010	25,643	1,992	6,995	14,471	40,600	86,000	389,382	6,106	0
108.	6,394	38,622	8,955	11,365	20,488	55,929	105,732	623,217	0	0
109.	1,213	4,217	935	1,428	2,148	5,645	18,500	100,000	0	0
110.	11,007	44,927	5,784	14,507	17,451	94,049	95,500	325,309	0	0
111.	30,966	140,813	15,624	71,050	122,062	253,401	299,751	1,616,757	151,741	70,708
112.	17,276	63,698	10,499	26,018	42,689	89,716	437,500	825,363	95,000	0
113.	20,344	59,472	6,924	19,928	30,241	89,667	224,752	522,971	0	0
114.	20,348	95,226	8,280	25,166	28,628	133,034	237,500	981,500	8,100	30,120
115.	13,895	43,673	11,183	27,912	26,503	93,597	132,000	563,180	0	0
116.	21,763	172,096	11,829	51,891	49,612	1,036,870	302,950	2,311,724	140,000	458,578
117.	4,760	39,617	2,234	215	9,515	47,863	83,782	242,747	16,595	46,500
118.	8,450	42,588	1,967	2,895	10,719	52,287	42,500	235,868	2,425	106,000
119.	5,452	28,629	41,461	11,278	9,913	40,264	78,000	134,020	0	0
120.	1,002	6,821	1,199	1,250	2,276	8,071	20,630	n.a.	0	0
121.	65,871	295,657	38,062	79,352	103,933	443,794	1,301,316	4,267,000	0	11,128
122.	8,180	65,981	5,435	18,683	21,677	96,581	96,000	1,067,549	8,855	0
123.	7,285	34,589	4,131	11,253	12,316	45,842	52,000	285,000	0	0
124.	9,835	54,170	2,622	15,030	23,429	110,639	57,924	474,783	49,763	316,945
125.	11,036	74,973	4,420	19,829	21,087	196,455	109,328	749,773	0	77,546

k.

Congregational Statistics
as of December 31, 1971 and December 31, 1987[1]

Congregation	Baptized 1971	Baptized 1987	Confirmed 1971	Confirmed 1987	Active (CCC) 1971	Active (CCC) 1987	Total Receipts 1971	Total Receipts 1987
126. St. Michael, Greenville	409	500	286	393	237	363	49,614	167,015
127. St. Michael, Moncks Corner	118	107	78	91	77	91	13,189	121,181
128. St. Nicholas, Fairfax	72	55	61	40	57	39	7,699	22,751
129. St. Paul, Aiken	501	606	353	417	330	417	44,839	158,168
130. St. Paul, Columbia	1,037	838	878	696	659	522	123,063	290,721
131. St. Paul, Gaffney	82	123	50	84	48	82	9,631	63,128
132. St. Paul, Gilbert	476	530	378	414	303	251	32,025	125,685
133. St. Paul, Mt. Pleasant	398	535	294	386	244	198	38,773	120,742
134. St. Paul, Pomaria	504	504	382	422	323	351	27,516	95,050
135. St. Peter, Batesburg	30	33	25	24	24	24	4,163	21,705
136. St. Peter, Chapin	752	833	543	680	474	545	38,501	156,854
137. St. Peter, Lexington	540	699	381	529	317	363	41,700	113,889
138. St. Peter, Litchfield Beach 1.	112	154	95	138	95	138	57,585	62,039
139. St. Philip, Myrtle Beach	318	486	220	398	191	359	35,315	298,873
140. St. Philip, Newberry	506	525	401	441	330	374	33,877	114,494
141. St. Stephen, Lexington	670	899	456	587	448	558	67,259	298,644
142. St. Thomas, Chapin	242	448	175	391	154	295	22,683	118,268
143. St. Timothy, Camden	241	340	169	275	139	183	29,820	113,094
144. St. Timothy, Goose Creek	222	463	113	309	89	246	17,493	113,482
145. St. Timothy, Whitmire	68	63	55	51	47	50	8,099	31,765
146. Sandy Run, Swansea	91	116	62	87	62	70	8,432	41,405
147. Shepherd of the Sea, Garden City m.	165	505	123	412	106	380	29,995	156,932
148. Silverstreet, Silverstreet	293	301	222	254	209	203	23,612	69,701
149. Summer Memorial, Newberry	312	338	269	288	264	243	30,091	93,396
150. Transfiguration, Cayce	553	467	404	386	315	359	54,449	131,128

	Current Oper. Expenditures		Benevolence Expenditures		Total Expenditures		Total Assets		Indebtedness	
	1971	1987	1971	1987	1971	1987	1971	1987	1971	1987
126.	19,306	104,000	6,516	35,396	64,466	152,362	276,000	1,129,296	157,489	62,047
127.	7,078	46,730	830	4,612	13,274	52,190	106,200	284,317	77,271	0
128.	5,055	9,929	2,252	4,096	7,699	17,824	37,250	167,792	0	0
129.	22,437	99,382	11,961	39,879	44,322	143,996	242,923	278,164	81,932	0
130.	55,995	185,043	45,612	88,246	137,421	274,289	712,102	2,065,290	0	0
131.	4,679	40,987	1,813	3,287	7,683	80,044	82,500	410,610	25,000	37,942
132.	14,384	73,700	9,470	26,923	30,848	103,823	181,200	548,559	0	0
133.	17,881	74,485	1,267	26,004	39,429	119,975	89,063	973,230	29,540	67,173
134.	13,397	52,921	9,030	22,444	26,974	98,987	131,868	1,466,258	1,574	0
135.	1,422	3,723	2,396	3,877	3,818	10,306	19,918	167,890	0	0
136.	12,300	90,475	11,375	32,632	38,177	197,008	214,159	759,910	48,008	59,772
137.	17,090	73,281	10,834	34,619	37,198	112,808	210,950	720,833	0	0
138. l.	43,236	49,881	3,428	5,439	55,186	61,147	120,230	161,183	95,350	93,400
139.	18,811	136,906	5,318	37,192	33,000	311,204	230,364	1,162,924	55,583	4,357
140.	12,047	56,258	8,217	22,121	34,170	80,879	255,600	945,722	22,624	0
141.	25,891	176,795	16,431	78,412	51,096	294,333	458,778	2,264,350	0	0
142.	4,756	77,847	5,208	23,929	10,388	114,362	66,574	746,211	0	20,000
143.	16,126	55,533	6,282	27,472	28,995	115,232	125,871	483,943	8,159	13,000
144.	7,487	72,828	1,646	12,636	17,785	119,490	130,200	705,360	0	157,252
145.	4,425	15,457	2,166	5,850	13,568	31,765	61,000	307,691	3,500	0
146.	3,270	34,260	2,179	5,618	7,002	40,459	33,100	213,453	0	0
147. m.	23,864	91,717	3,286	24,809	27,150	153,318	16,326	509,080	0	242,430
148.	9,658	44,102	6,369	13,396	22,825	61,013	77,500	1,053,900	0	0
149.	15,570	56,840	8,409	20,104	27,498	76,944	158,606	768,747	7,000	0
150.	17,233	81,164	11,835	10,975	53,754	133,495	138,000	752,651	8,800	62,500

Congregational Statistics
as of December 31, 1971 and December 31, 1987[1]

Congregation	Baptized 1971	Baptized 1987	Confirmed 1971	Confirmed 1987	Active (CCC) 1971	Active (CCC) 1987	Total Receipts 1971	Total Receipts 1987
151. Trinity, Columbia	142	478	94	360	86	228	9,036	110,958
152. Trinity, Elloree	232	208	171	179	125	151	20,020	50,613
153. Trinity, Fairfax	110	92	86	77	80	67	13,275	45,181
154. Trinity, Georgetown	149	160	106	134	92	82	20,920	47,907
155. Trinity, Greenville	822	985	622	780	450	659	111,293	462,758
156. Trinity, Saluda	97	106	74	90	74	59	6,003	20,827
157. Union, Leesville	333	324	245	261	209	172	19,620	70,585
158. University, Clemson	227	421	142	299	139	259	17,910	209,555
159. Wittenberg, Leesville	401	287	315	239	271	239	44,709	93,472
160. Zion, Lexington	357	474	272	377	235	294	35,546	139,452

	Current Oper. Expenditures		Benevolence Expenditures		Total Expenditures		Total Assets		Indebtedness	
	1971	1987	1971	1987	1971	1987	1971	1987	1971	1987
151.	6,962	66,722	382	13,359	7,344	121,224	42,244	473,228	34,600	177,000
152.	11,866	33,113	5,036	8,814	20,010	41,927	162,000	264,977	0	0
153.	6,232	32,461	3,190	6,435	13,275	46,652	62,250	237,000	4,737	0
154.	17,309	24,921	2,042	8,378	26,765	42,861	110,000	394,323	59,300	85,000
155.	41,011	204,664	20,037	84,769	203,909	448,397	1,103,500	2,536,944	206,779	123,595
156.	6,003	13,071	1,646	6,244	5,119	20,375	30,195	144,985	0	0
157.	6,671	42,344	5,860	13,344	19,941	57,308	108,000	437,065	28,300	0
158.	7,278	77,926	5,350	22,090	13,540	172,489	182,000	494,314	0	0
159.	24,433	55,936	11,246	19,523	47,040	100,656	152,660	515,561	0	0
160.	16,689	75,500	8,471	25,708	33,460	136,972	146,558	804,000	5,434	180,000

Baptized, Confirmed, and Confirmed
Communing Contributing (CCC) Members of
Congregations of South Carolina Synod,
1971-1987

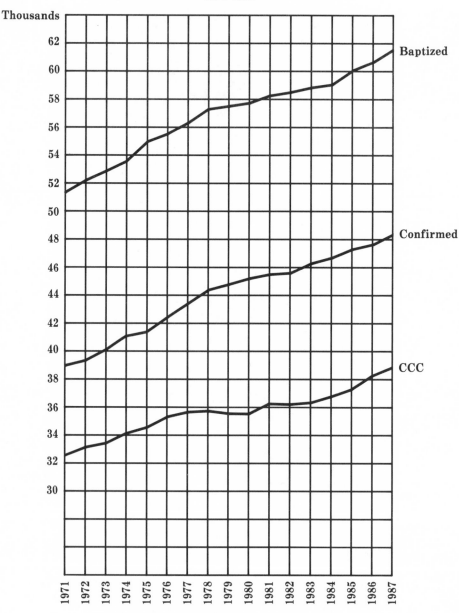

Total Income, Current Expenditures, Benevolence Expenditures, and Total Expenditures of
Congregations of South Carolina Synod,
1971-1987

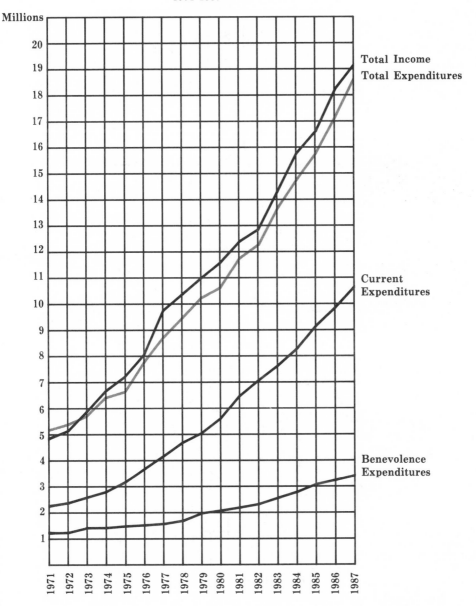

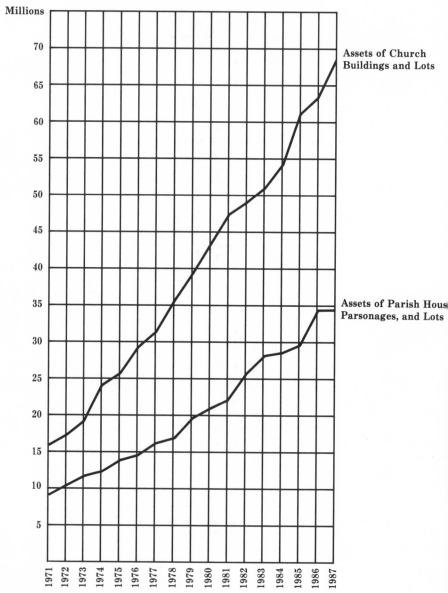

Assets of Church Buildings and Lots, and Assets
of Parish Houses, Parsonages, and Lots of
Congregations of South Carolina Synod,
1971-1987.

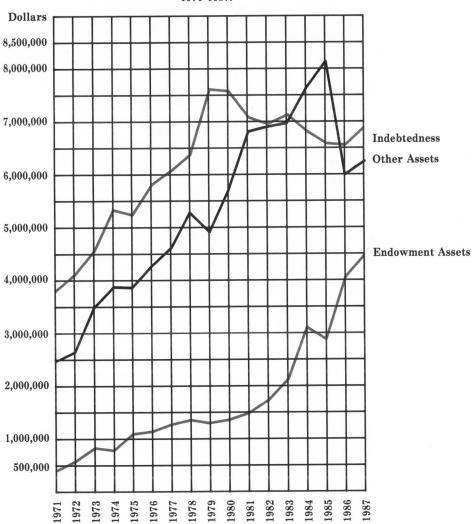

Endowment Assets, Other Assets, and Indebtedness of Congregations of South Carolina Synod
1971-1987.

Persons Elected to the Executive Board

1971 Convention
The Rev. Everette L. Lineberger   Mr. Edwin F. Brune
The Rev. Larry S. Long   Mr. Archie Dodgen

1972 Convention
The Rev. Guy C. Cruse   Mr. Roy H. Seay
The Rev. Leroy C. Trexler   Mr. Hubert E. Long

1973 Convention
The Rev. John L. Satterwhite   Mr. Wilbur B. Redd, Jr.
The Rev. Teddy P. Dominick, Jr.   Dr. Hal C. Anderson

1974 Convention
The Rev. Larry S. Long   Mr. Edwin F. Brune
The Rev. Harold G. Skinner   Mr. Raymond S. Caughman

1975 Convention
The Rev. Boyd F. Cook   Mrs. Mary Ann Shealy
The Rev. Earl H. Loadholdt   Mr. Harry C. Stoudenmire

1976 Convention
The Rev. Teddy P. Dominick, Jr.   Dr. Hal C. Anderson
The Rev. D. Luther Swicegood   Mr. Robert N. Hubbs

1977 Convention
The Rev. E. Armand Shealy   Mr. B. Cornell Bedenbaugh
The Rev. Harold G. Skinner   Mr. Raymond S. Caughman

1978 Convention
The Rev. Robert L. Dasher   Mrs. Mary Ann Shealy
The Rev. Earl H. Loadholdt   Mr. Harry C. Stoudenmire
The Rev. Boyd F. Cook

1979 Convention
The Rev. R. Delano Ricard   Mr. Robert N. Hubbs
The Rev. John L. Yost, Jr.   Dr. Richard L. Conn

1980 Convention
The Rev. E. Armand Shealy   Mr. Reid S. Wingard
The Rev. Guy C. Cruse   Mrs. Christine W. Shull

1981 Convention
The Rev. Robert L. Dasher   Mr. James N. Hallman
The Rev. Robert L. Swygert   Mrs. Heather W. Peacock

1982 Convention
The Rev. R. Delano Ricard   Dr. Richard L. Conn
The Rev. John L. Yost, Jr.   Mrs. Louise Waldrep

1983 Convention

The Rev. John L. Setzler   Mr. Wayne E. Caughman
The Rev. D. Luther Swicegood   Mr. Robert N. Hubbs

1984 Convention

The Rev. Marion C. Brazell   Mr. James N. Hallman
The Rev. Leon A. Rawl   Mr. R. Keith Hutto

1985 Convention*

The Rev. David A. Donges   Mr. Edward R. Morhmann, Sr.
The Rev. Gary L. Safrit   Mrs. Gloria D. Rast

1986 Convention*

The Rev. John L. Setzler   Mr. Robert N. Hubbs
The Rev. Donald E. Woolly   Mrs. Barbara Yingling

Delegates Elected to 1972 LCA Convention

Rev. Herman W. Cauble   Mr. Ben Bagwell
Rev. H. George Anderson   Mr. Raymond S. Caughman
Rev. Paulwyn L. Boliek   Mrs. J. Harry Crout
Rev. Robert L. Hock   Mr. Ralph D. Derrick
Rev. Larry S. Long   Mr. James N. Hallman
Rev. Lloyd W. Mitcham, Jr.   Mr. Mike Kohn
Rev. E. Armand Shealy   Mr. Harry C. Stoudenmire
Rev. Bernard L. Trexler   Mr. James B. Wessinger

Delegates Elected to 1974 LCA Convention

Rev. Herman W. Cauble   Mr. Robert A. Ballentine
Rev. Paulwyn L. Bolick   Mr. B. Cornell Bedenbaugh
Rev. Henry N. Brandt   Mr. Raymond S. Caughman
Rev. Earl H. Loadholdt   Mrs. Laura Pinner
Rev. Larry S. Long   Mrs. James B. Shealy
Rev. R. Earl McCombs, Jr.   Mr. Harry C. Stoudenmire
Rev. Ruben H. Olawsky   Mr. James B. Wessinger
Rev. Elford B. Roof   Mr. Reid S. Wingard, Jr.

Delegates Elected to 1976 LCA Convention

Rev. Herman W. Cauble   Dr. Dorothy Brandt
Rev. James W. Addy   Miss Selena Caughman
Rev. Paulwyn L. Boliek   Mrs. J. Harold Crout
Rev. Guy C. Cruse   Mr. Robert N. Hubbs
Rev. Teddy P. Dominick, Jr.   Mrs. Thomas R. Peacock
Rev. Everette L. Lineberger   Mr. Forrest M. Shealy
Rev. R. Delano Ricard   Mrs. James B. Shealy
Rev. Paul O. Slice   Mr. James B. Wessinger

Delegates Elected to 1978 LCA Convention

Rev. Herman W. Cauble
Rev. James W. Addy
Rev. James S. Aull
Rev. Charles E. Bernhardt
Rev. Everette L. Lineberger
Rev. Ruben H. Olawsky
Rev. Paul O. Slice
Rev. D. Luther Swicegood

Mr. Luther C. Boliek
Mr. Robert W. Carswell
Mrs. Chester M. Hawkins
Mrs. Thomas R. Peacock
Mrs. James B. Shealy
Mrs. D. Murray Shull, Jr.
Mr. James B. Wessinger
Dr. Glenn E. Whitesides
Mr. Reid S. Wingard, Jr.

Delegates Elected to 1980 LCA Convention

Rev. Herman W. Cauble
Rev. James W. Addy
Rev. James S. Aull
Rev. Henry N. Brandt
Rev. Everette L. Lineberger
Rev. Larry S. Long
Rev. John L. Setzler
Rev. Harold G. Skinner
Rev. Bernard L. Trexler

Mr. Robert A. Addy
Dr. Hal C. Anderson
Dr. Dorothy P. Brandt
Mr. Raymond S. Caughman
Mr. Richard L. Conn
Mrs. James B. Shealy
Mr. Harry C. Stoudenmire
Mr. James B. Wessinger
Dr. Glenn E. Whitesides

Delegates Elected to 1982 LCA Convention

Rev. Herman W. Cauble
Rev. James S. Aull
Rev. Robert L. Dasher
Rev. J. Hilton Roof
Rev. John L. Setzler
Rev. D. Murray Shull, Jr.
Rev. Dermon A. Sox, Jr.
Rev. Robert L. Swygert
Rev. Richard E. Webber

Dr. Hal C. Anderson
Mr. B. Cornell Bedenbaugh
Mr. Robert W. Carswell
Mr. Hal Kohn, Jr.
Mrs. Heather Peacock
Mr. Wayne Sease
Mrs. Bernice Shealy
Mrs. Jean Shealy
Mrs. Carolyn Torrence

Delegates Elected to 1984 LCA Convention

Rev. Herman W. Cauble
Rev. James W. Addy
Rev. Beverly D. Alexander
Rev. James S. Aull
Rev. Edward L. Counts
Rev. L. William Mitcham, Jr.
Rev. D. Murray Shull, Jr.
Rev. D. Luther Swicegood
Rev. John L. Yost, Jr.

Mr. J. Howard Cook, Jr.
Mr. James N. Hallman
Mr. Robert N. Hubbs
Mr. J. Larry Kyzer
Mrs. Jane P. Mitcham
Mrs. Heather W. Peacock
Mr. Wayne F. Sease
Mr. Roy H. Seay
Mrs. Mary Ann Shealy

Delegates Elected to 1986 LCA Convention

Rev. Herman W. Cauble
Rev. James W. Addy
Rev. Mary W. Anderson
Rev. James S. Aull
Rev. Bill B. Mims, Jr.
Rev. Amaretta J. Onstad
Rev. Gary L. Safrit
Rev. D. Murray Shull, Jr.
Rev. John L. Yost, Jr.

Mr. Robert A. Addy
Mr. Donald A. Caughman
Mr. Raymond S. Caughman
Mr. R. Keith Hutto
Mrs. Susan W. McArver
Mrs. Heather W. Peacock
Mr. Roy H. Seay
Mrs. Jean W. Shealy
Mrs. Mary Ann Shealy

Delegates Elected to Concluding Convention of the LCA and the Constituting Convention of the Evangelical Lutheran Church in America

Rev. Herman W. Cauble
Rev. Mary W. Anderson
Rev. James S. Aull
Rev. Robert L. Dasher
Rev. Gary L. Safrit
Rev. John L. Setzler
Rev. D. Murray Shull, Jr.

Dr. Dorothy P. Brandt
Mr. Raymond S. Caughman
Mr. James N. Hallman
Mrs. Clara S. Hawkins
Mr. Heber E. Rast, Jr.
Mrs. Gloria Rast
Mr. Miller W. Shealy, Sr.

DEANS

Central District

1972-1975	The Rev. Henry N. Brandt

Newberry District

1972-1973	The Rev. William H. Link
1973-	The Rev. William E. Stone
1974-1975	The Rev. G. Alvin Fulmer

Piedmont District

1972-1975	The Rev. Bernard L. Trexler

Southern District

1972-1973	The Rev. E. Armand Shealy
1973-1975	The Rev. Charles S. Wessinger

Western District

1972-1973	The Rev. Rudolf F. Ludwig
1973-1975	The Rev. Elford B. Roof, Sr.

Amelia District

1975-1980	The Rev. Robert L. Swygert
1980-1984	The Rev. Ralph H. Riddle
1984-1987	The Rev. Bill B. Mims, Jr.

Central District

1975-1980	The Rev. Edward L. Counts
1980-1984	The Rev. Larry S. Long
1984-1987	The Rev. James B. Park

Coastal District

1975-1976	The Rev. Charles S. Wessinger
1976-1980	The Rev. John L. Yost, Jr.
1980-1984	The Rev. Charles E. Bernhardt
1984-1987	The Rev. H. Wyman Dowd

Dutch Fork District

1975-1980	The Rev. Earl H. Loadholdt
1980-1984	The Rev. Guy C. Cruse
1984-1987	The Rev. Donald E. Woolly

Newberry District

1975-1979	The Rev. G. Alvin Fulmer
1979-1984	The Rev. Lester H. Cutter, Jr.
1984-1987	The Rev. James F. Shealy

Piedmont District

1975-1978	The Rev. Bernard L. Trexler
1978-1980	The Rev. Paul O. Slice
1980-1982	The Rev. Everette L. Lineberger
1982-1986	The Rev. D. Luther Swicegood
1986-1987	The Rev. Gary L. Safrit

Saxe-Gotha District

1975-1980	The Rev. Elford B. Roof, Sr.
1980-1984	The Rev. Charles W. Easley
1984-1986	The Rev. John L. Satterwhite
1986-1987	The Rev. Kay E. Overcash

Western District

1975-1980	The Rev. Harold G. Skinner
1980-1984	The Rev. J. Hilton Roof
1984-1987	The Rev. James W. Addy

Persons Elected to the Lowman Home for the Aged and Helpless Board of Trustees

1971 Convention   Mr. Deems Haltiwanger, Mr. William F. Austin, Mr. Harry C. Stoudenmire, the Rev. Robert L. Hock

1972 Convention   Mrs. Kay T. Cockwell, Dr. H. Harrison Jenkins, Mr. Howard A. Nilson, Dr. Carl W. Shealy, Mr. Robert A. Ballentine

1973 Convention   The Rev. Paul O. Slice, Mr. Harry O. Harman, Jr., Mr. James T. Brittingham, Mr. J. Howard Cook, Mrs. Caroline Kohn

1974 Convention   Mr. William F. Austin, Mr. Robert A. Ballentine, Mrs. Martha Counts, Mr. W. Archie Dodgen, Mr. Wilson W. Howard, Mr. J. Howard Cook, the Rev. C. P. Fisher, II, the Rev. Henry A. McCullough, Jr.

1975 Convention   Mr. Luther C. Boliek, Mrs. Caroline Kohn, the Rev. Henry A. McCullough, Jr., Mr. Howard A. Nilson, Dr. Carl J. Shealy

1976 Convention   Mr. J. Howard Cook, Jr., the Rev. C. P. Fisher, II, Mr. Harry O. Harman, Jr., Dr. Conrad B. Park, the Rev. Paul O. Slice

1977 Convention   The Rev. Paul Morgan, Mrs. Martha Counts, Mr. W. Archie Dodgen, the Rev. John L. Setzler, Mrs. Horry E. Wessinger

1978 Convention   Mr. Luther C. Boliek, Mrs. Caroline Kohn, the Rev. Henry A. McCullough, Jr., Mr. Virgil C. Summer, Dr. Carl J. Shealy, Mr. Howard A. Nilson

1979 Convention   Mrs. Bertha B. Ariail, Mr. J. Howard Cook, Jr., Mr. Harry O. Harman, Jr., Dr. Conrad B. Park, the Rev. Paul O. Slice

1980 Convention   Mr. Cecil H. Bowers, Mrs. Martha Counts, Mr. W. Archie Dodgen, the Rev. J. Hilton Roof, the Rev. John L. Setzler

1981 Convention   Mr. J. Kermit Addy, Mr. Luther C. Boliek, Mrs. Caroline Kohn, the Rev. Henry A. McCullough, Jr., Mr. Virgil C. Summer

1982 Convention   Mrs. Bertha Ariail, Mr. J. Howard Cook, Jr., Mr. Harry O. Harman, Jr., Dr. Conrad B. Park, the Rev. Paul O. Slice

1983 Convention   The Rev. Boyd F. Cook, the Rev. Edward L. Counts, the Rev. Charles B. Dawkins, the Rev. J. Hilton Roof, the Rev. Harry Weber

1984 Convention   Mr. J. Kermit Addy, Mr. Luther C. Boliek, Mrs. Caroline Kohn, Mr. Virgil C. Summer, Mrs. Sue Wingard

1985 Convention*   Mrs. Bertha Ariail, Mr. J. Howard Cook, Jr., Mr. Harry O. Harman, Jr., Dr. Conrad B. Park, the Rev. Robert F. Sims

1986 Convention*   Mr. Donald A. Caughman, the Rev. Boyd F. Cook, the Rev. Edward L. Counts, the Rev. Charles B. Dawkins, the Rev. Harry Weber

Persons Elected to the Lutheran Theological Southern Seminary Board of Trustees

1971 Convention   The Rev. Charles E. Bernhardt

1972 Convention   The Rev. Frank E. Lyerly, Mr. Grady B. Wingard

1973 Convention   The Rev. Charles E. Bernhardt, the Rev. Charles S. Wessinger

1974 Convention   Mr. Robert A. Darr

1975 Convention   The Rev. Bernard L. Trexler, Mr. Grady B. Wingard

1976 Convention   The Rev. Charles E. Bernhardt, the Rev. Elford B. Roof, Sr.

1977 Convention   Mr. Robert A. Darr

1978 Convention   The Rev. Bernard L. Trexler, Mr. Robert A. Addy

1979 Convention   The Rev. Charles E. Bernhardt, the Rev. Elford B. Roof, Sr.

1980 Convention   Mr. Robert A. Darr

1981 Convention   The Rev. Bernard L. Trexler, Mr. Robert A. Addy

1982 Convention   The Rev. Charles E. Bernhardt, the Rev. Elford B. Roof, Sr., Mr. Cletus W. S. Horne

1983 Convention   Mr. Thomas H. Kepley

1984 Convention   The Rev. Bernard L. Trexler, Mr. Robert A. Addy

1985 Convention*   The Rev. Charles E. Bernhardt, the Rev. John L. Yost, III

1986 Convention*   Mrs. Rebecca Wise Derrick

Persons Elected to the
Lutheridge Board of Trustees

1971 Convention	The Rev. J. Hilton Roof, Mr. Hal Kohn, Jr.
1972 Convention	The Rev. Harold F. Park, Mr. Albert J. Dooley
1973 Convention	Dr. Frank W. Shealy
1974 Convention	The Rev. J. Hilton Roof, the Rev. John E. Boyd, Jr.
1975 Convention	The Rev. Harold F. Park, Mrs. Hampton S. Caughman
1976 Convention	Mrs. Clara S. Hawkins, Mr. Frank W. Shealy, the Rev. Donald E. Woolly
1977 Convention	The Rev. John E. Boyd, Jr., the Rev. J. Hilton Roof
1978 Convention	The Rev. Dr. Harold F. Park, Mrs. Jean Derrick
1979 Convention	Mrs. Clara S. Hawkins
1980 Convention	The Rev. John E. Boyd, the Rev. Marion W. Clark, the Rev. Billy B. Mims, Jr.
1981 Convention	The Rev. Dr. Harold F. Park, the Rev. Billy B. Mims, Jr.
1982 Convention	Mrs. Clara S. Hawkins
1983 Convention	The Rev. John E. Boyd, Jr., Mrs. Martha F. Haigler
1984 Convention	The Rev. Dr. Harold F. Park, the Rev. Billy B. Mims, Jr.
1985 Convention*	Mrs. Clara S. Hawkins, Mr. Robert A. Ballentine
1986 Convention*	Mr. Robert A. Ballentine, Mrs. Martha F. Haigler

Persons Elected to the
Newberry College Board of Trustees

1971 Convention	Dr. C. A. Dufford, Jr., Mr. Porter O. Kinard, Mr. Otho L. Shealy, the Rev. Garth L. Hill, the Rev. Paulwyn L. Boliek
1972 Convention	Mr. John F. Clarkson, Dr. D. J. Haigler, Dr. Dorothy P. Brandt, the Rev. J. Milton Frick, the Rev. Dr. James S. Aull
1973 Convention	Mr. Gaines O. Boone, Dr. Homer M. Eargle, Mr. A. Hart Kohn, Jr., Mr. George D. Rast, Sr.
1974 Convention	Dr. C. A. Dufford, Jr., Mr. Porter O. Kinard, the Rev. Charles B. Dawkins, the Rev. Garth L. Hill

1975 Convention	Mr. John F. Clarkson, Mr. D. J. Haigler, Dr. Dorothy P. Brandt, the Rev. Dr. James S. Aull
1976 Convention	Mr. Gaines O. Boone, Mr. Homer M. Eargle, Mr. Philip T. Kelly, Jr., Mr. George D. Rast, Sr.
1977 Convention	The Rev. Charles W. Easley, Dr. H. Harrison Jenkins, Mr. Porter O. Kinard, the Rev. D. Murray Shull, Jr.
1978 Convention	The Rev. Dr. James S. Aull, Dr. Dorothy P. Brandt, Mr. Warren K. Giese, the Rev. Charles J. Shealy
1979 Convention	Mr. Gaines O. Boone, Mr. Gurdon W. Counts, Mr. Homer M. Eargle, Mr. Vernon F. Epting
1980 Convention	Mr. Porter O. Kinard, Mr. Hal Kohn, Jr., Mr. James R. Metts, the Rev. D. Murray Shull, Jr.
1981 Convention	The Rev. Dr. James S. Aull, Dr. Dorothy P. Brandt, the Rev. Charles W. Easley, Mrs. Marcia M. Loadholdt
1982 Convention	Mr. Homer M. Eargle, Mr. Vernon F. Epting, Dr. James L. Graham, Jr., Mrs. Mary Ann Shealy
1983 Convention	Mr. Porter O. Kinard, Mr. Eric B. Ficken, Mr. James R. Metts, the Rev. D. Murray Shull, Jr.
1984 Convention	The Rev. Dr. James S. Aull, the Rev. Hugh E. Baumgartner, Jr., Dr. Dorothy P. Brandt, Mrs. Marcia M. Loadholdt
1985 Convention*	Dr. James L. Graham, Jr., Mr. Philip T. Kelly, III, Mrs. Mary Ann Shealy, the Rev. John L. Yost, Jr.
1986 Convention*	Mr. Eric B. Ficken, Mr. James H. Riddle, Jr., the Rev. D. Murray Shull, Jr., the Rev. Charles W. Easley

Persons Elected to the Management Committee for Camp and Conference Ministries

1979 Convention	Mrs. Mickey Anderson, the Rev. Robert G. Coon, the Rev. William E. Stone, Mr. Roy H. Seay, Mr. Forrest M. Shealy, Jr., the Rev. Richard E. Webber, the Rev. James W. Addy, Mr. Raymond L. Boozer, the Rev. Larry S. Long
1980 Convention	Mrs. Mickey Anderson, the Rev. Robert G. Coon, the Rev. William E. Stone

1981 Convention   Mr. Roy H. Seay, Mrs. Sarah B. Frey, the Rev.
                   Richard E. Webber
1982 Convention   The Rev. James W. Addy, Mr. Raymond L.
                   Boozer, the Rev. Larry S. Long
1983 Convention   The Rev. Robert G. Coon, Mr. J. Larry Kyzer,
                   Mr. Wayne F. Sease
1984 Convention   Mr. Wilford C. Corbin, the Rev. Hollis A. Miller,
                   the Rev. James F. Kinsler
1985 Convention*   Mrs. Kathryn W. Mohrmann, the Rev. R. De-
                   lano Ricard, Mr. Roy H. Seay
1986 Convention*   Mrs. Celie Addy, Mr. Wayne F. Sease, the Rev.
                   Richard E. Webber, the Rev. H. Gene Beck

Persons Elected to the Lutheran Children's Home of the South Board of Trustees

1971 Convention   The Rev. Earl H. Loadholdt, Mr. R. D. Nilson

Corrections to *A History of the Lutheran Church in South Carolina* 1971

1. page 363—line 28—change "Francke" to "Franke".
2. page 403—line 3—change "Francke" to "Franke".
3. page 450—line 17—change "1959-61" to "1959-63".
4. page 494—line 28—delete "the only" and insert "only the second" (see page 391).
5. page 498—line 16—change "Harkens" to "Harkins".
6. page 500—line 35—change "James B." to "James W.".
7. page 560—Bachman Chapel, Prosperity—line 5—change "n" to "in".
8. page 561—Bethany, Lexington—line 14—change "Rawl's Hill" to "Rall's Hill".
9. page 567—Bethel, White Rock—line 4—after "Lowman Home" add "and others";
   line 8—after "1929" add "with the first service held September 14, 1930".
   lines 29 & 32—change "one son" to "three sons".

*Indicates terms scheduled to expire in 1988 and 1989 which expired December 31, 1987 with the merger and formation of the South Carolina Synod of the Evangelical Lutheran Church in America.

line 31 after "Virginia" add: "; Jesse B. Lowman and David Sheely."

line 40—change "Charles" to "Christian".

10. page 568—Bethel, White Rock—line 7—change "1875-1878" to "1876-1878".

 line 8—change "1879-1883" to "1879-1884".

 line 9—change the second "1884" to "1885".

 line 13—change "1891-1894" to "1891-1893".

 line 16—change "1922-1923" to "1922".

 line 17—after "1923-1926;" add "C.K. Derrick (supply), 1925-1926;".

11. page 595—Faith, West Columbia—lines 1 & 2—change "March 30, 1941" to "December 28, 1941".

12. page 606—Good Shepherd, Swansea—line 4—change "1925-1927" to "1925-1926" and add: "C.K. Derrick, 1926-1929".

 line 5—change "1942-" to "1946-".

 line 6—change "1952-61" to "1952-63".

 line 7—change "1963" to "1964".

13. page 612—Holy Cross, Charleston—line 5—Change "Robinson" to "Robertson".

14. page 626—Mayer Memorial, Newberry—line 17—after "New church." add: "An additional lot was purchased and the parsonage moved on it. The new church was then erected on the old church and parsonage lots."

15. page 631—Mount Calvary, Johnston—line 12—change "Sigmon" to "Sigman".

16. page 632—Mt. Hebron, Leesville—line 32—change "J." to "F."

17. page 650—Nazareth, Lexington—lines 13 & 14—delete "The present building ... third structure." and add: "The present sanctuary was constructed around the frame of the third structure in 1956."

18. page 658—Pilgrim, Lexington—after line 4 add the following paragraph: "The Rev. J. L. Drafts is a son of this congregation."

19. page 661—Pisgah, Lexington—delete lines 11-17 and replace with: "following: Barnabas Kreps, 1879-1884; Drewry Kyzer, 1885-1888; John G. Graichen, 1889-1891; S. P. Shumpert, 1894-1895; Jefferson D. Shealy, 1896-?: Jacob W. Nease, 1905-1907; Benjamin W. Cronk, 1907-1910; Paul D. Risinger, 1911-1916; Oswell B. Shearouse, 1917-1934; L. Legare Swygert, 1934-1941; Edgar T. Chisemer, 1942-1952; Vernon A. Frick, 1953-1957; Thomas H. Weeks, 1958-1964; William E. Stone, 1966-1969; Dermont F. Swicegood, 1969-."

20. page 668—Redeemer, Newberry—line 6—change "1856' to "1853".

21. page 670—Reformation, Columbia—line 31—change "1961" to "1960."

22. page 683—St. Barnabas, Charleston—line 25—change "Paschal" to "Pascal".

23. page 672—Reformation, Lancaster—line 21—change "W." to "M."

24. page 679—St. Andrew's, Charleston—line 26—change "sister" to "Sister".

25. page 690—St. James, Leesville—line 16—change "surplus" to "surplice".

26. page 700—St. John's, Charleston—line 11—change "bonk" to "bank".

27. page 702—St. John's, Charleston—line 5—change "John" to "Jehu".

28. page 702—St. John's, Clinton—last line—change "Shealy" to "Sheely".

29. page 704—St. John's, Clinton—line 31—change "Allen" to "Allan".
    line 34—change "Clarke" to "Clark".

30. page 712—St. John's, Pomaria—line 19—delete "A new parsonage was constructed in 1956."
    after line 29 add the following paragraph: "According to the memory of some older members, the parsonage was shared with St. Peter's, Chapin, located at St. Peter's prior to 1920. From 1920 to 1956, the parsonage was located in Chapin across the street from Mt. Horeb, and shared with St. Jacob's and Mt. Olivet. In 1956, a new parsonage was constructed at St. John's."

31. page 714—St. John's, Spartanburg—line 32—change "Women's" to "Woman's".
    line 37—add "South" after "415".

32. page 715—St. John's, Spartanburg—line 1—add "Jr." after "Shealy".
    line 6—add at the beginning of this paragraph: "The first service was held in the new church in 1949."
    lines 7 & 8—delete: "Which included the first service in the beautiful church".
    line 16—change "1964" to "1963".

33. page 723—St. Luke's, Summerville—line 5—after "and" add: "in 1931".
    line 24—after "1917-18;" add: "A.J. Bowers, 1919-20;".

34. page 725—St. Mark's, Sullivan's Island—line 33—change "1963-." to "1964-."

35. page 727—St. Mark's, Prosperity—line 28—after "1959-63;" add: "Charles B. Dawkins, 1964-65;".

36. page 730—St. Matthew's, Charleston—line 7—change "steepe" to "steeple".

37. page 748—St. Paul's, Gilbert—line 13—after "1959-62;" add: "John F. Fischer, 1964-1965;".

38. page 749—St. Paul's, Mt. Pleasant—line 23—delete phrase: "Referred to now as the Lutheran Cemetery,".

39. page 778—Trinity, Georgetown—line 27—Change "M." to "N."

40. page 797—Bethlehem, Clear Pond—line 14—change "M.W.C." to "H.W.C."

41. page 824—St. Martin's, White Rock—line 10—change "Directl" to "directly".

42. page 832—AULL, J. HERMAN—change "probably Beaufort, S.C." to "Orangeburg District, S.C."

43. page 832—AULL, JAMES STROUD—lines 3 & 4—change "S.T.M. So. Sem.;' to "S.T.M. Lutheran School of Theology at Chicago;".

44. page 834—BALLENTINE, S.C.—full name is "SIDNEY CALHOUN".
    line 3—after "1894-1905:" add "Luther Chapel (now Wittenburg), Leesville, 1908-1915;".

45. page 839—change "BLOMGREEN" to "BLOMGREN".

46. page 846—COBB, JAMES KIVETT—line 4—change "1946-1949" to "1946-1951", and delete "Pa., 1949-1952".
    lines 4 & 5—change "Va., 1952-1955. Tenn., 1955-1958." to "Va., 1951-1954; S.E., 1954-1958."

47. page 846—COOK, BOYD F.—change birthdate to "May 8, 1941".

48. page 851—DOWD, HUGH WYMAN—change birthplace to "Prosperity, S.C."

49. page 852—DUNLAP, HUBERT A.—change birthdate to "June 1, 1907".

50. page 853—EFIRD, ADAM—change "Stanley" to "Stanly".

51. page 854—EFIRD, DANIEL—change "Stanley" to "Stanly".

52. page 860—HAIGLER, ALVIN HAYNE, SR.—line 4—change "1961-1966;" to "1961-1964;".

53. page 863—HENDRIX, WILFORD PASCHAL, JR.—change "PASCHAL" to "PASCAL".

54. page 865—HOLLAND, GEORGE W.—last line—after "1877-1895" add: "; President of South Carolina Synod, 1880."

55. page 867—HOUCK, WILLIAM ALEXANDER—change birth-
    place to "Lexington County".
56. page 869—change "JORDON" to "JORDAN."
57. page 870—KEISLER, JAMES ALBERT, JR.—last line—delete
    "Ret. 1969."
58. page 872—KLEINDT, F. ADOLF—line 3—change "Ga." to
    "Fla."
        line 4—change "1957-1963" to "1957-1964" and "1963-." to
        "1964-."
59. page 880—MEALY, STEPHEN ALBION—last line—change
    date of death to "1855".
60. page 887—POOLE, DONALD RAYMOND, SR.—line 6—delete:
    "Author of Centennial History, SE. Synod." and replace with:
    "Author: 'The History of the Georgia/Alabama Synod,
    1860-1960'."
61. page 895—SCHOTT, G.F., JR.—line 2—change "1939" to
    "1937".
        last line—change "June 1939" to "June 1937".
62. page 900—SIGMON, WALTER A.—change "SIGMON" to
    "SIGMAN".
63. page 933—delete reference: "Addy, James B., 451, 500, 510."
64. page 933—to "Addy, James Wilbur," add "451, 500, 510".
65. page 942—change both listings of "Francke" to "Franke".

ENDNOTES
Chapter One

[1] *S. C. Synod Minutes,* 1976, page 30.
[2] *S. C. Synod Minutes,* 1977, page 27.
[3] *S. C. Synod Minutes,* 1985, page 42.
[4] *S. C. Synod Minutes,* 1986, page 42.
[5] *S. C. Synod Minutes,* 1974, page 31.
[6] *S. C. Synod Minutes,* 1975, page 34.
[7] *S. C. Synod Minutes,* 1976, page 30.
[8] *S. C. Synod Minutes,* 1981, page 39.
[9] *S. C. Synod Minutes,* 1972, page 29.
[10] *S. C. Synod Minutes,* 1975, page 34.
[11] *S. C. Synod Minutes,* 1981, page 39.
[12] *Final Reports, S. C. Synod, LCA,* 1987, unpublished.
[13] *S. C. Synod Minutes,* 1985, page 41.
[14] *S. C. Synod Minutes,* 1978, page 171.
[15] *S. C. Synod Minutes,* 1979, page 110.
[16] *S. C. Synod Minutes,* 1984, page 93.
[17] *S. C. Synod Minutes,* 1985, page 150.
[18] *South Carolina Lutheran,* Vol. LXVII, No. 4 (April 1988), page 7.
[19] *S. C. Synod Minutes,* 1972, page 53.
[20] *Final Reports, S. C. Synod, LCA,* 1987, unpublished.
[21] *A History of the Lutheran Church in South Carolina* (Columbia: The R. L. Bryan Co., 1971), page 498. (Hereafter referred to as *History,* 1971.)
[22] *S. C. Synod Minutes,* 1979, page 134.
[23] *Minutes Tenth Biennial Convention of the LCA,* 1980, pages 256-258.
[24] *S. C. Synod Minutes,* 1981, page 45.
[25] *S. C. Synod Minutes,* 1981, page 91.
[26] *S. C. Synod Minutes,* 1985, page 50.
[27] *Final Reports, S. C. Synod, LCA,* 1987, unpublished.
[28] *Final Reports, S. C. Synod, LCA,* 1987, unpublished.
[29] *S. C. Synod Minutes,* 1984, page 43.
[30] *S. C. Synod Executive Board Minutes,* January 29, 1973, December 11, 1973, and April 1, 1984.
[31] *S. C. Synod Minutes,* 1975, page 94.
[32] *S. C. Synod Constitution,* Article Four, 2.
[33] *S. C. Synod By-Laws,* Article V, Section 1.
[34] *S. C. Synod Minutes,* 1974, pages 84-89.
[35] *Final Reports, S. C. Synod, LCA,* 1987, unpublished.
[36] *History,* 1971, page 501.
[37] *S. C. Synod Minutes,* 1985, page 156.
[38] *S. C. Synod Minutes,* 1981, page 107-108.

39 *S. C. Synod Minutes*, 1984, page 204.

40 *S. C. Synod Minutes*, 1982, page 219.

41 *S. C. Synod Minutes*, 1983, page 42 and 1984, page 55.

42 *S. C. Synod Minutes*, 1976, pages 131-132.

43 *S. C. Synod Minutes*, 1977, pages 64-65.

44 *S. C. Synod Minutes*, 1982, page 188.

45 *S. C. Synod Minutes*, 1982, pages 199-200.

46 *S. C. Synod Minutes*, 1983, pages 161-162.

47 *S. C. Synod Minutes*, 1984, pages 205-206.

48 *S. C. Synod Minutes*, 1985, page 105.

49 *S. C. Synod Minutes*, 1983, page 165.

50 *S. C. Synod Minutes*, 1986, page 122.

51 *S. C. Synod Minutes*, 1986, page 214.

52 *S. C. Synod Minutes*, 1973, page 147.

53 *S. C. Synod Minutes*, 1983, page 111.

54 *S. C. Synod Minutes*, 1986, page 215.

55 *S. C. Synod Minutes*, 1984, page 49.

56 *Final Reports, S. C. Synod, LCA*, 1987, unpublished.

57 *S. C. Synod Minutes*, 1967, page 87.

58 *S. C. Synod Minutes*, 1968, page 70.

59 *S. C. Synod Minutes*, 1977, page 75.

60 *History*, 1971, page 468.

61 *Final Reports, S. C. Synod, LCA*, 1987, unpublished.

62 *History*, 1971, page 469.

63 *S. C. Synod Minutes*, 1982, page 155.

64 *S. C. Synod Minutes*, 1985, page 202.

65 *S. C. Synod Minutes*, 1976, page 129.

66 *S. C. Synod Executive Board Minutes*, November 30, 1978.

67 *S. C. Synod Minutes*, 1979, pages 144-146.

68 *S. C. Synod Minutes*, 1981, page 136.

69 *S. C. Synod Minutes*, 1982, pages 130-131.

70 *S. C. Synod Minutes*, 1983, pages 148-149.

71 *S. C. Synod Minutes*, 1984, page 50.

72 *S. C. Synod Minutes*, 1981, page 138.

73 *S. C. Synod Minutes*, 1984, pages 132-133.

74 *S. C. Synod Minutes*, 1984, pages 169-170.

75 *S. C. Synod Minutes*, 1985, page 104.

76 *S. C. Synod Minutes*, 1985, pages 203-204.

77 *S. C. Synod Minutes*, 1985, page 104.

78 *S. C. Synod Minutes*, 1986, page 125.

79 *S. C. Synod Minutes*, 1986, pages 55-56.

80 *S. C. Synod Minutes*, 1986, pages 132-133.

81 *S. C. Synod Minutes*, 1986, pages 133-140.

82 *S. C. Synod Minutes*, 1986, pages 190-192.

83 *Minutes of the South Carolina Synod of the Evangelical Lutheran Church in America Constituting Convention*, May 29-30, 1987, page 19.

Chapter Two

[1] *S. C. Synod By-Laws*, Article IV, Section 1.
[2] *S. C. Synod Minutes*, 1971, page 153.
[3] *S. C. Synod Minutes*, 1973, pages 126-127 and 1974, pages 161-166.
[4] *S. C. Synod Minutes*, 1975, page 132.
[5] *S. C. Synod Minutes*, 1984, page 207.
[6] *S. C. Synod Executive Board Minutes*, September 28, 1976.
[7] *S. C. Synod Minutes*, 1972, page 141.
[8] *S. C. Synod Minutes*, 1976, page 149.
[9] *S. C. Synod Minutes*, 1971, page 74-77.
[10] *S. C. Synod Executive Board Minutes*, September 11, 1973.
[11] *S. C. Synod Executive Board Minutes*, December 3, 1984.
[12] *S. C. Synod Minutes*, 1985, page 105.
[13] *S. C. Synod Minutes*, 1972, page 126.
[14] *S. C. Synod Minutes*, 1983, pages 107-108.
[15] *S. C. Synod Minutes*, 1985, page 206.
[16] *S. C. Synod Minutes*, 1986, page 212.
[17] *History*, 1971, page 497.
[18] *S. C. Synod Minutes*, 1985, page 58.
[19] *S. C. Synod Minutes*, 1972, page 58.
[20] *S. C. Synod Minutes*, 1979, page 81.
[21] *S. C. Synod Minutes*, 1972, page 58.
[22] *S. C. Synod Executive Board Minutes*, June 13, 1979.
[23] *S. C. Synod Minutes*, 1981, page 179.
[24] *S. C. Synod Minutes*, 1984, page 92.
[25] *S. C. Synod Minutes*, 1981, page 107.
[26] *S. C. Synod Minutes*, 1976, page 109.
[27] *S. C. Synod By-Laws*, Article V, Section 7.
[28] *S. C. Synod Executive Board Minutes*, September 21, 1982.
[29] *S. C. Synod Minutes*, 1979, page 131.
[30] *S. C. Synod Minutes*, 1982, page 219.
[31] *S. C. Synod Minutes*, 1986, page 69.
[32] *S. C. Synod Executive Board Minutes*, April 19, 1983.
[33] *Final Reports, S. C. Synod, LCA*, 1987, unpublished.
[34] *S. C. Synod Minutes*, 1978, page 174.
[35] *S. C. Synod Minutes*, 1984, page 93.
[36] *S. C. Synod Executive Board Minutes*, September 26, 1979; and February 19, 1980.
[37] *S. C. Synod Minutes*, 1972, page 173.
[38] .*S. C. Synod Minutes*, 1983, page 196.
[39] *S. C. Synod Minutes*, 1986, page 220.
[40] *S. C. Synod Minutes*, 1975, page 79.
[41] *S. C. Synod Minutes*, 1976, page 93.
[42] *S. C. Synod Minutes*, 1983, page 147.
[43] *S. C. Synod Minutes*, 1986, page 219.

44 *S. C. Synod Minutes*, 1985, page 175.

45 *S. C. Synod Minutes*, 1986, page 219.

46 *S. C. Synod Executive Board Minutes*, April 1, 1974; and September 17, 1974.

47 *S. C. Synod Minutes*, 1980, page 172.

48 *S. C. Synod Minutes*, 1972, page 120.

49 *S. C. Synod Minutes*, 1978, page 94.

50 *S. C. Synod Minutes*, 1971, pages 159-162.

51 *S. C. Synod Minutes*, 1979, page 129.

52 *S. C. Synod Minutes*, 1978, pages 95 and 100.

53 *S. C. Synod Minutes*, 1978, pages 95-101.

54 *S. C. Synod Executive Board Minutes*, December 11, 1973.

55 *S. C. Synod Minutes*, 1976, page 112.

56 *S. C. Synod Executive Board Minutes*, June 7, 1977.

57 *S. C. Synod Executive Board Minutes*, February 12-13, 1984.

58 *S. C. Synod Minutes*, 1967, pages 103, 145-148.

59 *S. C. Synod Minutes*, 1969, page 127.

60 *S. C. Synod Minutes*, 1970, page 56.

61 *S. C. Synod Minutes*, 1971, page 116.

62 *S. C. Synod Minutes*, 1972, page 77.

63 *S. C. Synod Minutes*, 1974, page 172.

64 *S. C. Synod Minutes*, 1974, page 172.

65 *S. C. Synod Minutes*, 1973, page 168.

66 *S. C. Synod Minutes*, 1974, page 172.

67 *S. C. Synod Minutes*, 1974, page 97.

68 *S. C. Synod Minutes*, 1975, page 103.

69 *S. C. Synod Minutes*, 1977, page 69.

70 *S. C. Synod Minutes*, 1978, pages 152-153

71 *S. C. Synod Minutes*, 1979, pages 34-35, 172, and 174.

72 *S. C. Synod Minutes*, 1980, page 101.

73 *S. C. Synod Minutes*, 1981, page 193.

74 *S. C. Synod Minutes*, 1982, page 100.

75 *S. C. Synod Minutes*, 1983, page 183.

76 *Final Reports, S. C. Synod, LCA*, 1987, unpublished.

77 *S. C. Synod Minutes*, 1977, page 154.

78 *S. C. Synod Minutes*, 1978, pages 145-146.

79 *S. C. Synod Minutes*, 1979, page 34.

80 *S. C. Synod Executive Board Minutes*, February 8-9, 1983.

81 *S. C. Synod Minutes*, 1985, page 194.

82 *S. C. Synod Minutes*, 1969, page 34.

83 *S. C. Synod Minutes*, 1969, page 109.

84 *S. C. Synod Minutes*, 1969, page 31.

85 *S. C. Synod Minutes*, 1970, page 150.

86 *S. C. Synod Minutes*, 1976, page 109.

87 *South Carolina Lutheran*, Vol. LIV, Number 9 (October 1975), page 10.

88 *S. C. Synod Minutes*, 1977, page 179.

[89] *S. C. Synod Minutes*, 1985, page 58.
[90] *Final Reports, S. C. Synod, LCA*, 1987, unpublished.
[91] *Final Reports, S. C. Synod, LCA*, 1987, unpublished.
[92] *S. C. Synod Minutes*, 1975, page 120.
[93] *S. C. Synod Minutes*, 1984, page 81.
[94] *S. C. Synod Minutes*, 1986, page 198.
[95] *S. C. Synod Minutes*, 1975, page 196.
[96] *S. C. Synod Minutes*, 1976, page 183.
[97] *S. C. Synod Minutes*, 1986, page 125.
[98] *S. C. Synod Minutes*, 1986, page 199.
[99] *S. C. Synod Minutes*, 1972, page 172.
[100] *S. C. Synod Minutes*, 1976, page 159.
[101] *S. C. Synod Minutes*, 1978, page 137.
[102] *Final Reports, S. C. Synod, LCA*, 1987, unpublished.
[103] *Final Reports, S. C. Synod, LCA*, 1987, unpublished.

Chapter Three

[1] *Final Reports, S. C. Synod, LCA*, 1987, unpublished.
[2] *Final Reports, S. C. Synod, LCA*, 1987, unpublished.
[3] *S.C.L.C.W. Minutes*, 1981, page 16.
[4] *Final Reports, S. C. Synod, LCA*, 1987, unpublished.
[5] *Final Reports, S. C. Synod, LCA*, 1987, unpublished.
[6] *S. C. Synod Minutes*, 1975, page 150.
[7] *S. C. Synod Minutes*, 1975, page 151.
[8] *Final Reports, S. C. Synod, LCA*, 1987, unpublished.
[9] *S. C. Synod Minutes*, 1977, page 154.
[10] *S. C. Synod Minutes*, 1978, pages 137-138.
[11] *S. C. Synod Minutes*, 1979, page 156.
[12] *Constitution for State LCY Organization.* 1981, Article II.
[13] *Final Reports, S. C. Synod, LCA*, 1987, unpublished.
[14] *Lutheran Men of the South Carolina Synod Directory*, 1988, pages 48-49.
[15] *S. C. Synod Minutes*, 1981, page 185.
[16] *Lutheran Men of the South Carolina Synod Directory*, 1988, page 42.
[17] *Lutheran Men of the South Carolina Synod Directory*, 1988, page 43.
[18] *Lutheran Men of the South Carolina Synod Directory*, 1988, pages 40-41.
[19] *Lutheran Men of the South Carolina Synod Directory*, 1988, page 8.

Chapter Four

[1] *History*, 1971, page 363.
[2] *S. C. Synod Minutes*, 1975, page 154.
[3] *S. C. Synod Minutes*, 1976, page 119.
[4] *S. C. Synod Minutes*, 1978, page 167.
[5] *S. C. Synod Minutes*, 1979, page 161.
[6] *S. C. Synod Minutes*, 1982, page 201.
[7] *S. C. Synod Minutes*, 1984, page 145.
[8] *S. C. Synod Minutes*, 1986, page 127.
[9] *S. C. Synod Minutes*, 1984, page 145.
[10] *S. C. Synod Minutes*, 1985, page 129.
[11] *S. C. Synod Minutes*, 1986, page 156.
[12] *S. C. Synod Minutes*, 1986, page 157.
[13] *Final Reports, S. C. Synod, LCA*, 1987, unpublished.
[14] *Final Reports, S. C. Synod, LCA*, 1987, unpublished.
[15] *Final Reports, S. C. Synod, LCA*, 1987, unpublished.
[16] *Minutes of the Board of Trustees*, Lutheran Theological Southern Seminary, May 15, 1970, page 12. (Hereafter referred to as *Minutes*.)
[17] *Minutes*, October 3, 1969, page 5; see also H. George Anderson, "The Seminary and the Church, 1930-1980," in H. George Anderson and Robert M. Calhoon, eds., *"A Truly Efficient School of Theology: The Lutheran Theological Southern Seminary in Historical Context 1830-1980* (Columbia: LTSS, 1981), page 79.
[18] *Minutes*, October 16, 1975, page 26.
[19] *Minutes*, November 17, 1972, page 3; and May 17, 1973, page 14.
[20] *Minutes*, May 7-8, 1979, page 3; see also *The Bulletin of Lutheran Theological Southern Seminary*, No. 7 (August 1973), page 1. (Hereafter referred to as *The Bulletin*.)
[21] *Minutes*, May 15, 1974, page 41; *The Bulletin*, No. 9 (May 1976), page 4.
[22] *Minutes*, May 14, 1976, pages 13 & 33; *The Bulletin*, No. 9 (February 1976), pages 4-5.
[23] *Minutes*, May 12, 1972, page 12.
[24] *Minutes*, May 12, 1972, page 13; October 31, 1973, page 53; October 15, 1974, page 9.
[25] *Minutes*, May 15, 1974, page 9.
[26] *Minutes*, May 15, 1974, pages 20-22.
[27] *Minutes*, May 17, 1973, pages 47-78.
[28] *Minutes*, May 12, 1972, page 12.
[29] *Minutes*, October 16, 1974, page 8.
[30] *Minutes*, May 15, 1974, pages 6 & 11.
[31] *Minutes*, May 14, 1976, page 44.
[32] *Minutes*, May 12, 1972, page 17.

[33] *Minutes*, May 14, 1976, page 13; May 7-8, 1979, page 54; *The Bulletin*, No. 12 (May 1979), page 3.

[34] Lutheran Theological Southern Seminary, *The Catalogue: Announcements for 1984-86* (Columbia: LTSS, 1984), page 3.

[35] *Minutes*, May 14, 1975, page 23; May 8-9, 1978, page 28; May 7-8, 1979, pages 55-56; May 12-13, 1980, pages 7-8.

[36] *Minutes*, May 8-9, 1978, page 28; October 24-25, 1978, page 12.

[37] *Minutes*, October 6, 1971, page 11; October 15-16, 1975, pages 40-41; May 7-8, 1979, page 28; May 12-13, 1980, pages 24-25.

[38] *Minutes*, May 7-8, 1979, pages 55-56; October 10-11, 1979, page 19.

[39] *Minutes*, May 15, 1974, pages 8-9; October 16, 1974, page 44.

[40] *Minutes*, October 31, 1973, page 54; May 7-8, 1979, pages 26-27.

[41] *Minutes*, May 12-13, 1977, pages 30-31; April 15-16, 1982, pages 33-34.

[42] *The Bulletin*, No. 9 (November 1976), page 3; No. 12 (May, 1979), page 3.

[43] *The Bulletin*, No. 10 (November 1977), page 1.

[44] *The Bulletin*, No. 12 (February 1979), page 4.

[45] *Minutes*, October 24-25, 1978, page 12.

[46] *Minutes*, April 27-28, 1981, page 13; November 5-6, 1981, pages 15 & 20.

[47] *Minutes*, November 5-6, 1981, page 16; May 14, 1976, page 38.

[48] *Minutes*, April 27-28, 1981, page 14.

[49] *Executive Committee Minutes*, July 28, 1981, page 1; *Minutes*, November 5-6, 1980, page 13-14.

[50] *Minutes*, November 4-5, 1982, pages 10-11; *The Bulletin*, No. 15 (November 1982), page 1.

[51] *The Bulletin*, No. 16 (February 1983), pages 1 & 3.

[52] *Minutes*, November 4-5, 1982, page 15; October 31-November 1, 1985, page 5.

[53] *Minutes*, May 9-10, 1984, pages 3-4; *The Bulletin*, No. 17 (September 1984), page 1.

[54] *Minutes*, April 16-17, 1985, page 3; *The Bulletin*, No. 18 (February 1985), page 1.

[55] *Minutes*, November 17, 1972, page 22; April 16-17, 1985, page 32.

[56] *Minutes*, October 31-November 1, 1985, page 5; October 30-31, 1986, pages 5-6; *The Bulletin*, No. 18 (September 1985), page 1; No. 19 (August 1986), page 10; No. 19 (October 1986), page 2.

[57] *Minutes*, May 9-10, 1984, page 14; October 31-November 1, 1985, page 15; *The Bulletin*, No. 18 (September 1985), page 1.

[58] *Executive Committee Minutes*, November 1, 1984, page 2; *The Bulletin*, No. 17 (November 1984), page 1.

[59] *Minutes*, November 1-2, 1984, page 10; *The Bulletin*, No. 17 (November 1984), page 1.

[60] *Minutes*, May 13, 1980, page 33; November 4-5, 1982, pages 42 & 48.

61 *Minutes*, April 27-28, 1981, page 4; April 16-17, 1985, page 16; *The Bulletin*, No. 14 (May 1981), page 2.

62 *Minutes*, November 1-2, 1984, pages 10, E. 3-5, & E. 24-25.

63 *Minutes*, May 20-21, 1986; *The Bulletin*, No. 20 (January 1987), page 1; *Vision 21* (Columbia: LTSS, 1986).

64 *Minutes*, May 20-21, 1986, pages 20-21; *The Bulletin*, No. 19 (October 1986), pages 1-2.

65 *Minutes*, April 22-23, 1986, pages 3 & E. 6-11; October 30-31, 1986, pages 50-56; *The Bulletin*, No. 19 (October 1986), page 1.

66 *Minutes*, May 20-21, 1986, pages 17-19; *The Bulletin*, No. 19 (October 1986), page 1.

67 *Minutes*, October 30-31, 1986, pages 52-55.

68 *Minutes*, May 9-10, 1984, pages 44-45; April 16-17, 1985, pages 30-31.

69 *Minutes*, October 31-November 1, 1985, page 19; October 30-31, 1986, page 37.

70 *Minutes*, October 30-31, 1986, pages 7 & 37.

71 *Minutes*, October 30-31, 1986, pages 9 & 37.

72 *Minutes*, May 18, 1948, page 6.

73 *Minutes*, April 6-7, 1987, page 31.

74 *Minutes*, October 28-29, 1987, pages 47-48.

75 *The Bulletin*, No. 19 (April 1986), page 2; *Taproot*, No. 1 (Summer 1986).

76 *Final Reports, S. C. Synod, LCA*, 1987, unpublished.

77 *Minutes*, April 15-16, 1982, pages 32-33 & E. 12-18.

78 *Minutes*, November 3-4, 1983, pages 3, 41, & E. 20-21.

79 For a description of this program see Professor Schultz's *Internship Manual*, Part I, *Introducing the Internship Program*, Part II, *Function of the Internship Committee and Learning Covenant*, Part III, *Evaluation/Feedback; Internship Committee* (Columbia: LTSS, 1984).

80 *Minutes*,November 5-6, 1981, pages 22-25 & 46; November 4-5, 1982, pages 43-45.

81 *Minutes*, October 30-31, 1986, page 12.

82 Lutheran Theological Southern Seminary, *The Catalogue: Announcements for 1986-87* (Columbia: LTSS, 1986), pages 26-27.

83 *Minutes*, November 4-5, 1982, page 50; May 5-6, 1983, pages 19-20; April 16-17, 1985, page 33; October 31-November 1, 1985, pages 15-17; October 30-31, 1986, pages 15-17; *The Bulletin*, No. 17 (September 1984), page 1.

84 *Minutes*, October 30-31, 1986, pages 66-68; *The Bulletin*, No. 20 (Fall 1987), page 5.

85 *Minutes*, October 30-31, 1986, pages 45-48.

86 *The Bulletin*, No. 11 (November 1978), page 3.

87 *S. C. Synod Minutes*, 1976, page 175.

88 *S. C. Synod Minutes*, 1985, page 122.

[89] *S. C. Synod Minutes*, 1984, page 151.

[90] *S. C. Synod Minutes*, 1984, page 151.

[91] *S. C. Synod Minutes*, 1984, page 151.

[92] *S. C. Synod Minutes*, 1981, page 195.

[93] *S. C. Synod Minutes*, 1983, page 184.

[94] *Final Reports, S. C. Synod, LCA*, 1987, unpublished.

[95] *S. C. Synod Minutes*, 1975, page 109.

[96] *S. C. Synod Minutes*, 1984, page 151.

[97] *S. C. Synod Minutes*, 1977, page 113.

[98] *S. C. Synod Minutes*, 1980, page 129.

[99] *S. C. Synod Minutes*, 1975, page 109.

[100] *S. C. Synod Minutes*, 1976, page 175.

[101] *S. C. Synod Minutes*, 1971, page 119.

[102] *S. C. Synod Minutes*, 1986, page 162.

[103] *S. C. Synod Minutes*, 1973, page 160.

[104] *S. C. Synod Minutes*, 1973, page 162.

[105] *Final Reports, S. C. Synod, LCA*, 1987, unpublished.

[106] *Dimensions*, Newberry College, Vol. 5, No. 1 (October 1971), page 5. (Hereafter referred to as *Dimensions.*)

[107] *Dimensions*, Vol. 11, No. 5 (May 1978), page 1.

[108] *Dimensions*, Vol, 11, No. 5 (May 1978), page 4.

[109] *Dimensions*, Vol. 17, No. 4 (April 1984), page 1.

[110] *Dimensions*, Vol. 17, No. 4 (April 1984), page 10.

[111] *Dimensions*, Vol. 18, No. 2 (December 1984), page 1.

[112] *Dimensions*, Vol. 18, No. 3 (February 1985), page 1.

[113] *Dimensions*, Vol. 18, No. 3 (February 1985), page 1-2.

[114] *Dimensions*, Vol. 19, No. 2 (December 1985), page 1.

[115] *Dimensions*, Vol. 18, No. 4 (April 1985), page 1.

[116] *Dimensions*, Vol. 20, No. 2 (December 1986), page 3.

[117] *Dimensions*, Vol. 20, No. 2 (December 1986), page 3.

[118] *Dimensions*, Vol. 19, No. 5 (June 1986), page 1.

[119] *Dimensions*, Vol. 19, No. 5 (June 1986), page 3.

[120] *Dimensions*, Vol. 20, No. 1 (October 1986), page 40.

[121] *Dimensions*, Vol. 20, No. 1 (October 1986), page 36.

[122] *Dimensions*, Vol. 20, No. 3 (February 1987), page 1.

[123] *Dimensions*, Vol. 6, No. 3 (January 1973), page 1.

[124] *Dimensions*, Vol. 13, No. 4 (February 1980), page 1.

[125] *Dimensions*, Vol. 11, No. 3 (January 1978), page 2.

[126] *Dimensions*, Vol. 6, No. 1 (October 1972), page 1.

[127] *Dimensions*, Vol. 6, No. 1 (October 1972), page 6.

[128] *Dimensions*, Vol. 10, No. 1 (October 1976), page 2.

[129] *Dimensions*, Vol. 10, No. 1 (October 1976), page 1.

[130] *Dimensions*, Vol. 10, No. 5 (May 1977), page 1.

[131] *Dimensions*, Vol. 14, No. 2 (October 1980), page 3.

[132] *Dimensions*, Vol. 15, No. 2 (October 1981), page 12.

[133] *Dimensions*, Vol. 20, No. 3 (February 1987), page 1; Vol. 20, No. 4 (May 1987), page 1.

[134] *Dimensions*, Vol. 21, No. 2 (December 1987), page 19.

[135] *Dimensions*, Vol. 17, No. 4 (April 1984), page 6.

[136] *Dimensions*, Vol. 17, No. 4 (April 1984), page 7.

[137] *Dimensions*, Vol. 17, No. 4 (April 1984), page 2.

[138] *Dimensions*, Vol. 18, No. 3 (February 1985), page 11.

[139] *Dimensions*, Vol. 10, No. 2 (November 1976), page 9.

[140] *Dimensions*, Vol. 15, No. 2 (October 1981), page 1.

[141] *Dimensions*, Vol. 13, No. 5 (April 1980), page 1; Vol. 14, No. 2 (October 1980), page 1.

[142] *Dimensions*, Vol. 20, No. 1 (October 1986), page 38.

[143] *Dimensions*, Vol. 12, No. 1 (August 1978), page 1.

[144] *Dimensions*, Vol. 21, No. 1 (October 1987), page 1.

[145] *Dimensions*, Vol. 21, No. 2 (December 1987), page 1.

[146] *S. C. Synod Minutes*, 1985, page 199.

[147] McCullough, Henry A., Jr., J. Obert Kempson, Helen S. Sanders, *50 Years of Ministry in Christ's Name*, LSS/CSC, 1988.

Appendix

[1] *S. C. Synod Minutes*, 1972 and *Final Reports, S. C. Synod*, 1987.

a. Organized 1975; statistics as of Dec. 31, 1976 from *S. C. Synod Minutes*, 1977.

b. Organized 1981; statistics as of Dec. 31, 1981 from *S. C. Synod Minutes*, 1982.

c. Organized 1974; statistics as of Dec. 31, 1974 from *S. C. Synod Minutes*, 1975.

d. Organized 1986; statistics as of Dec. 31, 1986 from *Final Reports, S. C. Synod*, 1987.

e. Organized 1986; statistics as of Dec. 31, 1986 from *Final Reports, S. C. Synod*, 1987.

f. Organized 1981; statistics as of Dec. 31, 1981 from *S. C. Synod Minutes*, 1982.

g. Organized 1977; statistics as of Dec. 31, 1977 from *S. C. Synod Minutes*, 1978.

h. Organized 1985; statistics as of Dec. 31, 1985 from *S. C. Synod Minutes*, 1986.

i. Organized 1974; statistics as of Dec. 31, 1975 from *S. C. Synod Minutes*, 1976.

j. Organized 1972; statistics as of Dec. 31, 1972 from *S. C. Synod Minutes*, 1973.

k. Organized 1974; statistics as of Dec. 31, 1975 from *S. C. Synod Minutes*, 1976.

l. Organized 1984; statistics as of Dec. 31, 1985 from *S. C. Synod Minutes*, 1986.

m. Organized 1976; statistics as of Dec. 31, 1976 from *S. C. Synod Minutes*, 1977.

n.a. Not Available.

Index